AF618568

Easy Rider
Road Book

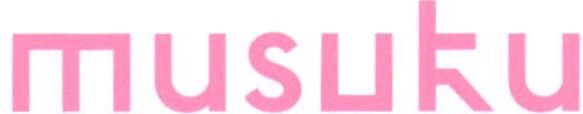

A Tour through the Wild and Inspiring Side of Bicycle Culture

Easy Rider Road Book

Edited by Anke Fesel & Chris Keller
musuku — Museum der Subkulturen

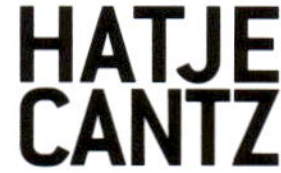

Photos

Adam Corbett

Christophe Gateau

Julie Glassberg

Jeoffrey Guillemard

Tod Seelie

Prologue

The bicycle is an ever-more popular mode of transportation. The pioneers of this new bike culture can be found in subcultures across the globe. In New York and Berlin, bike-freaks are building vehicles, at once fantastic and sustainable, out of scrap metal and old bike frames. Celebrating their creativity on wheels, their do-it-yourself endeavors provide an alternative to the omnipresent consumer culture. These bike-punk's wild creations push the boundaries well beyond their intended use. At the same time, most of these creators are largely self-taught, having compiled their knowledge about materials and mechanics themselves. They love the tall bike, which evokes the early days of the bicycle at the end of the nineteenth century. Some like to take those tall bikes out to cruise around town, while others prefer to use them for an excursion across the country.

Over a century ago, women fought for the right to ride a bicycle. With a bicycle, they could travel from village to village or across a city without depending upon a man. Riding a bike still is a form of emancipation, for both the individual as well as the community. The rolling "Critical Mass" demonstration is a worldwide movement wherein individuals meet up to become a swarm, illustrating what a city without automobiles could look like. When thousands of teenagers ride through London during "BikeStormz," they express their hope for a better future. In a similar vein, the Chilangos Lowbike Club provide a symbol against violence during their Sunday rides across Mexico City.

The bicycle is a promise of freedom. While most of the time one rides solo on a bicycle, riding together can be a powerful manifestation of solidarity and community—an expression of the ways in which we're all equal in the saddle.
Bicycling is not just a form of locomotion. Bike culture is in constant interaction with fashion, music, design, politics, city planning, and transportation concepts. Biking is both a form of protest and a vision for a better world. The more people ride bicycles, the more changes can be envisioned. The bicycle has the potential to change life in the city and, ultimately, change the city itself.

Contents

"Knives down, bikes up!"

London—A bike movement changing the lives of young riders

Photos
Adam Corbett

For teenagers, London can be a dangerous place. Every year dozens die from knife crime perpetrated by their own peers. Although politicians and the police have done little to counter this epidemic, the bicycle has meanwhile become a vehicle for curbing it. During the biannual "BikeStormz" thousands of minors, mostly male bicyclists, ride across the city in a positive protest against knife violence. Their motto is "knives down, bikes up!"

In 2014 Mac Ferrari and Jake O'Neill came up with the idea for BikeStormz. After losing his best friend, Mac Ferarri decided to radically change his life and turned his back on street crime. Meanwhile when he was a teenager, O'Neill was already a well-established bike virtuoso. Being greatly admired for his acrobatic skills, the youth of London imitate O'Neill by performing a wheelie—riding together with their front wheels in the air.

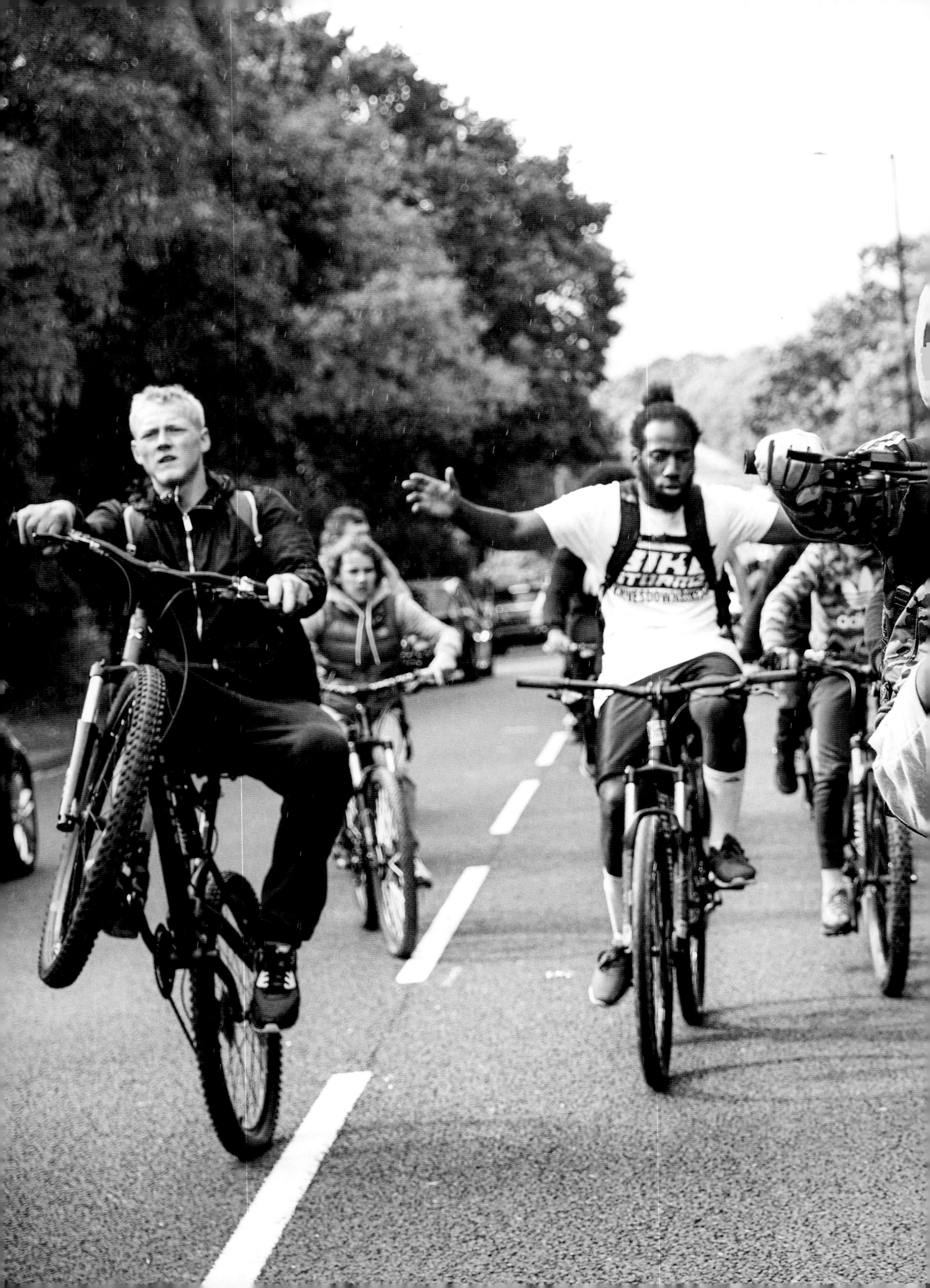

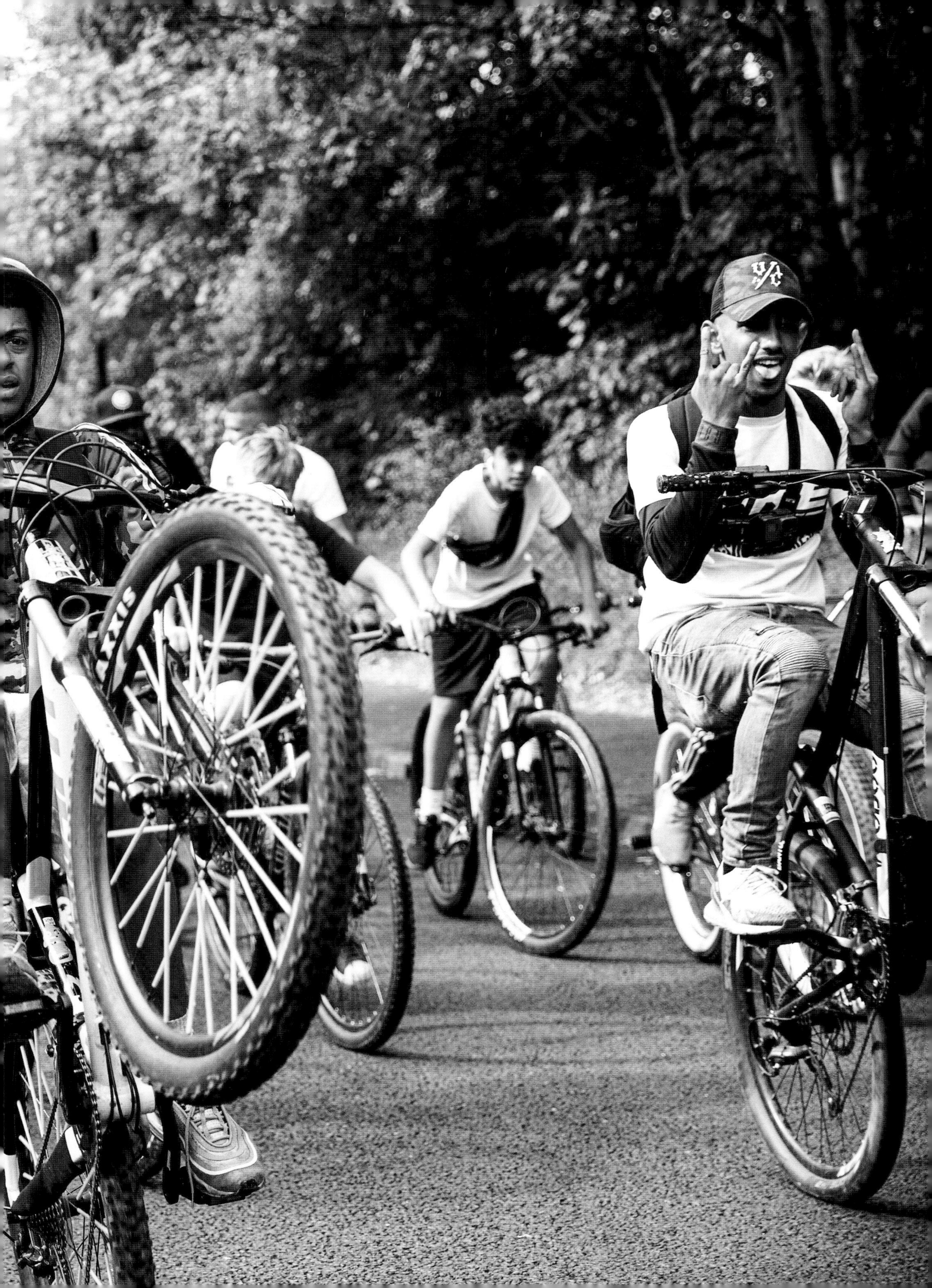

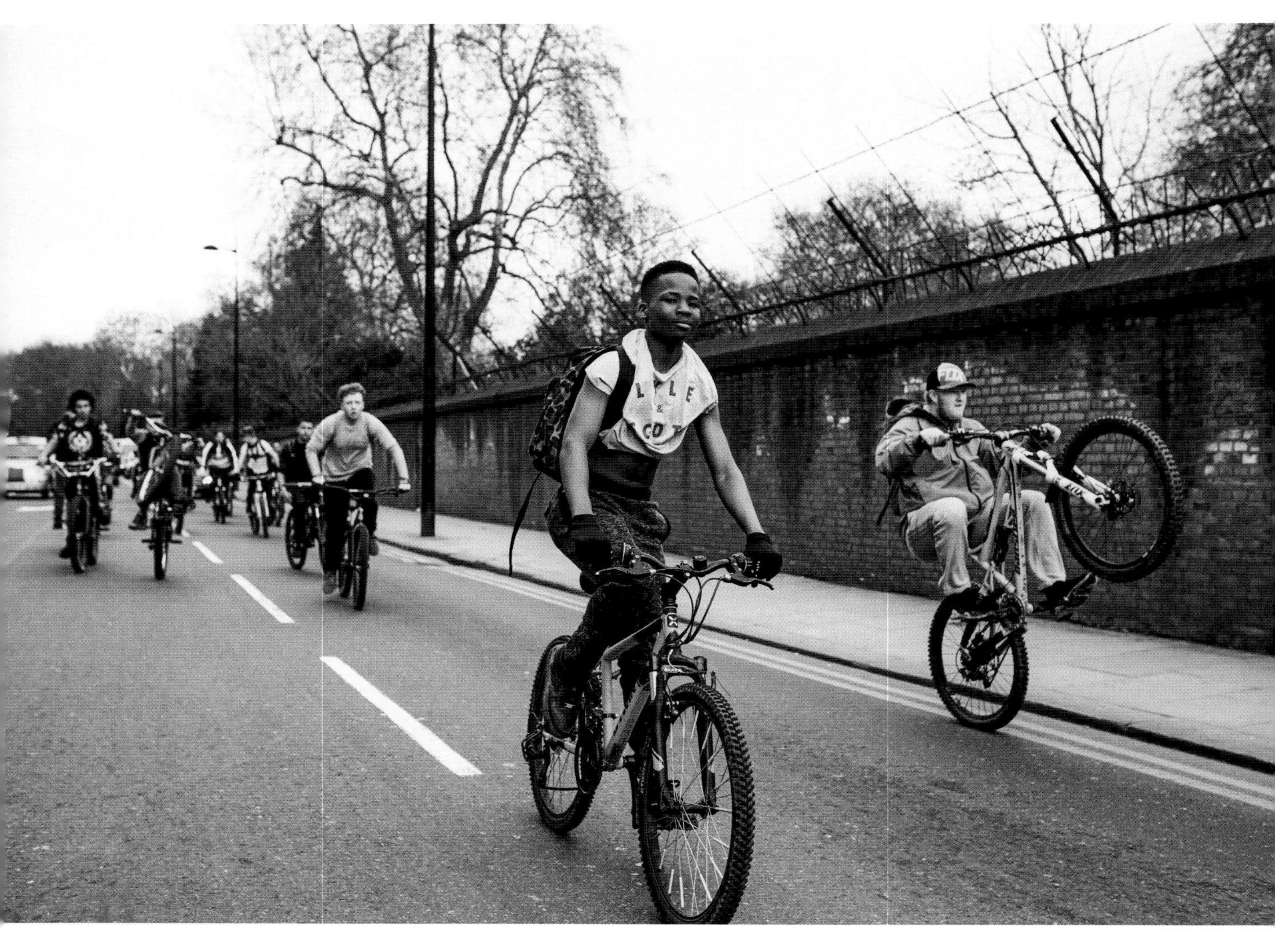

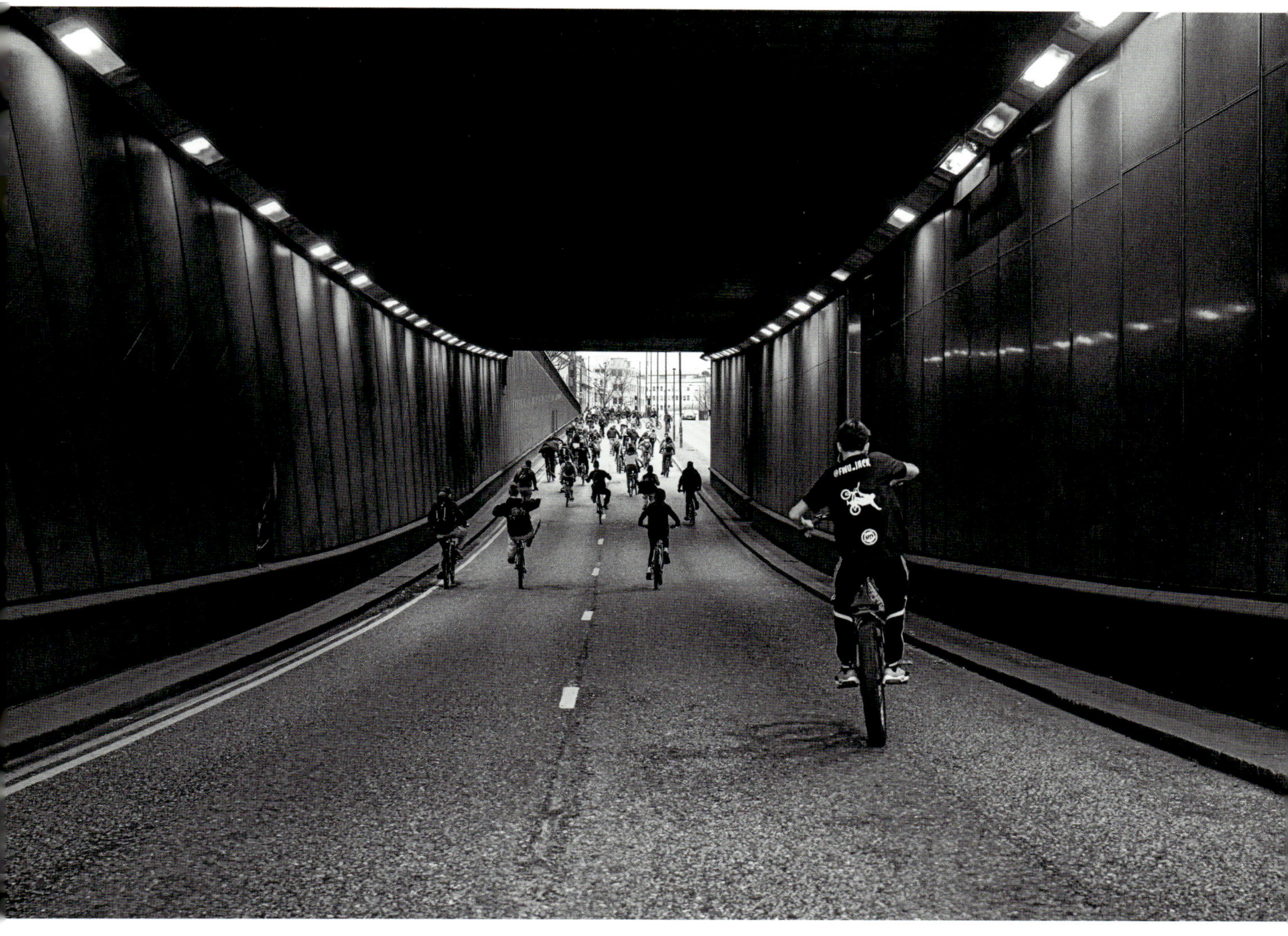

"It's about unity, coming out and facing your fears. Meeting people you can trust and build long-term friendships with, beating the stereotype of what people expect from you."

Mac Ferrari

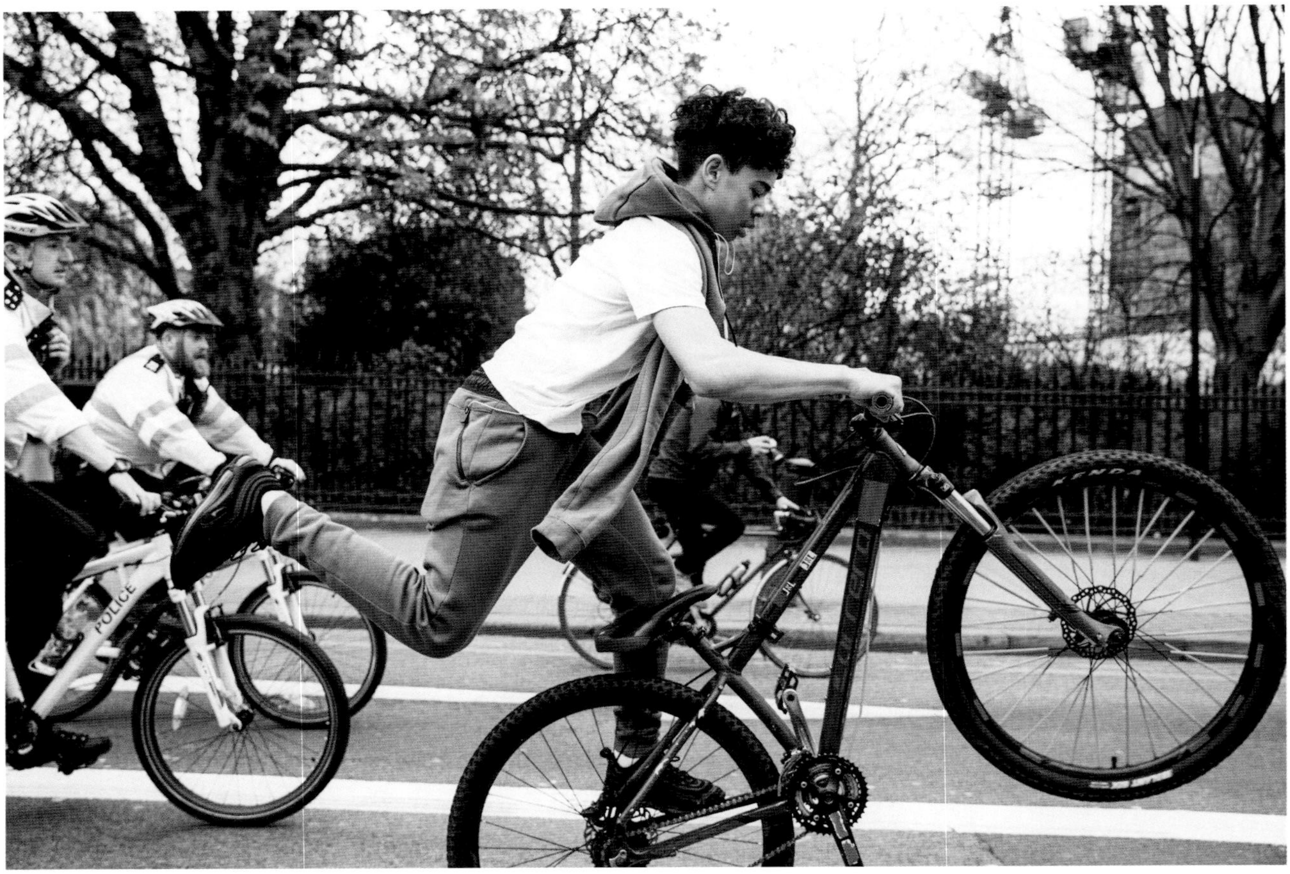
POLICE
KENDA

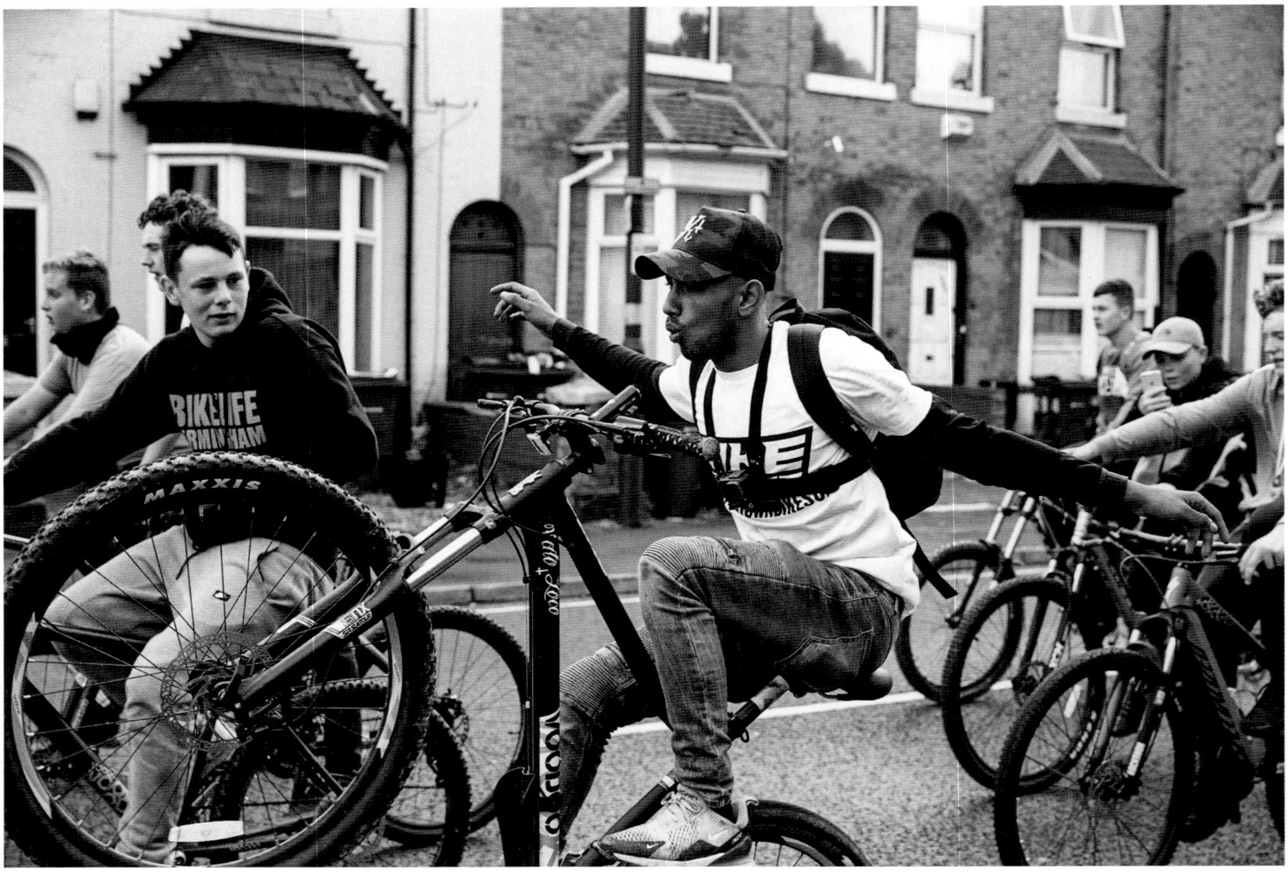
MAXXIS
BIKELIFE

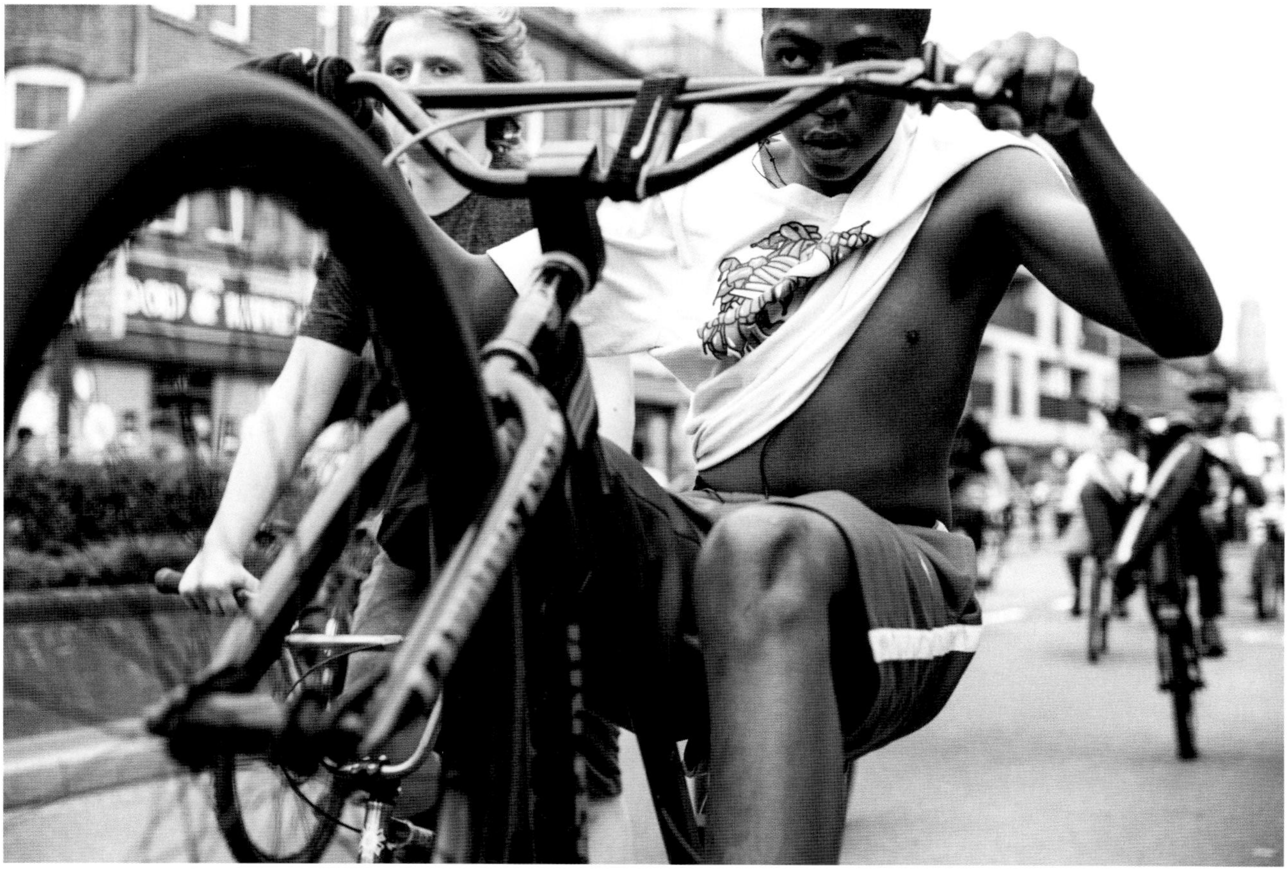

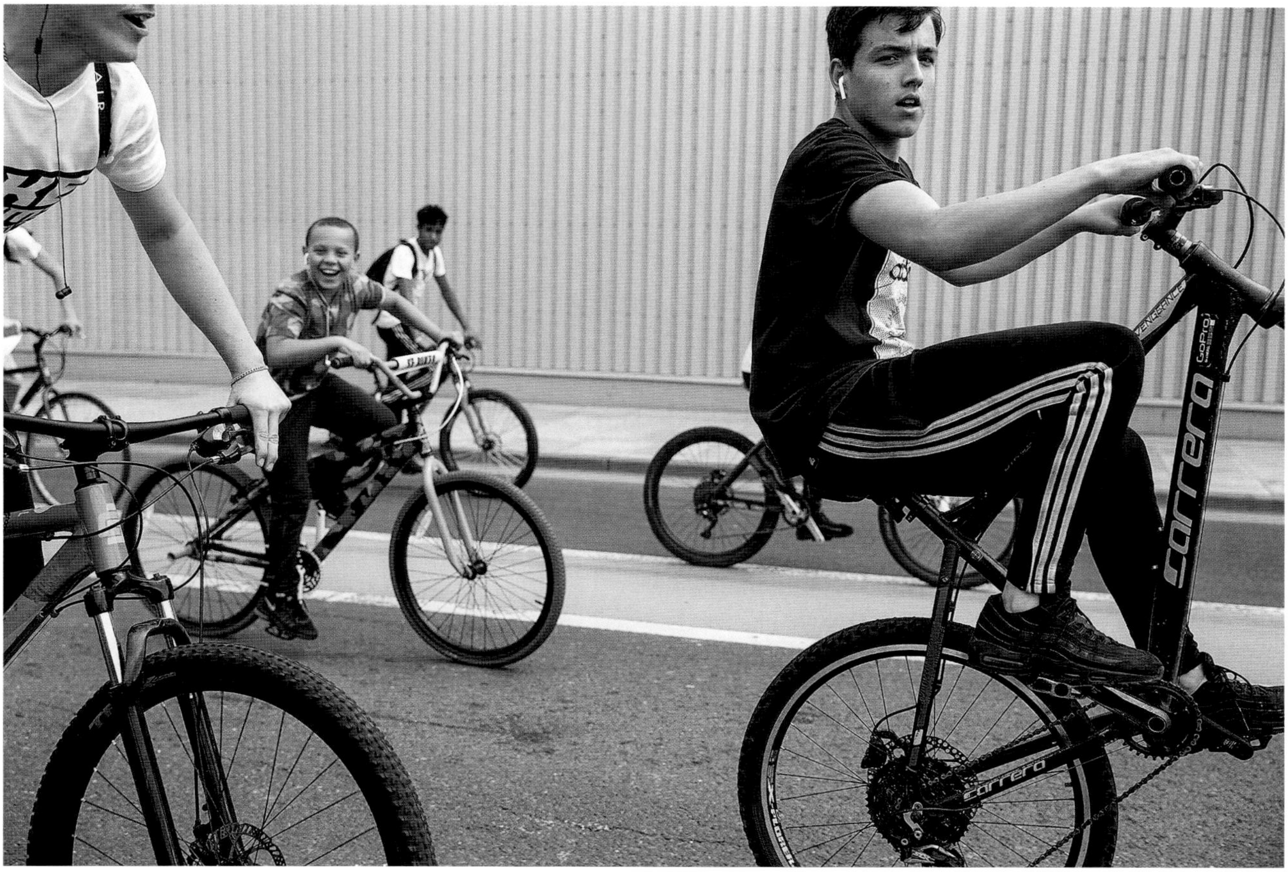

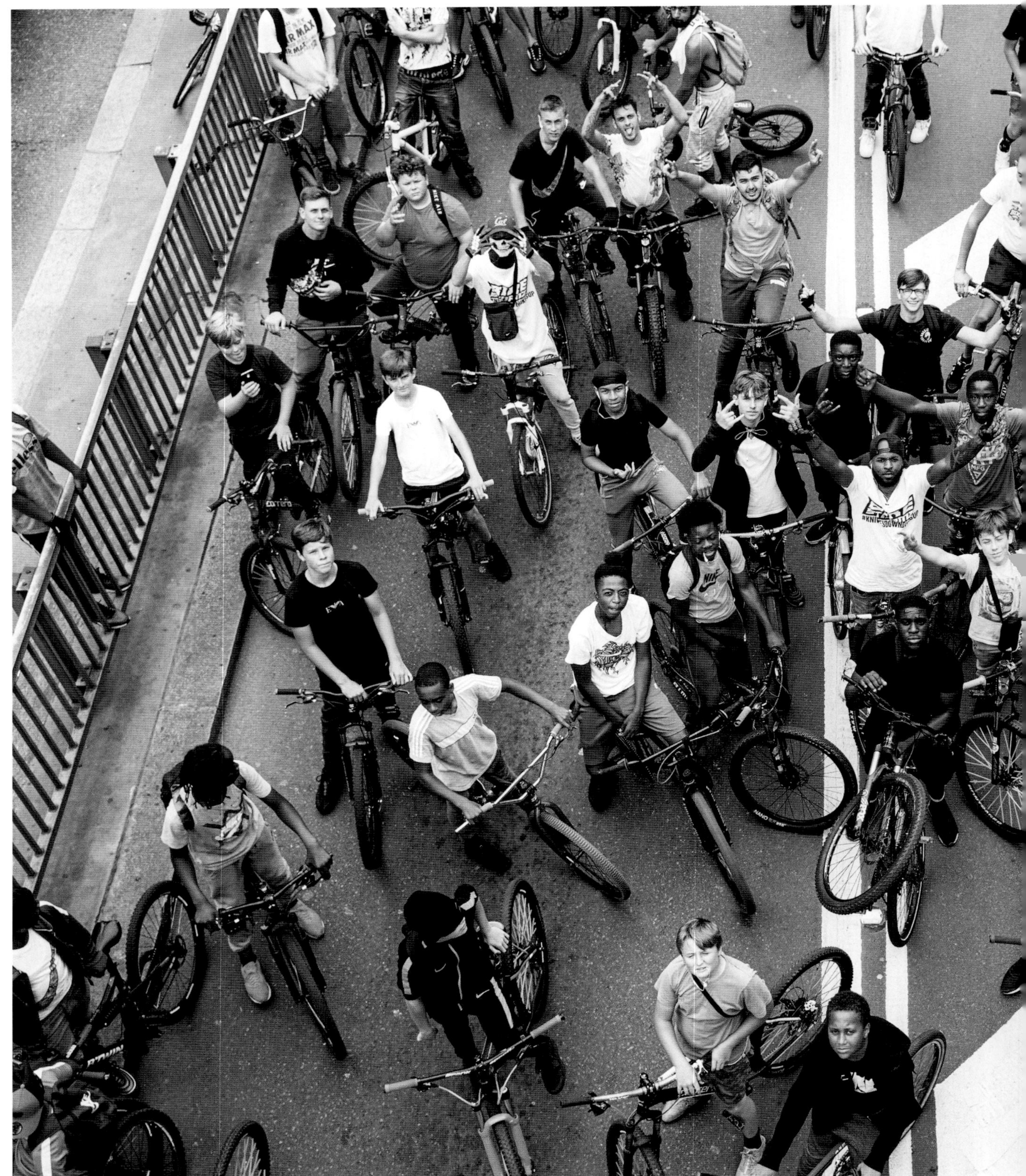
NIKE

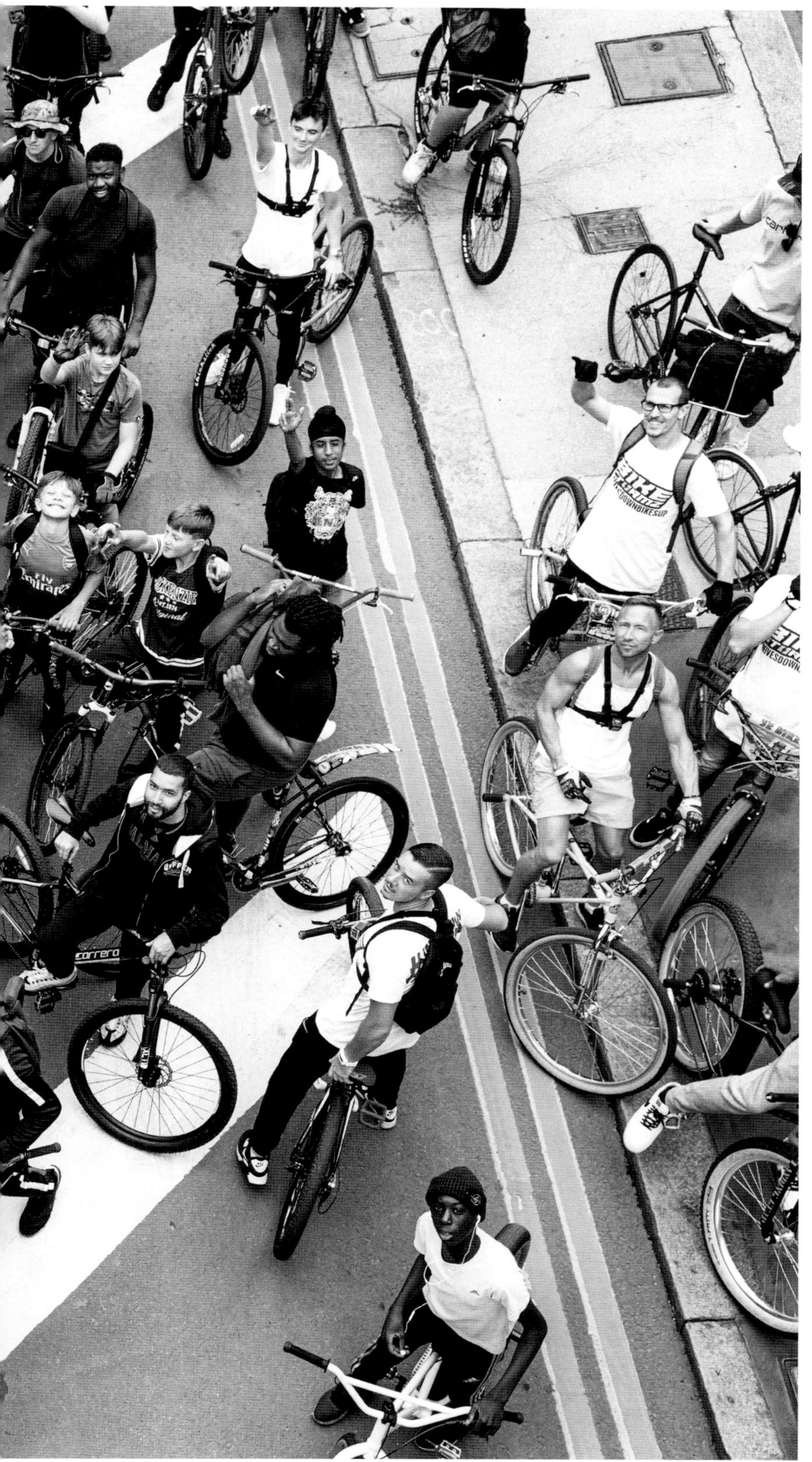
carrera

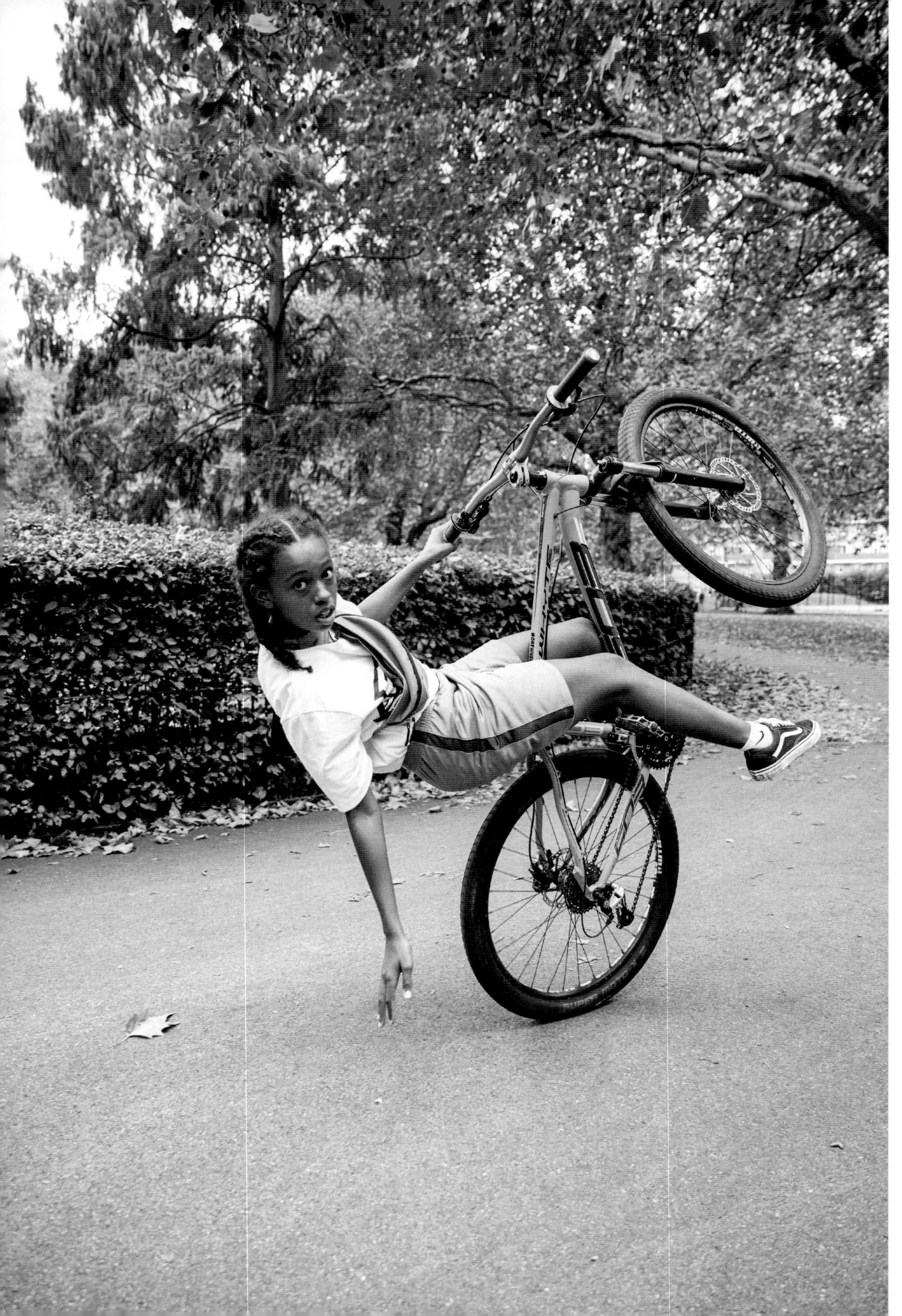

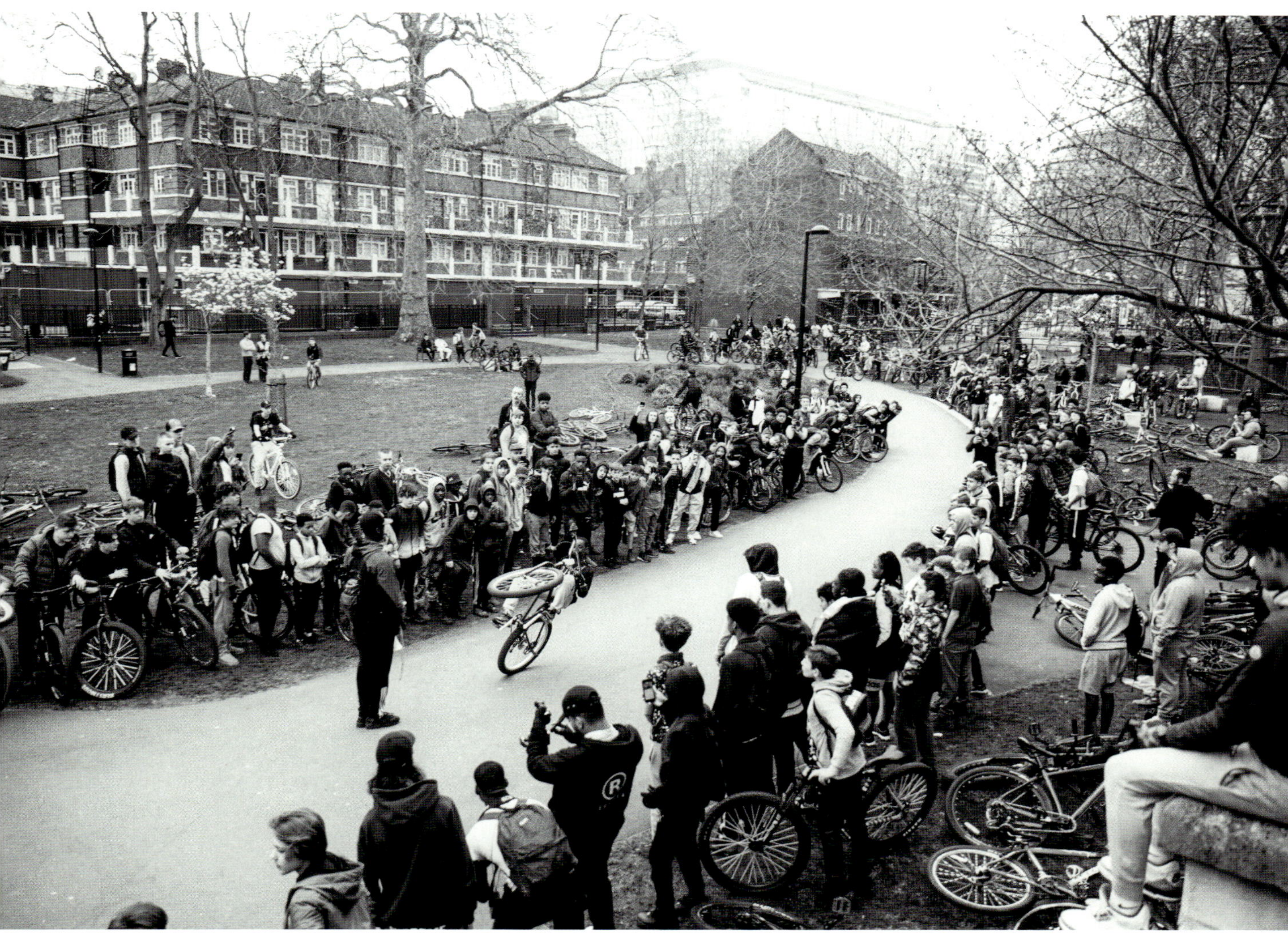

"It's an amazing feeling being surrounded by hundreds
of people who share the same passion as you.
I never thought something like this could happen here.
All you can see is a storm of positivity."

Jake O'Neill

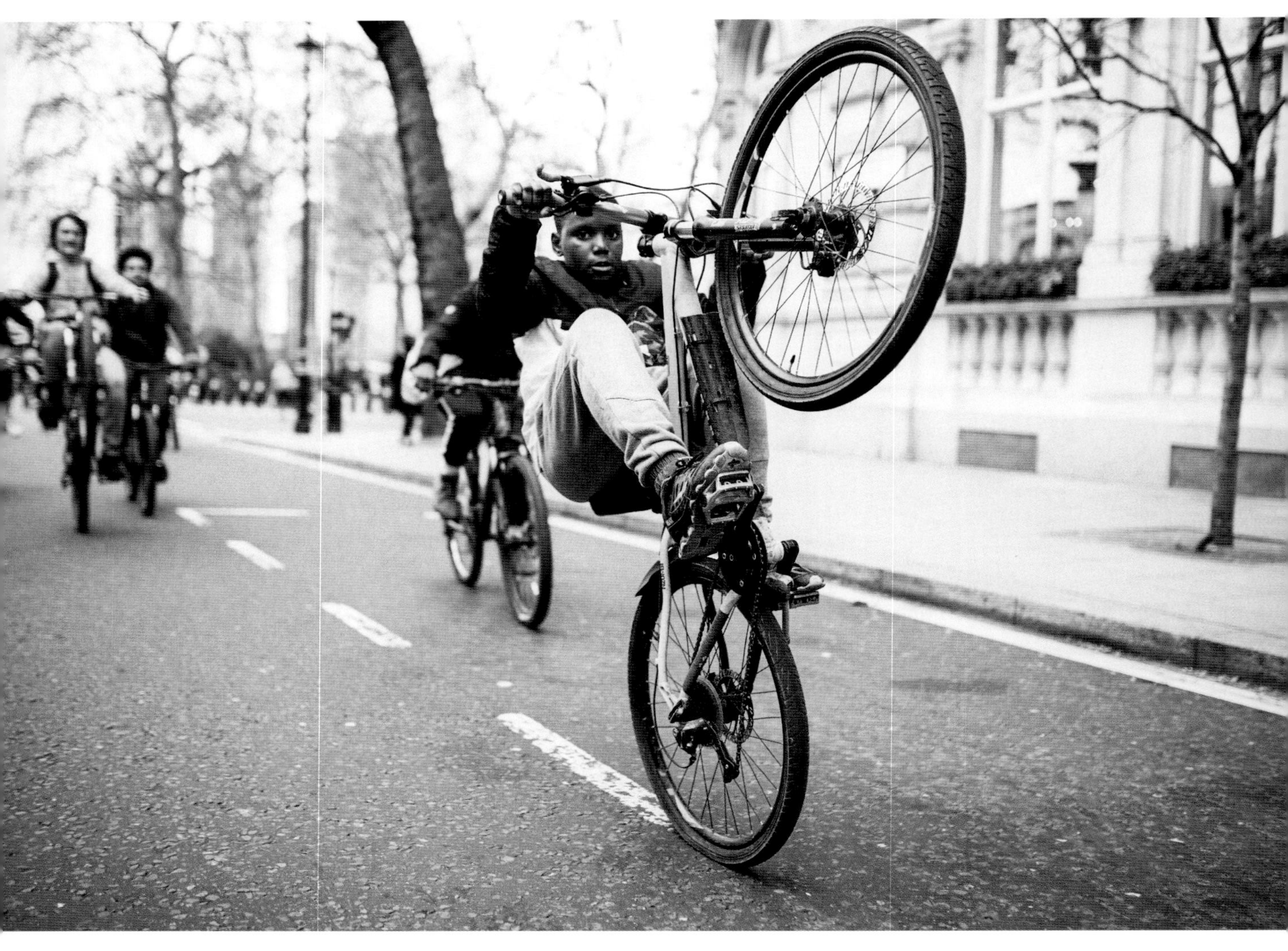

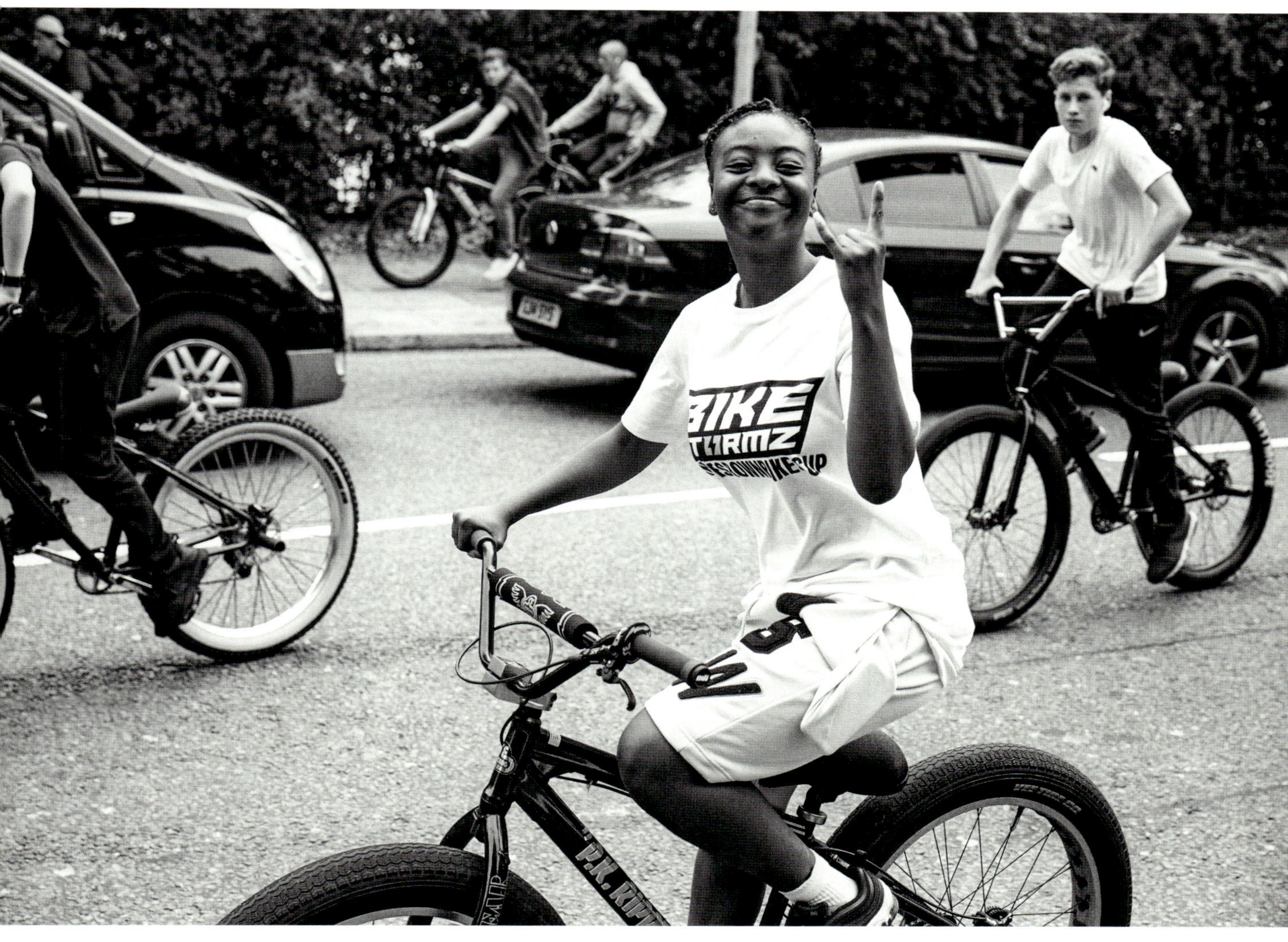

"When I was their age, I didn't think I would survive. I've gone through everything in my life: I've dealt drugs, I've stolen, I've hurt people. But now I'm here to listen to anything they have to tell me… and I'll put myself in harm's way to ensure they make it to 25."

Mac Ferrari

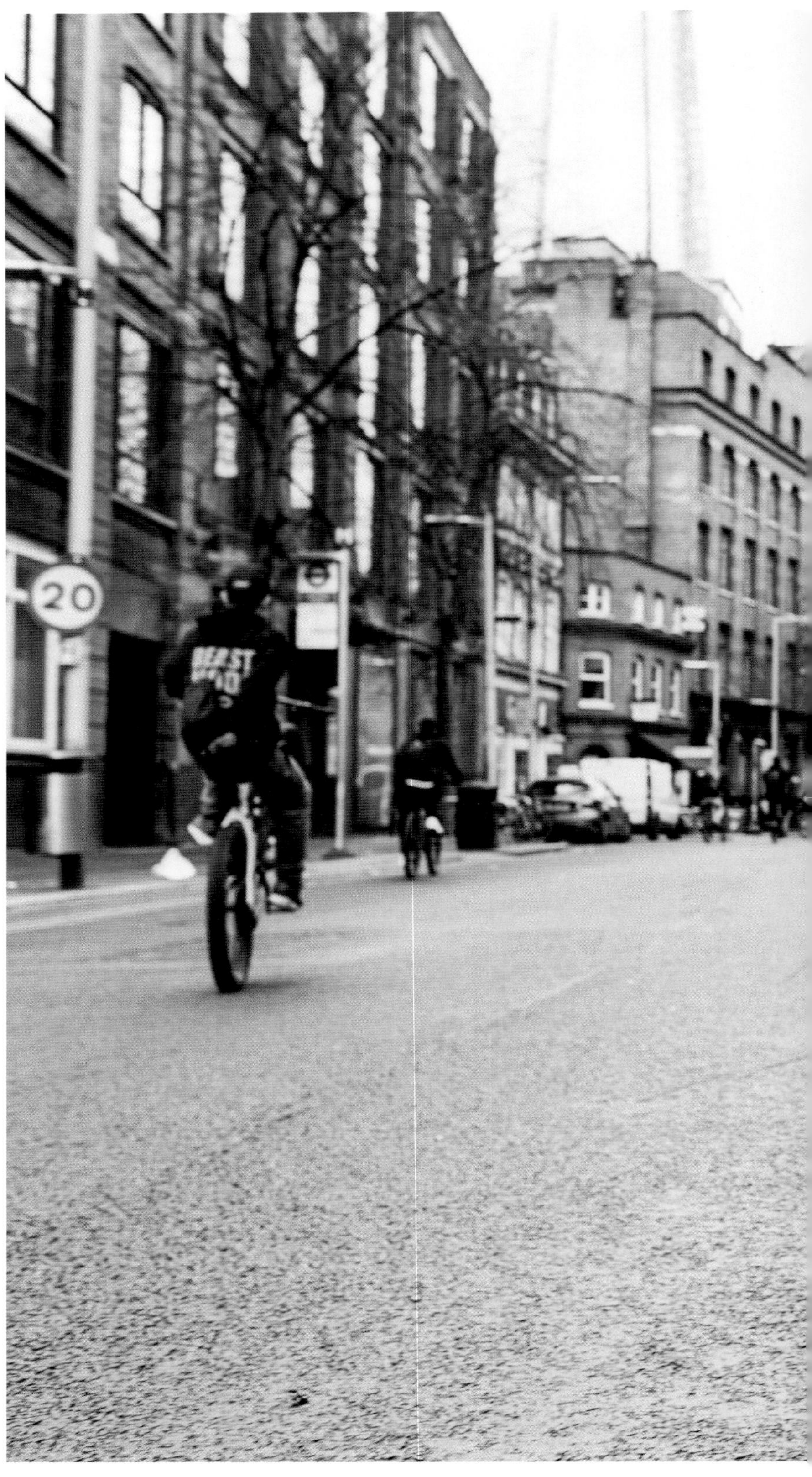
20

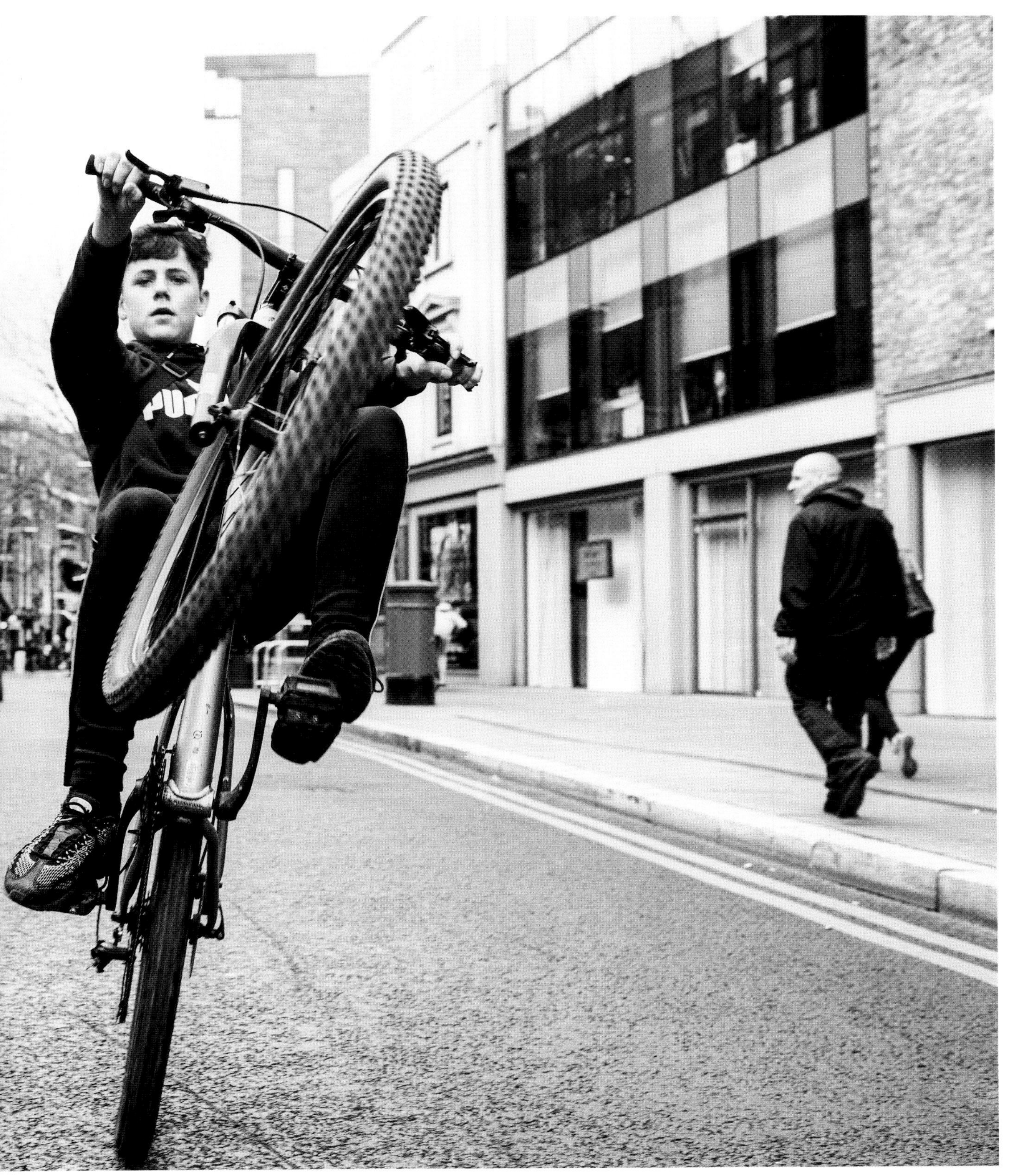

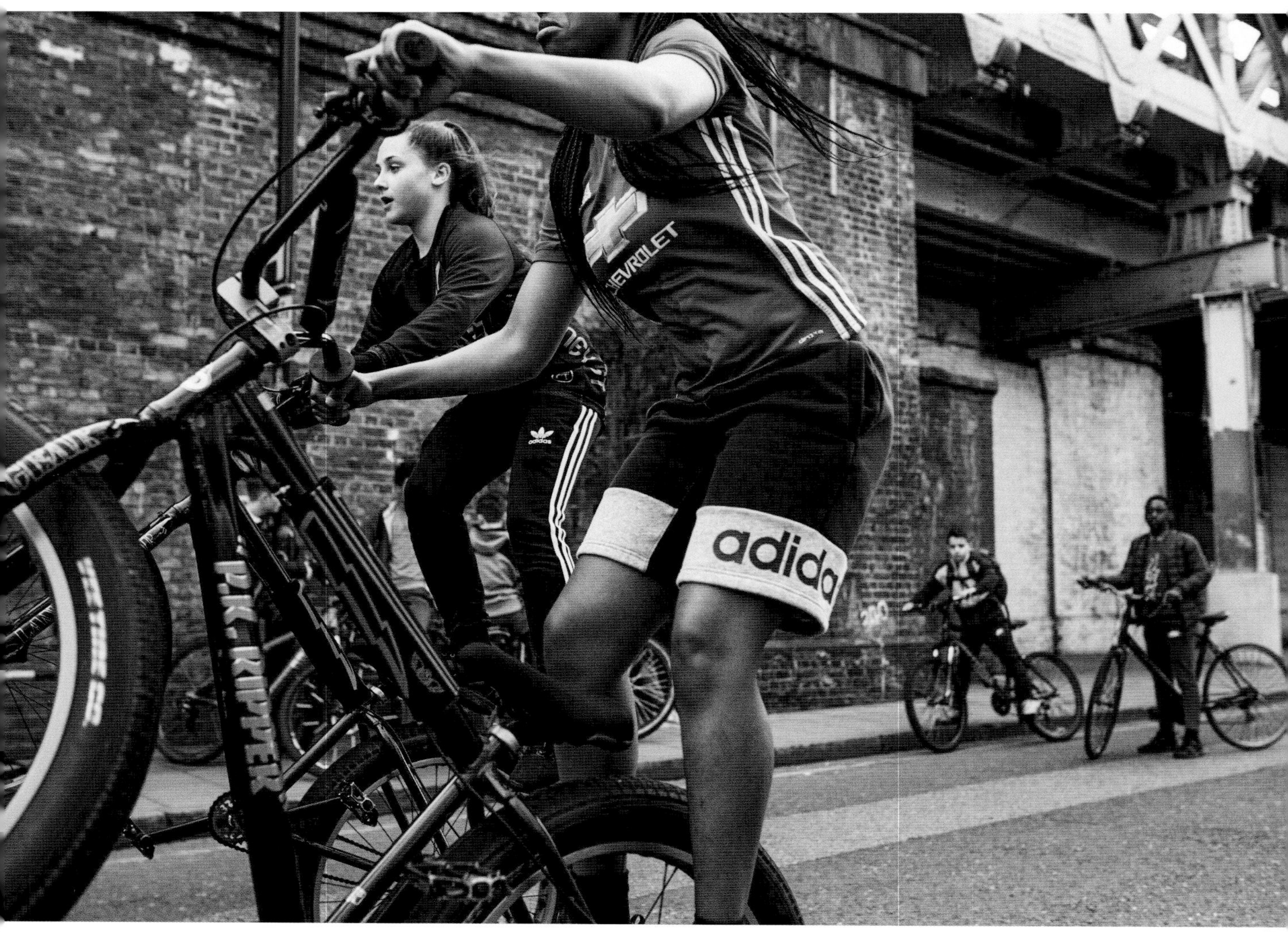
HEVROLET
adida
PK RIPPER
adidas

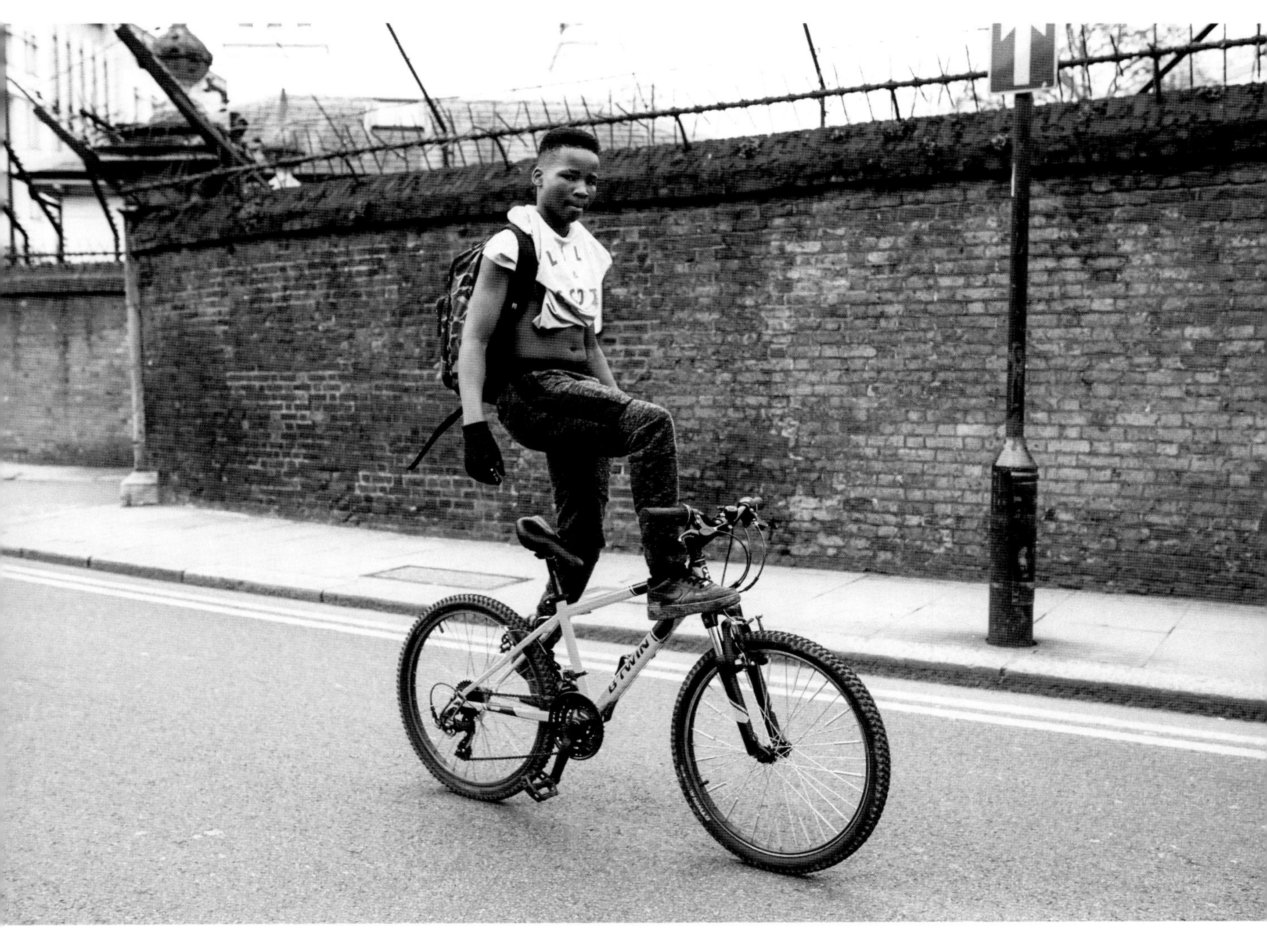
B'TWIN

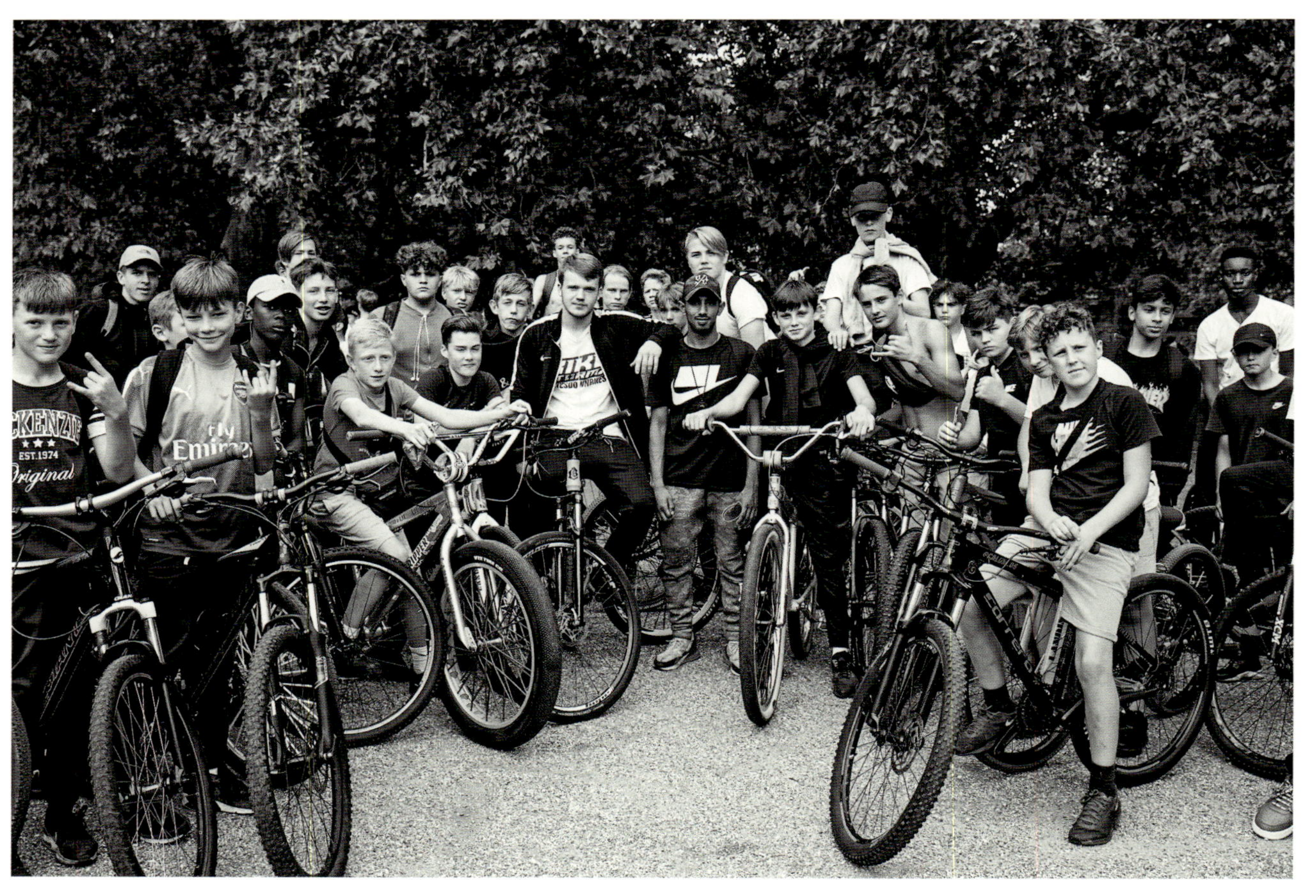

"As 3,000 riders prepare to shut down traffic in the capital to make a unified stand against violence, it's clear that the voices of young people can no longer be ignored. This is what London looks like with one wheel raised to the sky."

Alex King

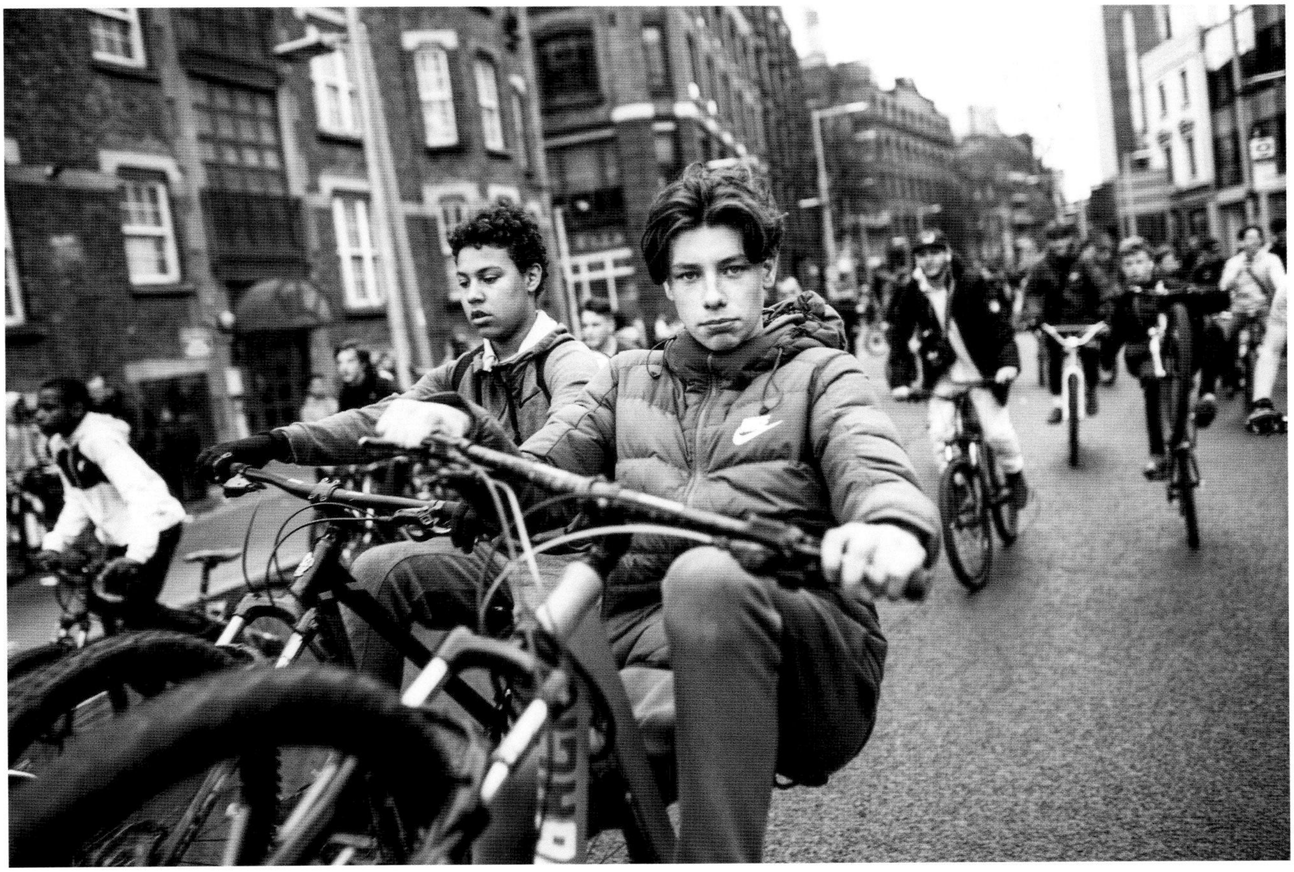

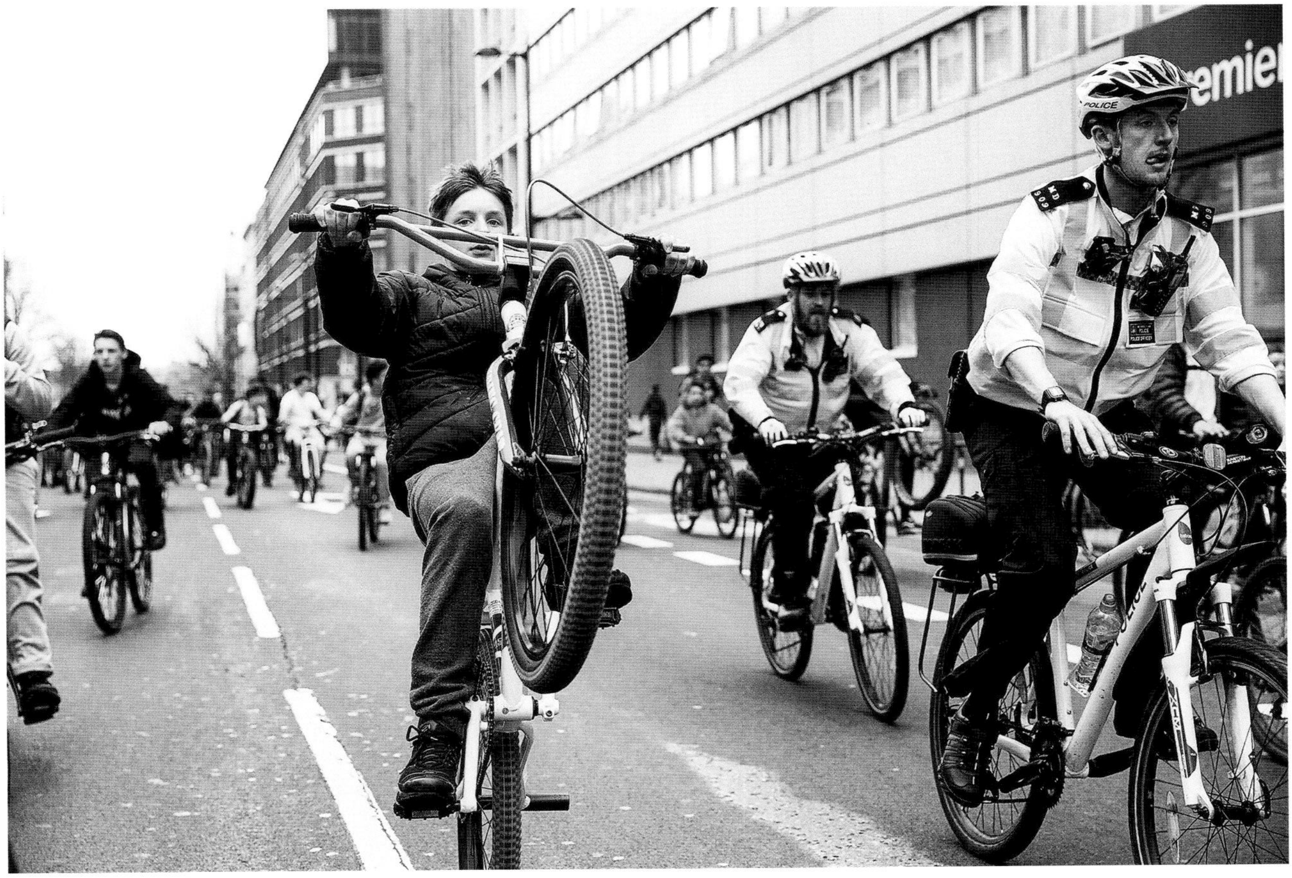

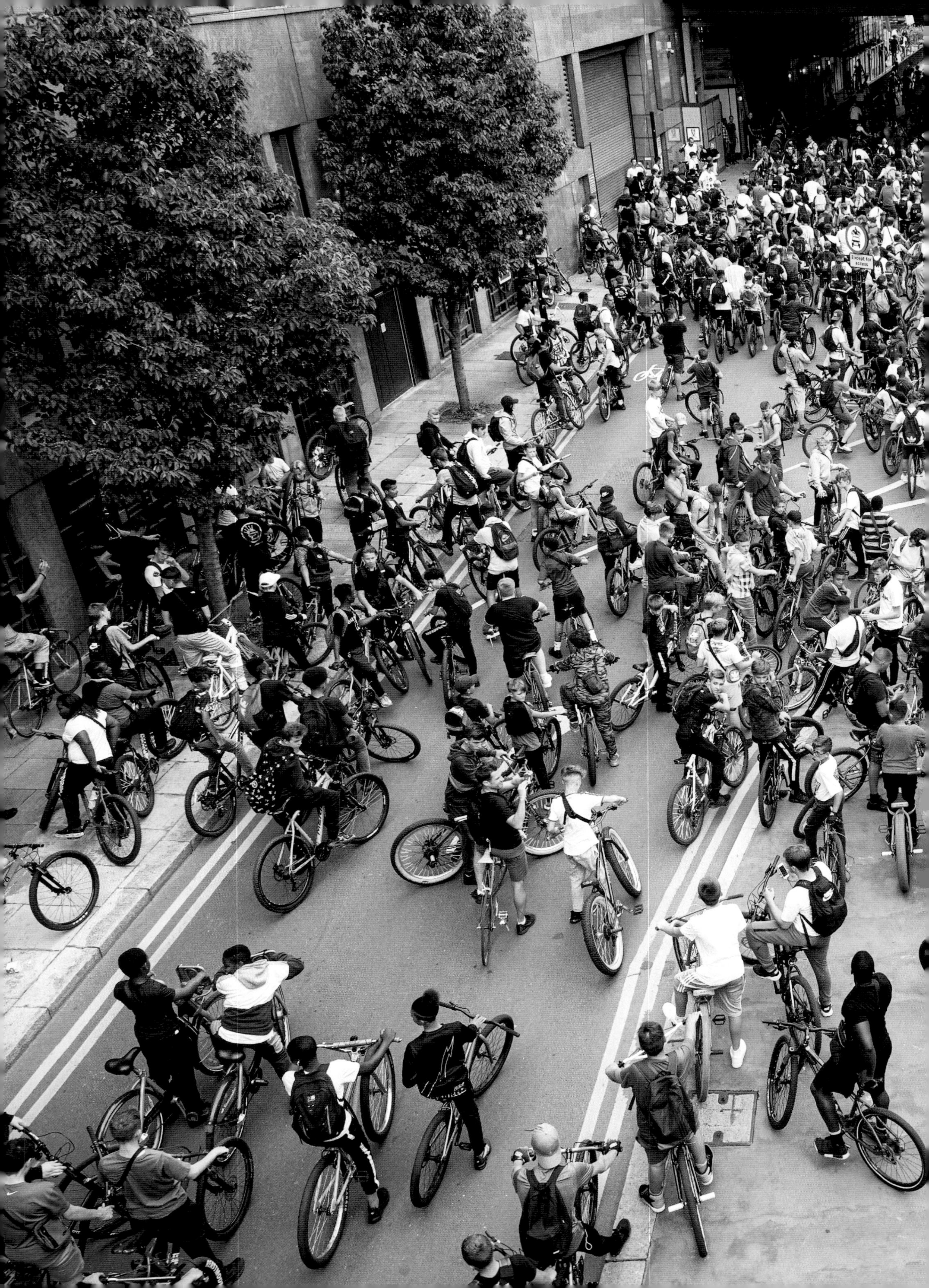
Except for
access

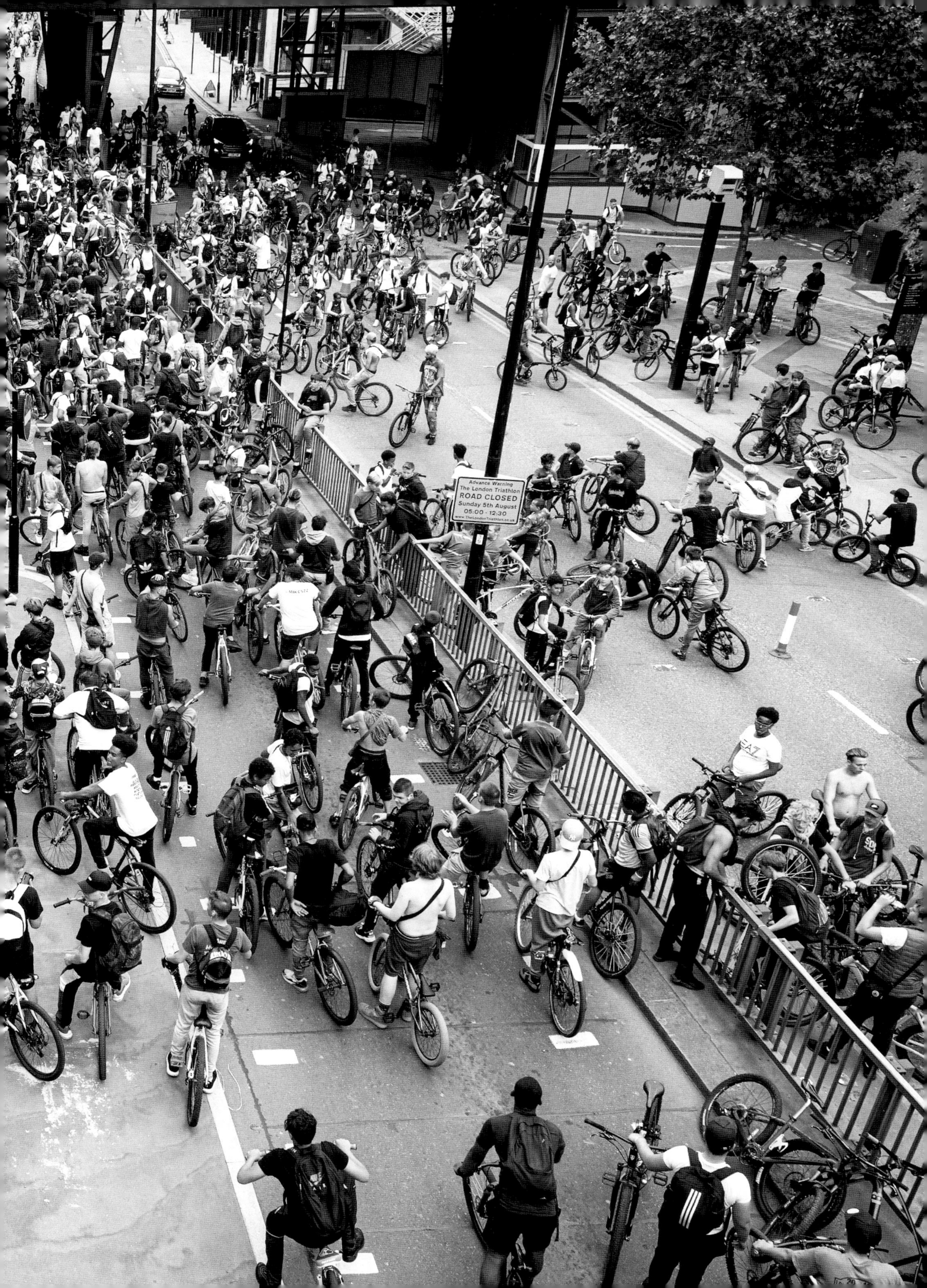
Advance Warning
The London Triathlon
ROAD CLOSED
Sunday 5th August
05:00 - 12:30
www.TheLondonTriathlon.co.uk

The World from Above

Havana—A bike builder who touches the sky

Photos
Tod Seelie

When Félix Ramón Guirola Cepero saw his first tandem bike as a child, he had a vision. One day he would build a bike that would not stretch horizontally, but vertically. The Cuban built his first tall bike as a teenager. Since then, he's built several more, some of which are made from thirty-year-old Chinese bike frames he has welded together. Sitting at a height of three meters, he joyfully rides his creations across Havana. To the amazement of passengers—and irritation of drivers—he rests at red lights by leaning against the city buses.

Cepero dreams of building a bike ten meters tall. With such a bike, he would break the existing record and be added to the *Guinness Book of World Records*. But for him, this is secondary to his friendship with fellow North American Richie Trimble, a world record holder from the USA. Trimble has even traveled to Havana to visit Félix, whom he regards as an equally talented bike builder. Together, the pair rode their tall bikes through the streets, Cepero leading the way, a fraternity of two, framed against the sky.

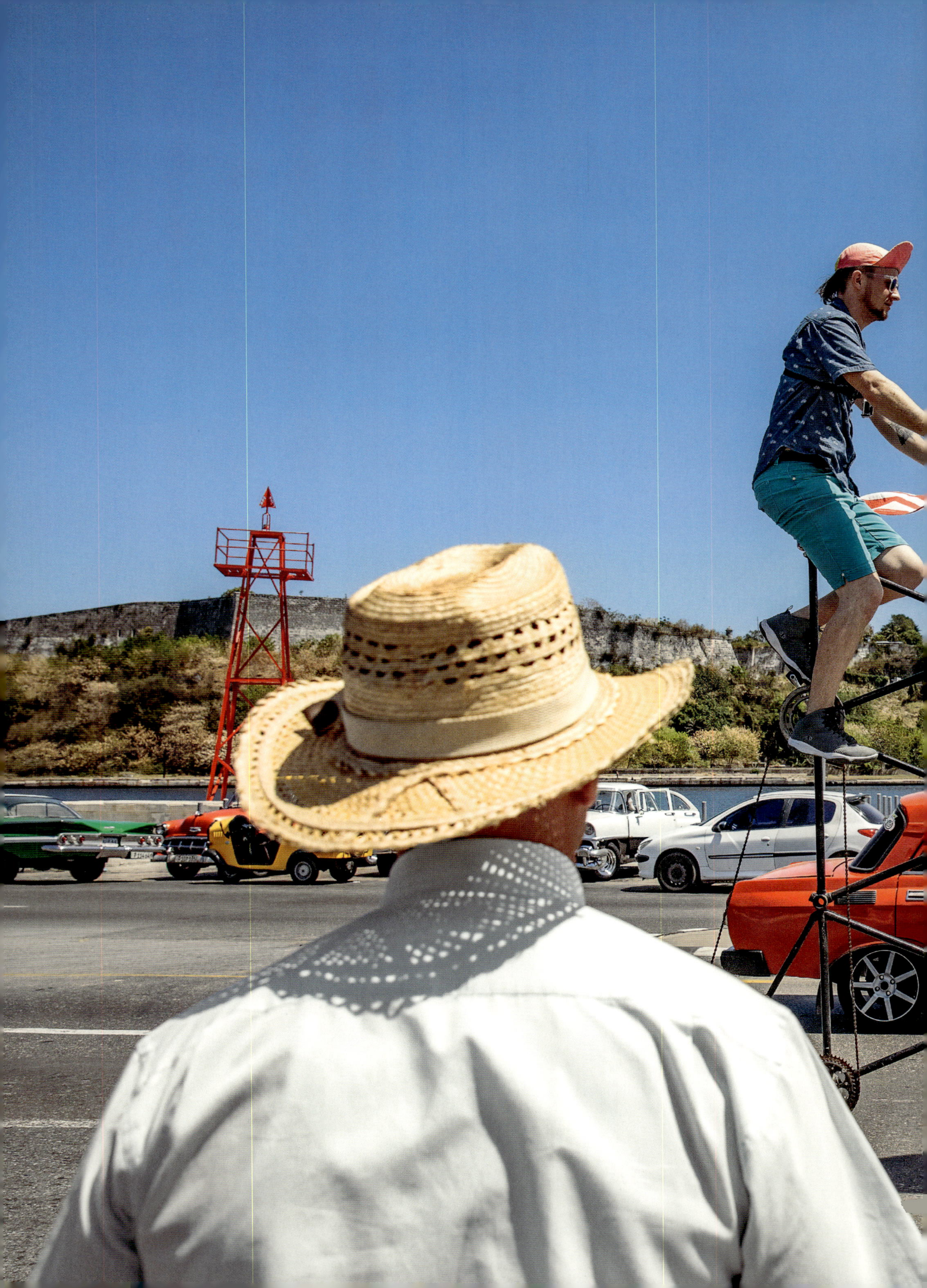

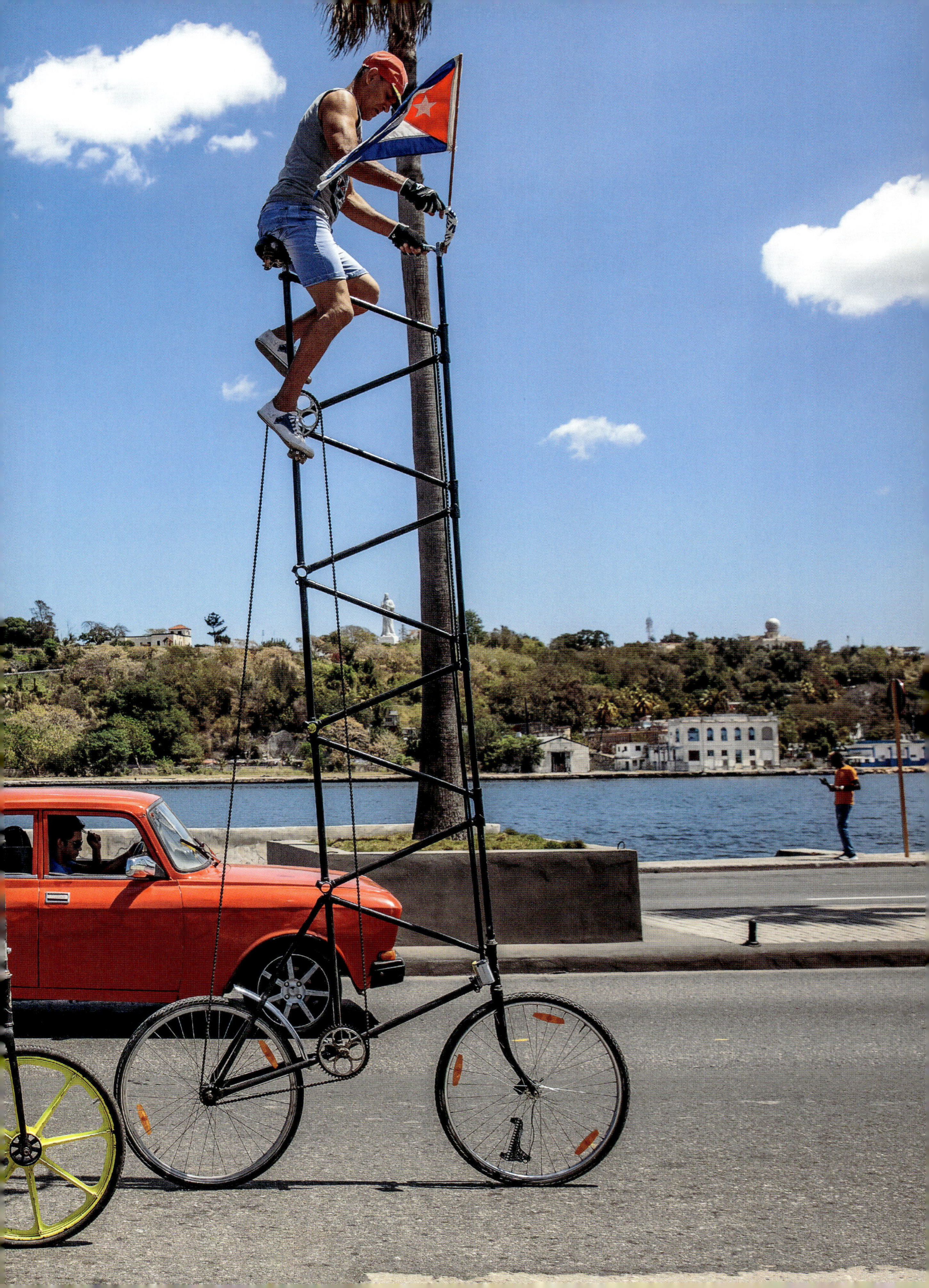

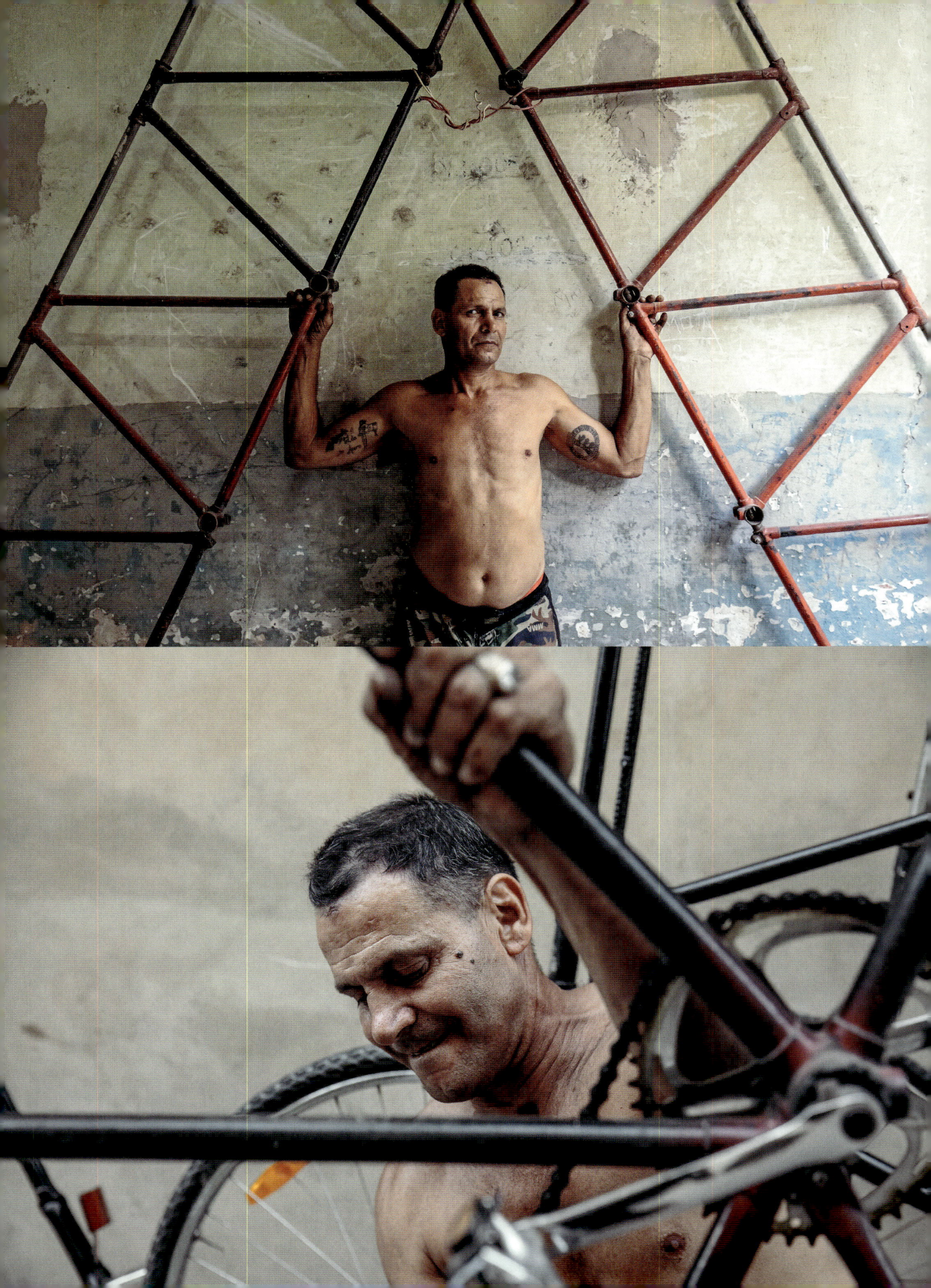

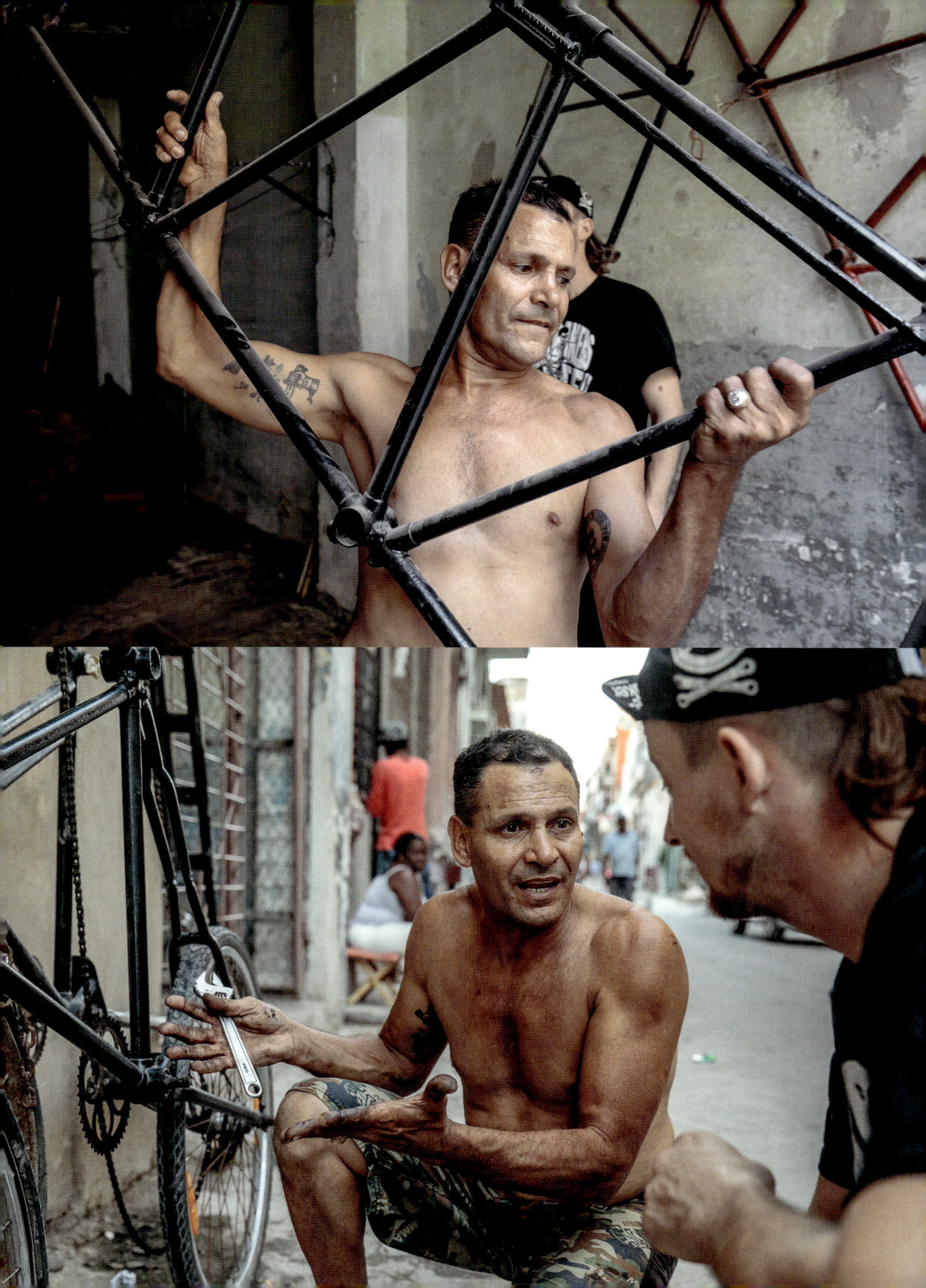

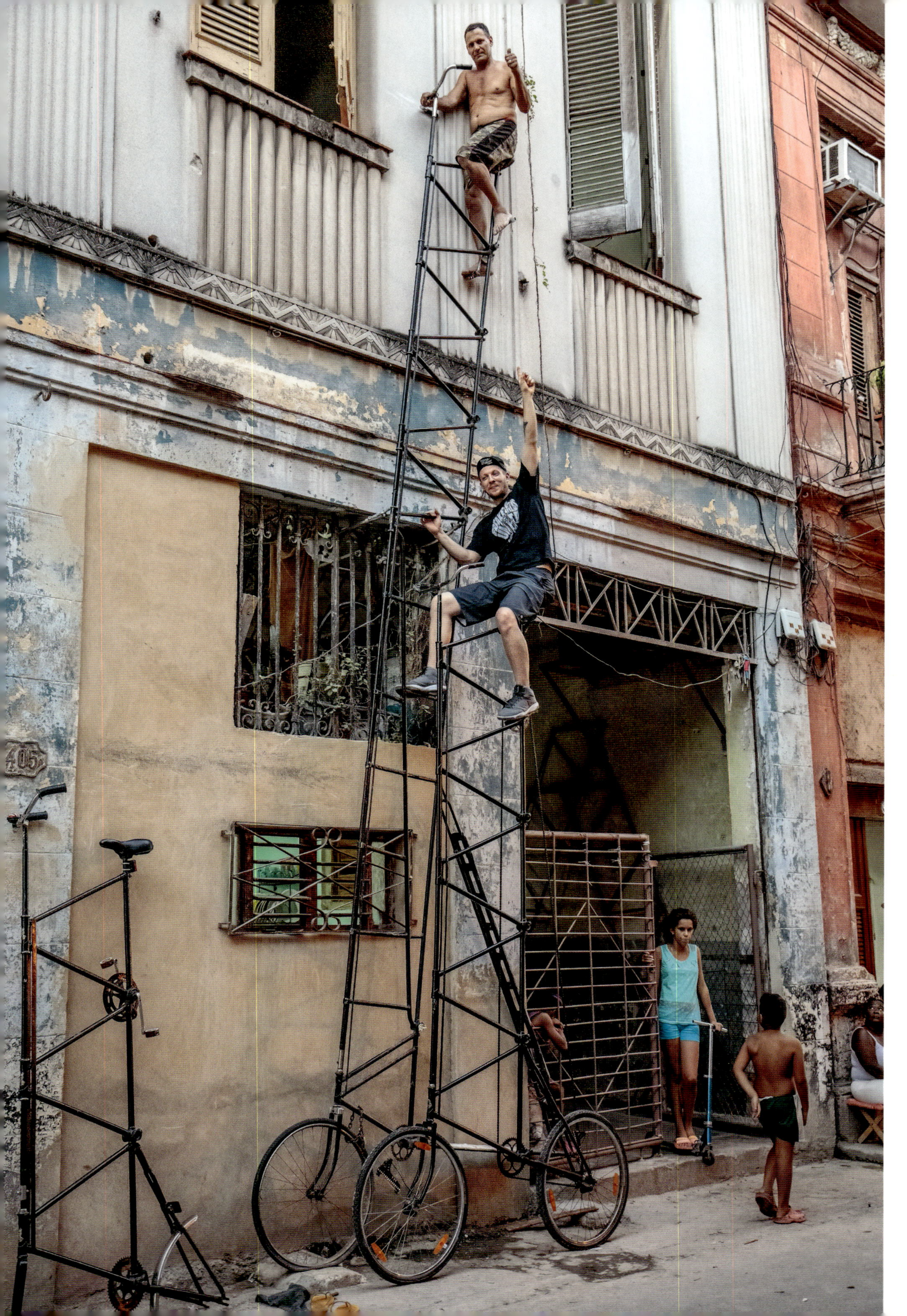
405

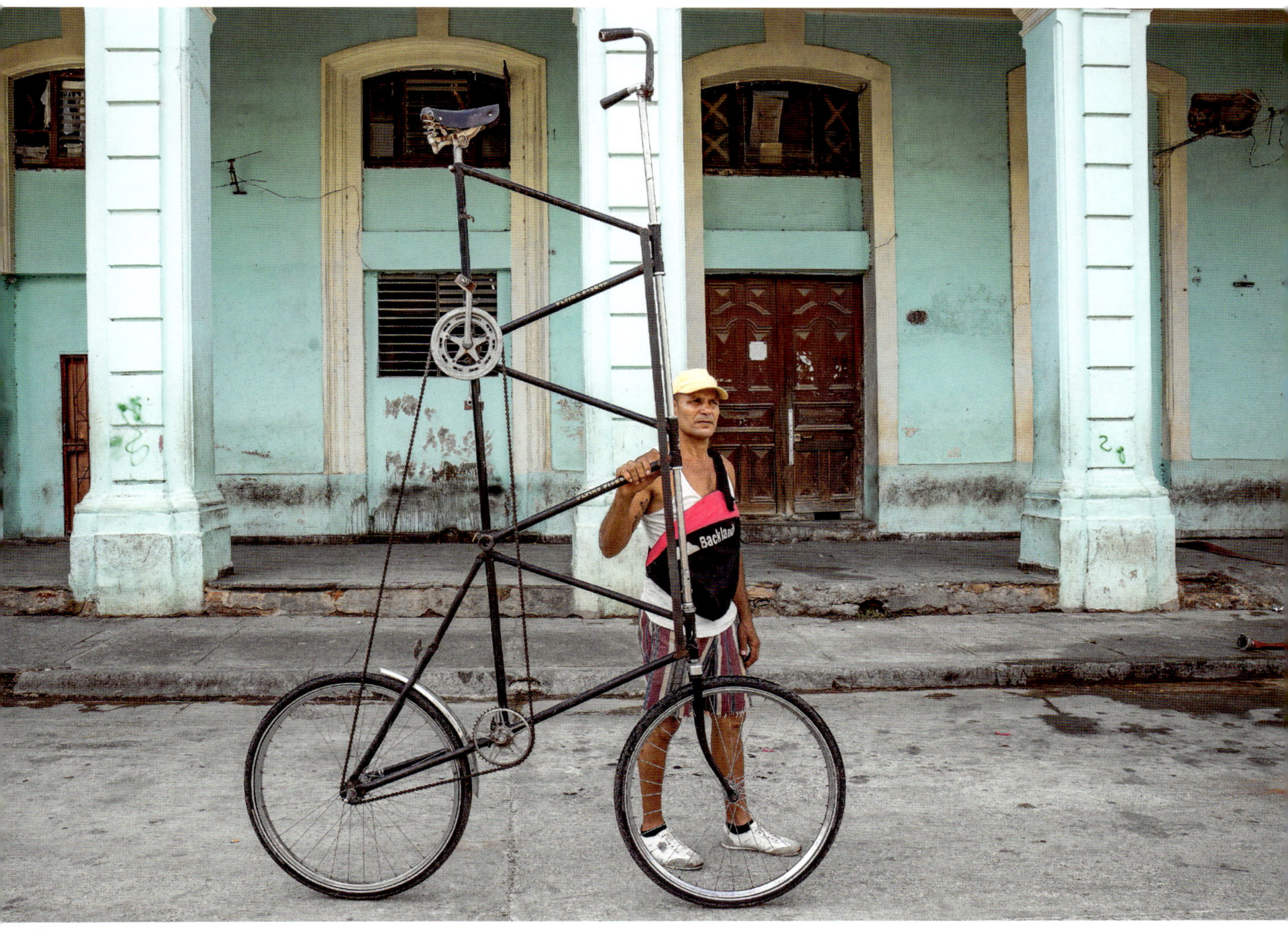

"For me it is an honor that the guy who holds the world record came to meet me, and that makes me a record holder in itself. This record of friendship is more important than Guinness."

Félix Ramón Guirola Cepero

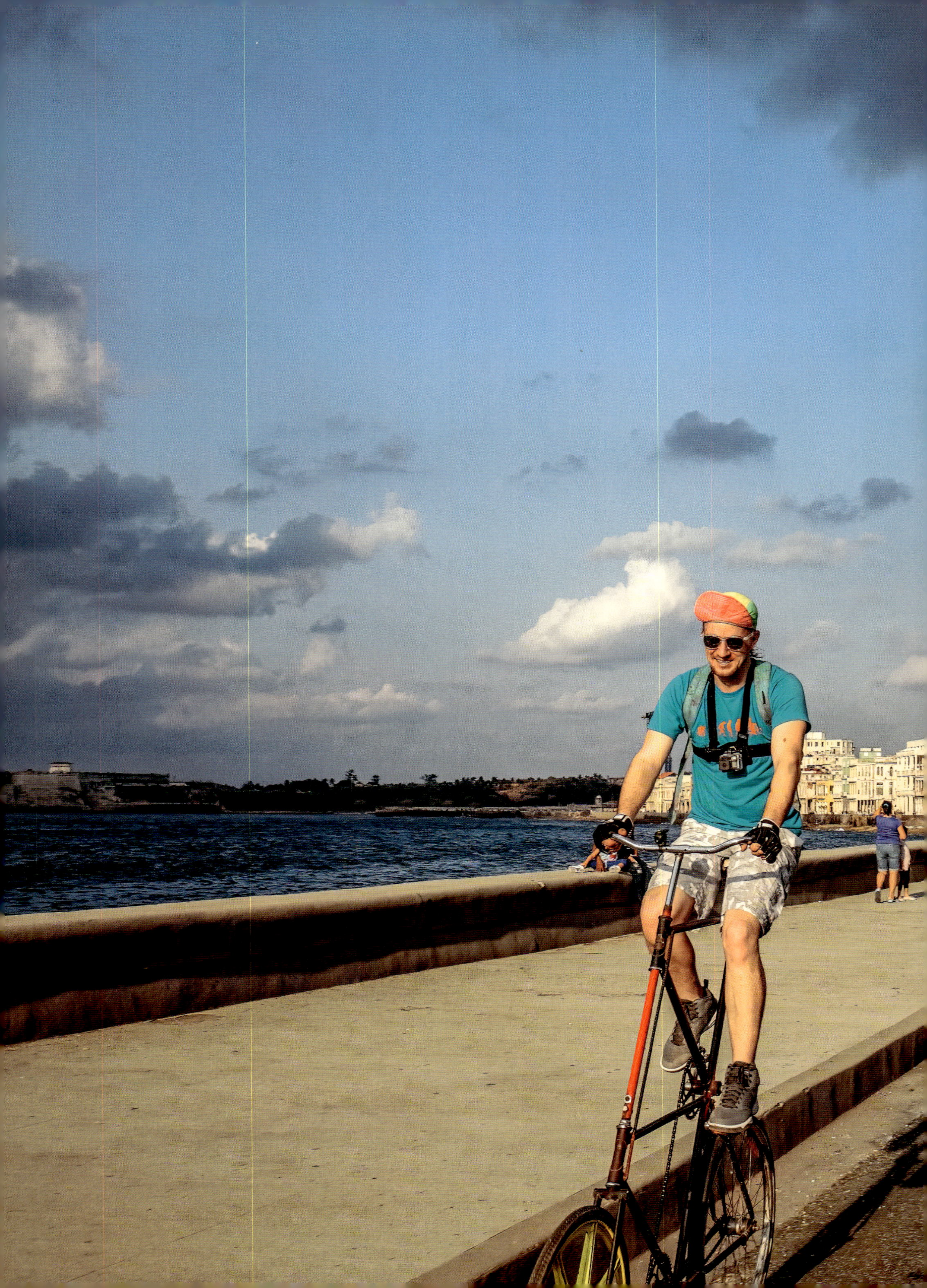

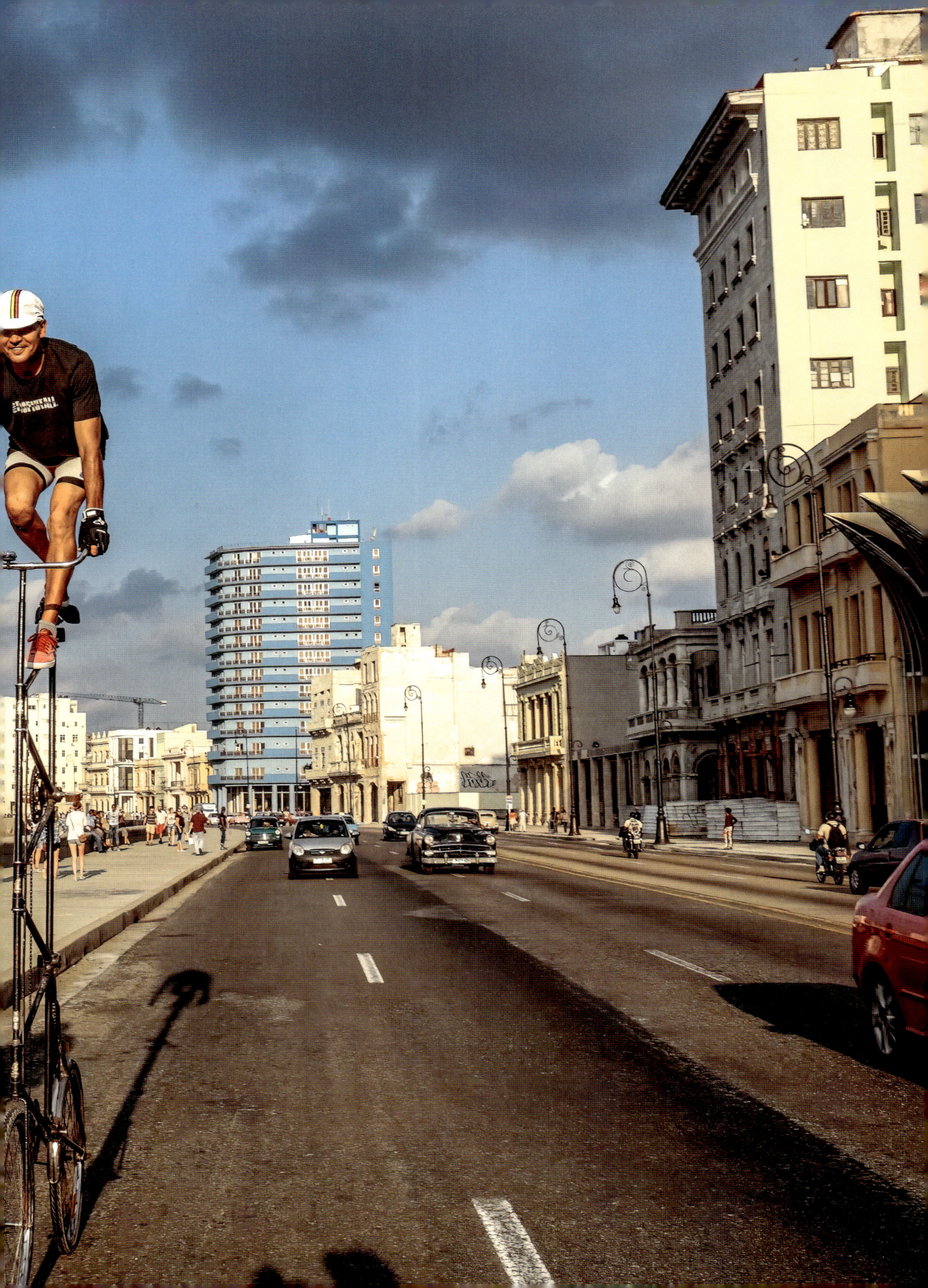

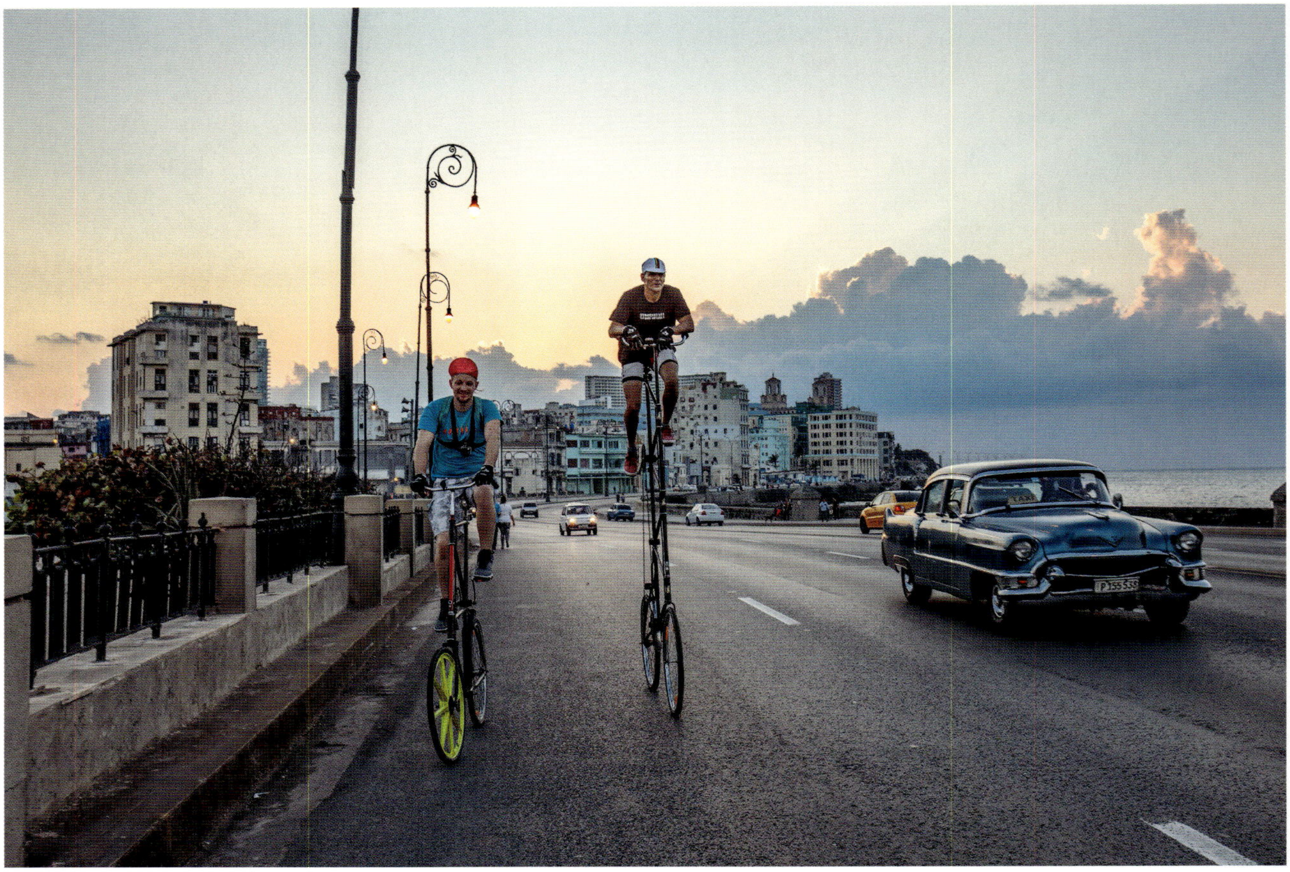

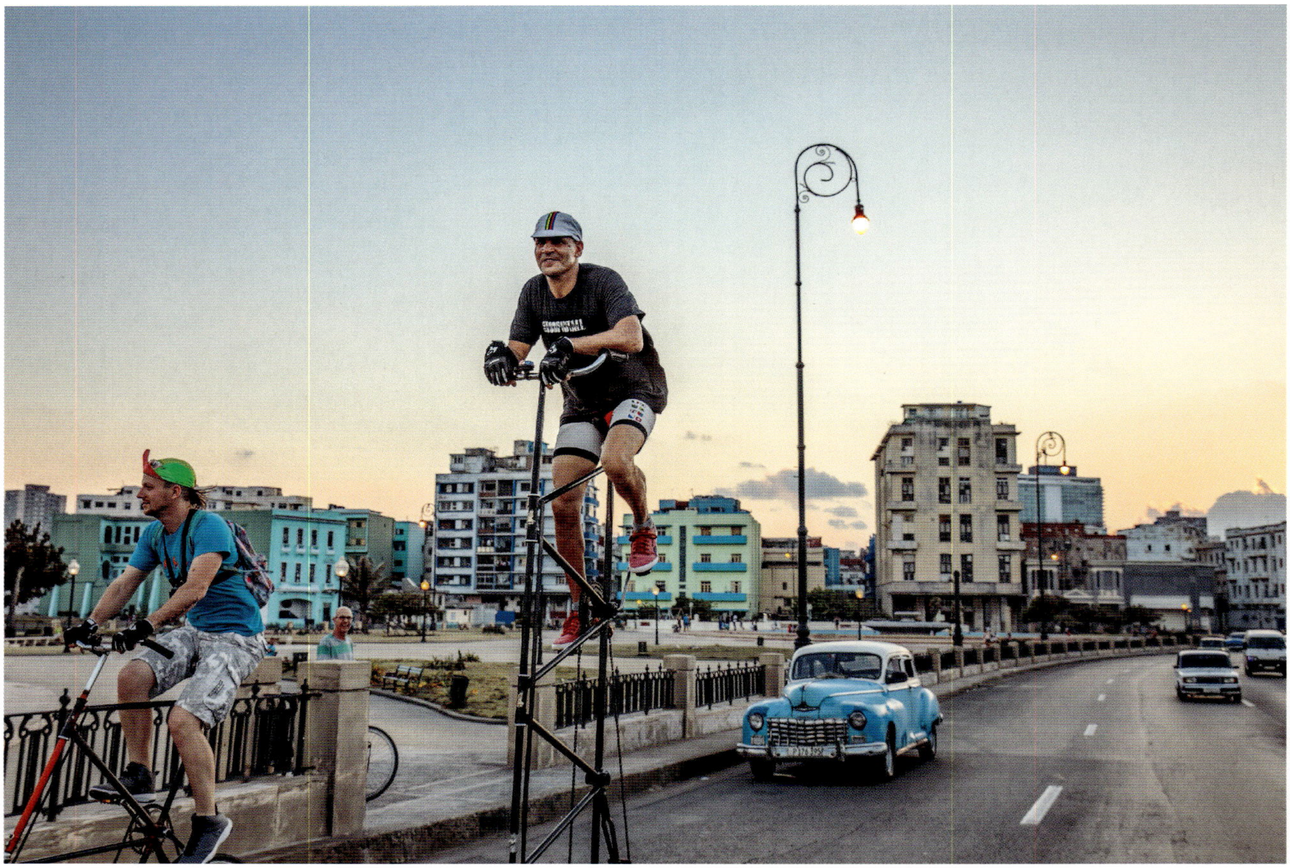

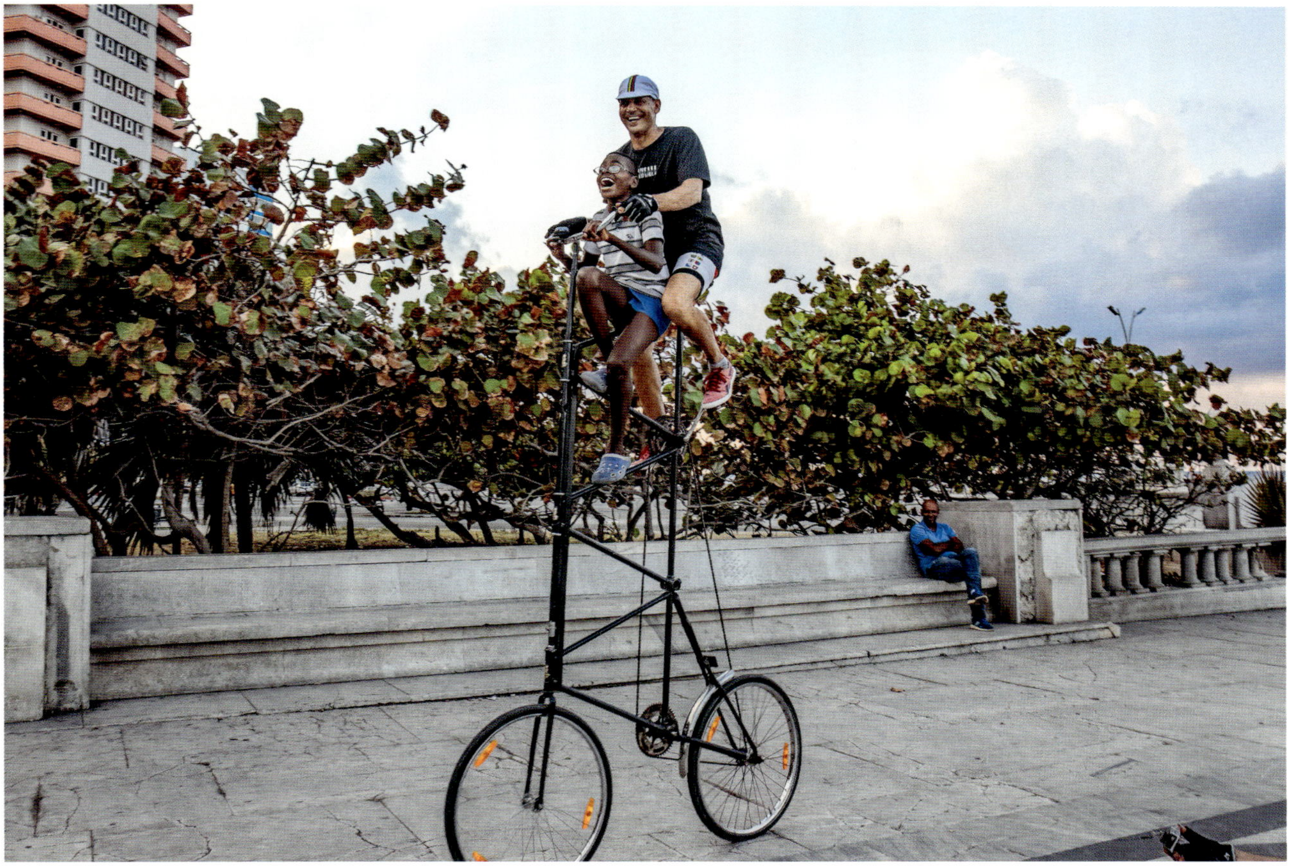

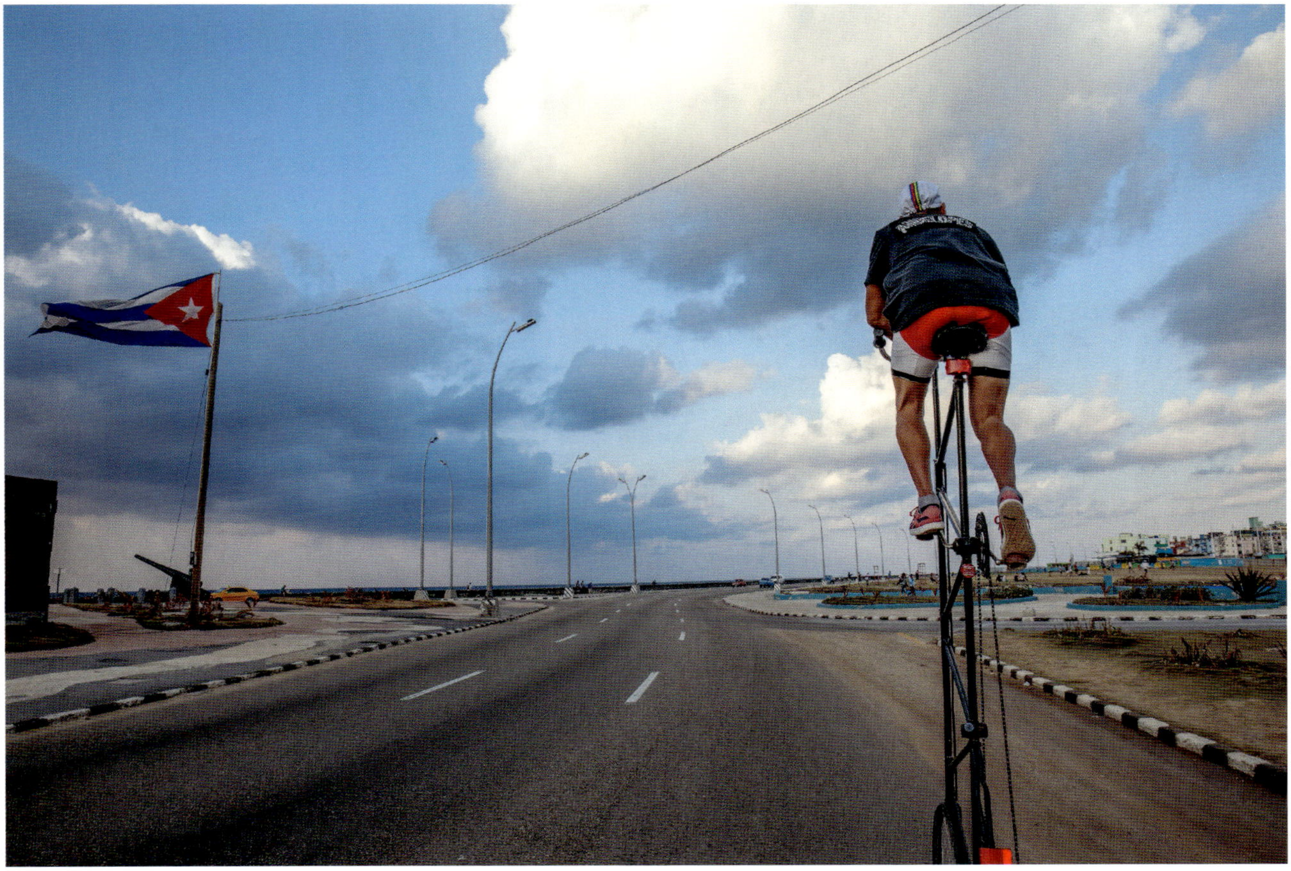

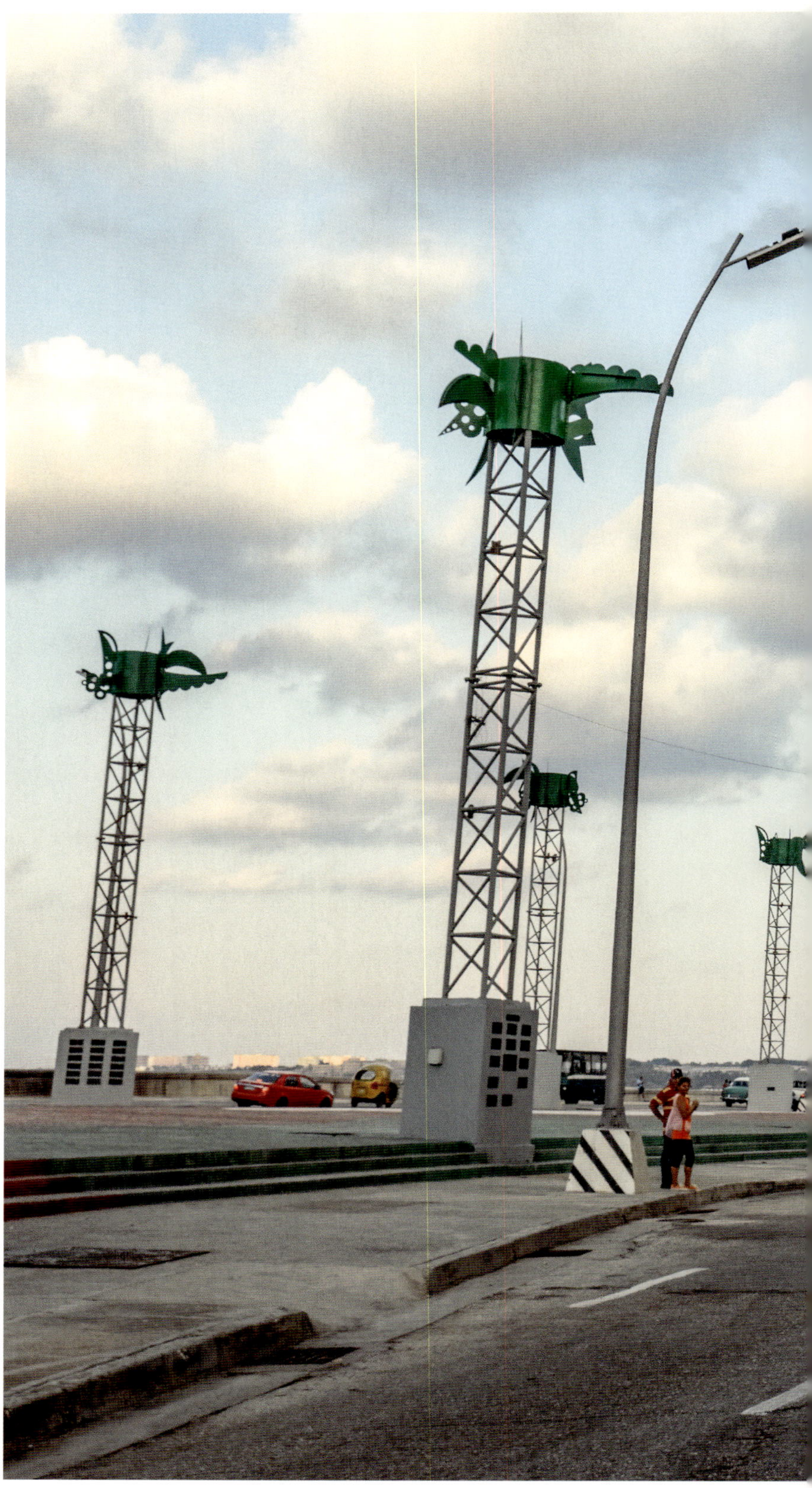

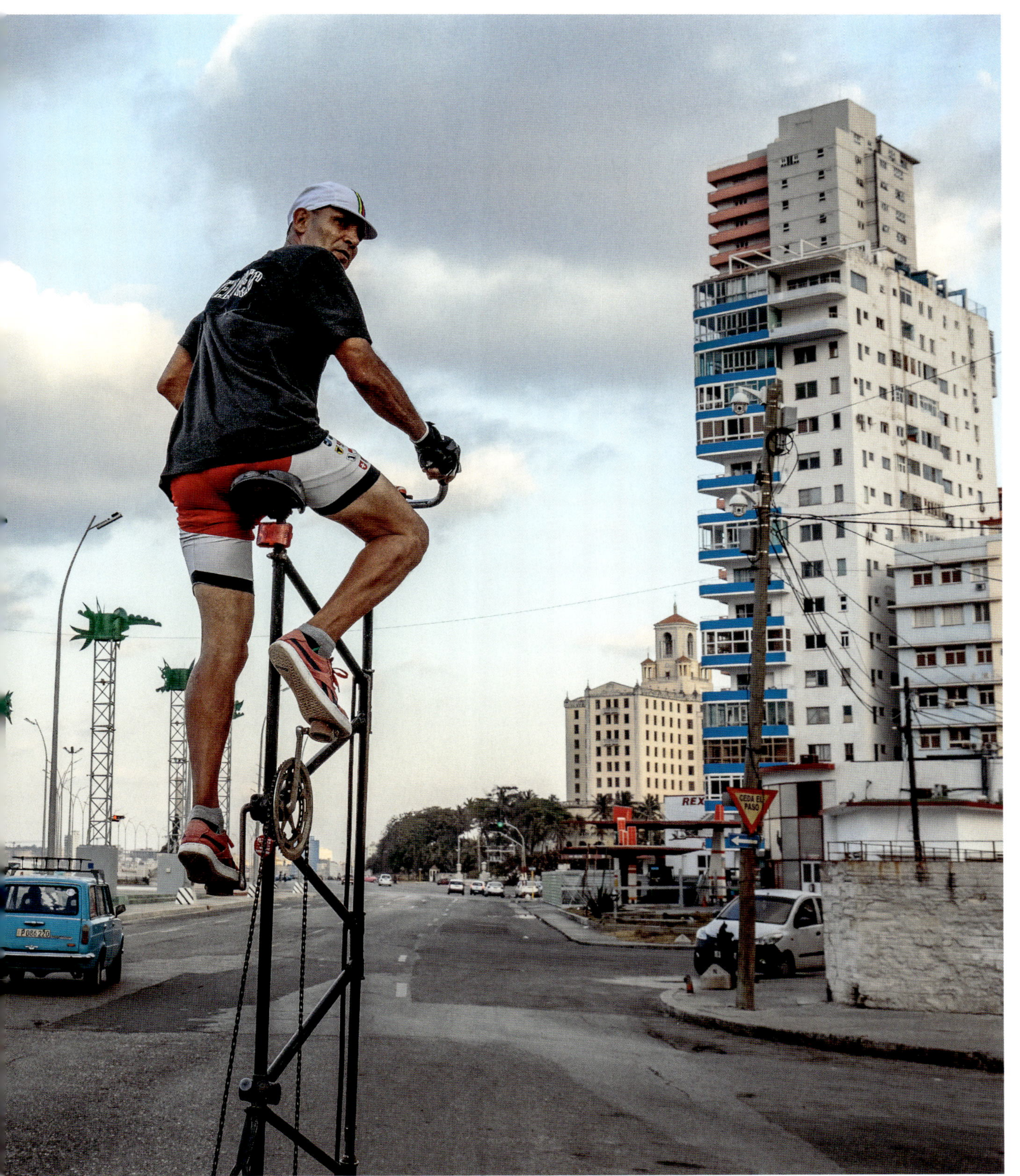
REX
CEDA EL PASO

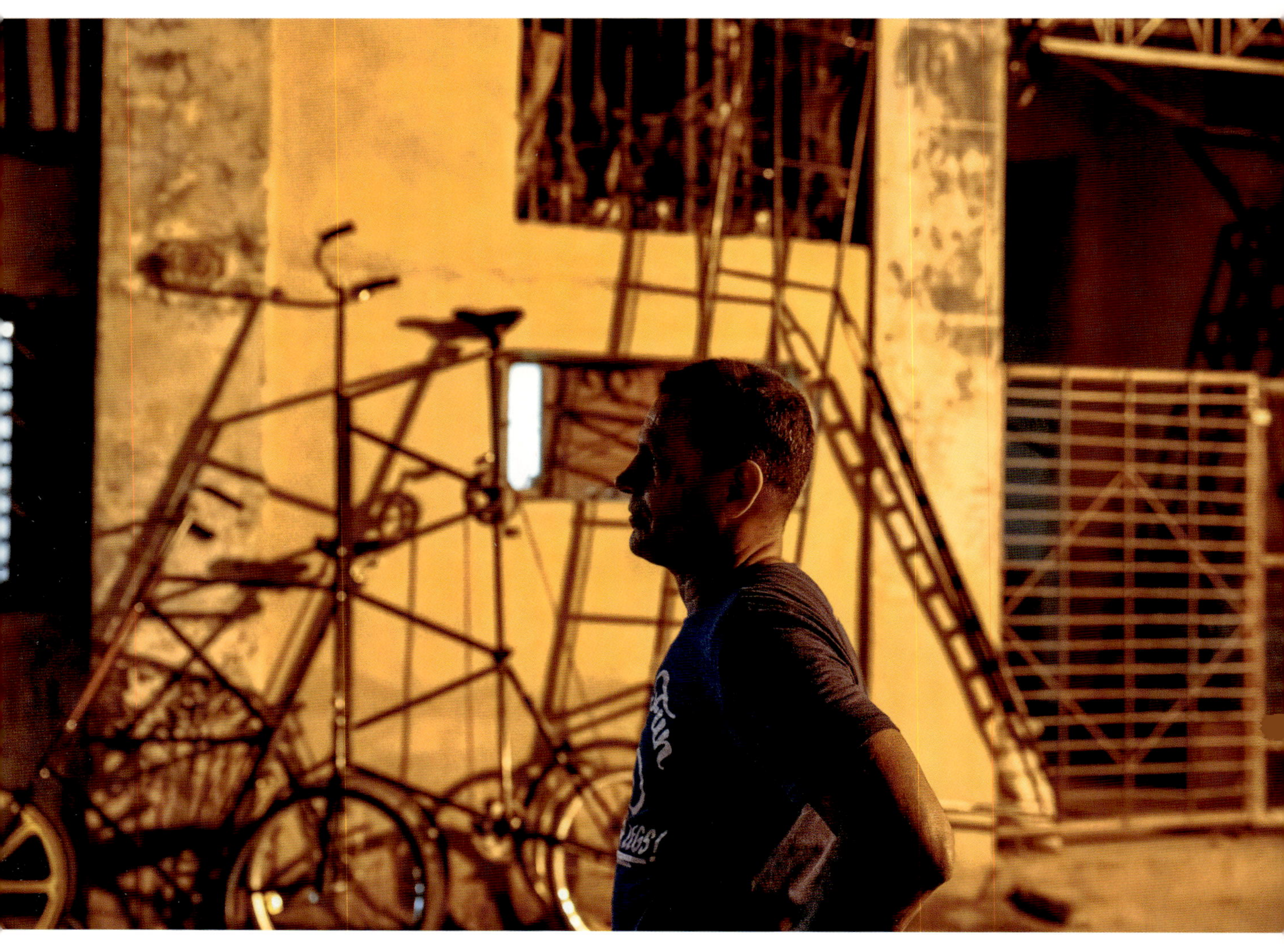

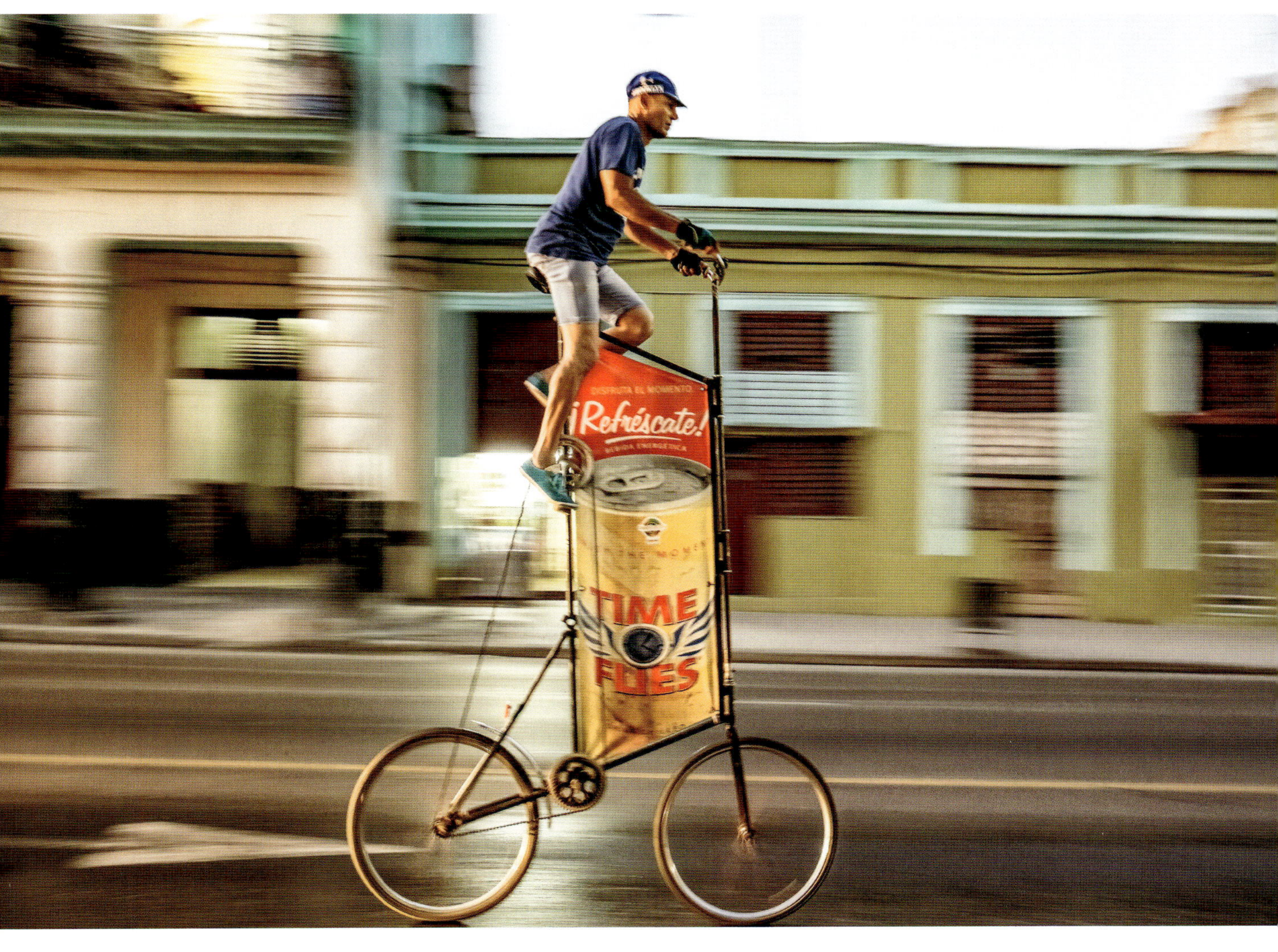

"When I saw a tandem for the first time, it was horizontal.
I said, 'Well, I'm going to build upwards.'"

Félix Ramón Guirola Cepero

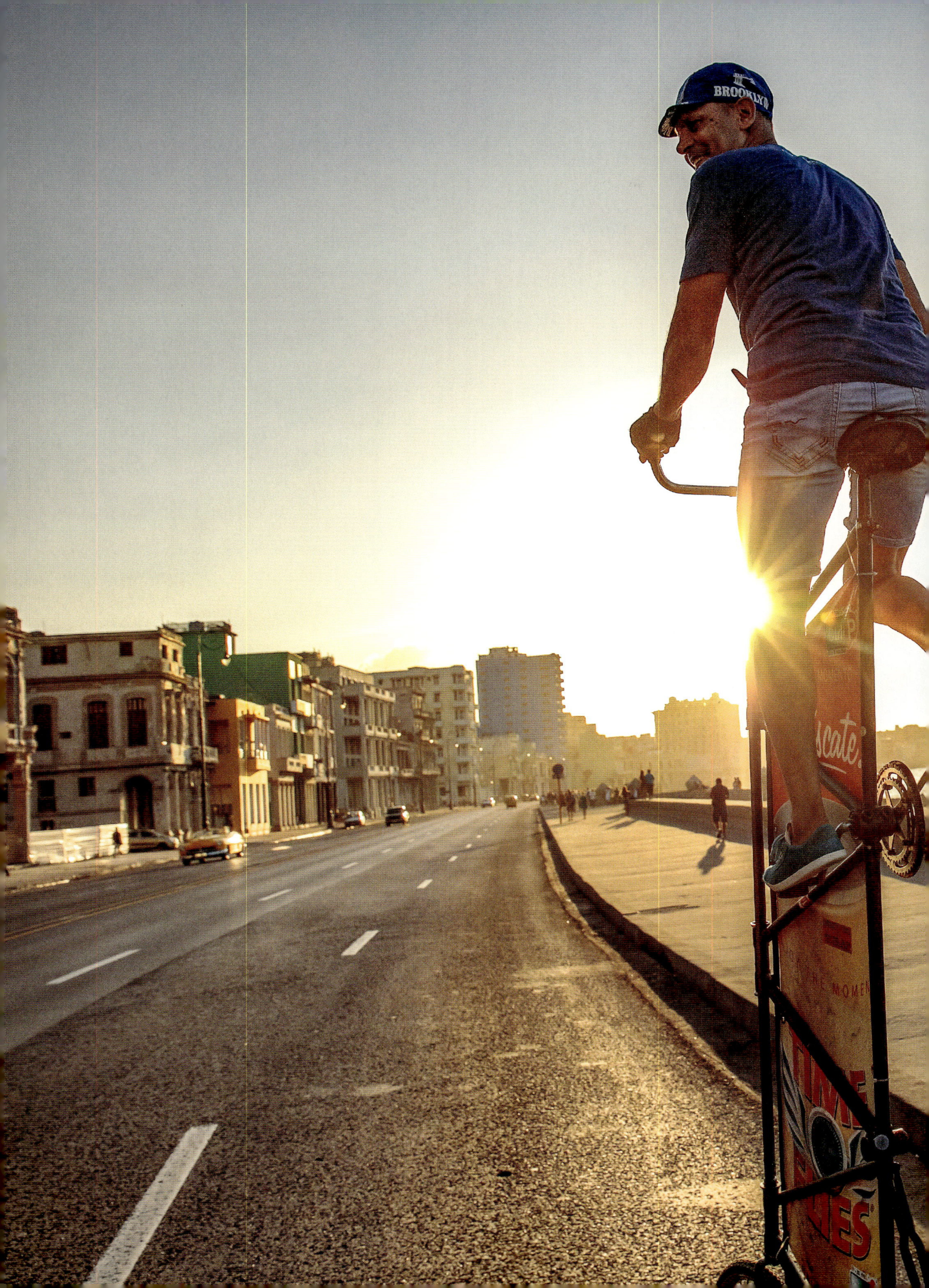

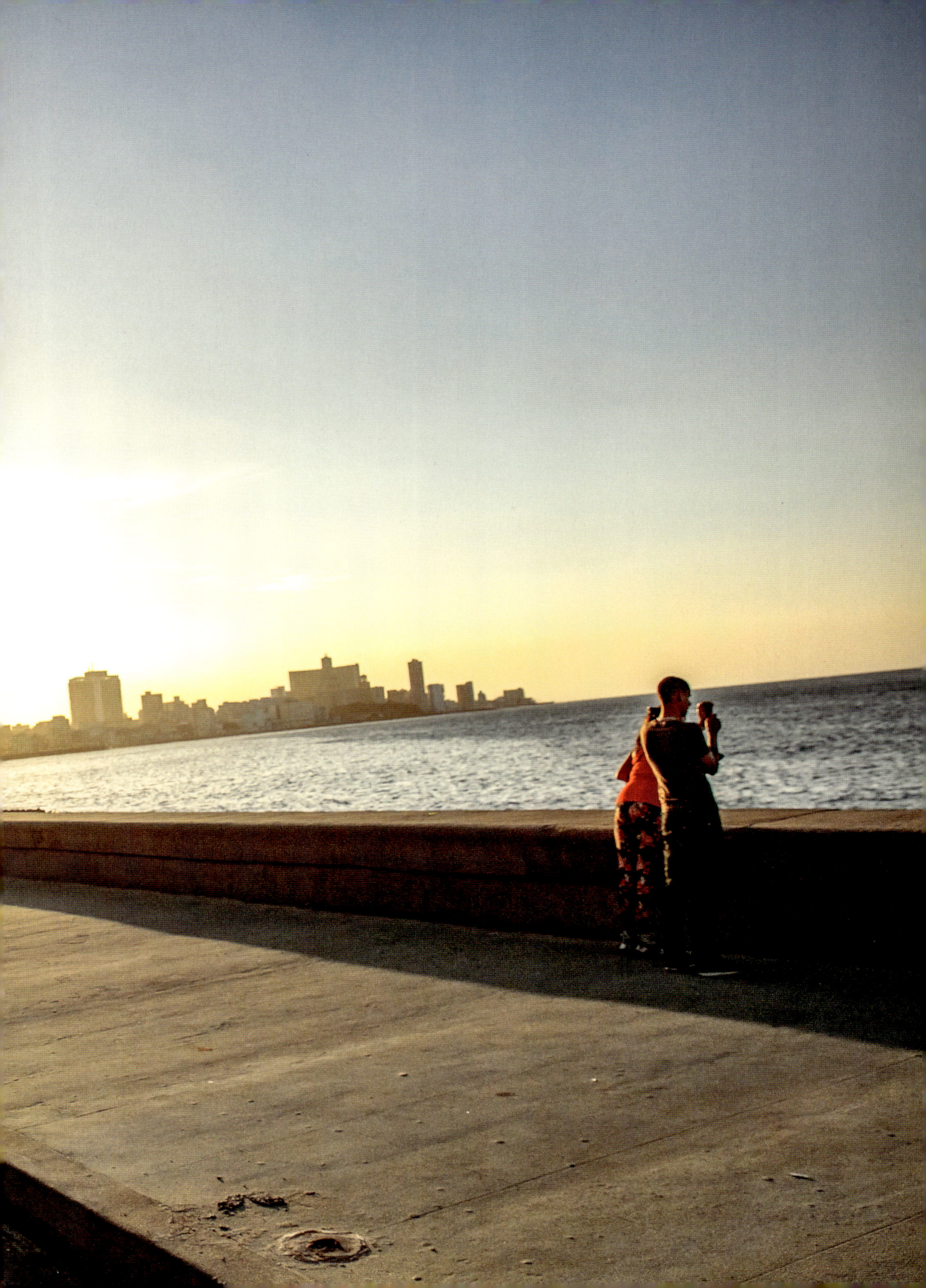

Chilangos Lowbike Club

Mexico City—A shared, peaceful passion for lowbikes

Photos
Jeoffrey Guillemard

On Sundays, the main streets in the center of Mexico City are closed to vehicle traffic. This is where the Chilangos Lowbike Club rides. The appearance of their male and female members and their bikes often attract attention. The members of the bike club, founded in 2014, appear like gangsters from poorer districts of the city, with their tattoos, shaved heads, and piercings. However, the Chilangos have sworn off violence and drugs and are even committed to not drink alcohol in public. Many of them bring their children and partners along when traveling to conventions across the country.

Their bikes, chromed and gilded, are unique specimens to behold, often featuring banana seats, mirrors attached to the handlebars, and even mock exhaust pipes. The roots of low-rider culture can be traced back to migrant culture in the USA, where subcultures lower their cars and bikes alike.

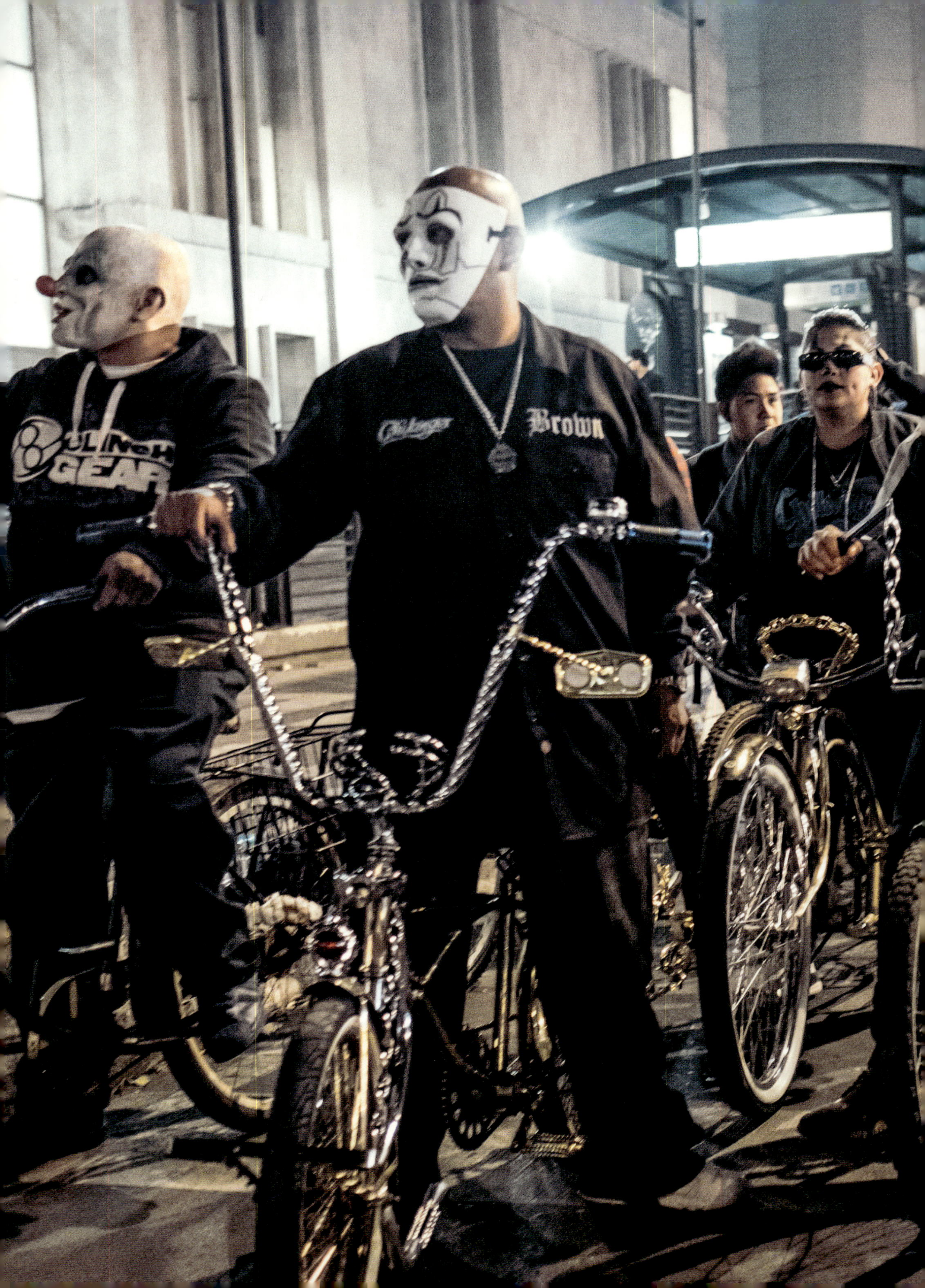

GEAR
Brown

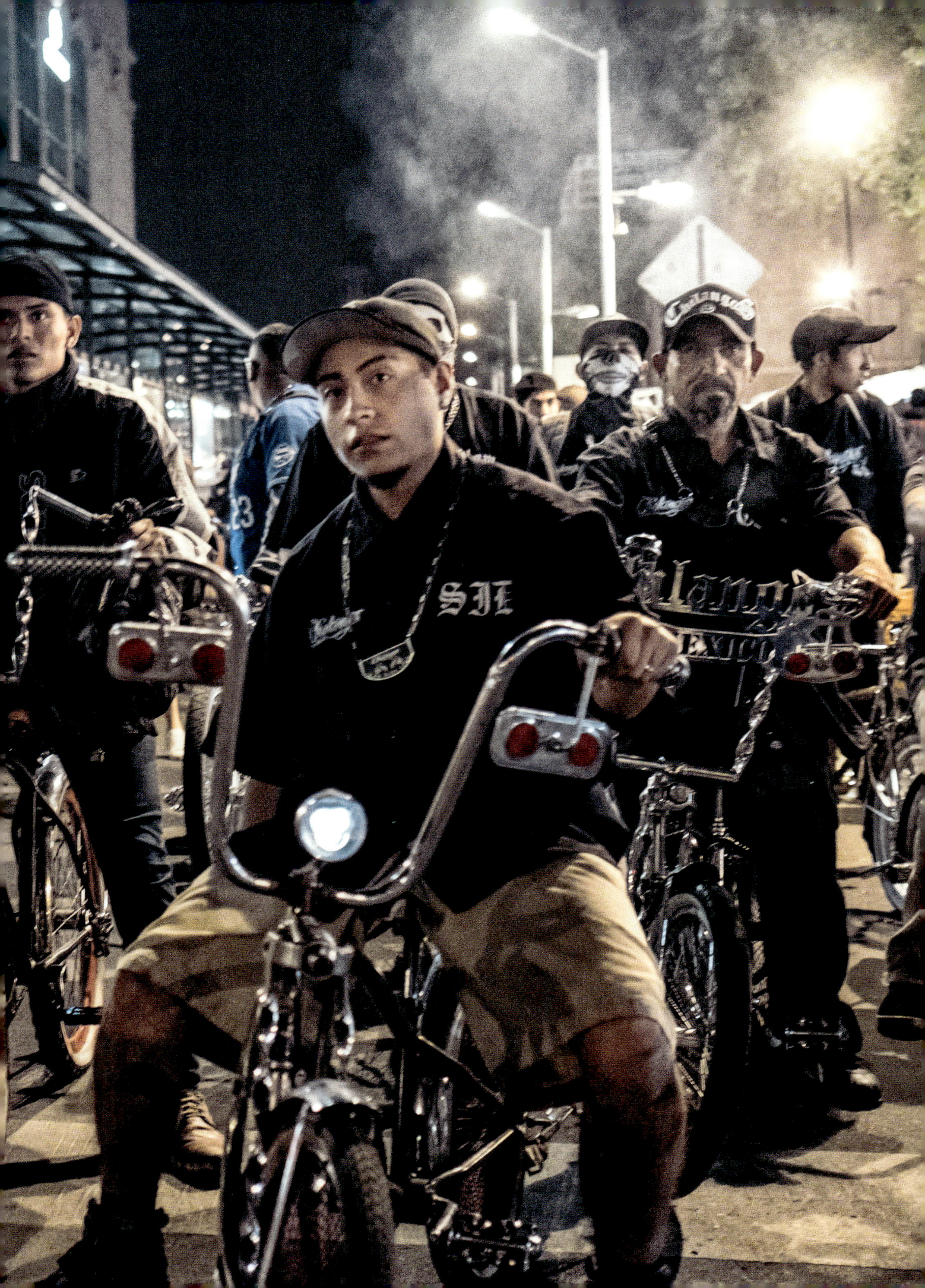

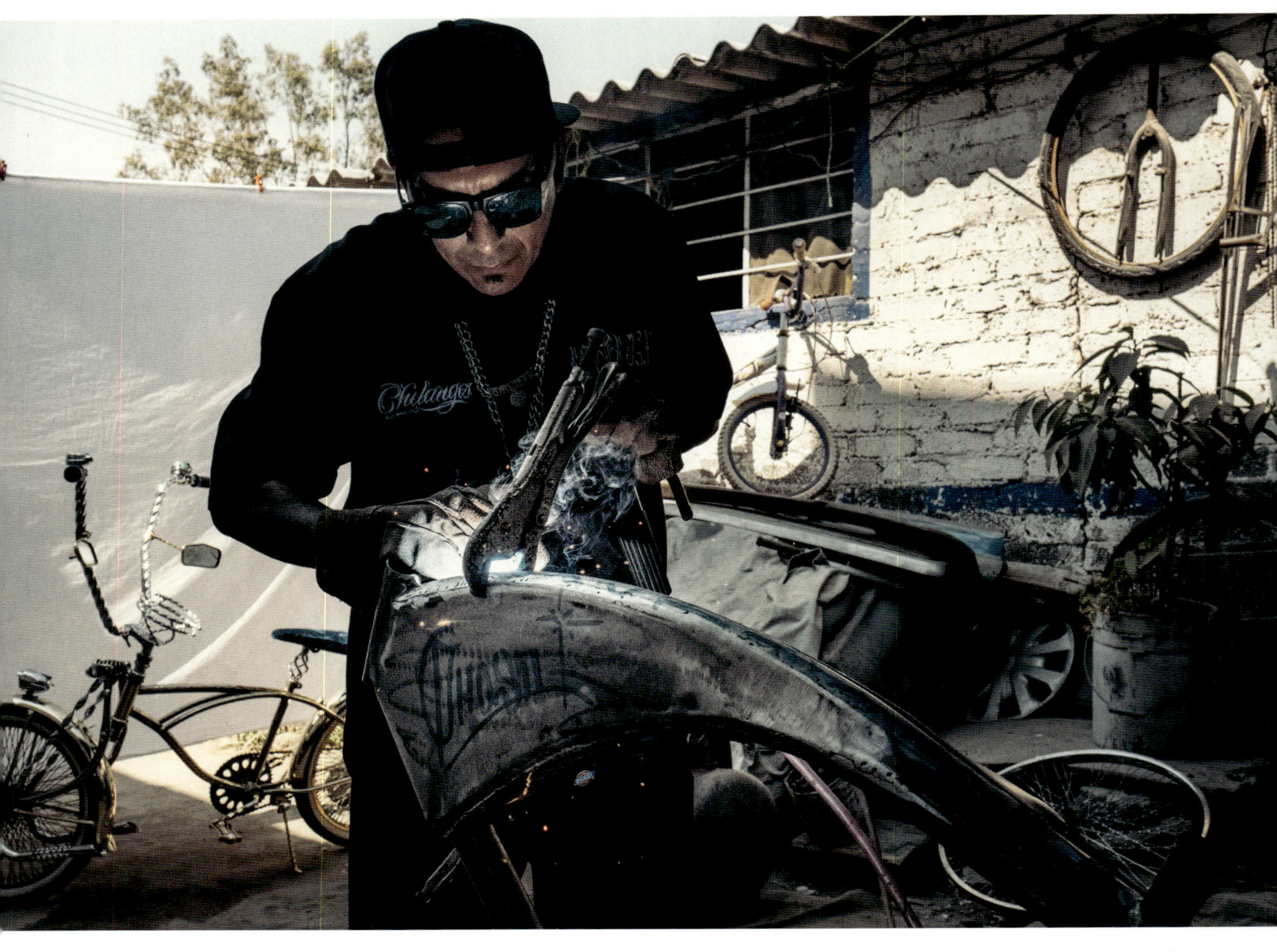
Chilangos

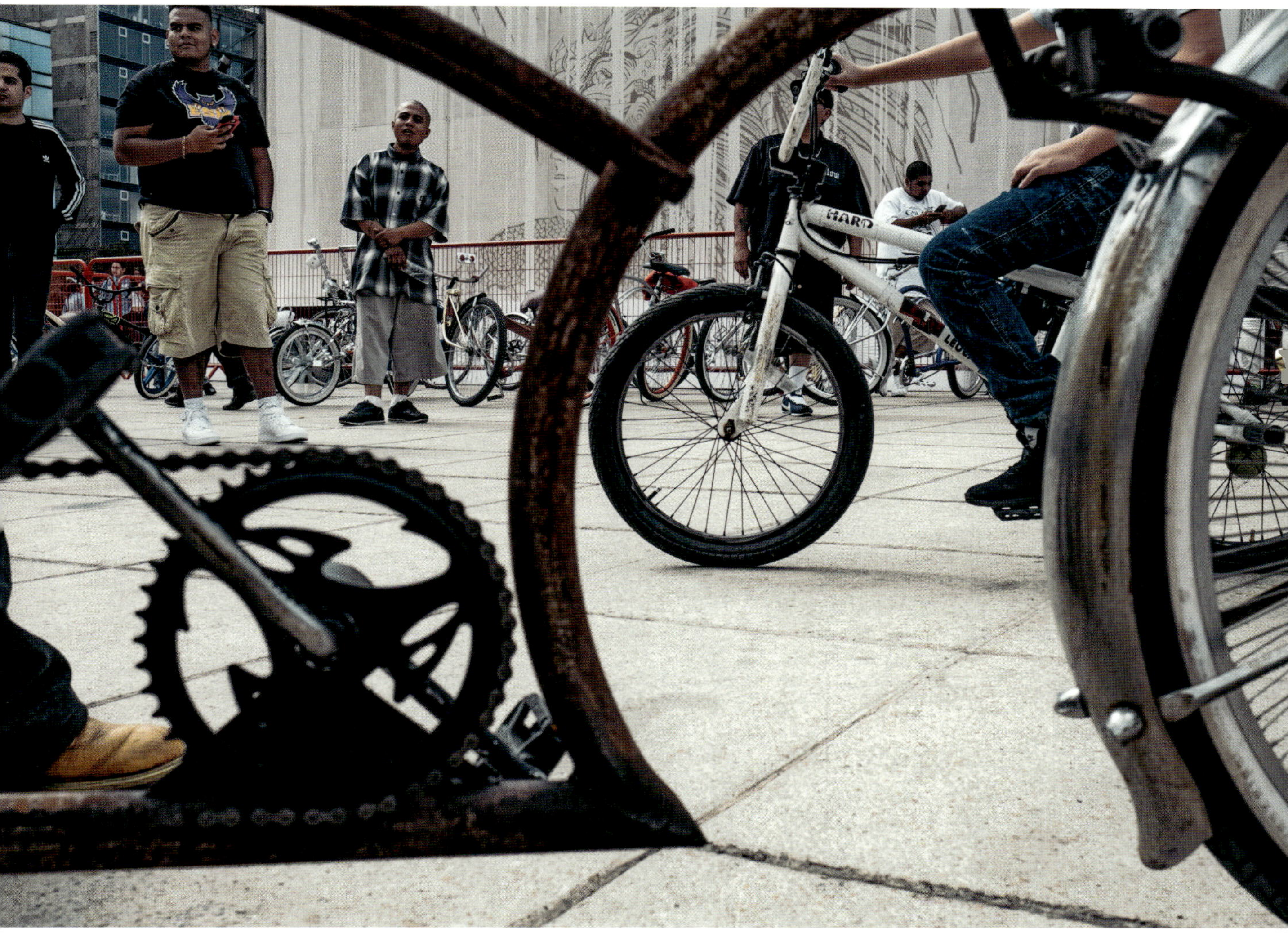

"Lowrider culture was born out of Mexican immigration to the United States. Today, many migrants have returned to Mexico and brought this culture back with them."

Juan Carlos Jasso

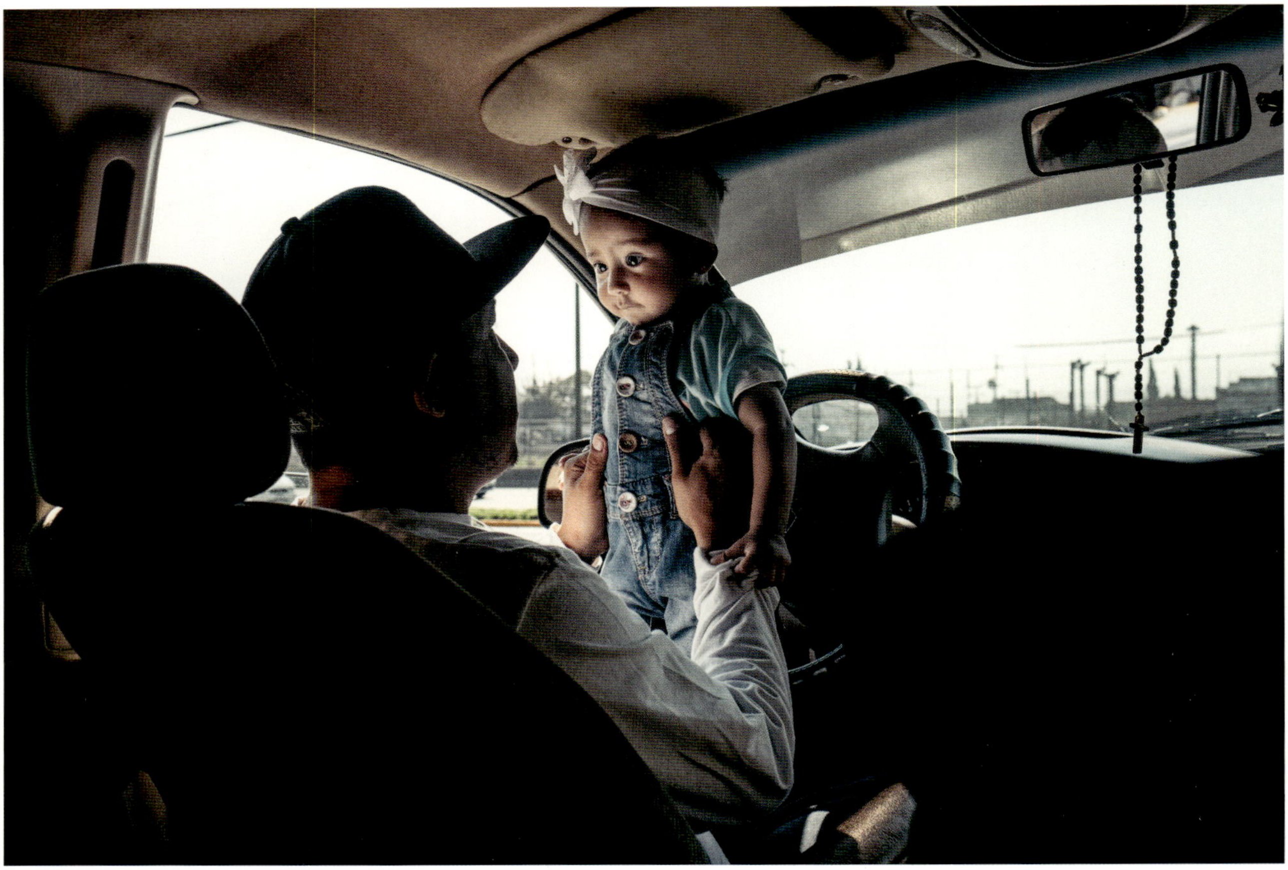

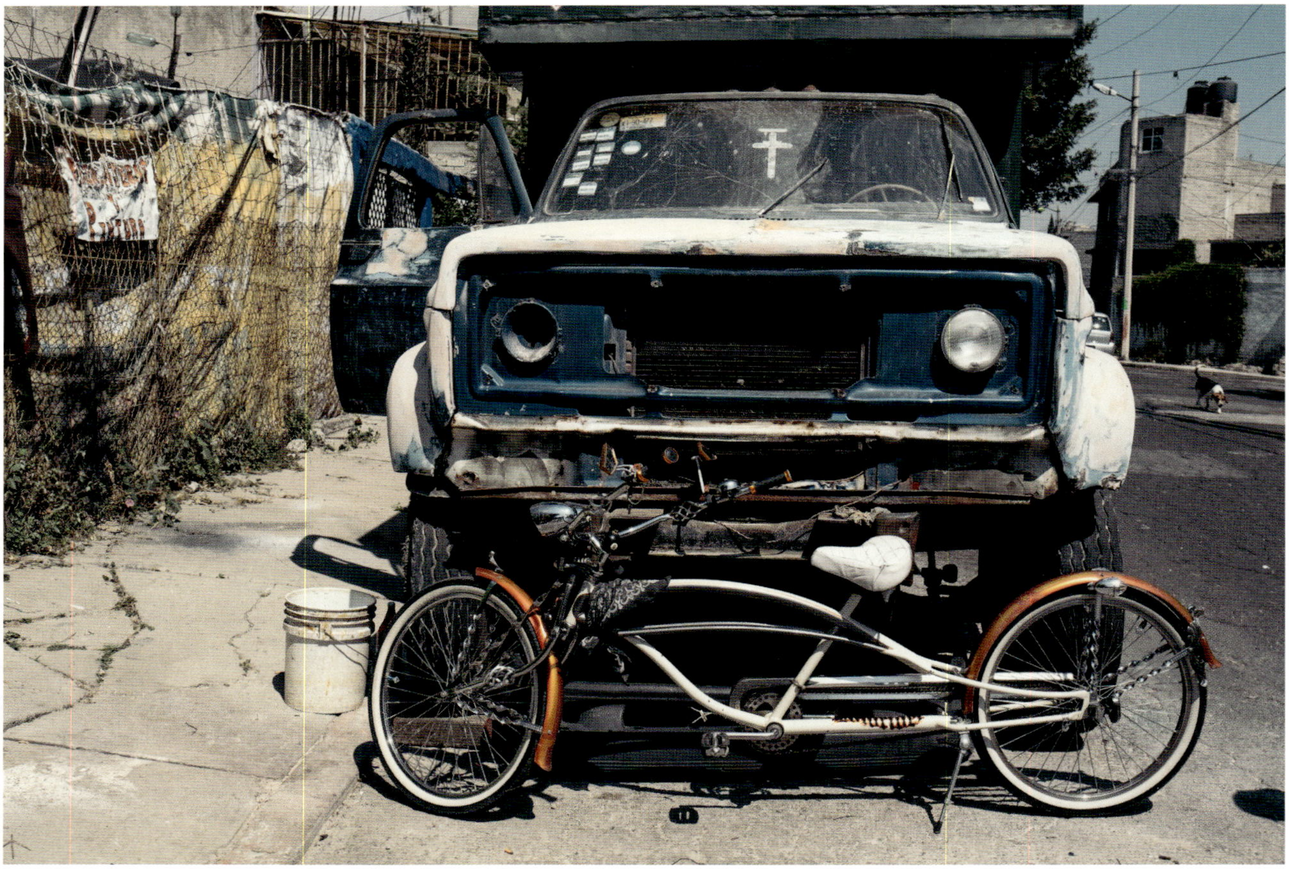

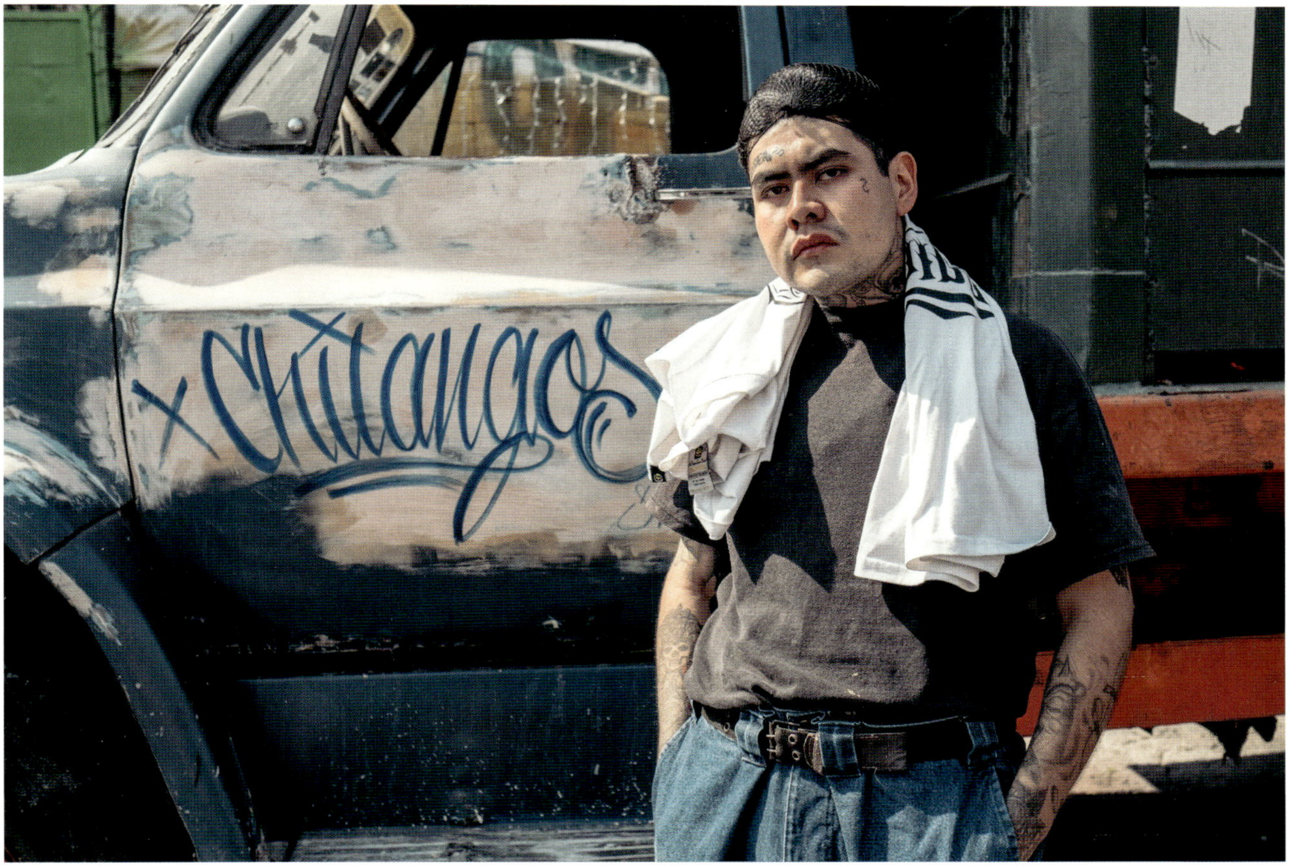
Chilangos

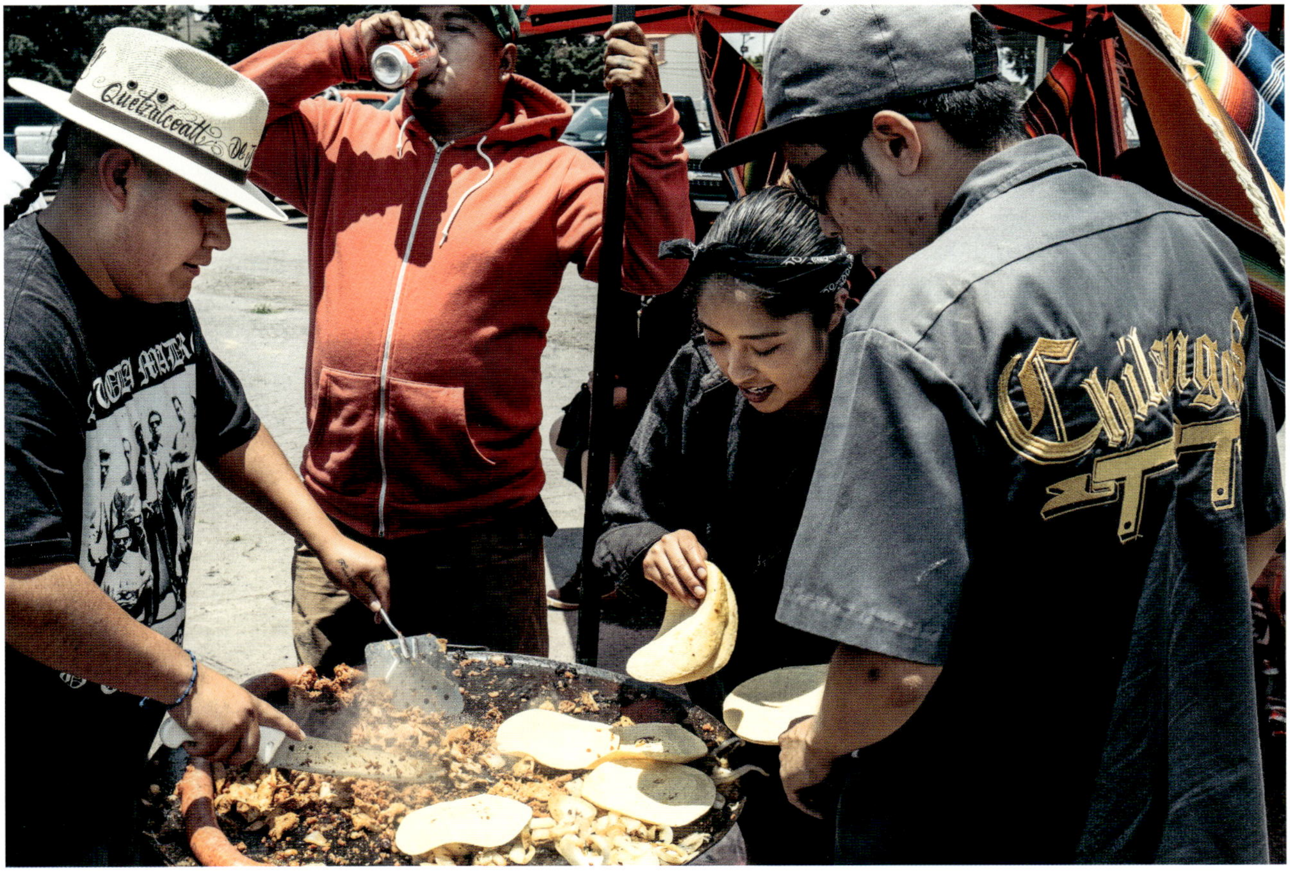
Quetzalcoatl
Chilangos

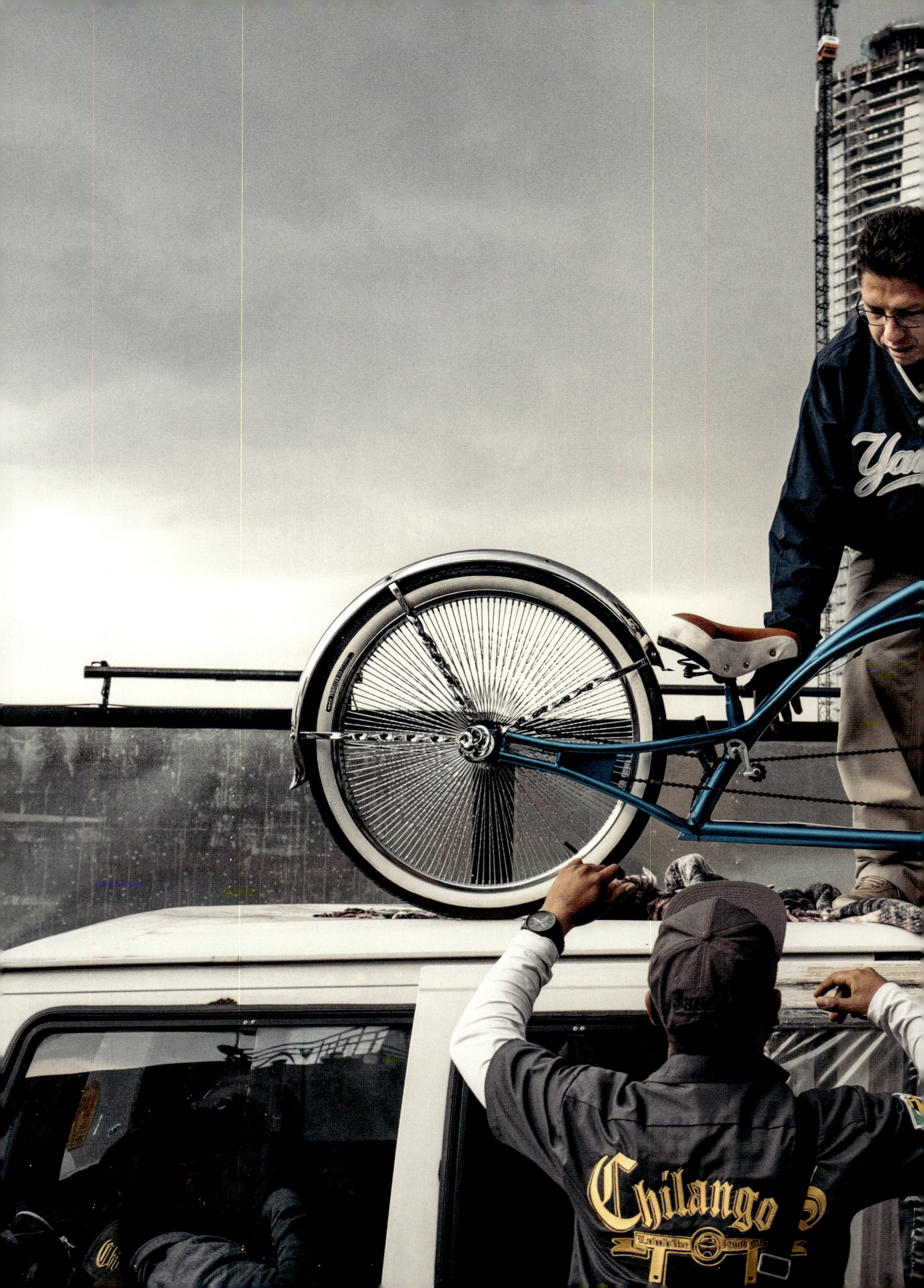
Chilango

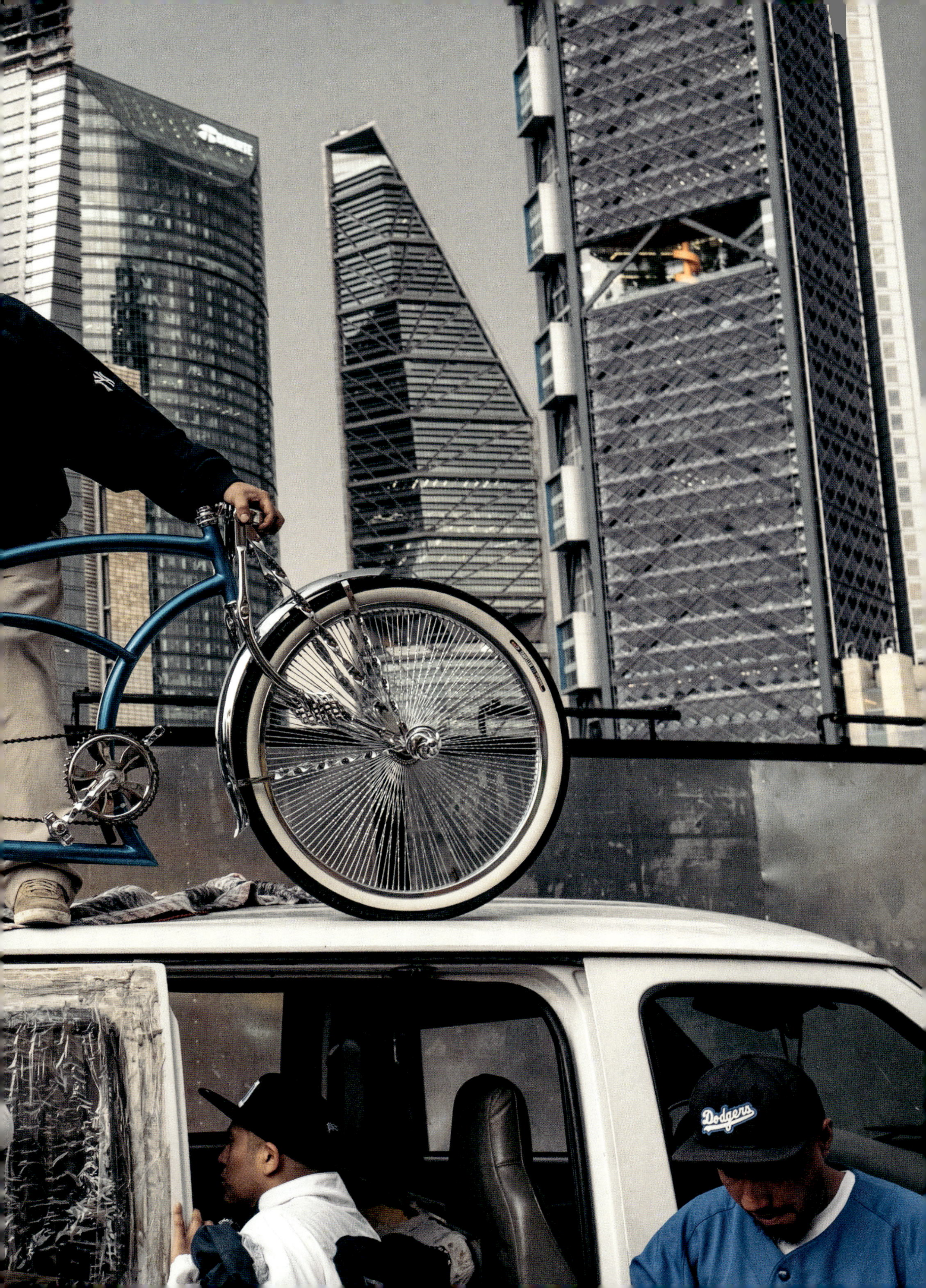
Dodgers

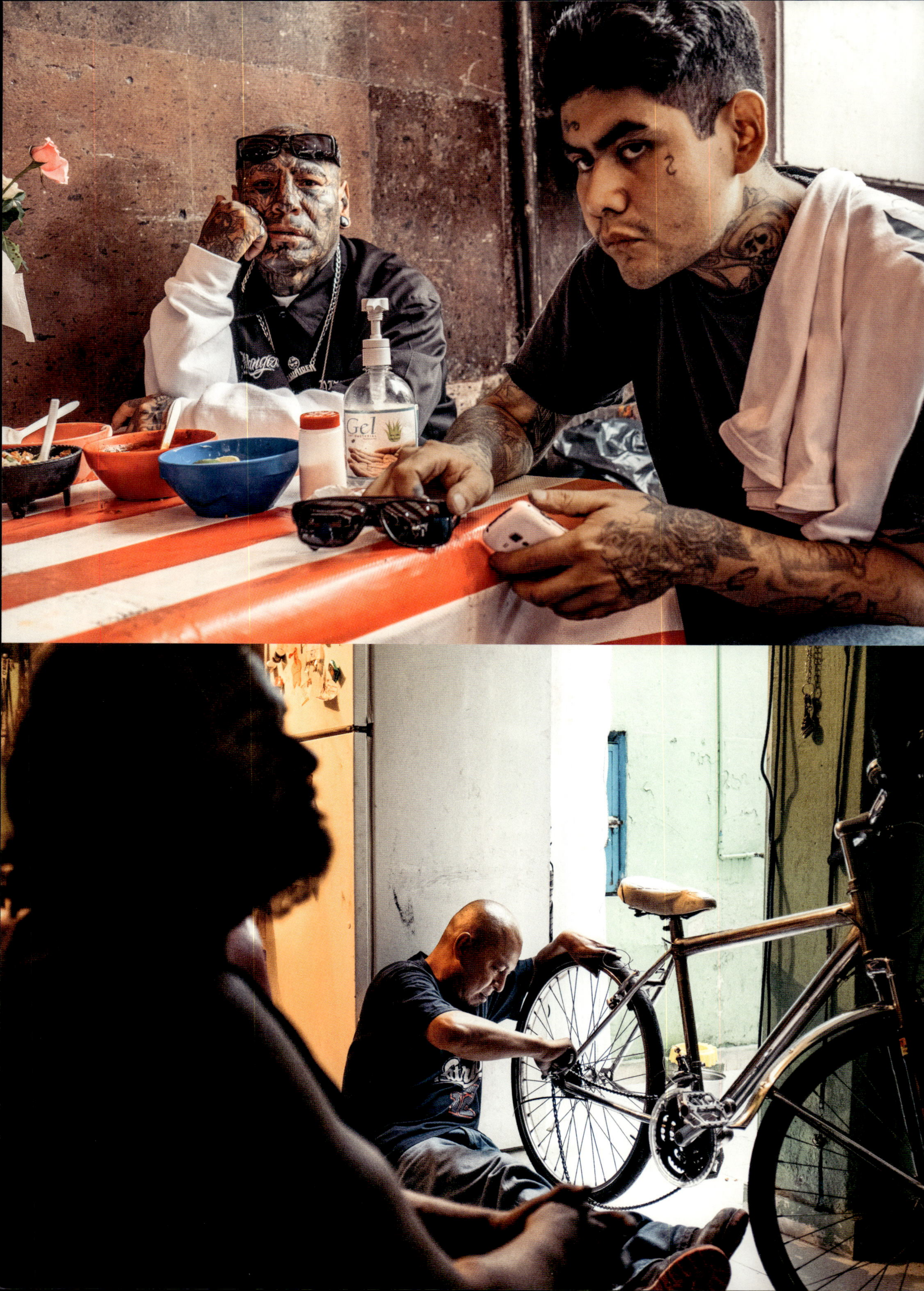
Gel

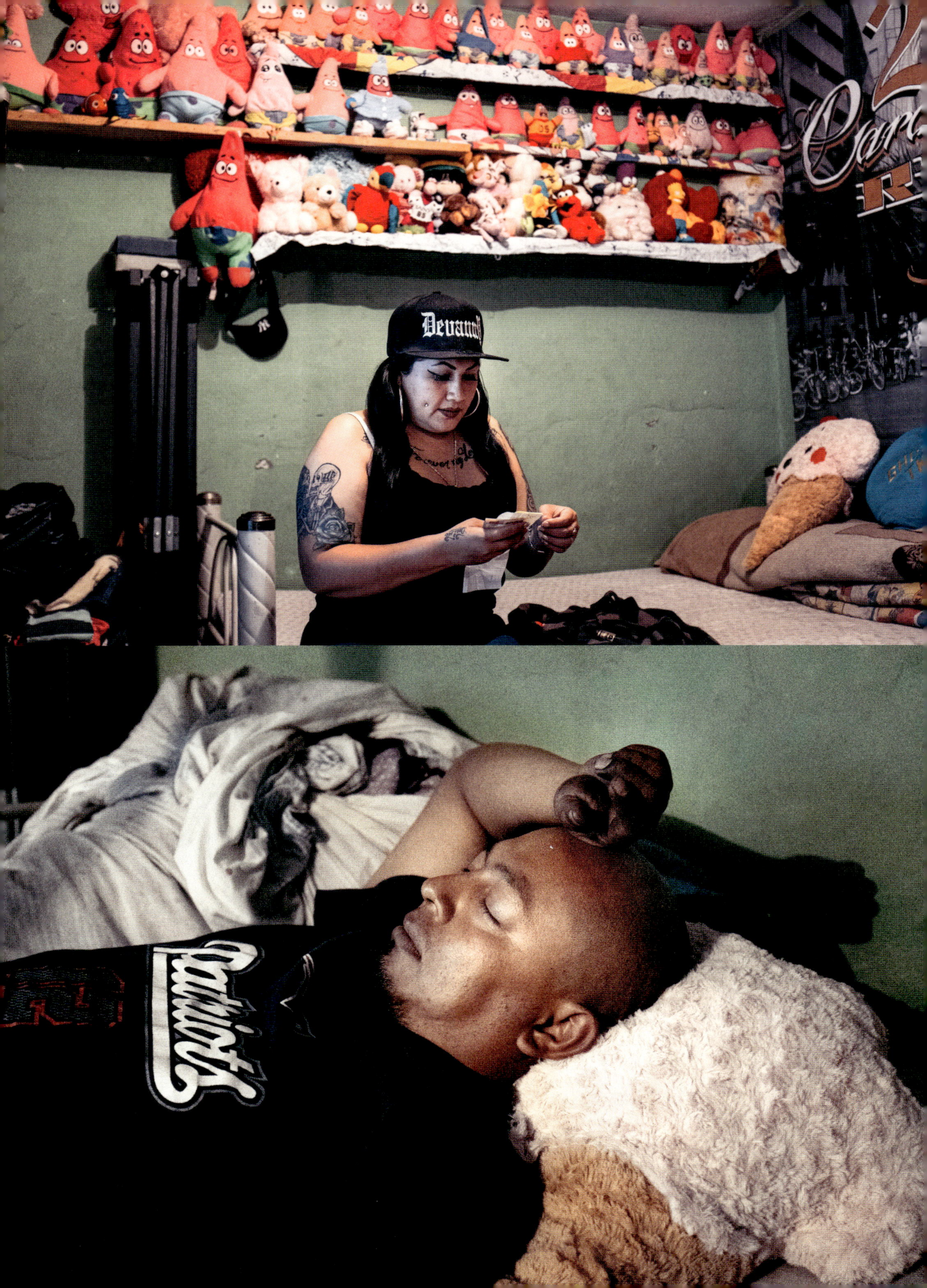
Patriots

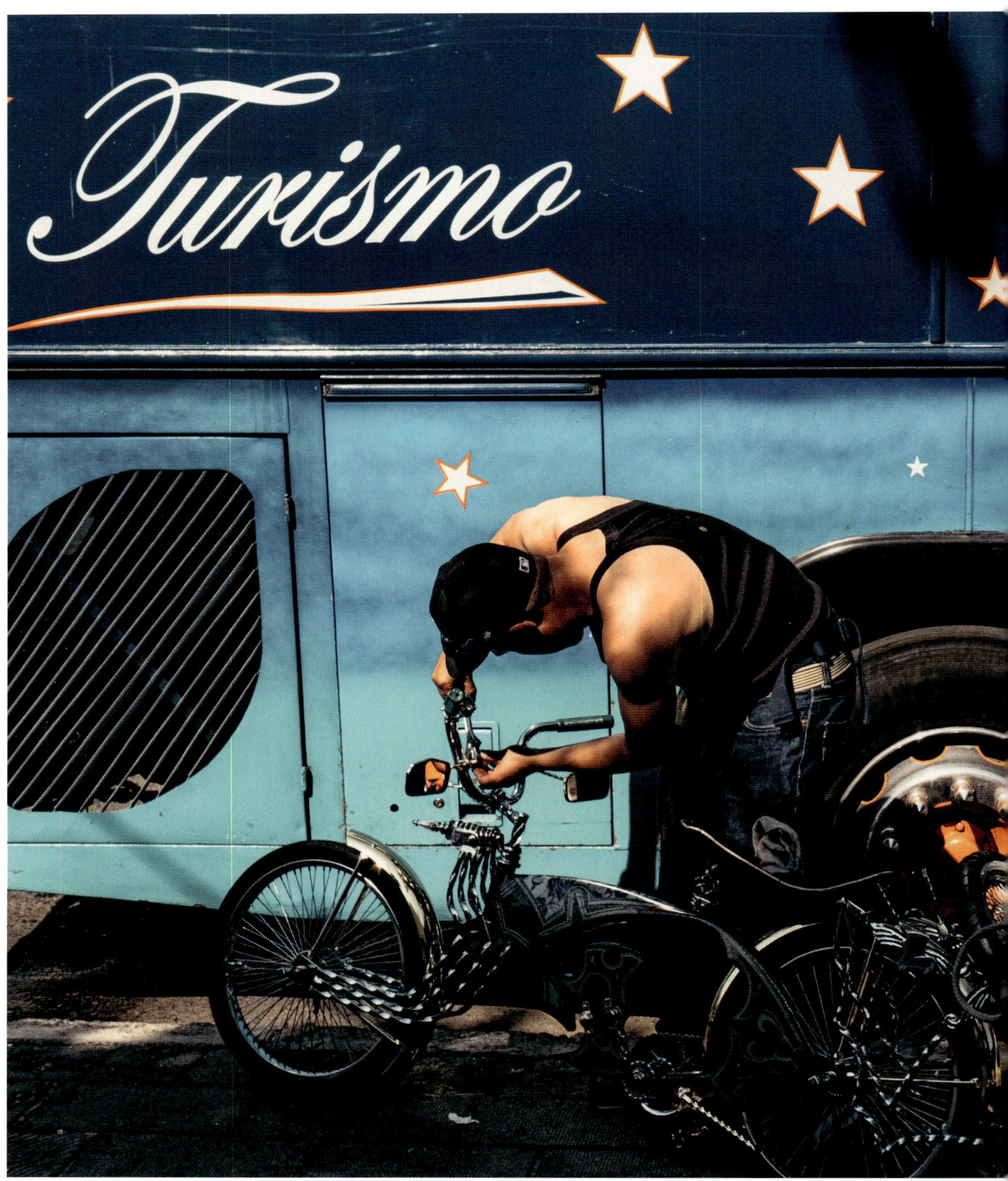
Turismo

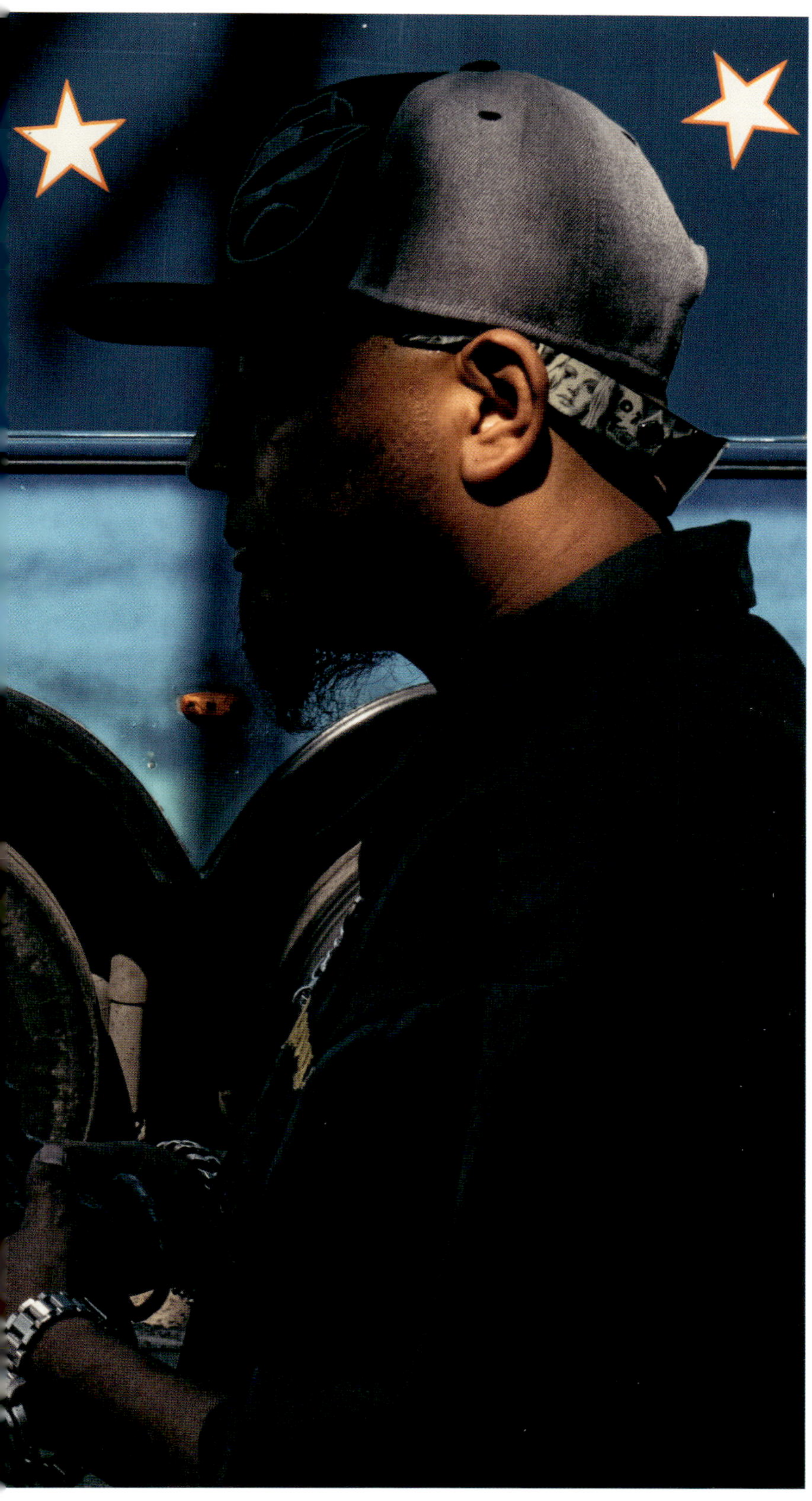

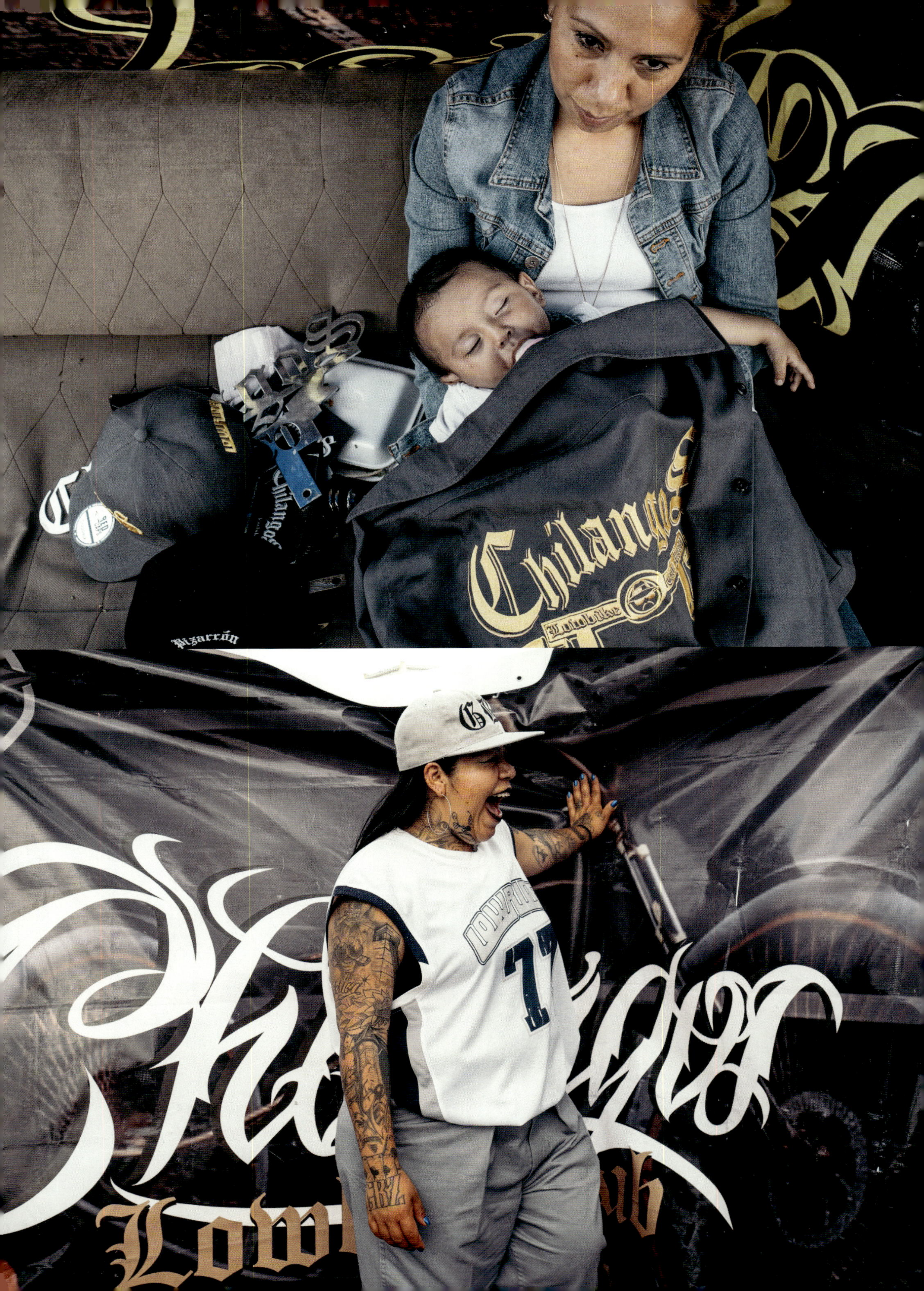

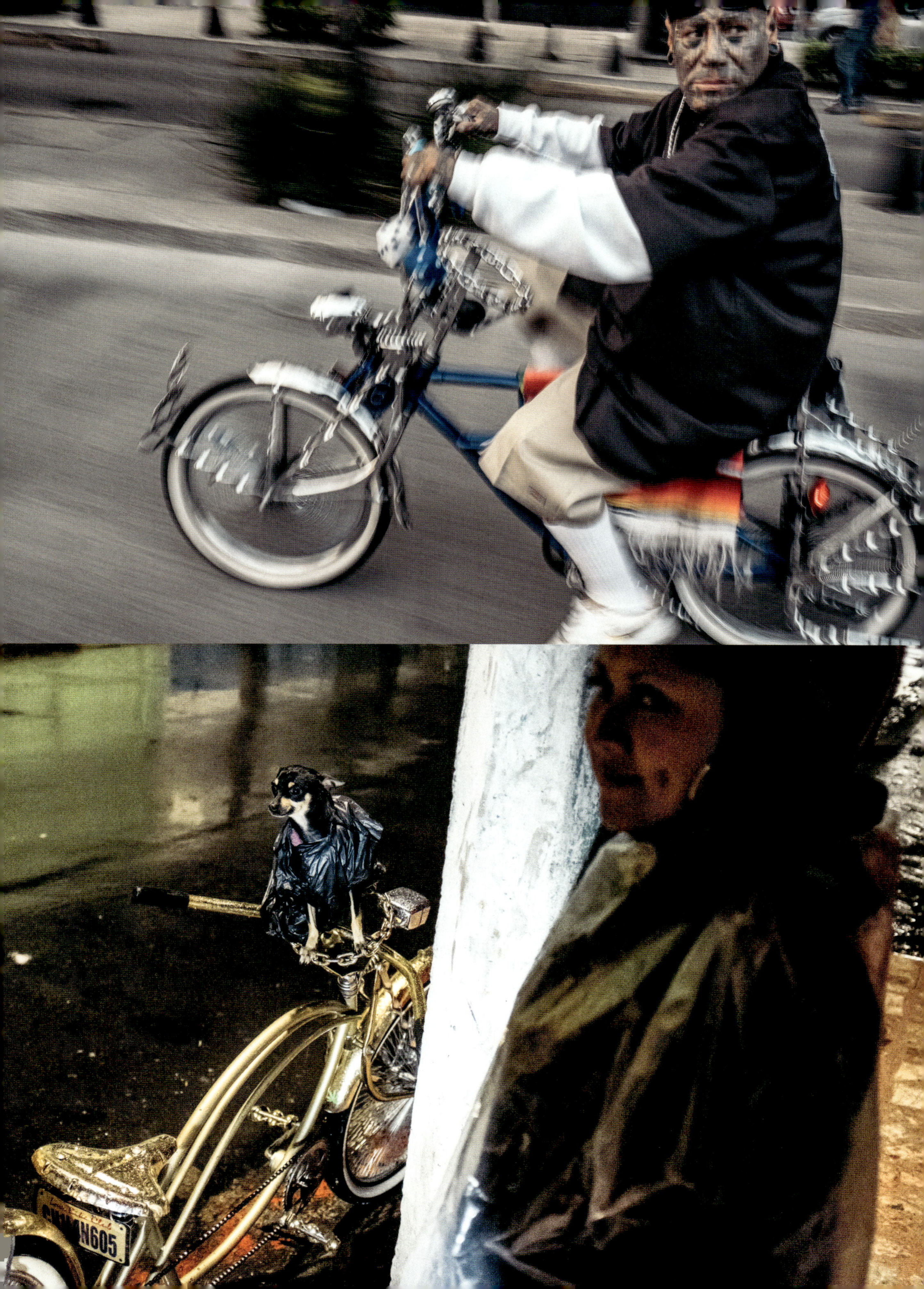

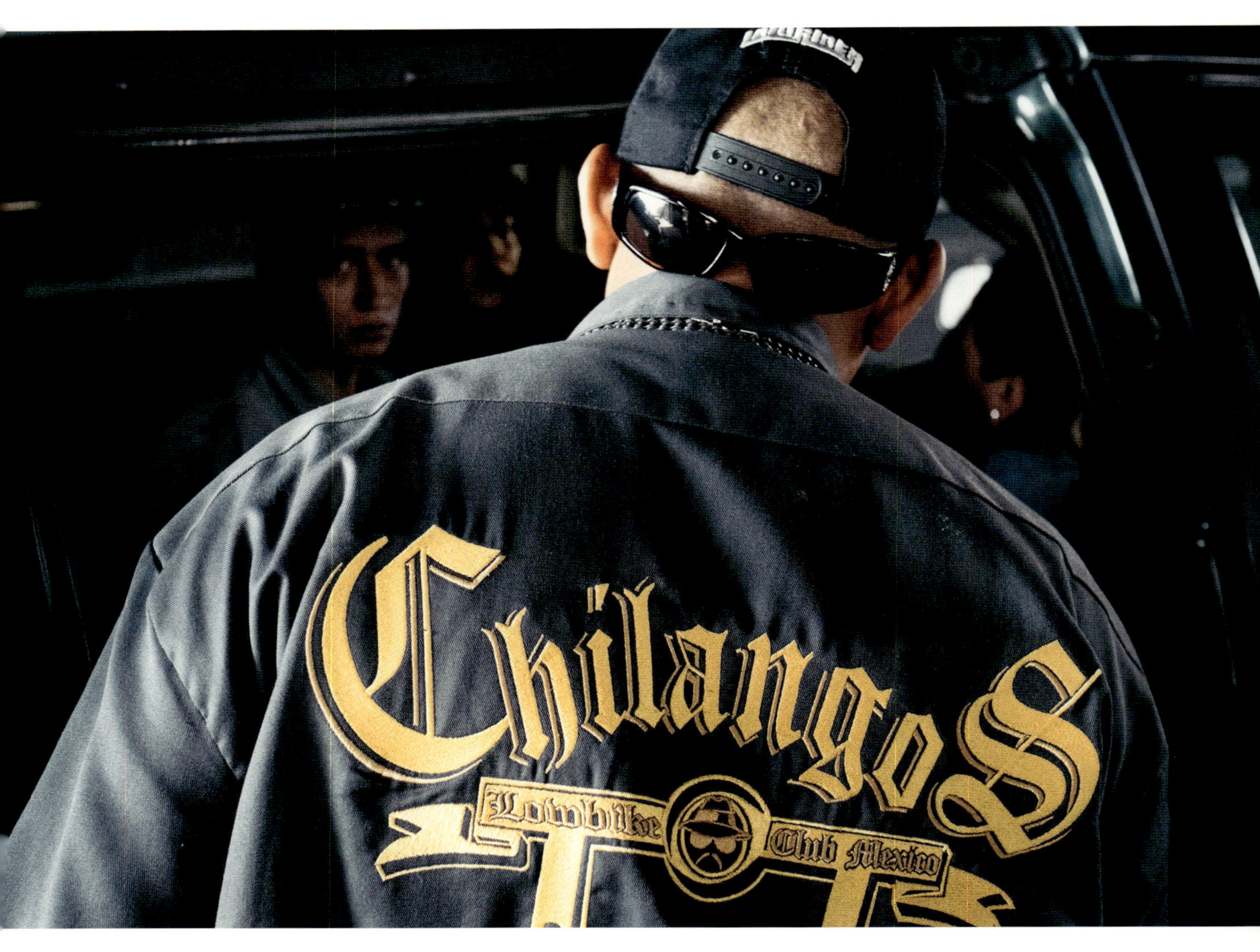
Chilangos
Lowbike
Club Mexico

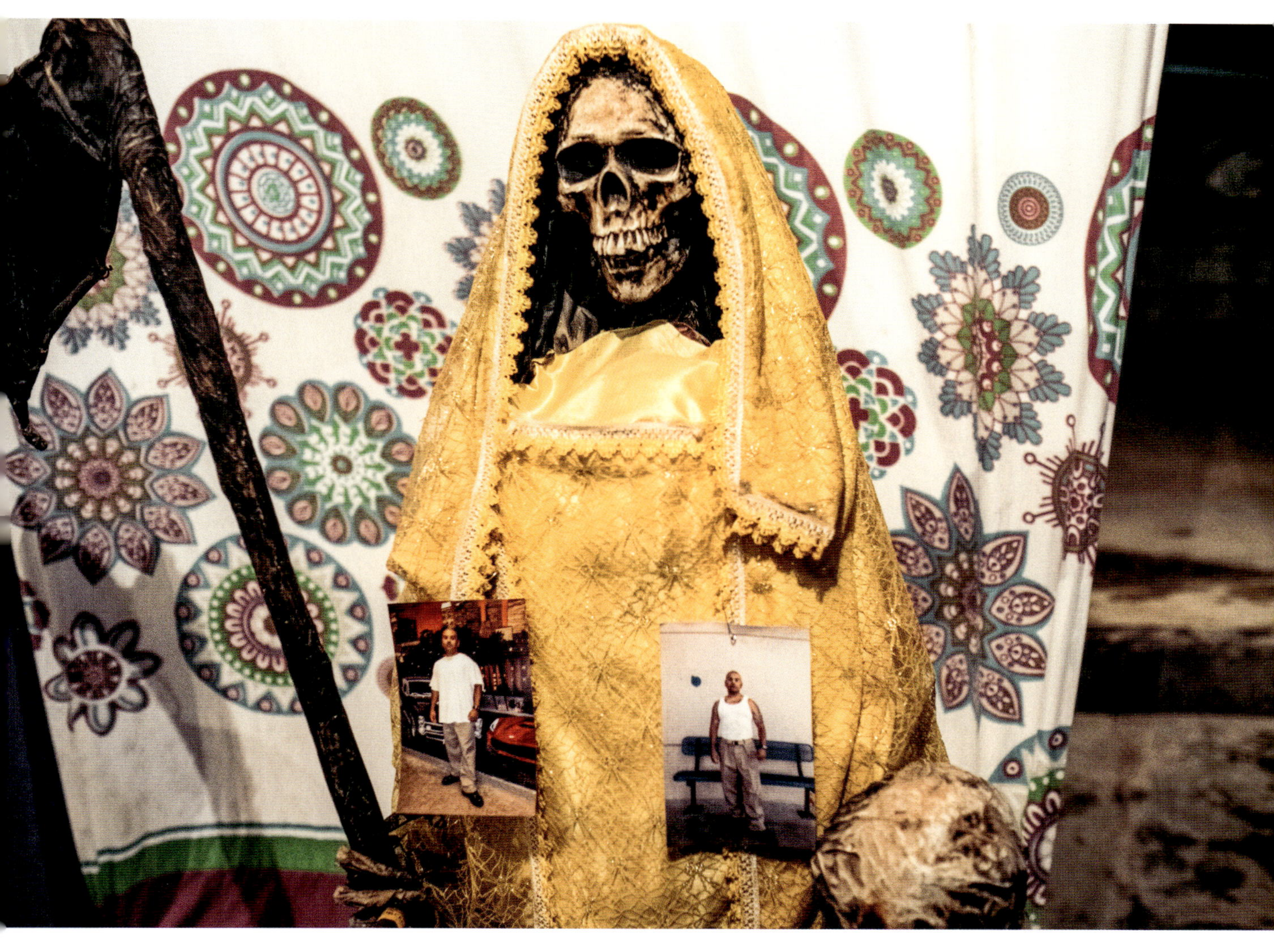

"*Chilango*, in Mexican slang, refers to an inhabitant of Mexico City."

Juan Carlos Jasso

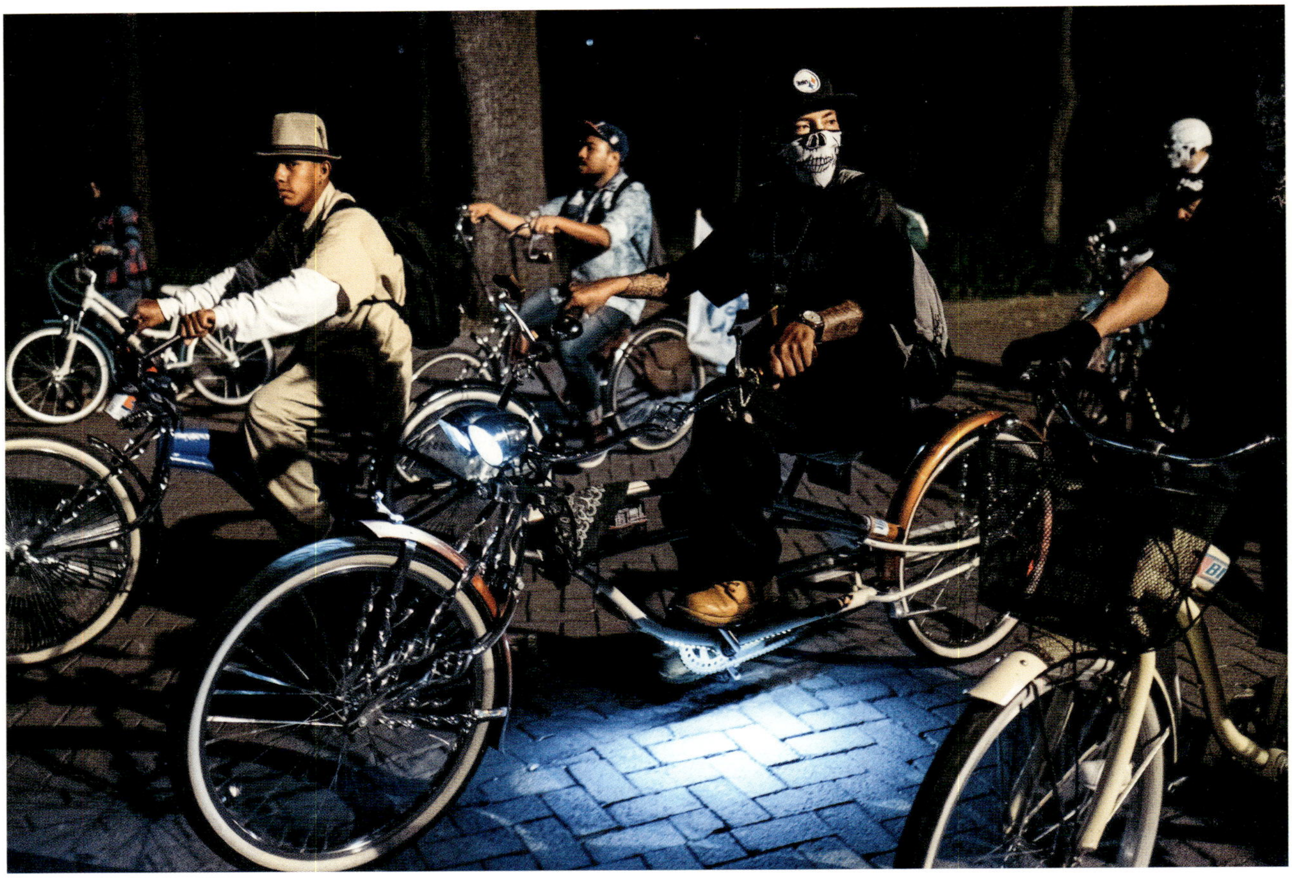

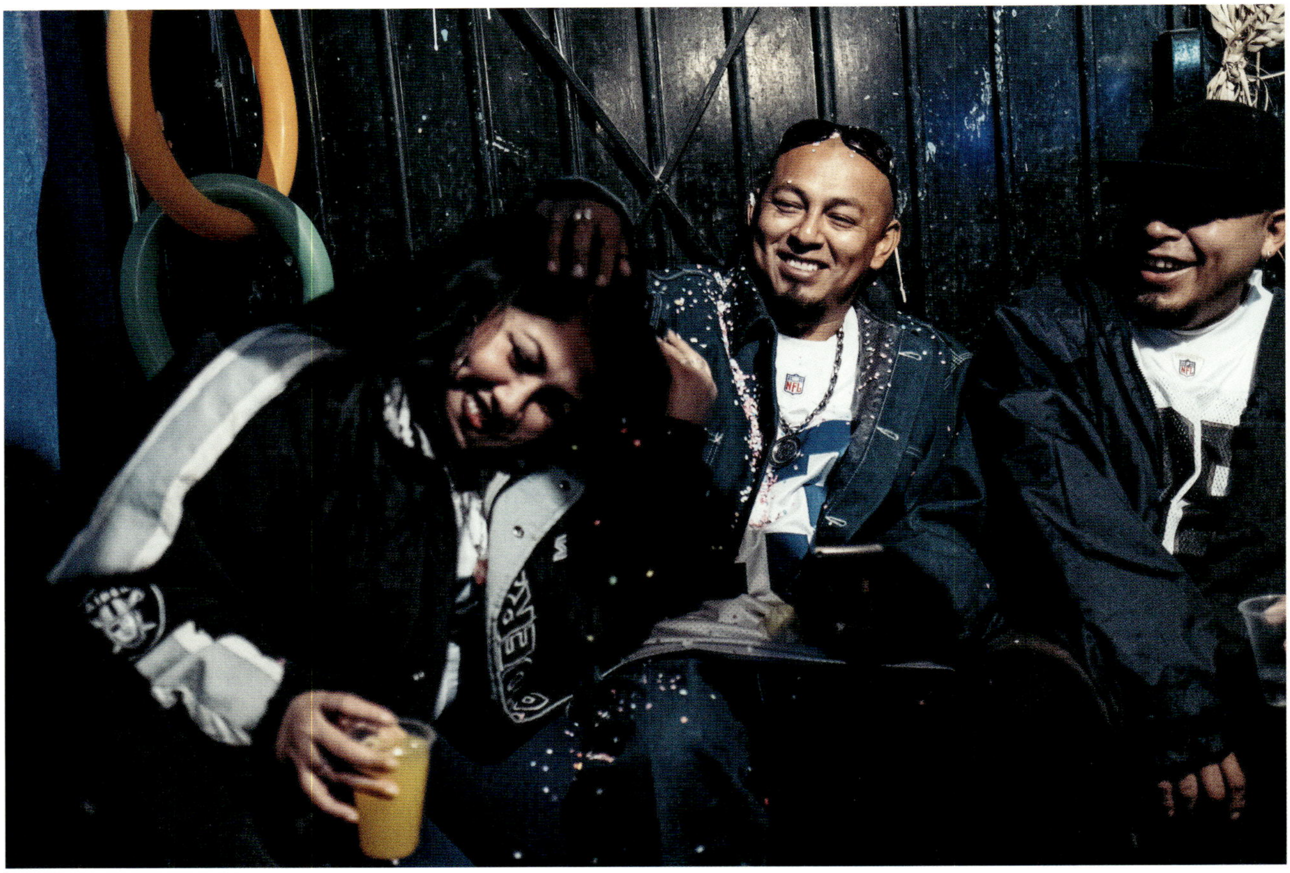

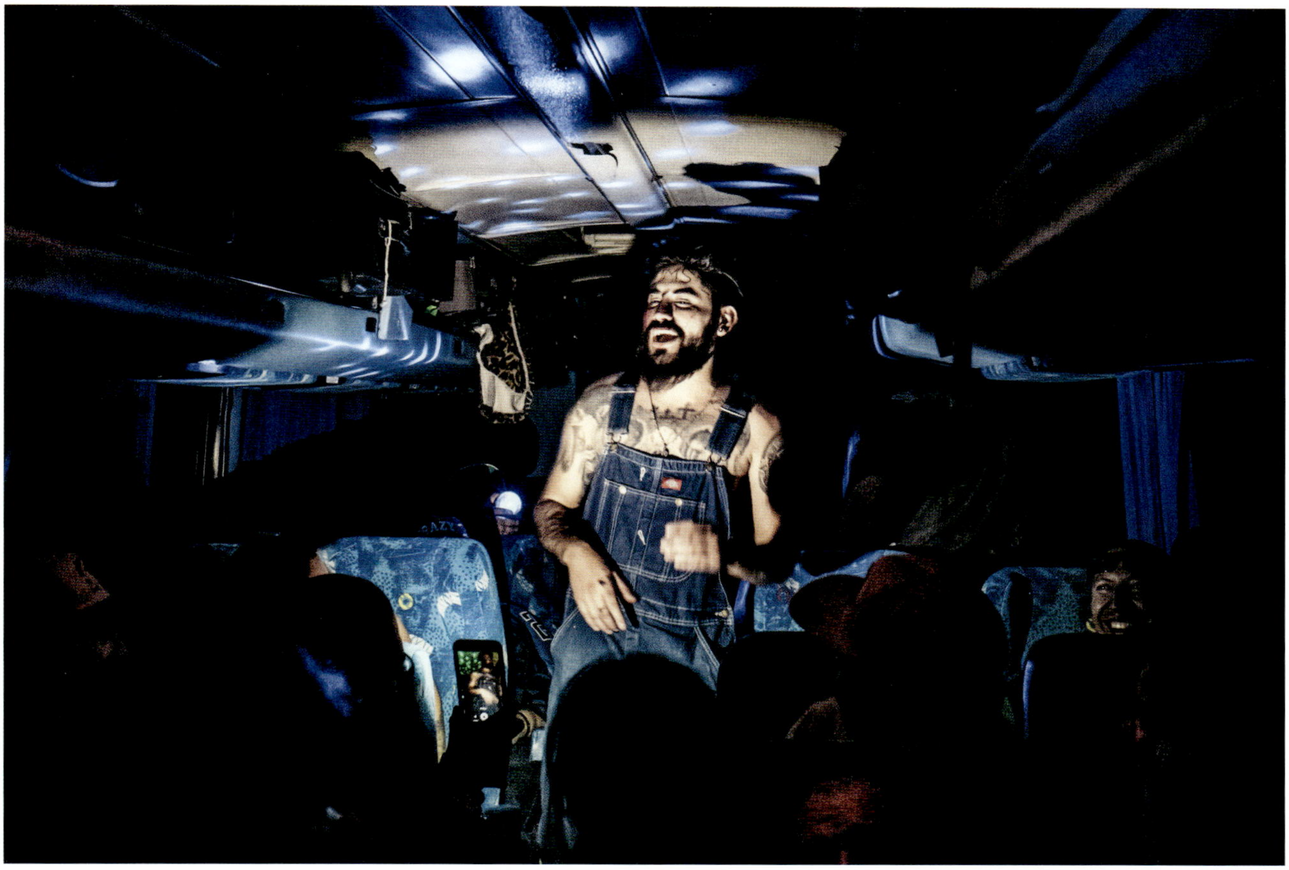

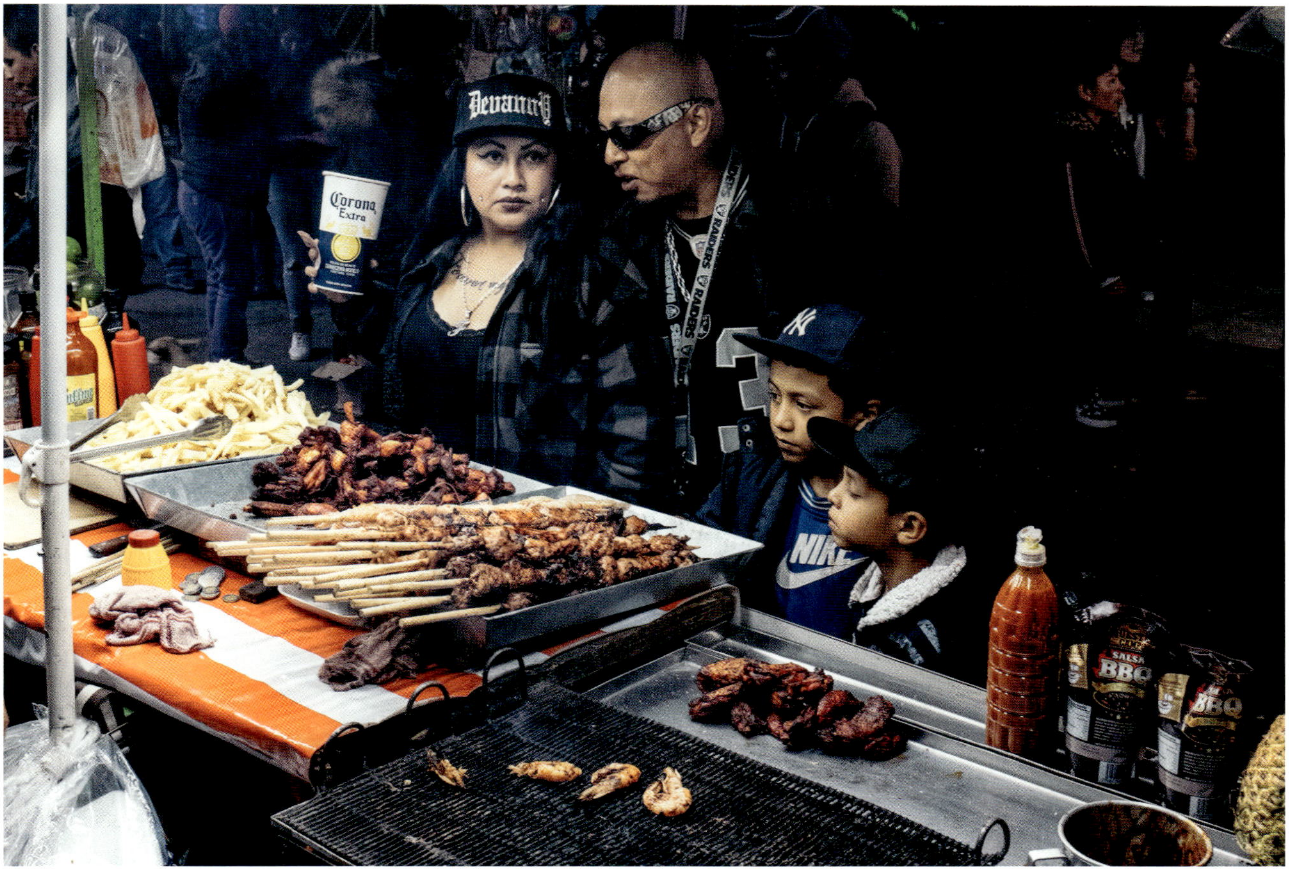

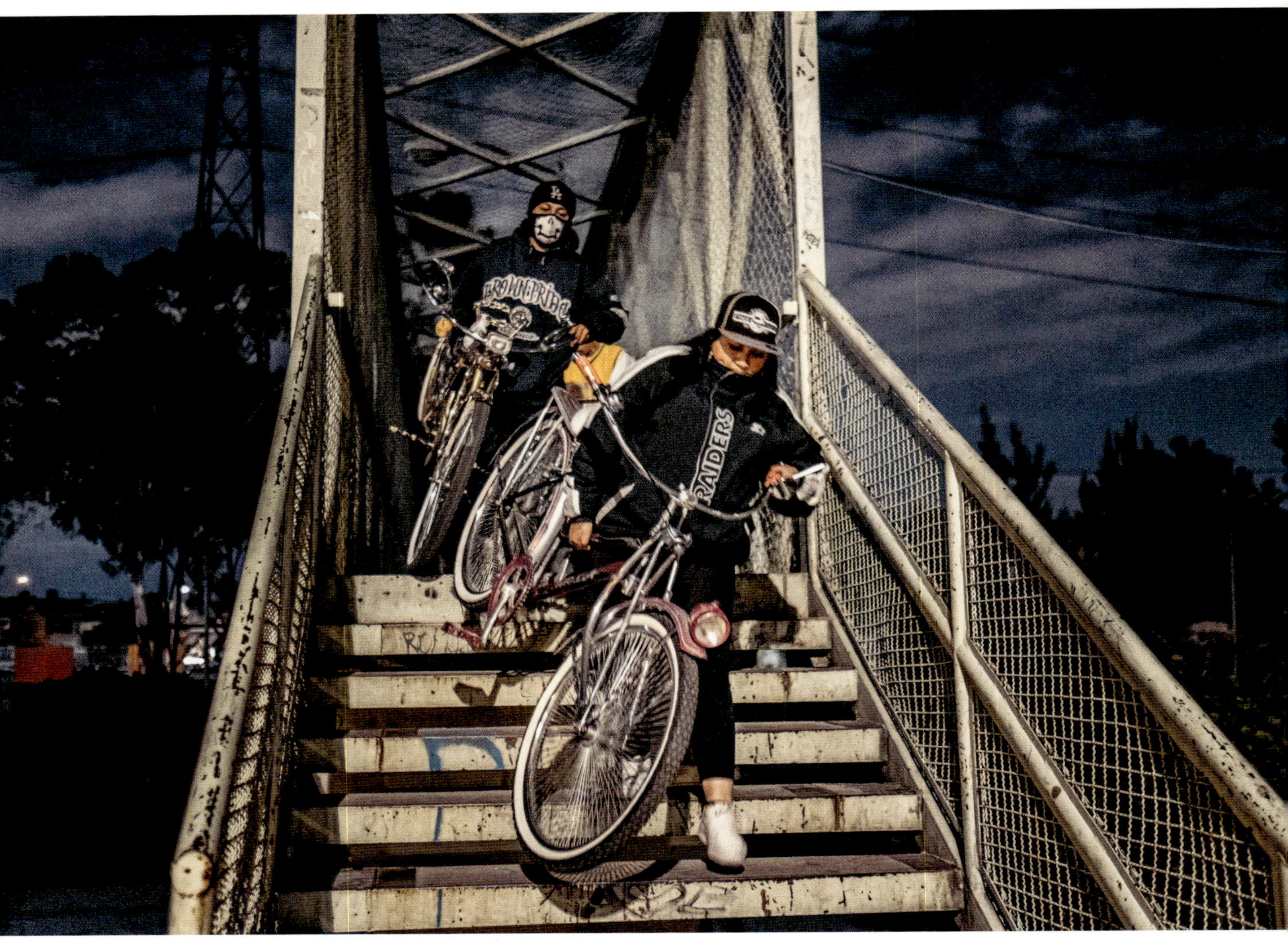

"We like to make Lowrider culture accessible to everyone. Our aim is to escape gang violence while preserving a culture that we consider our own. People often confuse us just because of the way we dress or look. Our aim is to show that we're not associated with crime and gangs, and that it's something completely different."

Juan Carlos Jasso

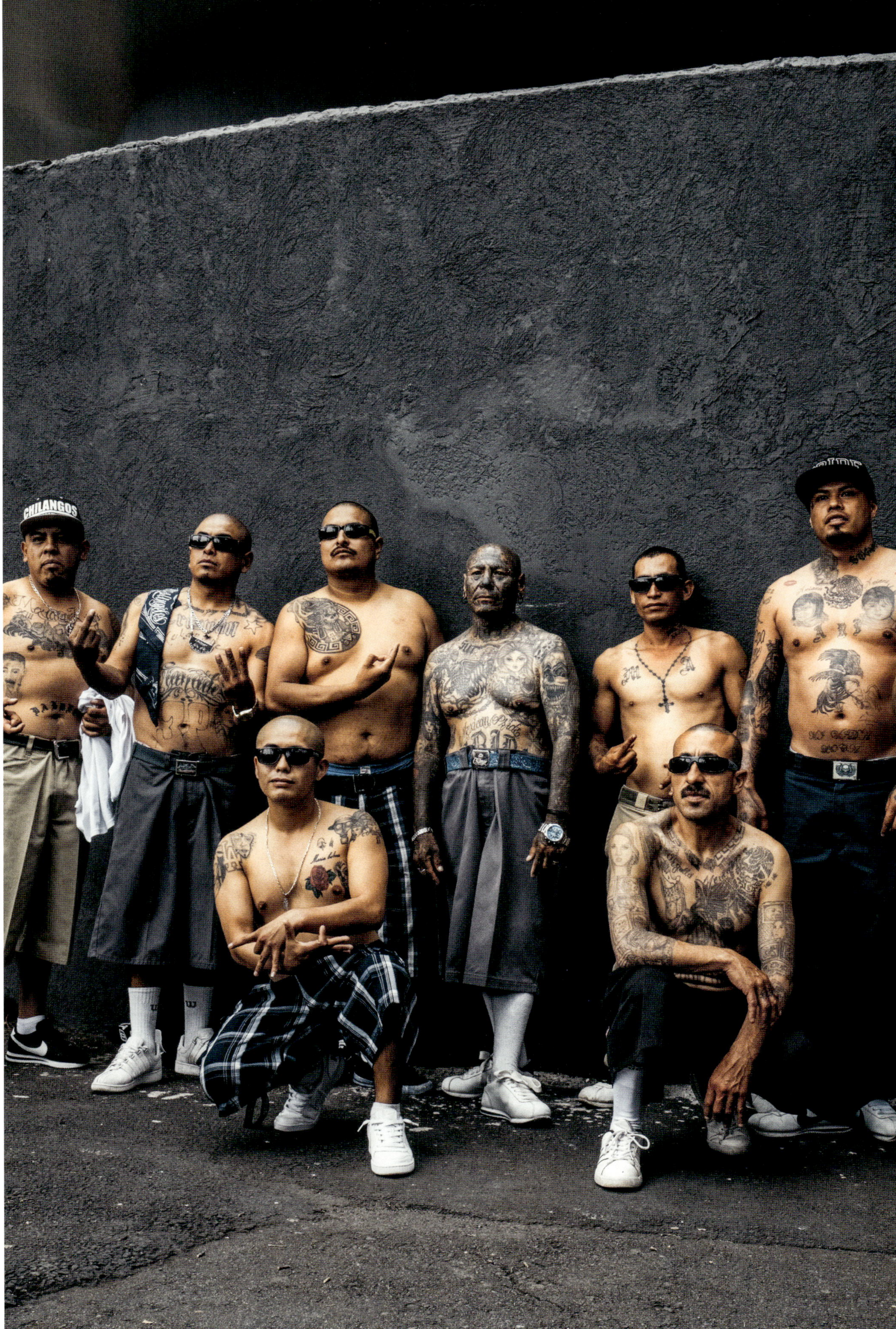
CHILANGOS

Into the Wild

USA—A long, slow journey with friends

Photos
Tod Seelie

A group of people, some friends, some strangers, meet up and set off on a bicycle tour. They ride through strikingly beautiful and sparsely populated landscapes. For some it's about escaping the trappings of daily life, while for others it's the draw of pedaling through gorgeous scenery. Within days, bonds begin to form between previous strangers. Watching the sunset in front of a panoramic landscape or bathing in the biting cold of a mountain lake is all the more enjoyable when done together.

The bicycle is both a mode of transport and a companion. A long ride is a form of wordless conversation. Bike touring offers a chance to learn about oneself—not just one's physical abilities, but where one's mind goes while meditating in motion through the long days of pedaling. As with so many journeys, the destination is an afterthought. The point is rather how, and with whom, we get there.

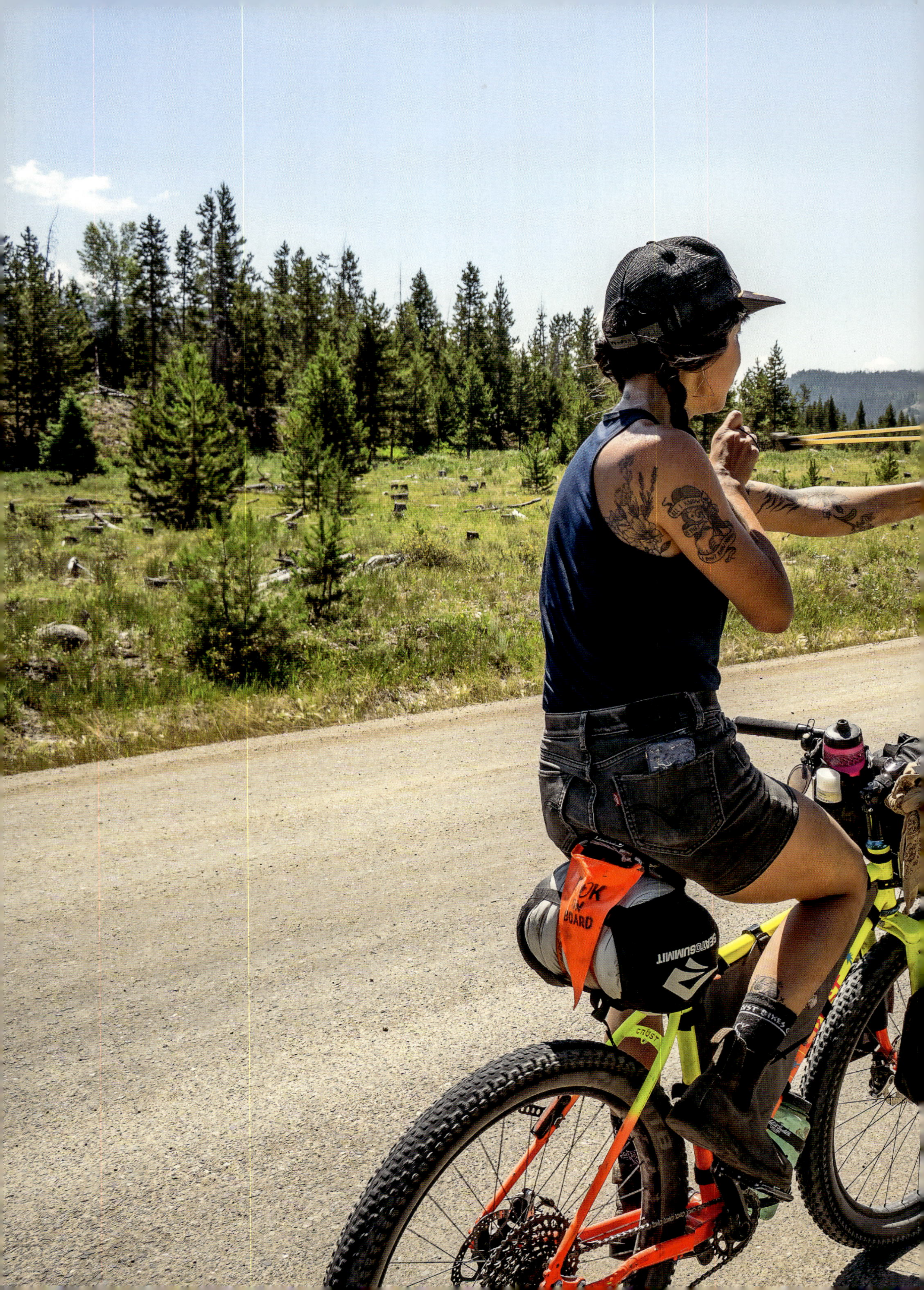
BOARD

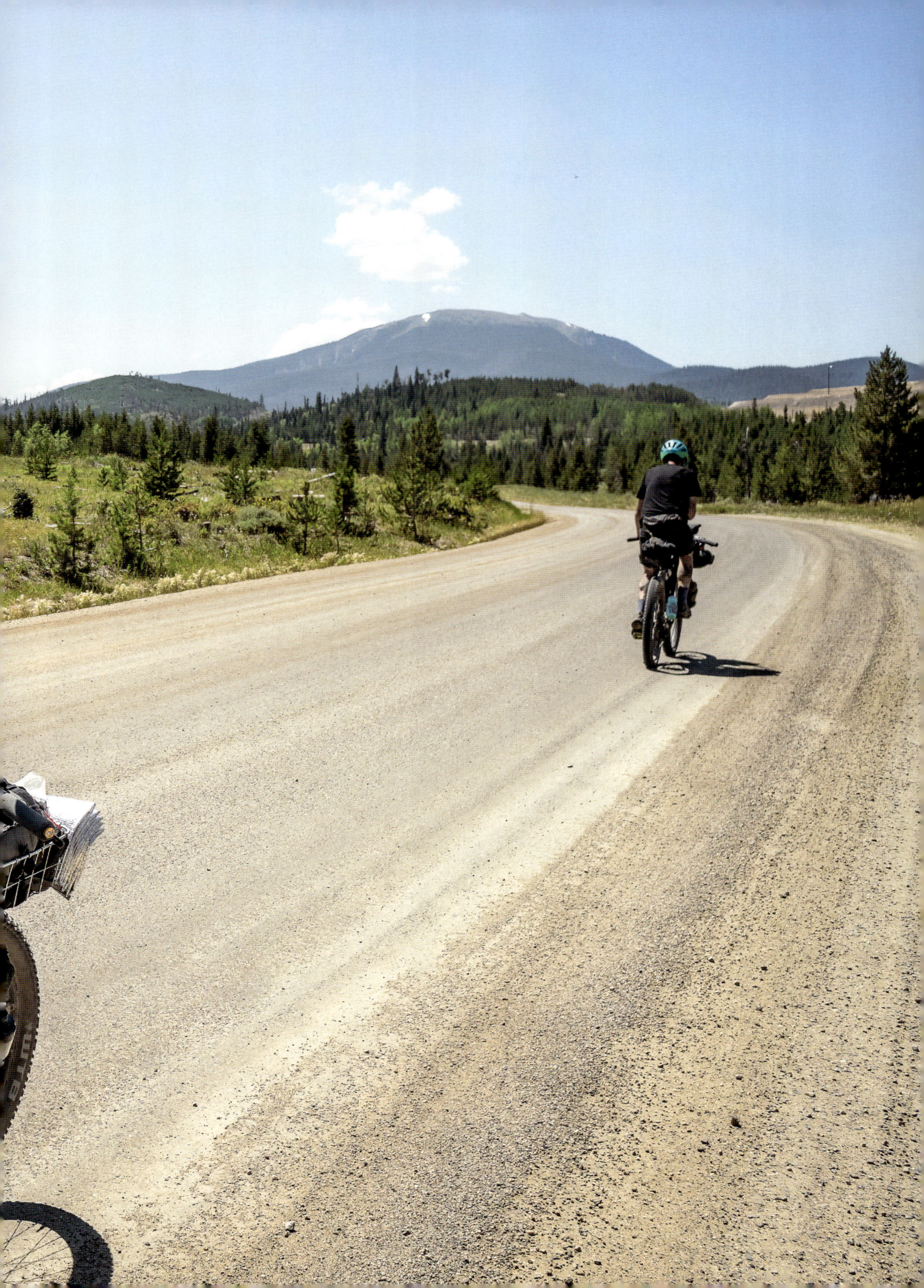

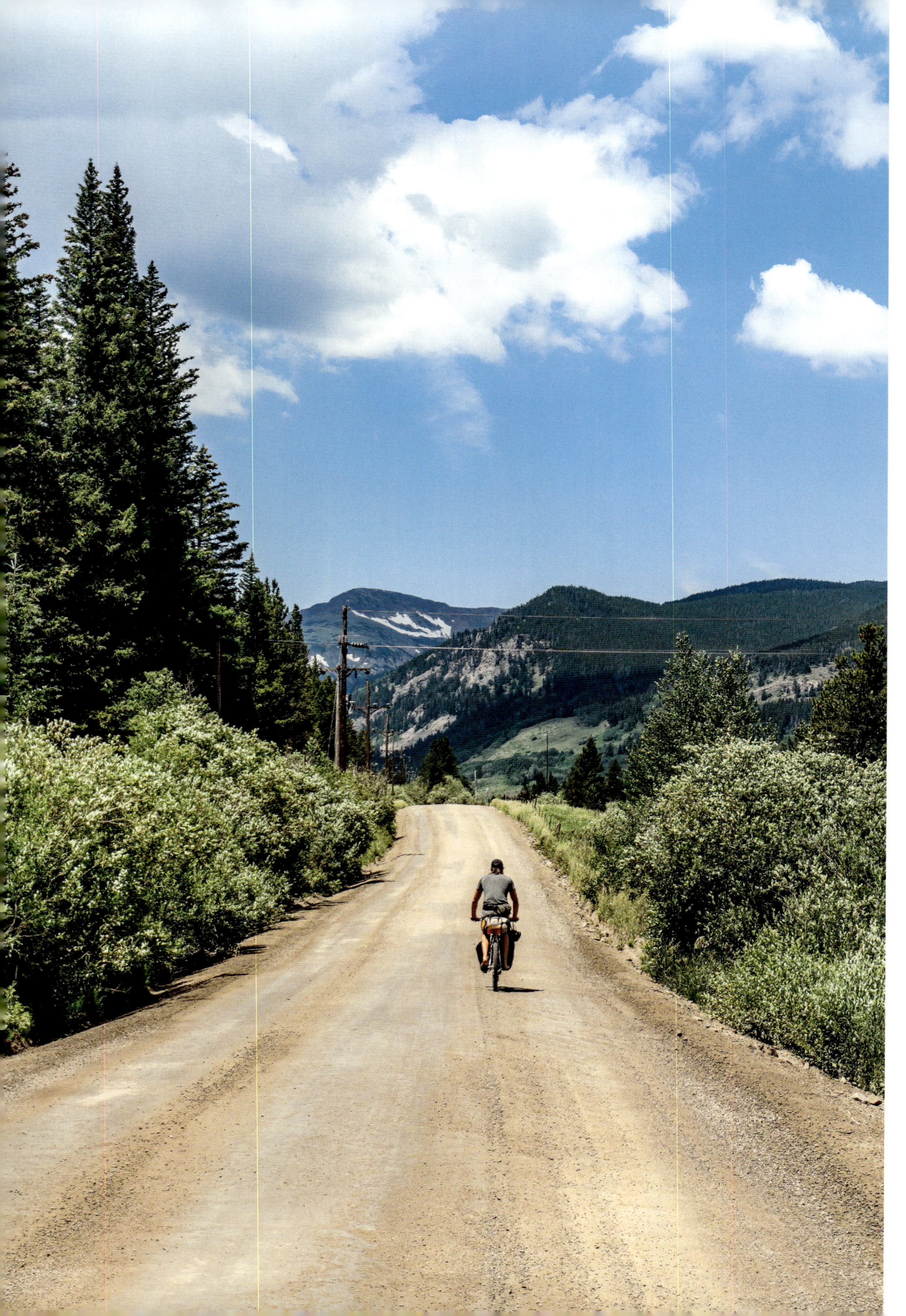

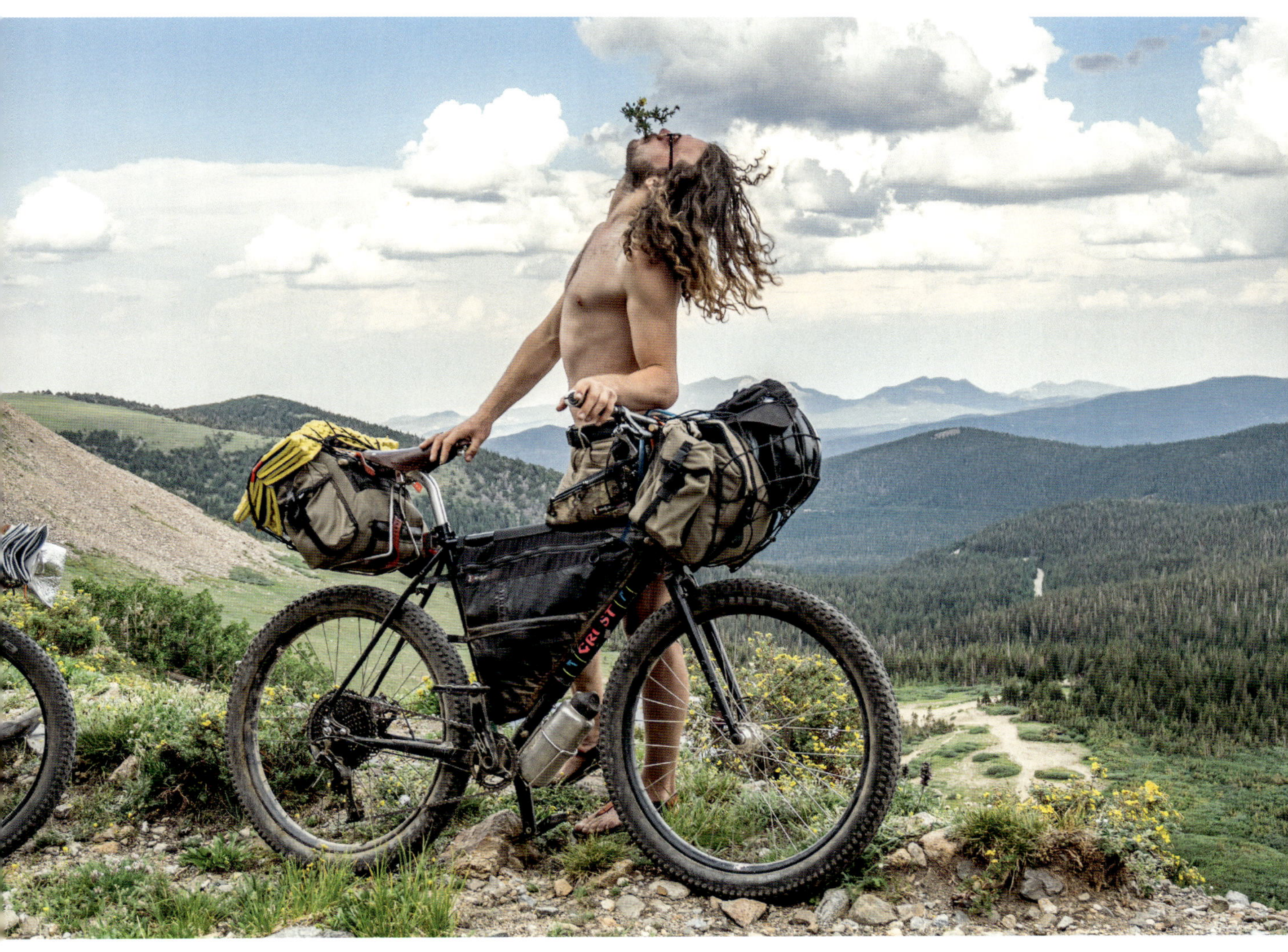

"Up and down are different planes of existence while touring. Each with their own personalities and experiences, pitfalls and triumphs. And, when you expect to be doing one forever, the transition to the other is jarring and delightful."

Adam

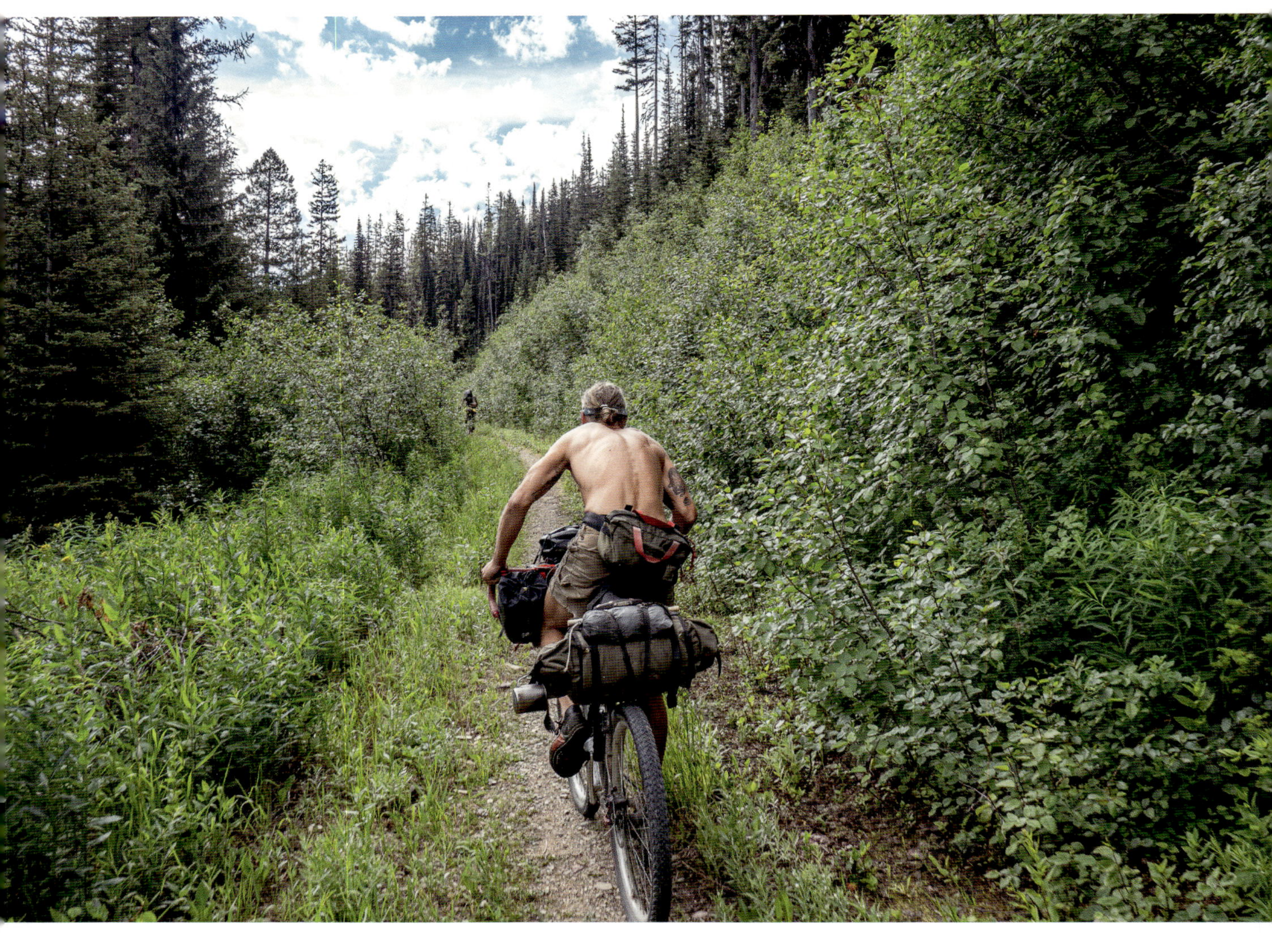

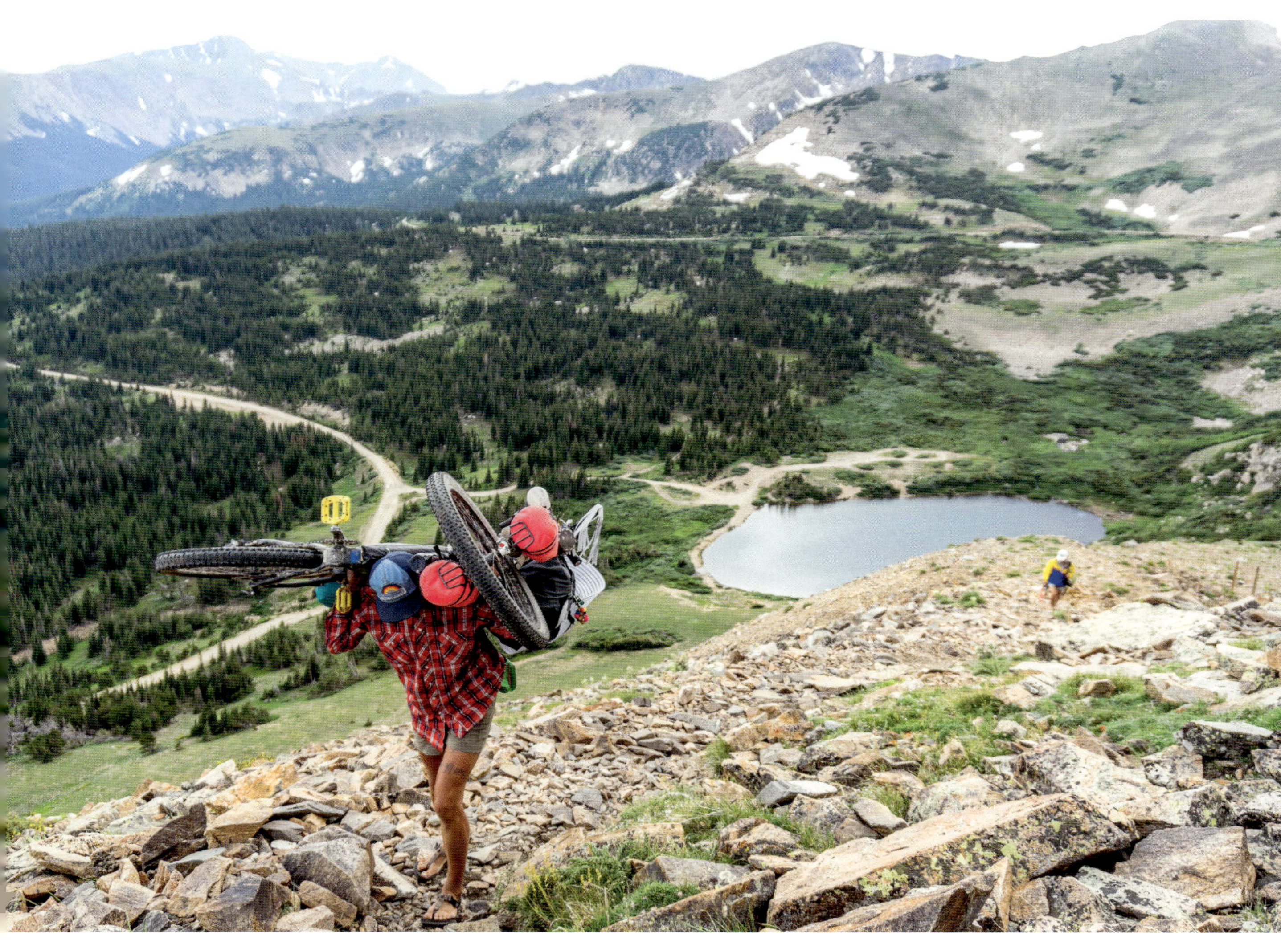

"Days went by slowly and quickly at the same time,
so much happened in one day
that yesterday seemed like last week."

Hannah Kirby

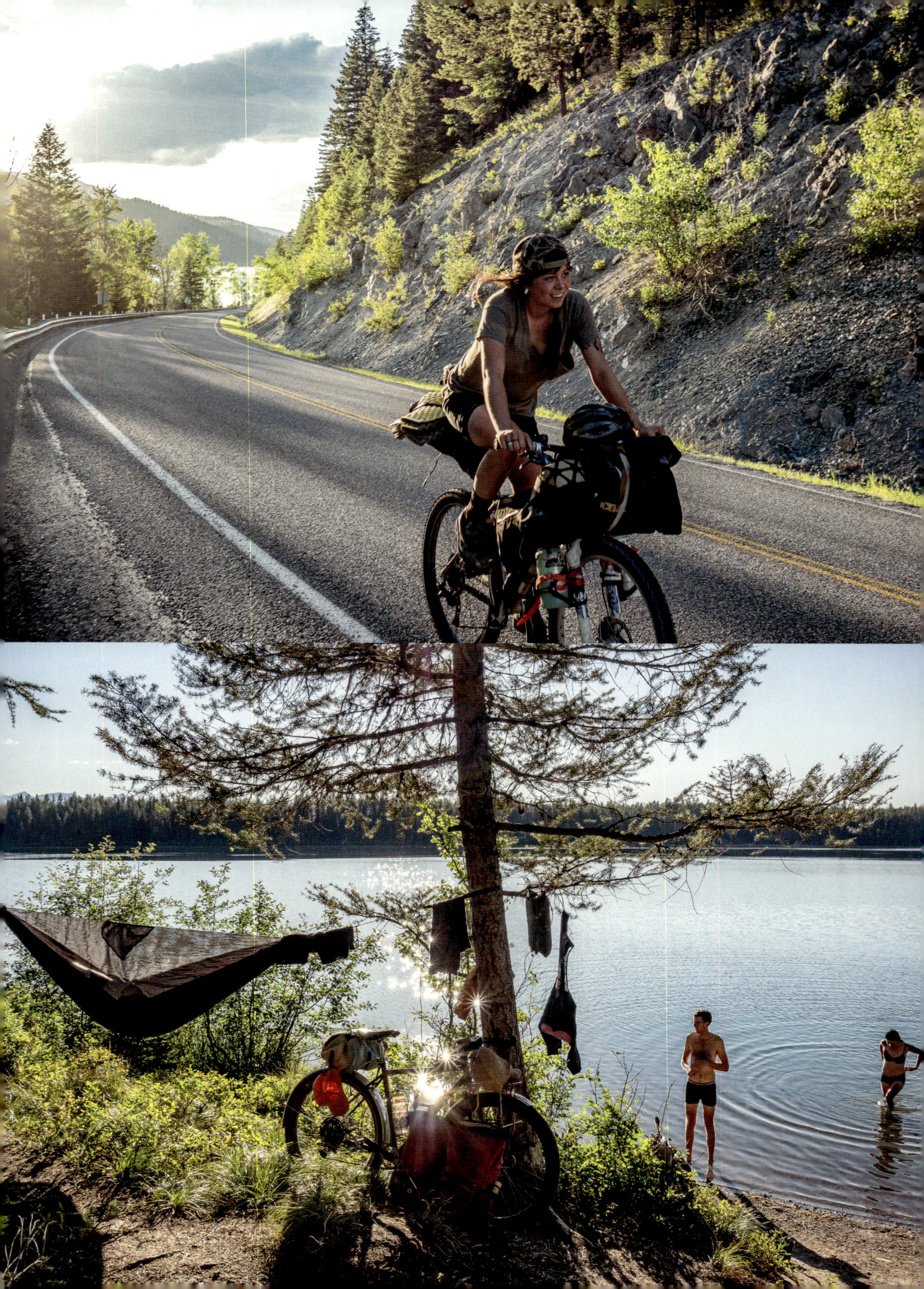

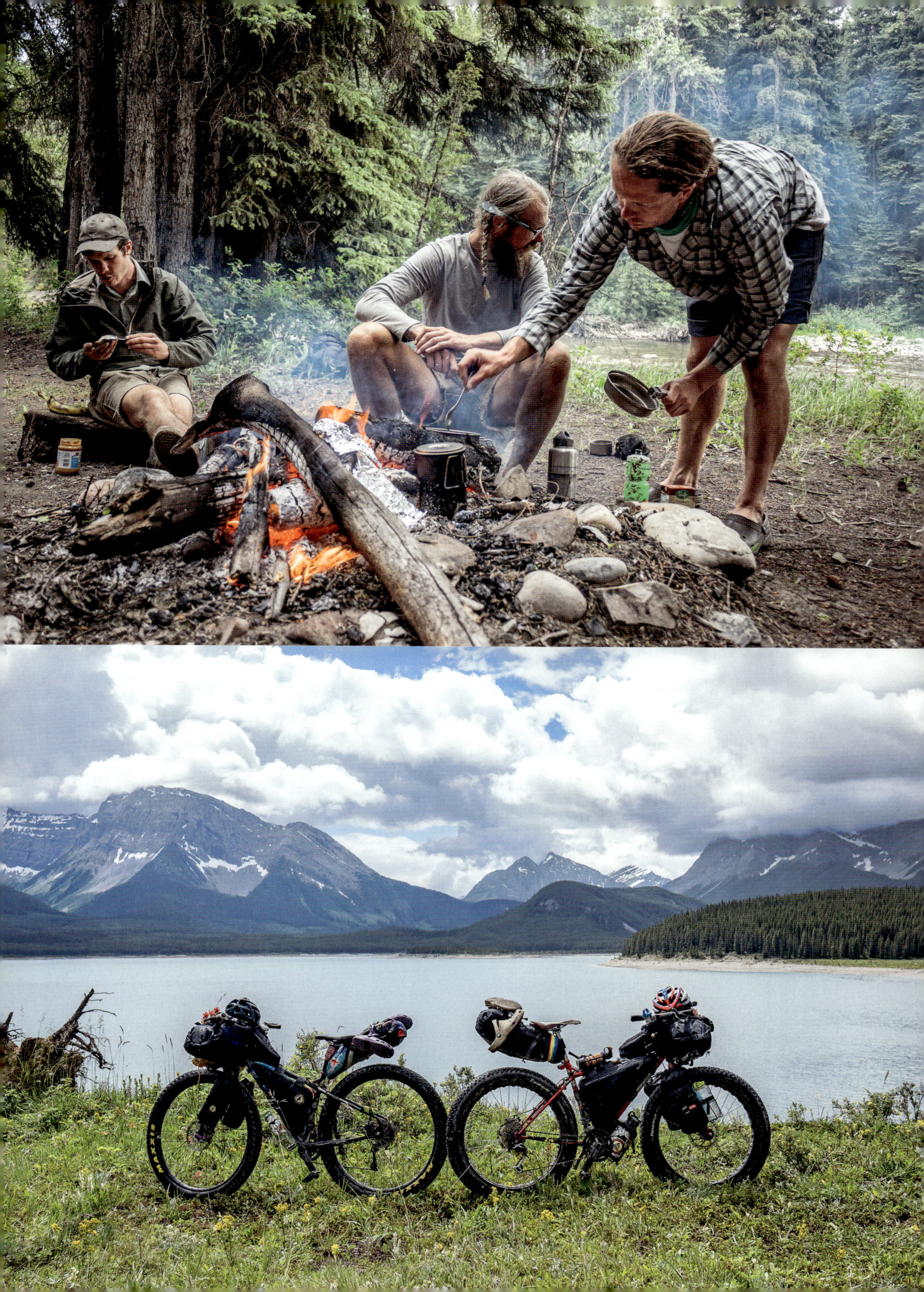

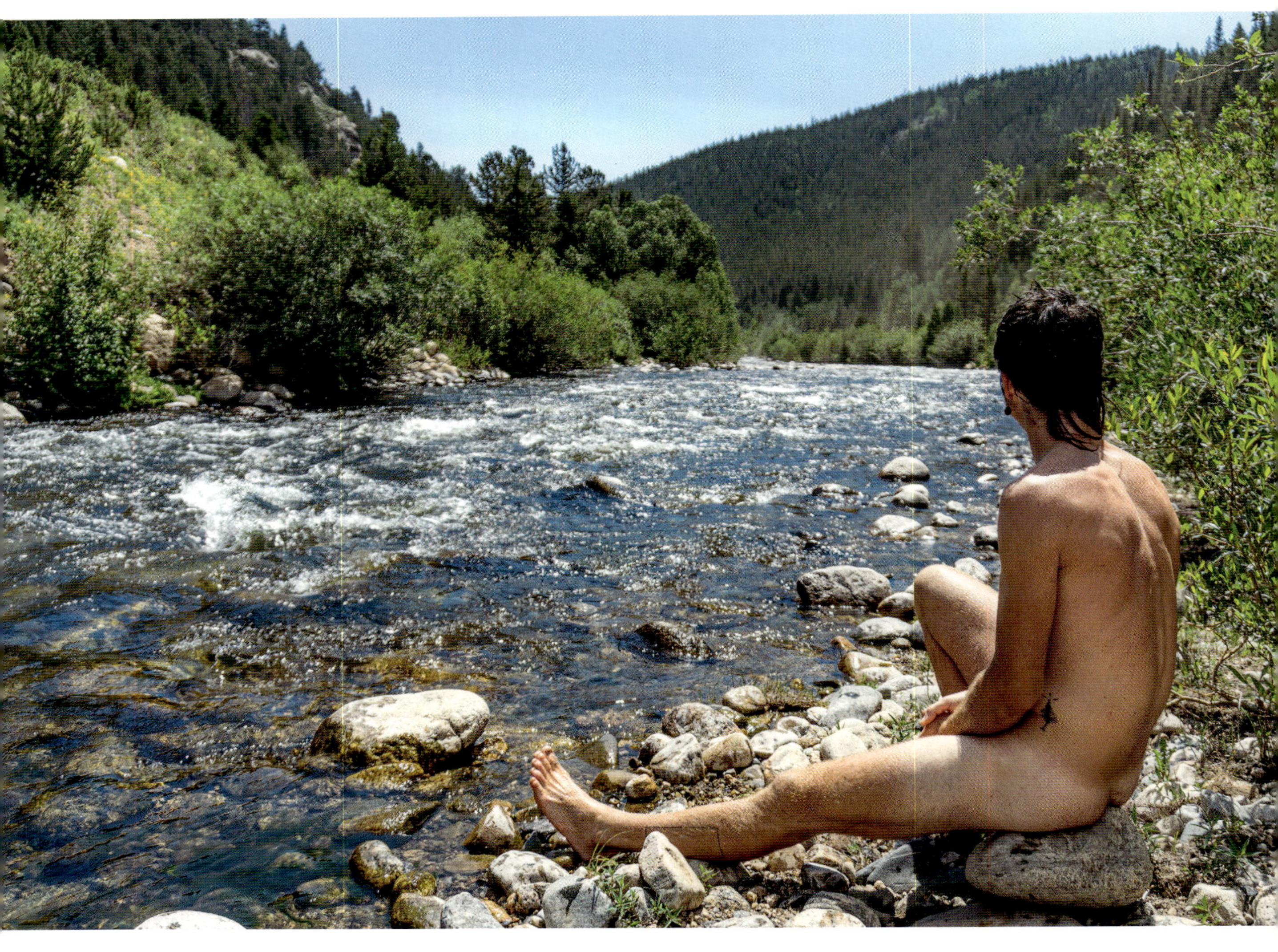

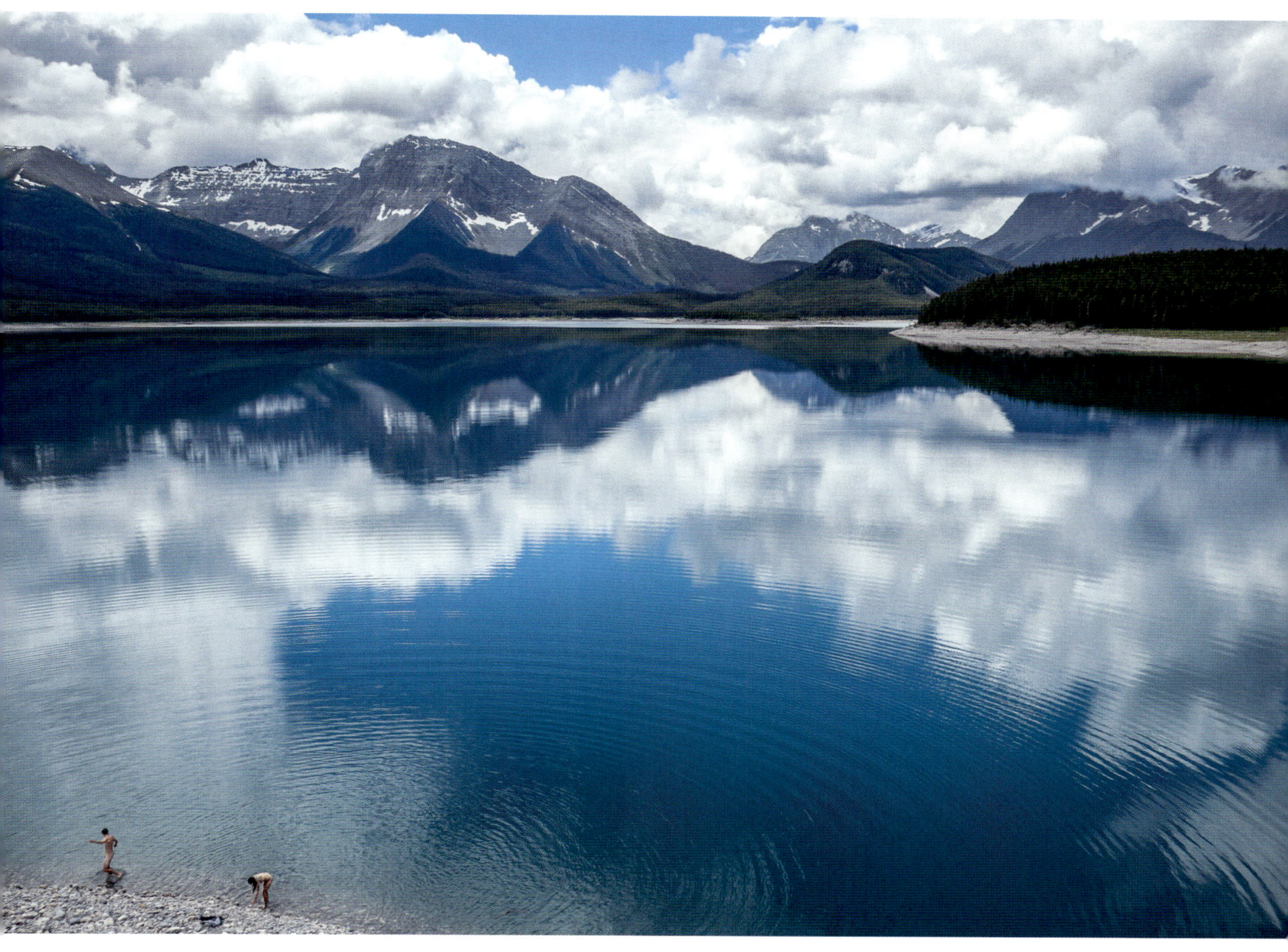

"We change with the sun and sink back into the tranquil again. We laugh, we're naked, we bathe, we cook in groups, we set up our personal chrysalises, we alter ourselves however we deem fit, we stare, we hug, we love this shit and each other and we go the fuck to bed."

Adam

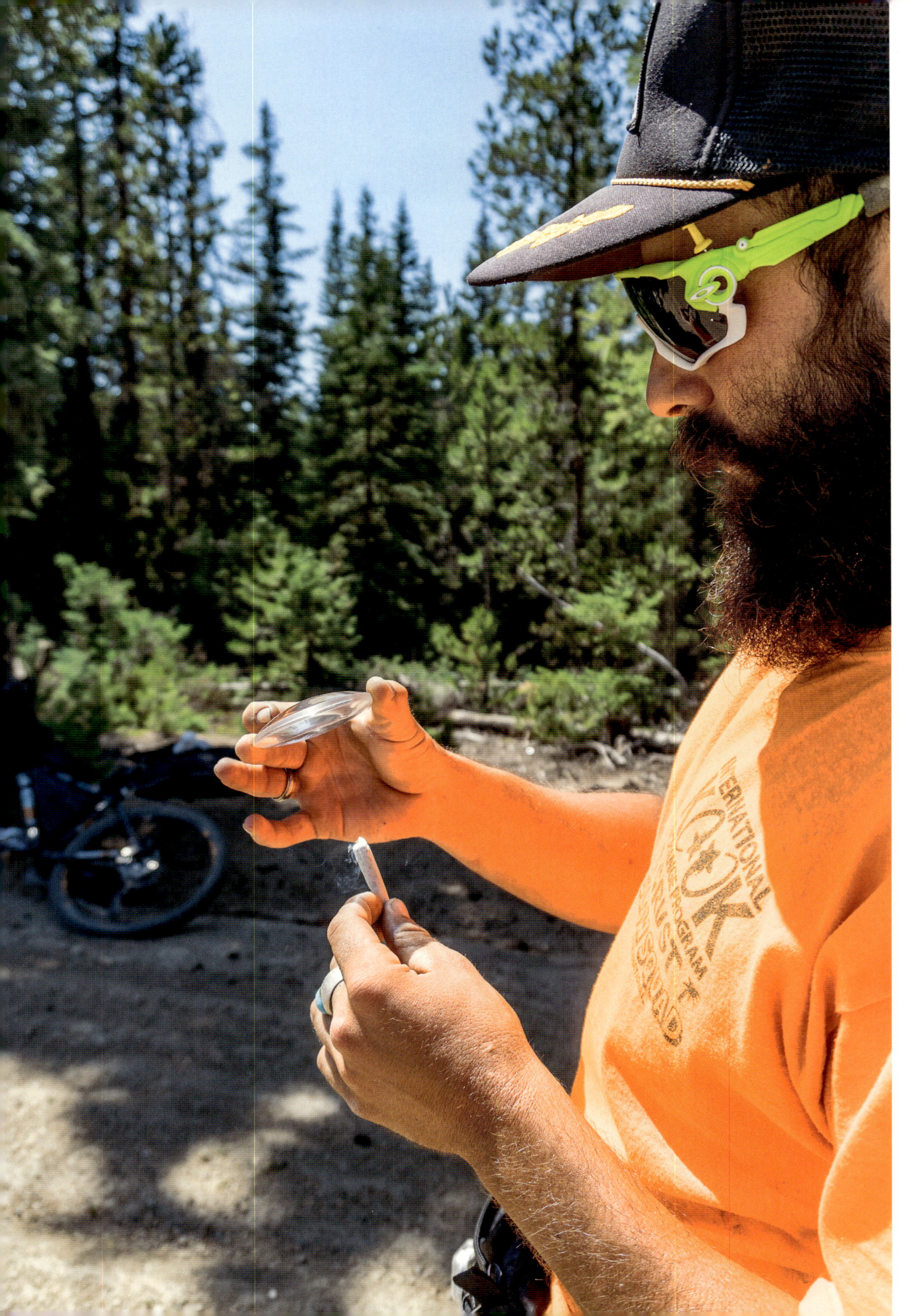
PROGRAM

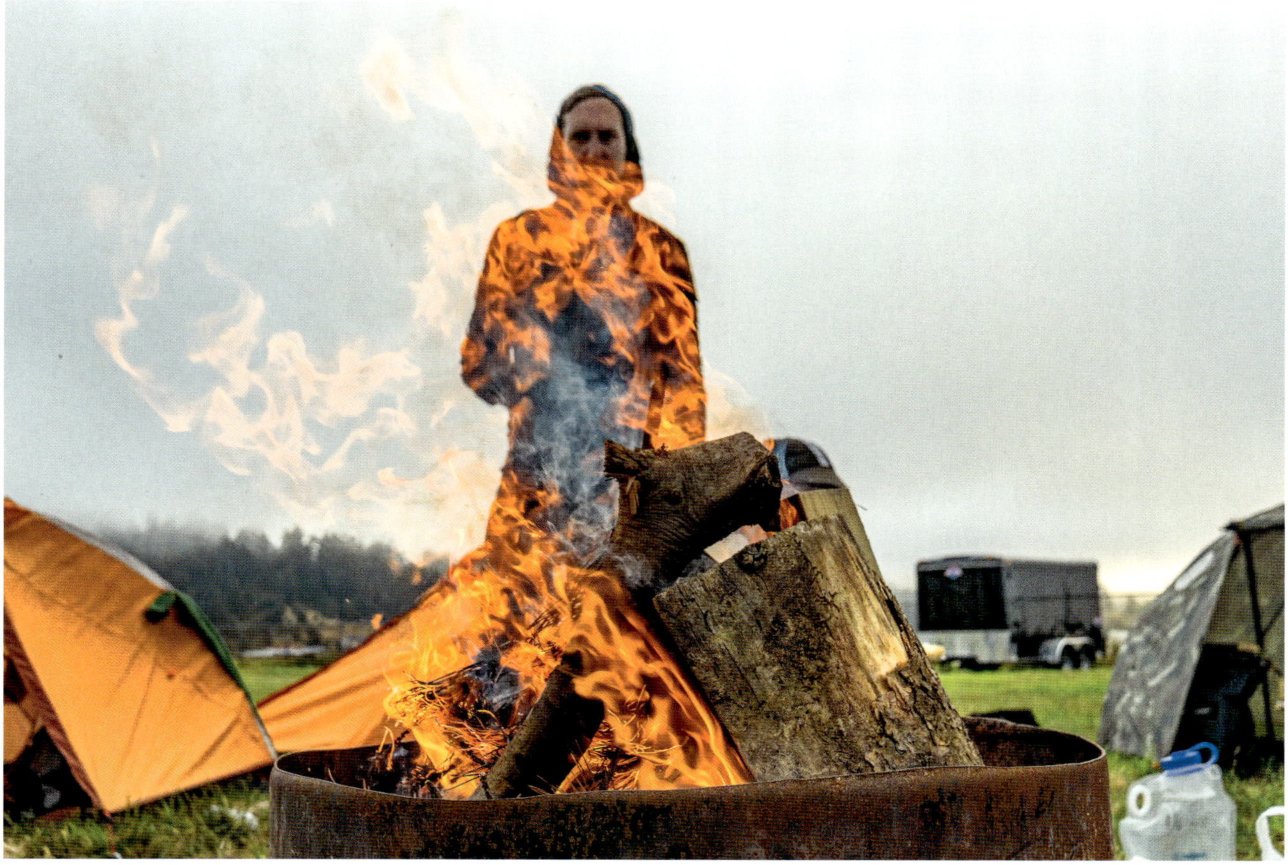

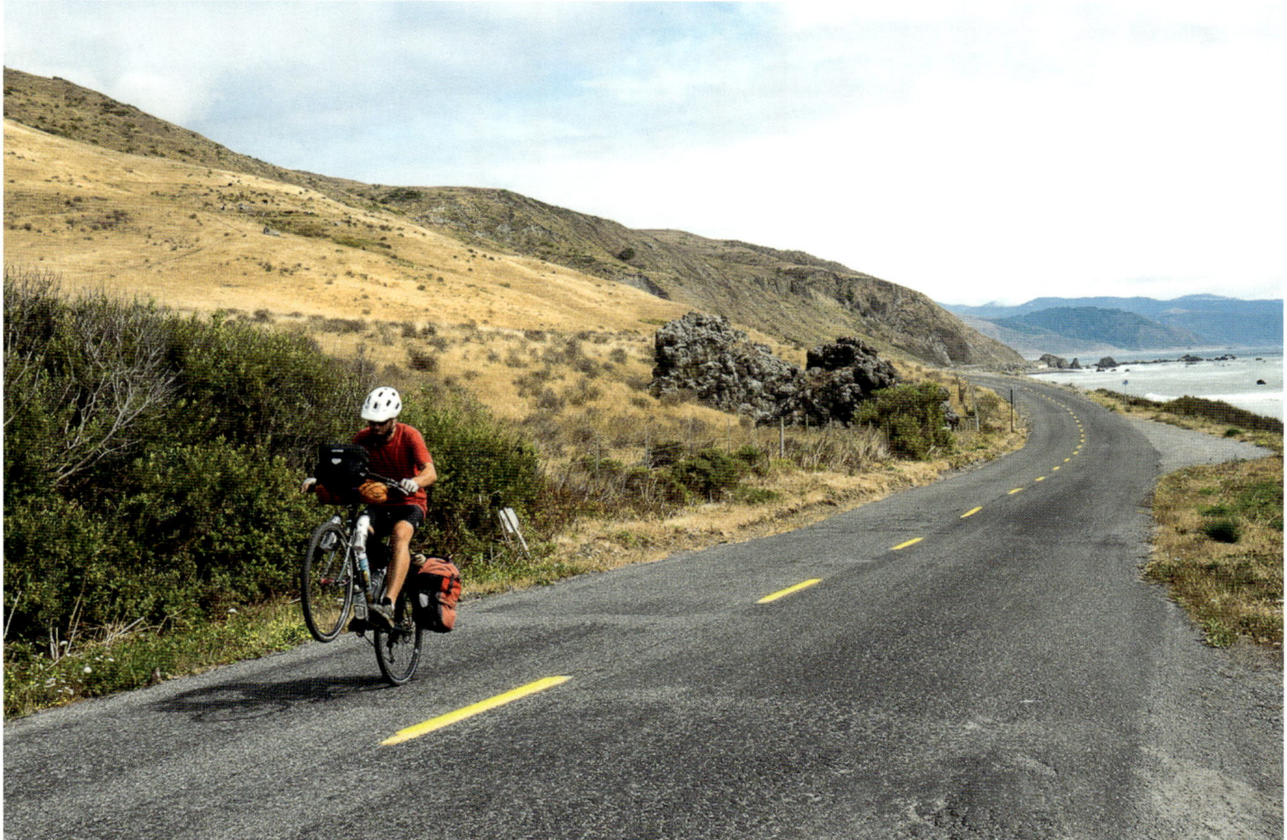

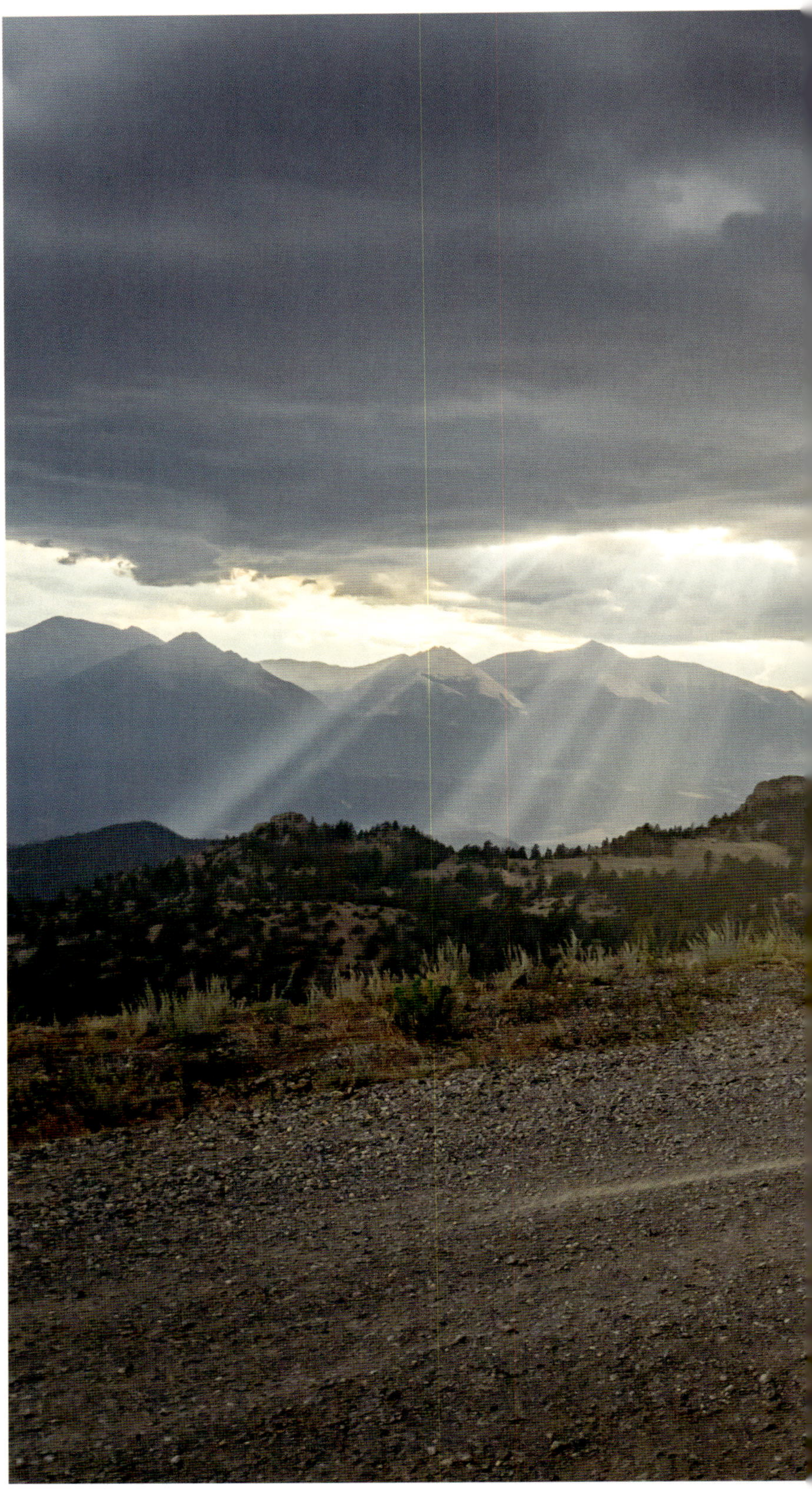

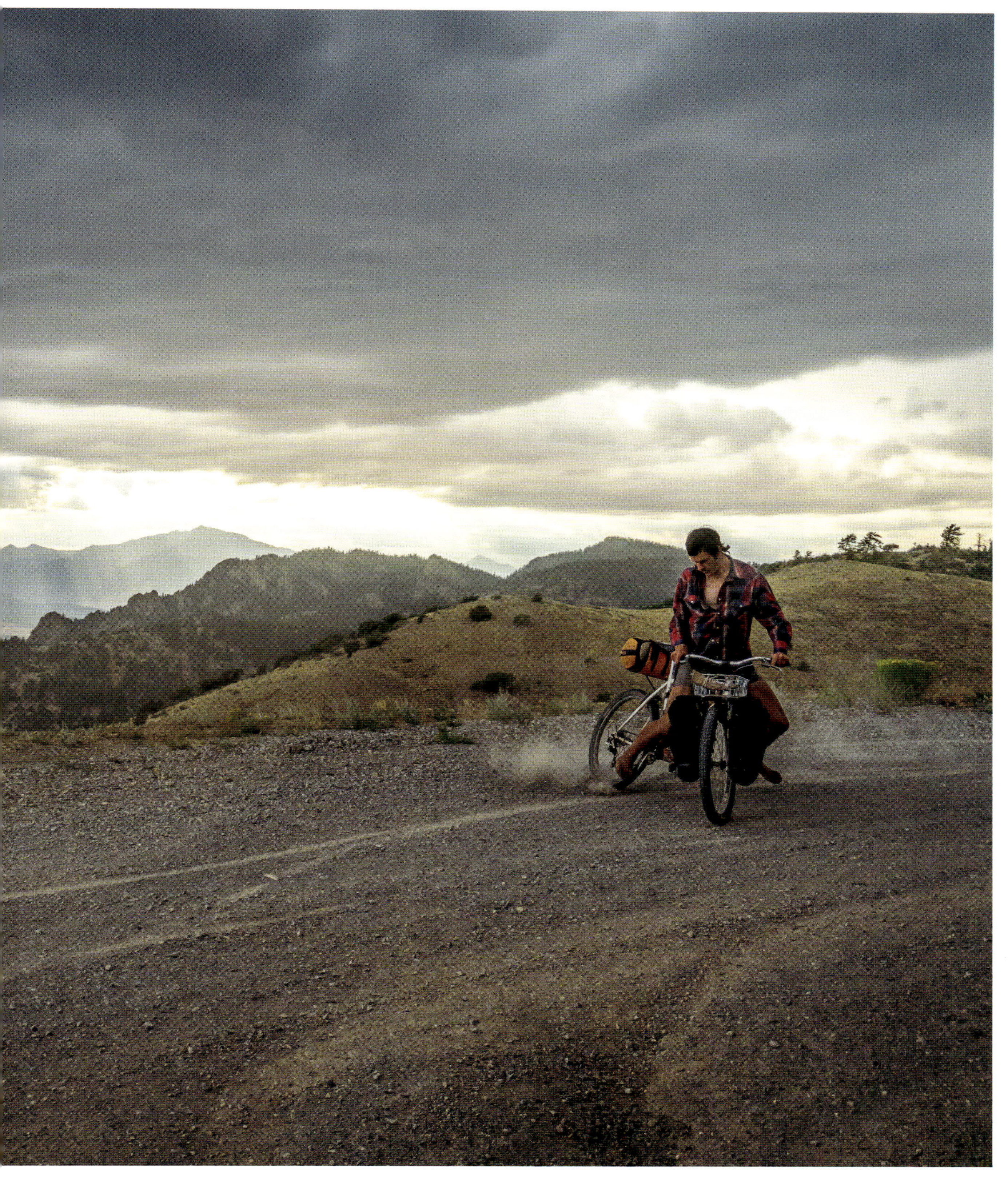

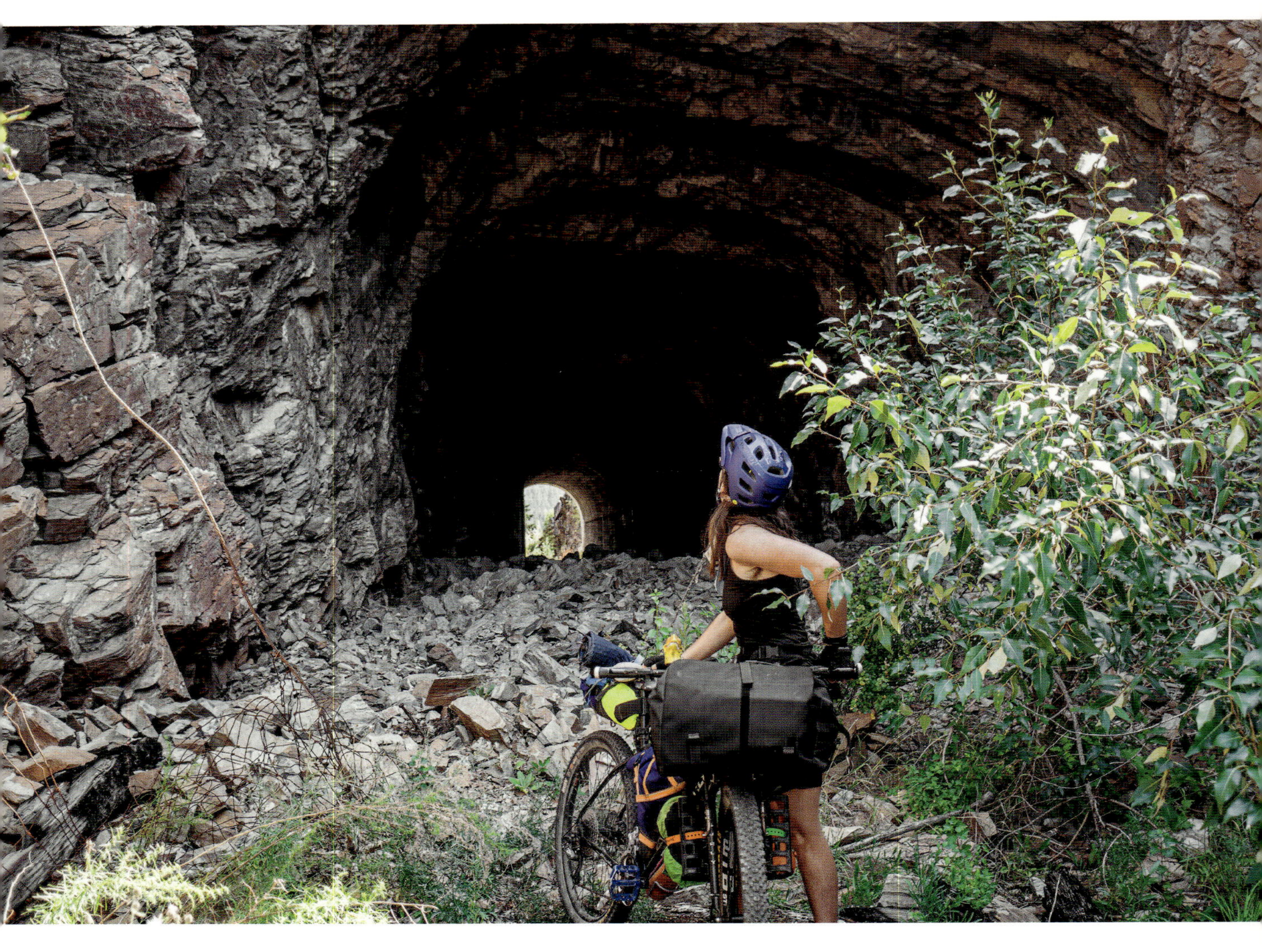

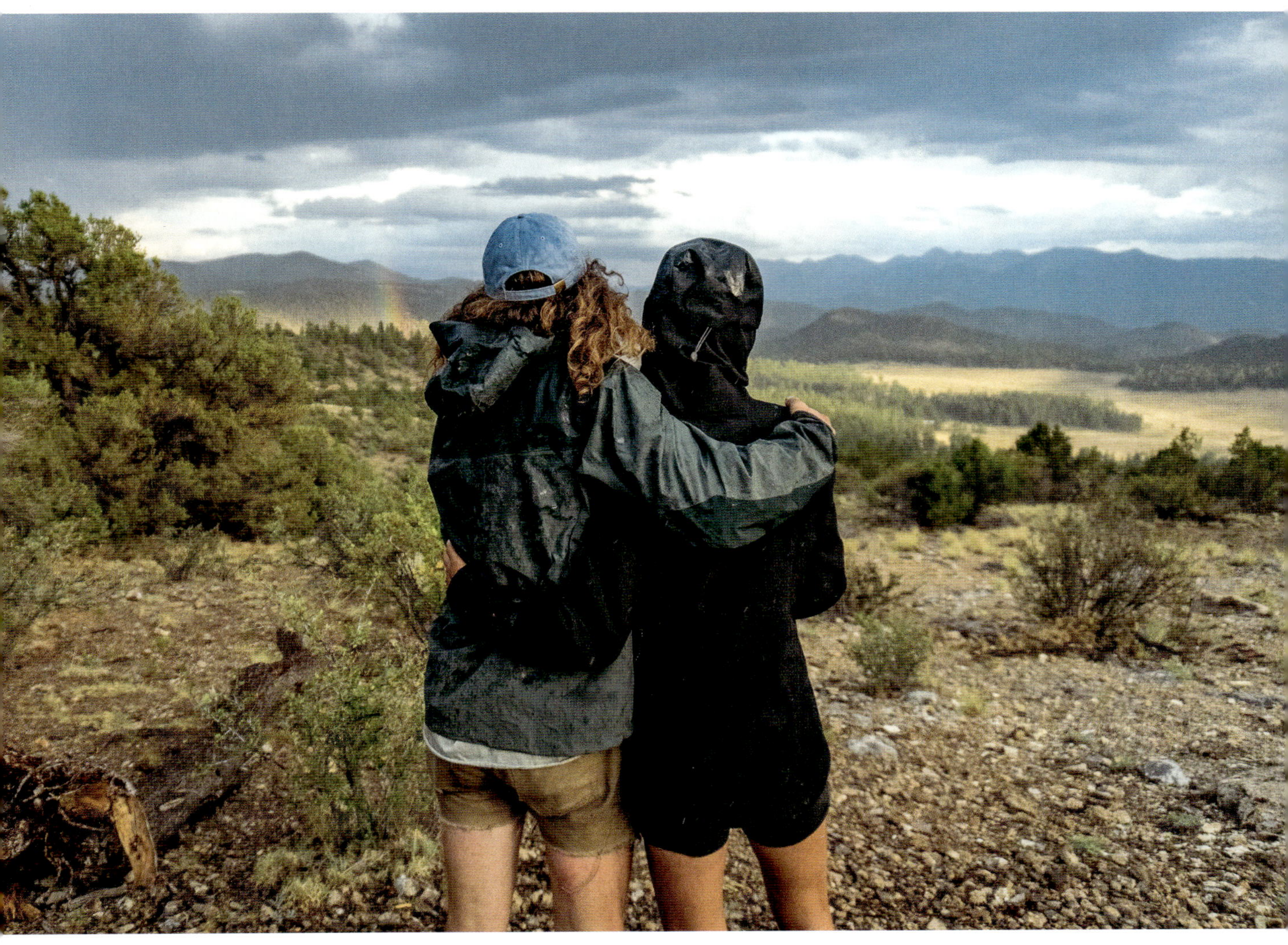

"As we rambled we managed to keep our panties unbunched and worked together to make the adventure as magical, restorative, contemplative, and liberating as it could be. You may think you can plan for a good time but happiness is best when it's unexpected."

Hannah Kirby

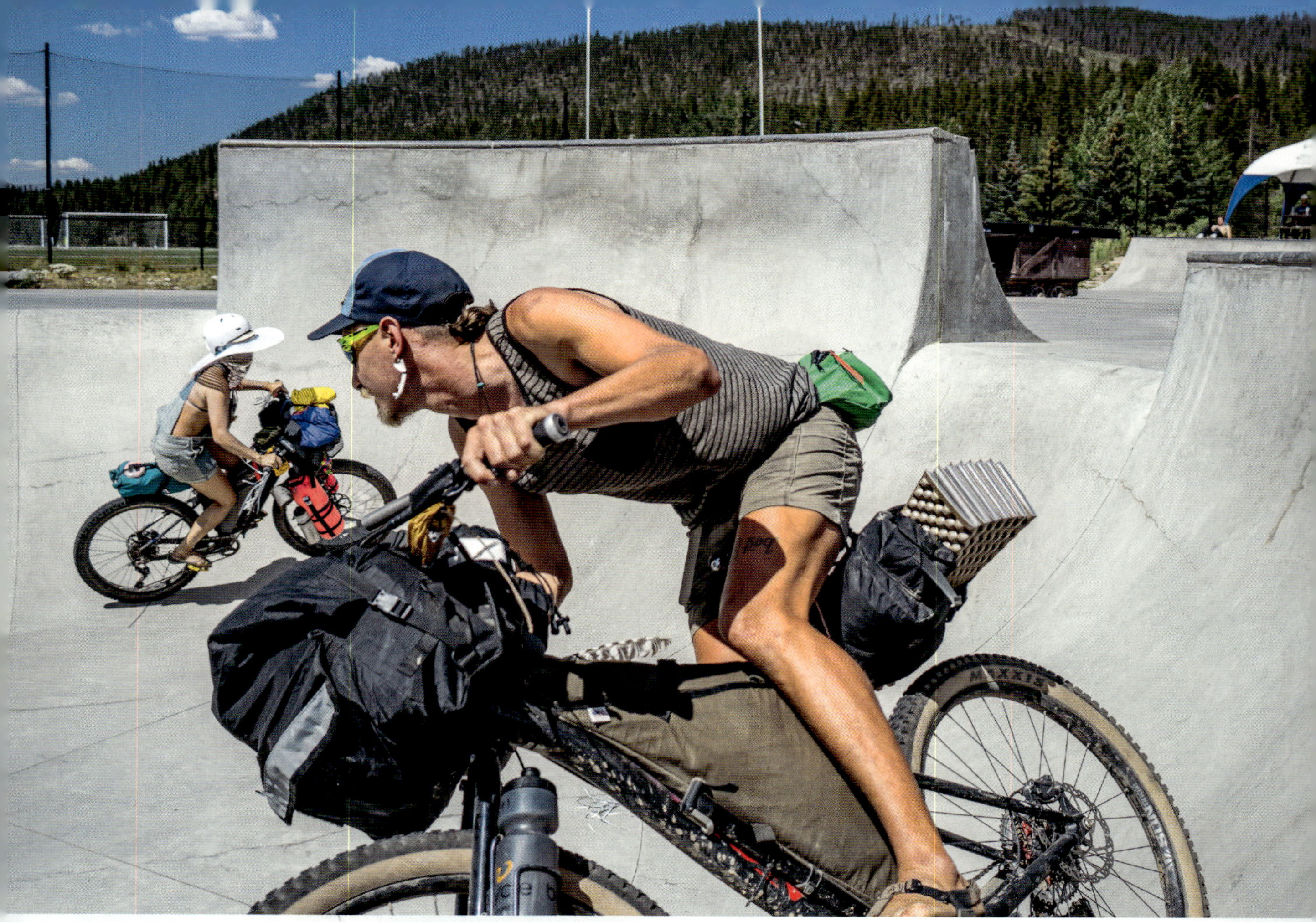

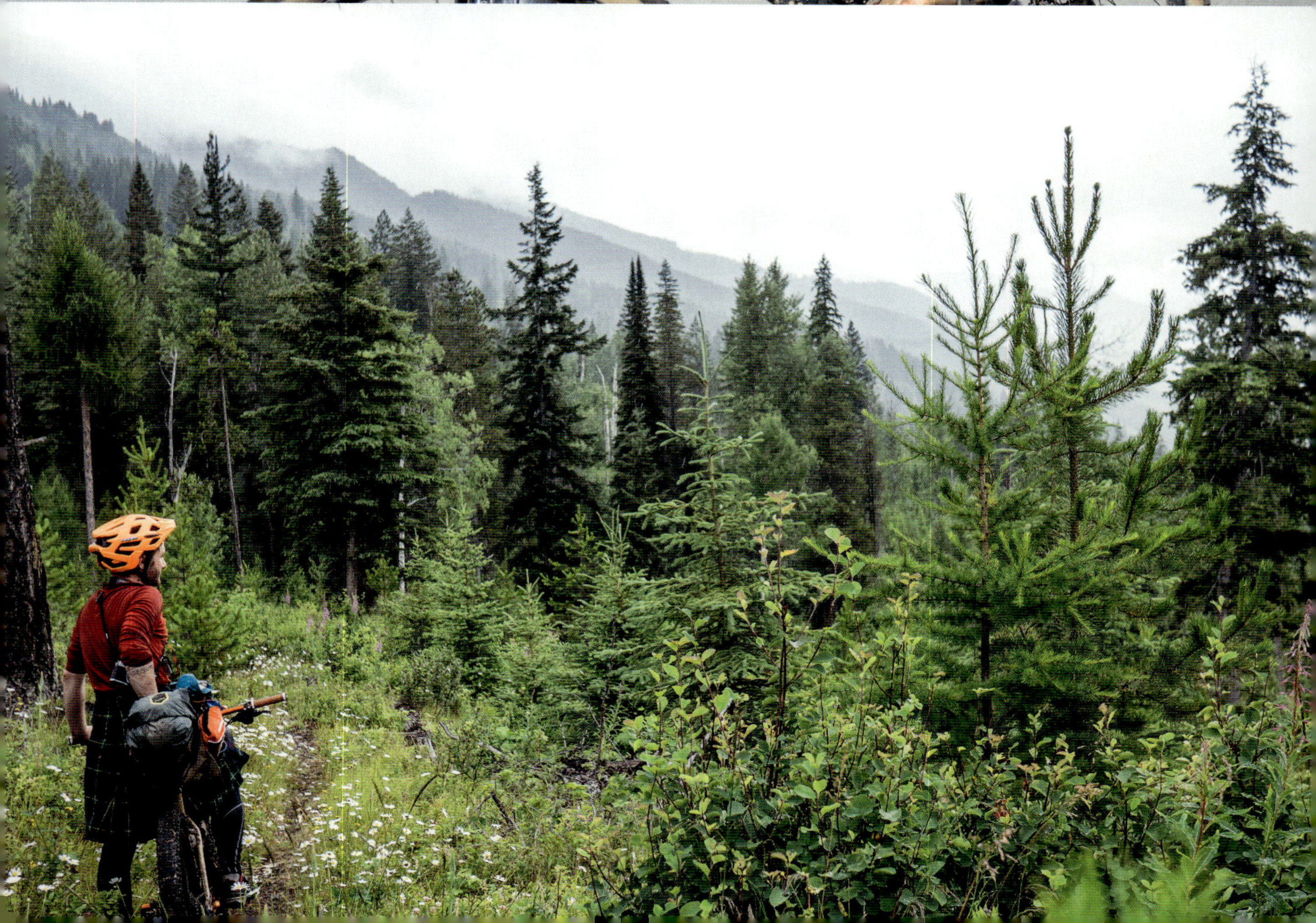

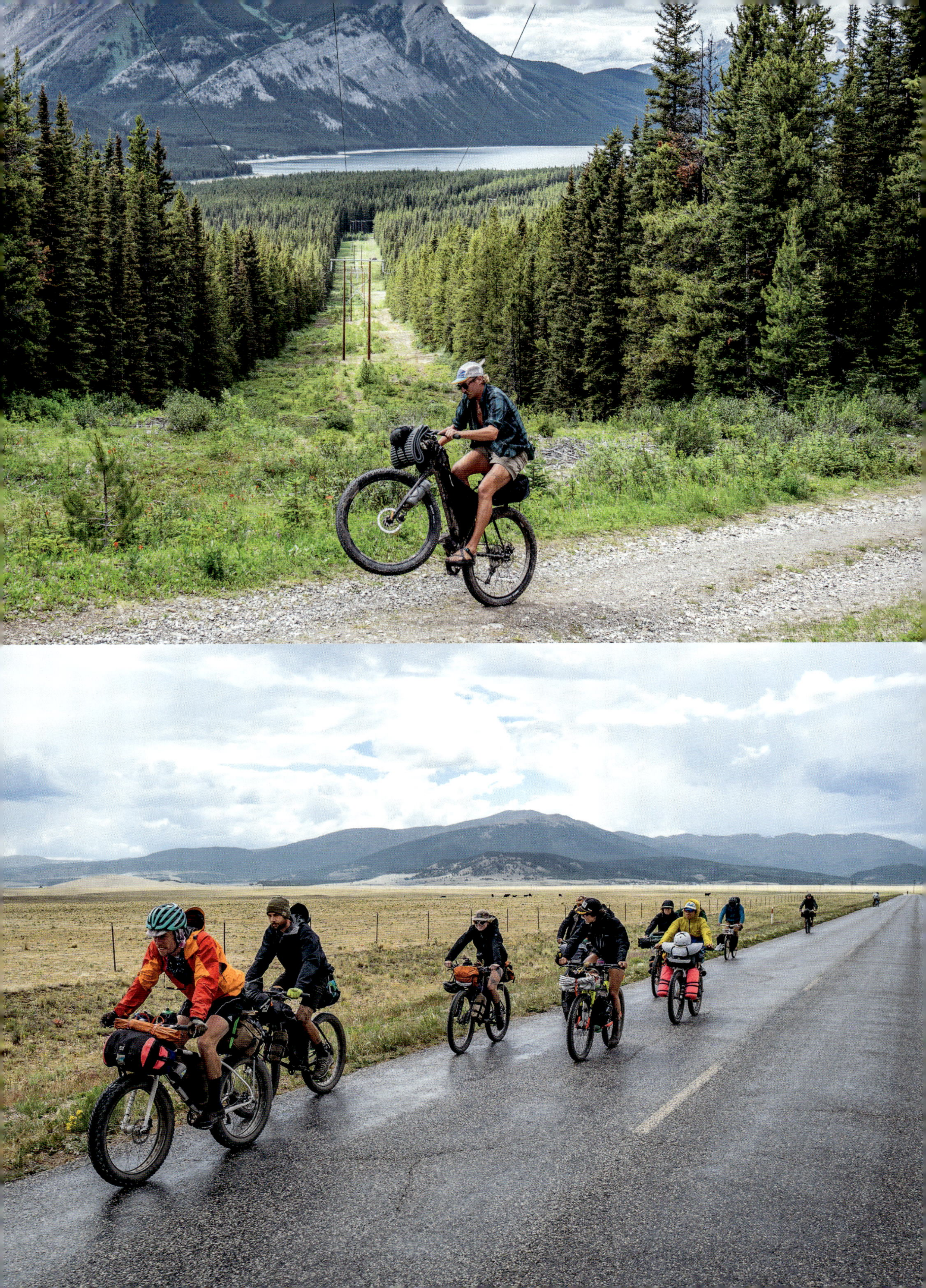

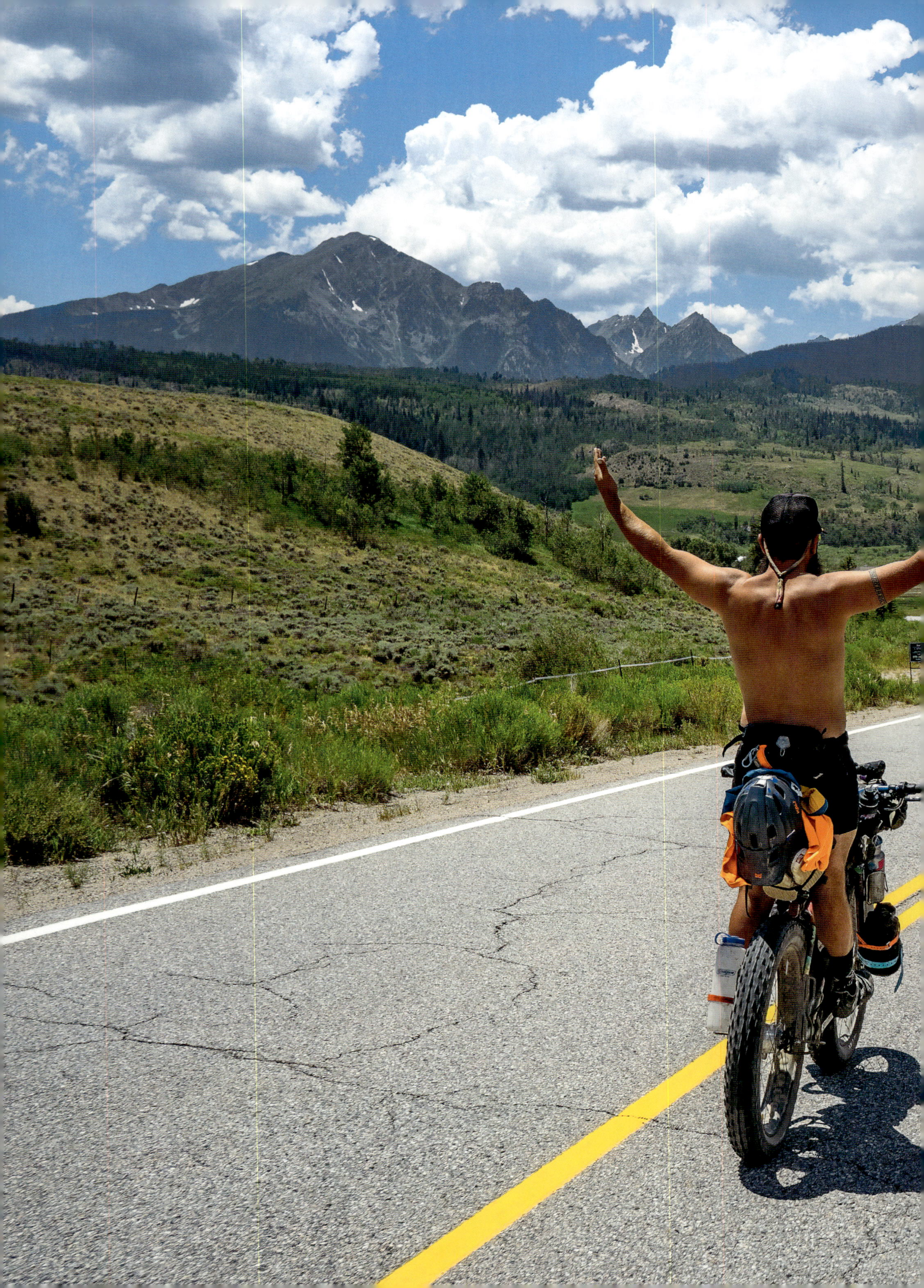

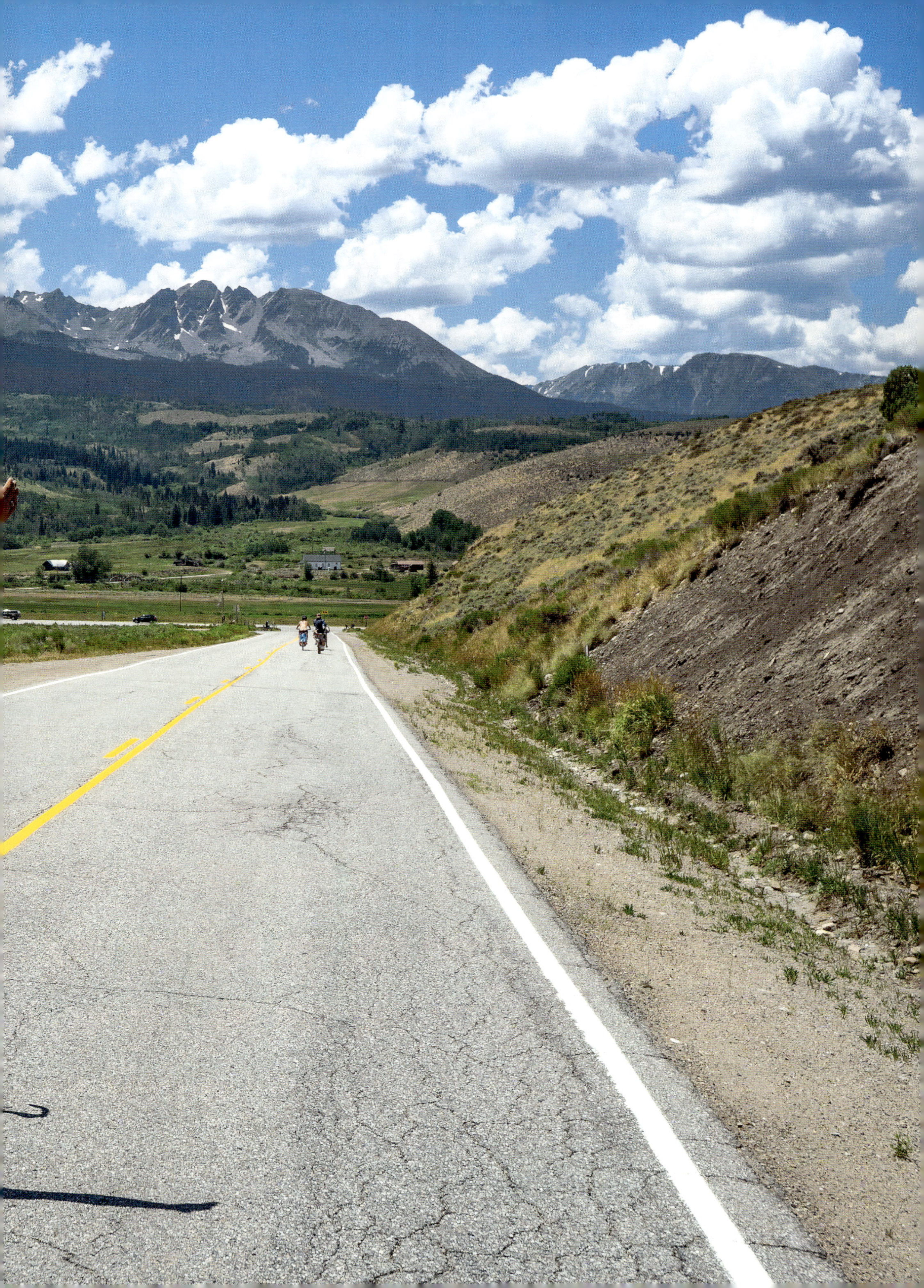

Black Label Bike Club

New York—A tight-knit group of bikers

Photos
Julie Glassberg

The Black Label Bike Club was formed in Minneapolis in 1992 by Jake Houle and Per Hanson. There are now chapters in New York, Austin, New Orleans, Tokyo, Stockholm, Malmö, and other cities. In keeping with the DIY ethos members began to build their own tall bikes. Many of the bikes seen at Bike Kill are self-welded tall bikes, which are a distant reminder of their late nineetenth-century predecessors. The Black Label Bike Club scene is bustling with punks, artists, and people from all walks of life who come together to work on their bikes and ride around the city.

The photographer Julie Glassberg spent three years with these bicycle-punks. Thus, she was able to produce these intimate photos from the inner workings of the New York Black Label Bike Club and extended family. Wherever they meet, they will ride and party—and sleep it off the next day.

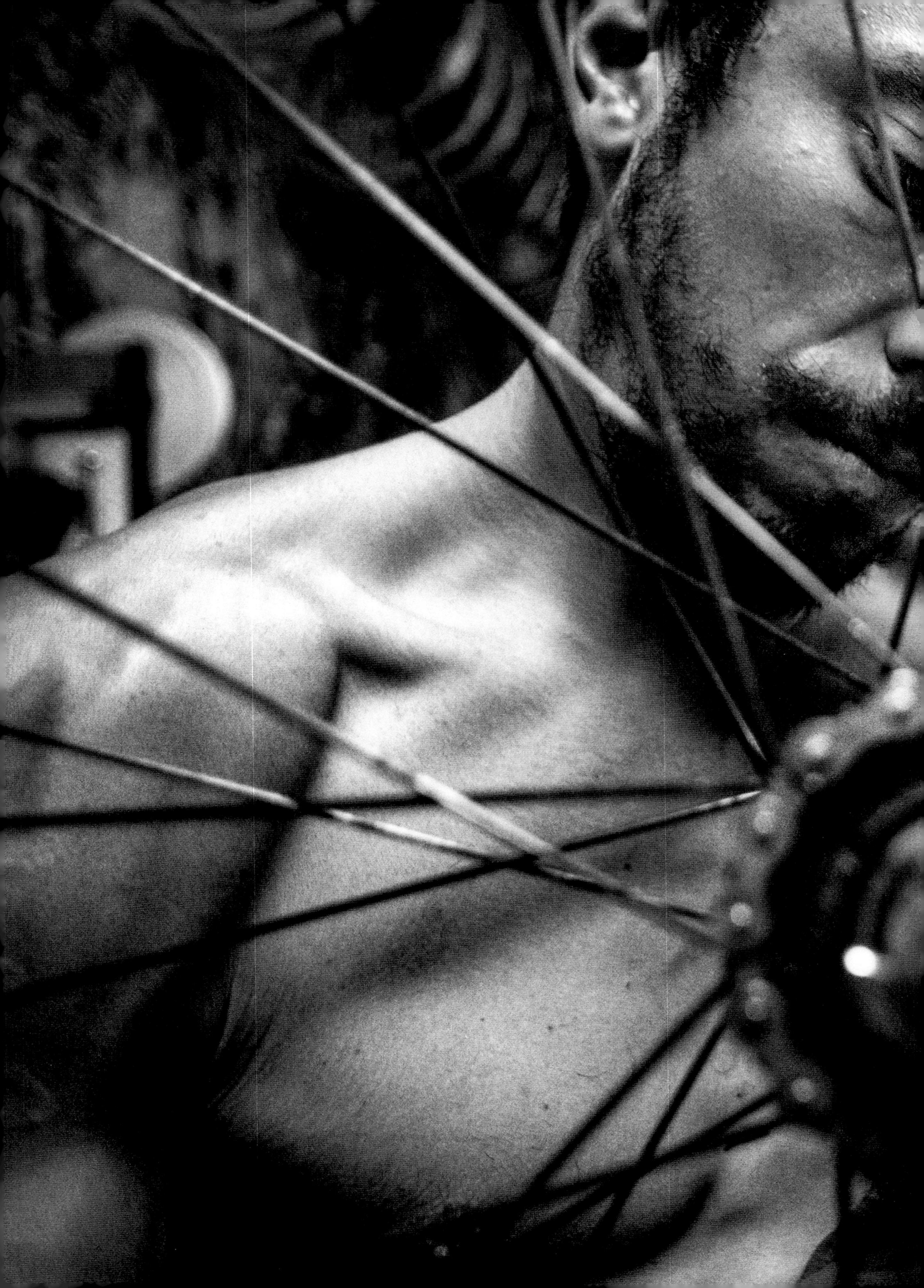

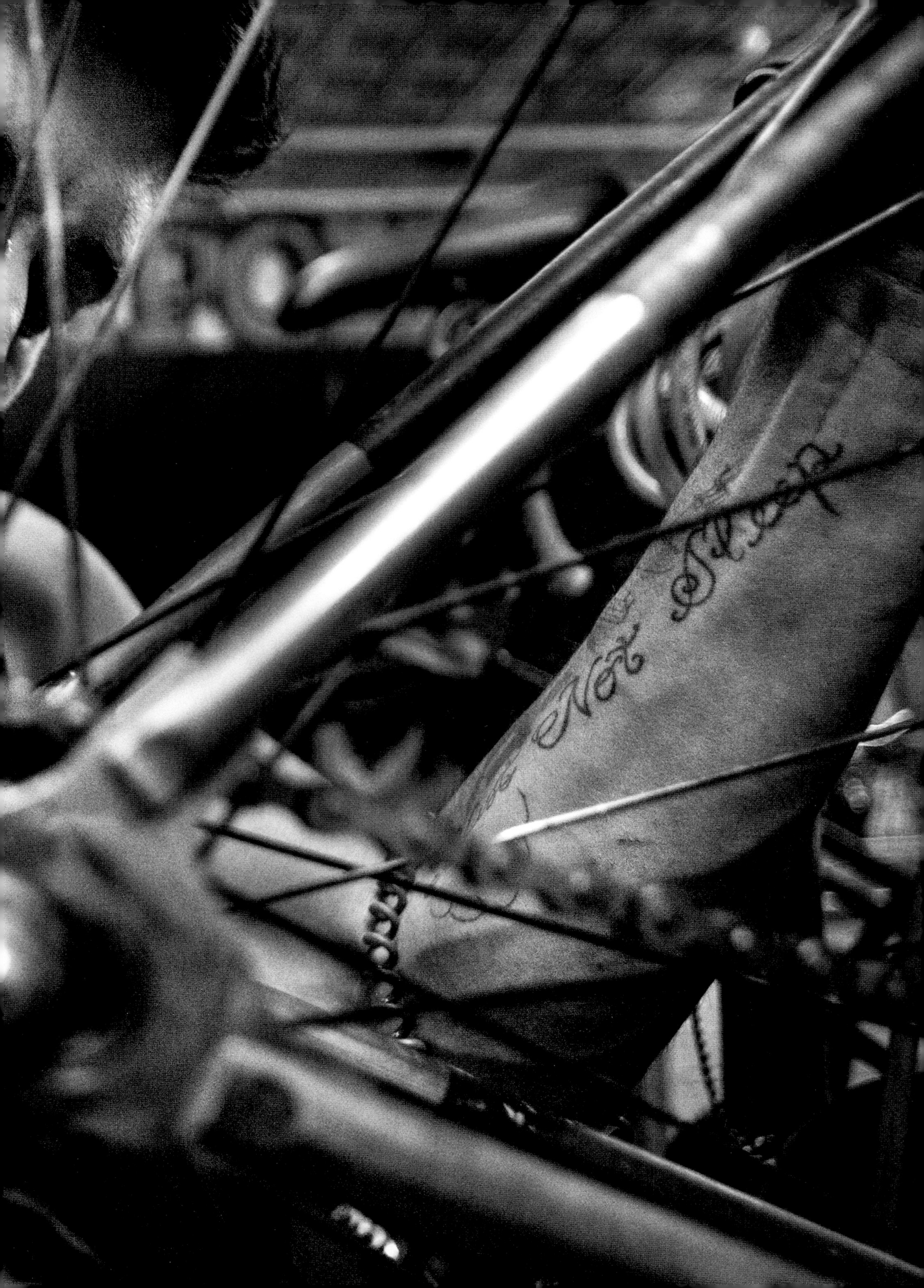

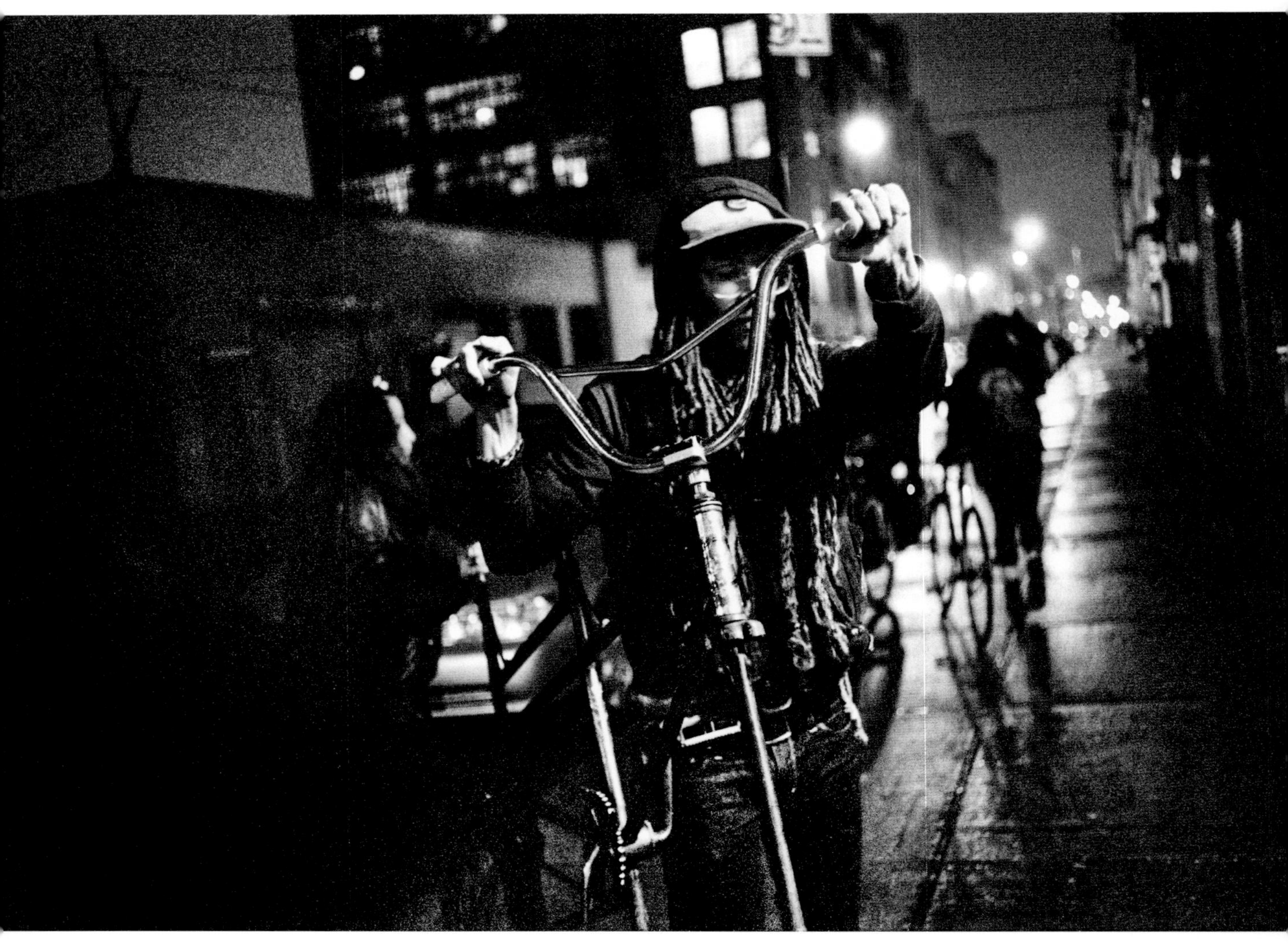

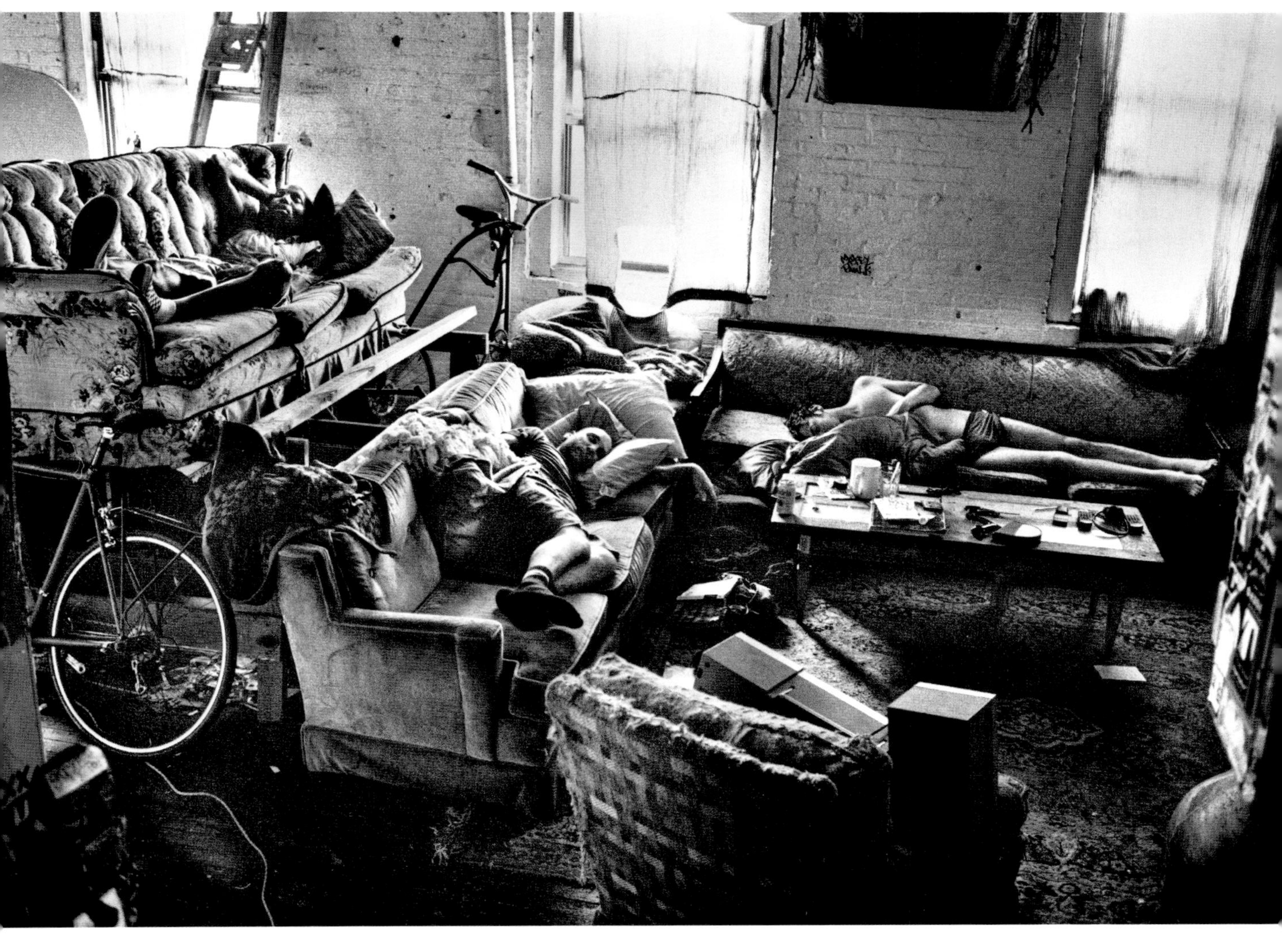

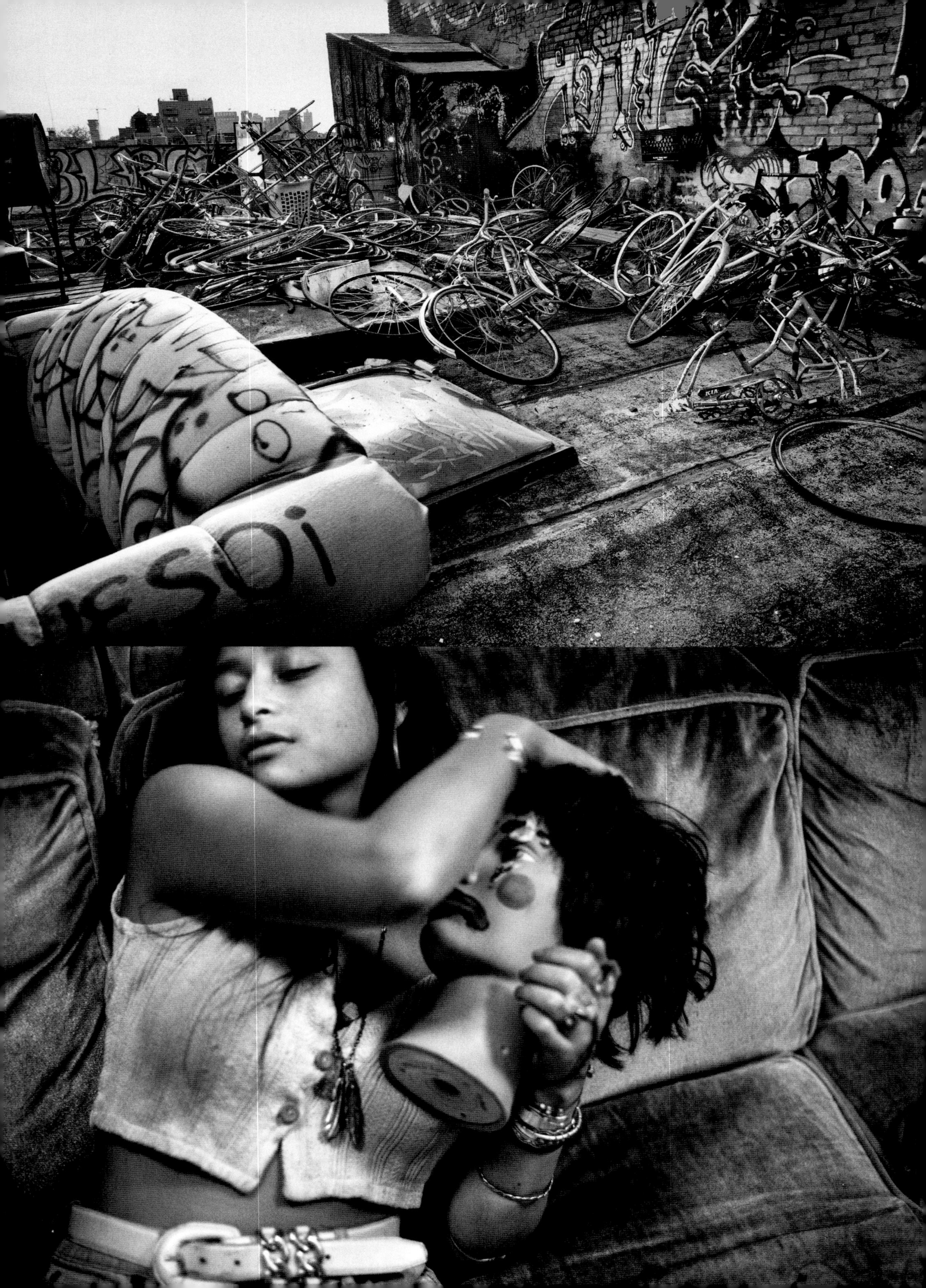

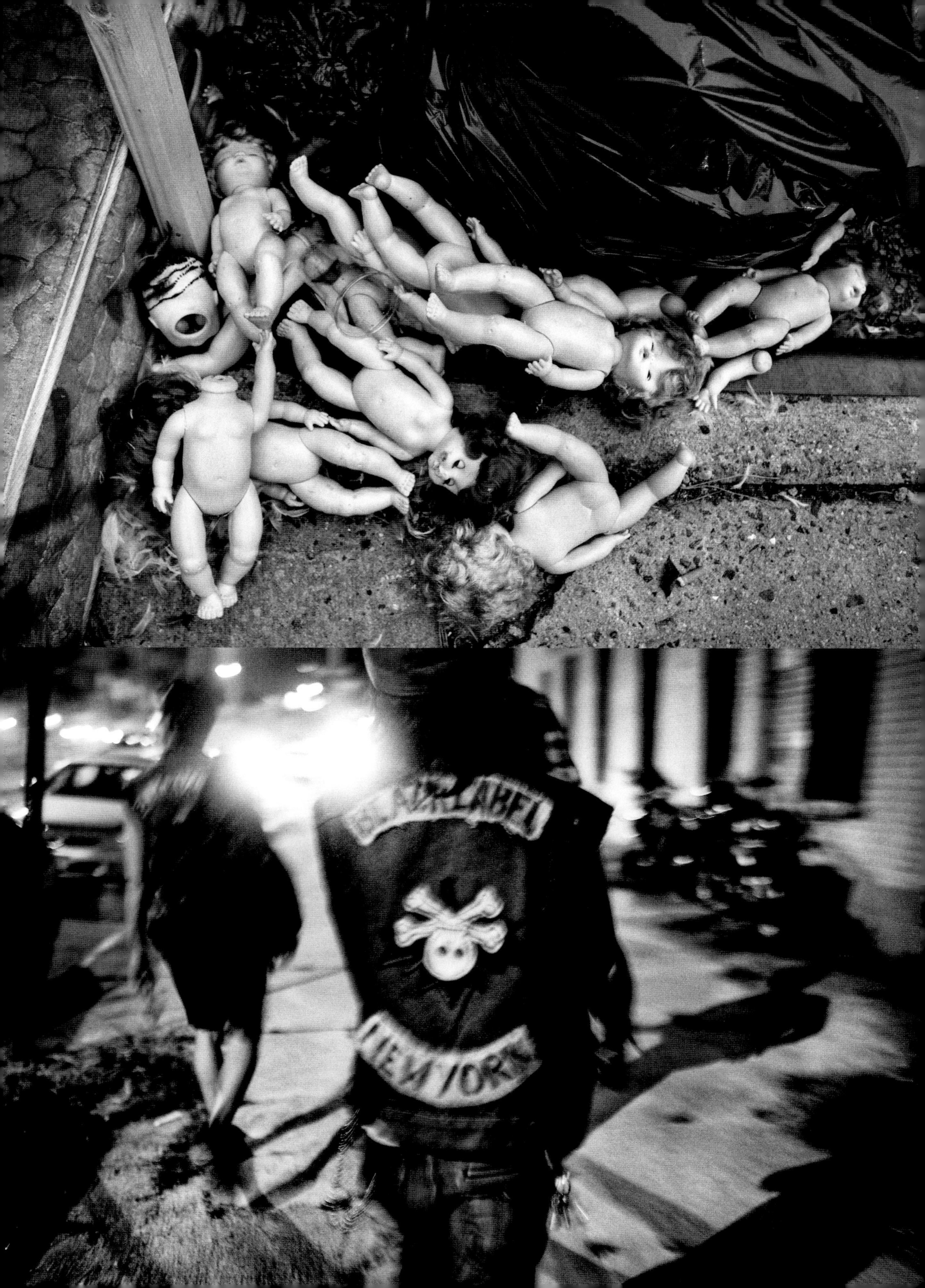
NEW YORK

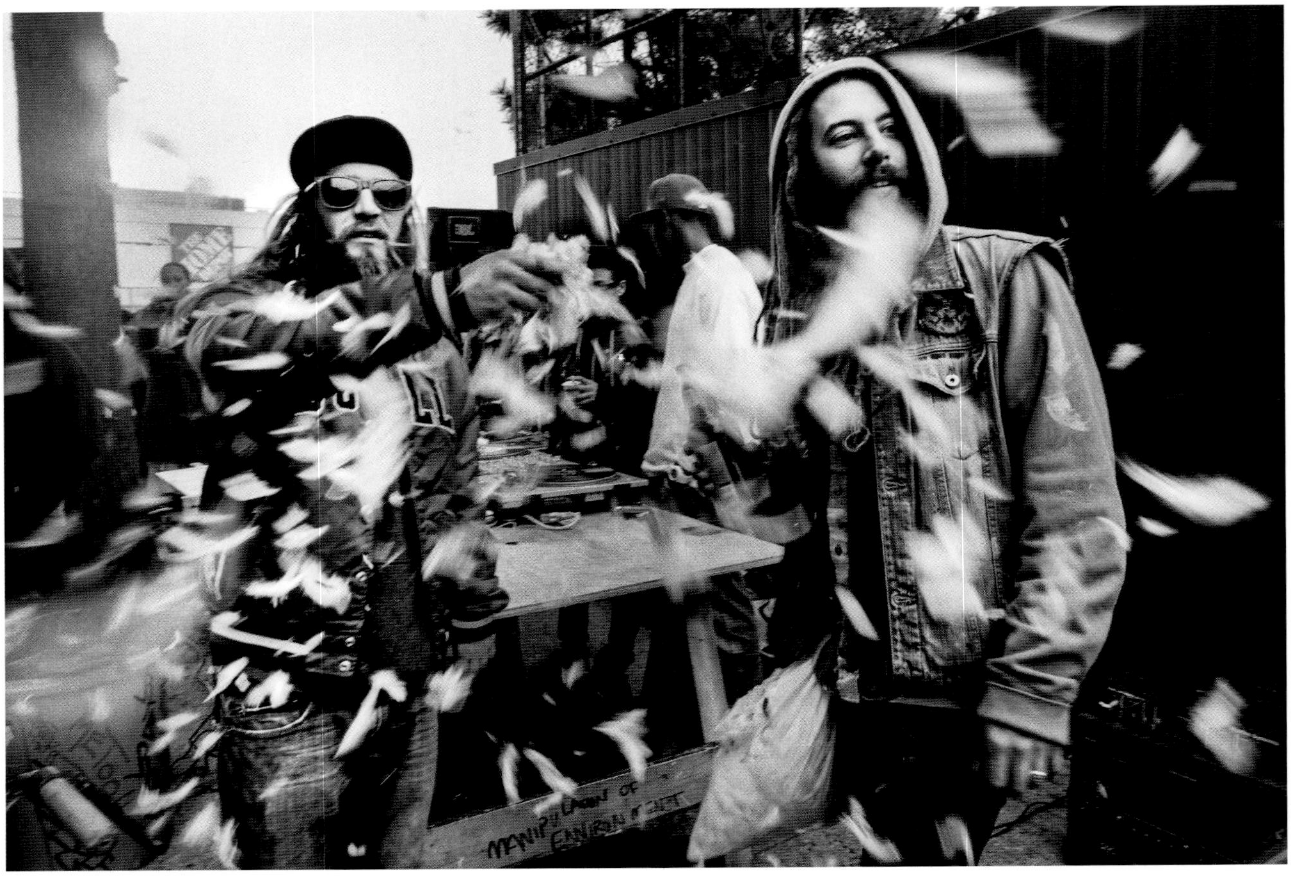

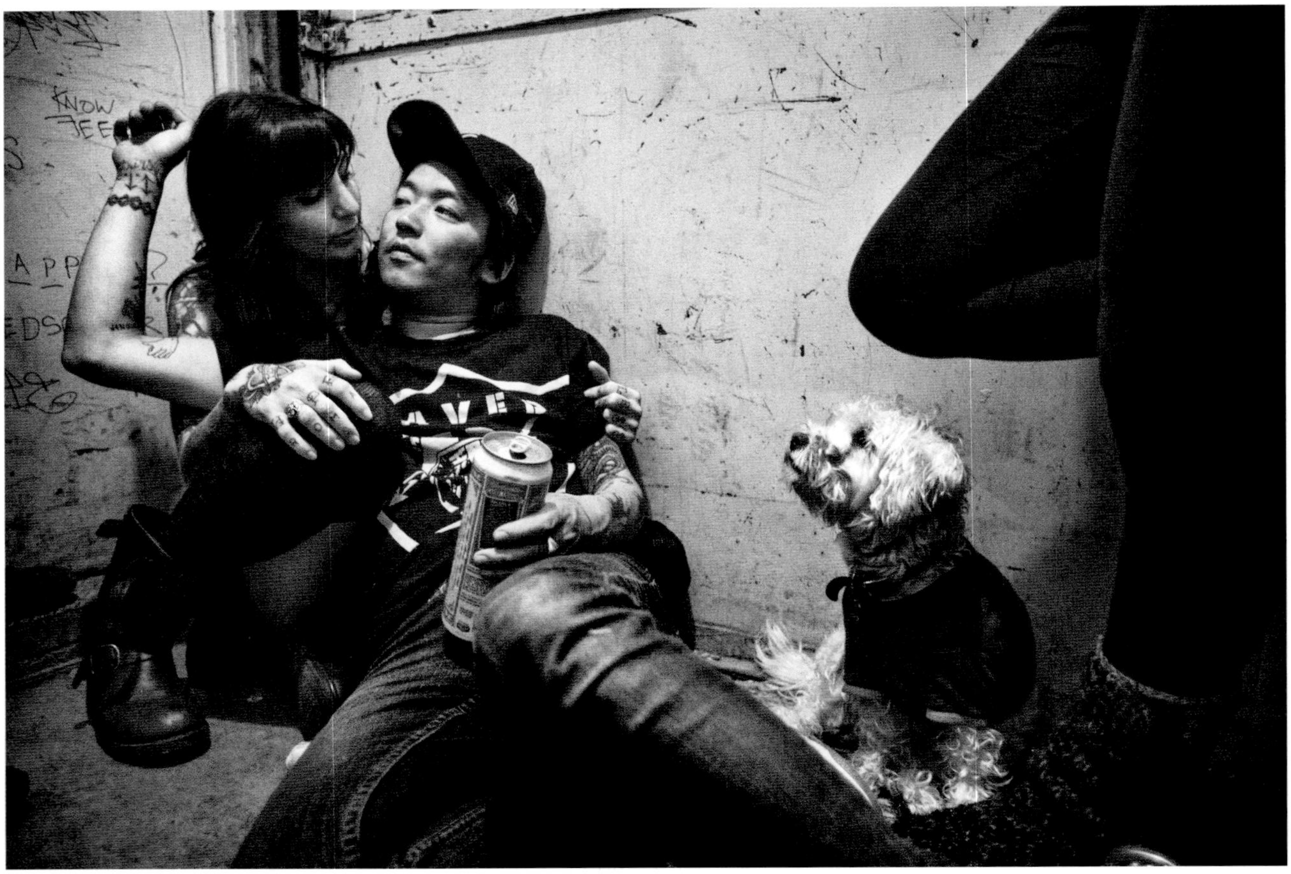

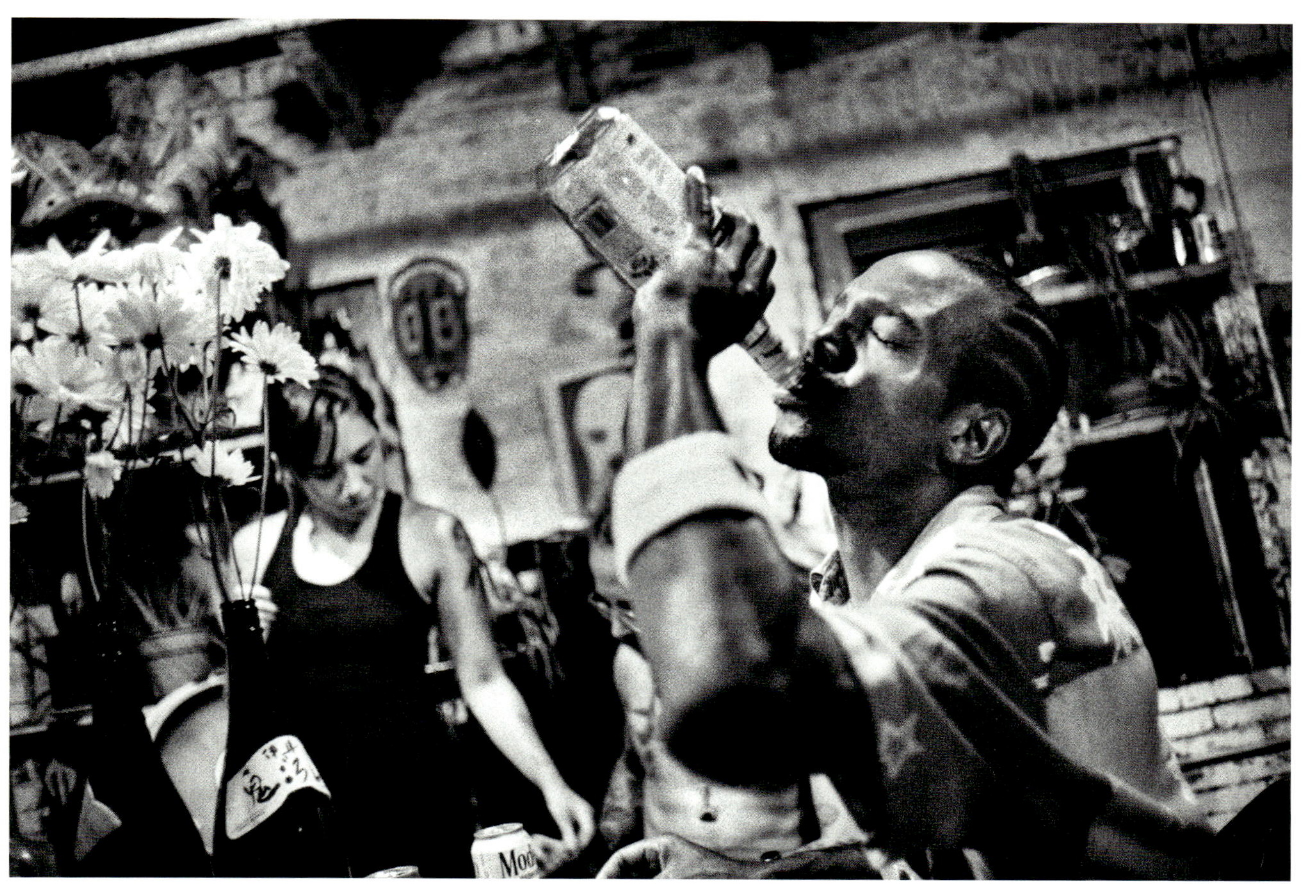

"They are an independent community rebelling against the system. In a society that pushes us to consume, focus on money, and overly use technology, it is interesting to see a group of young people resisting and fighting against it."

Julie Glassberg

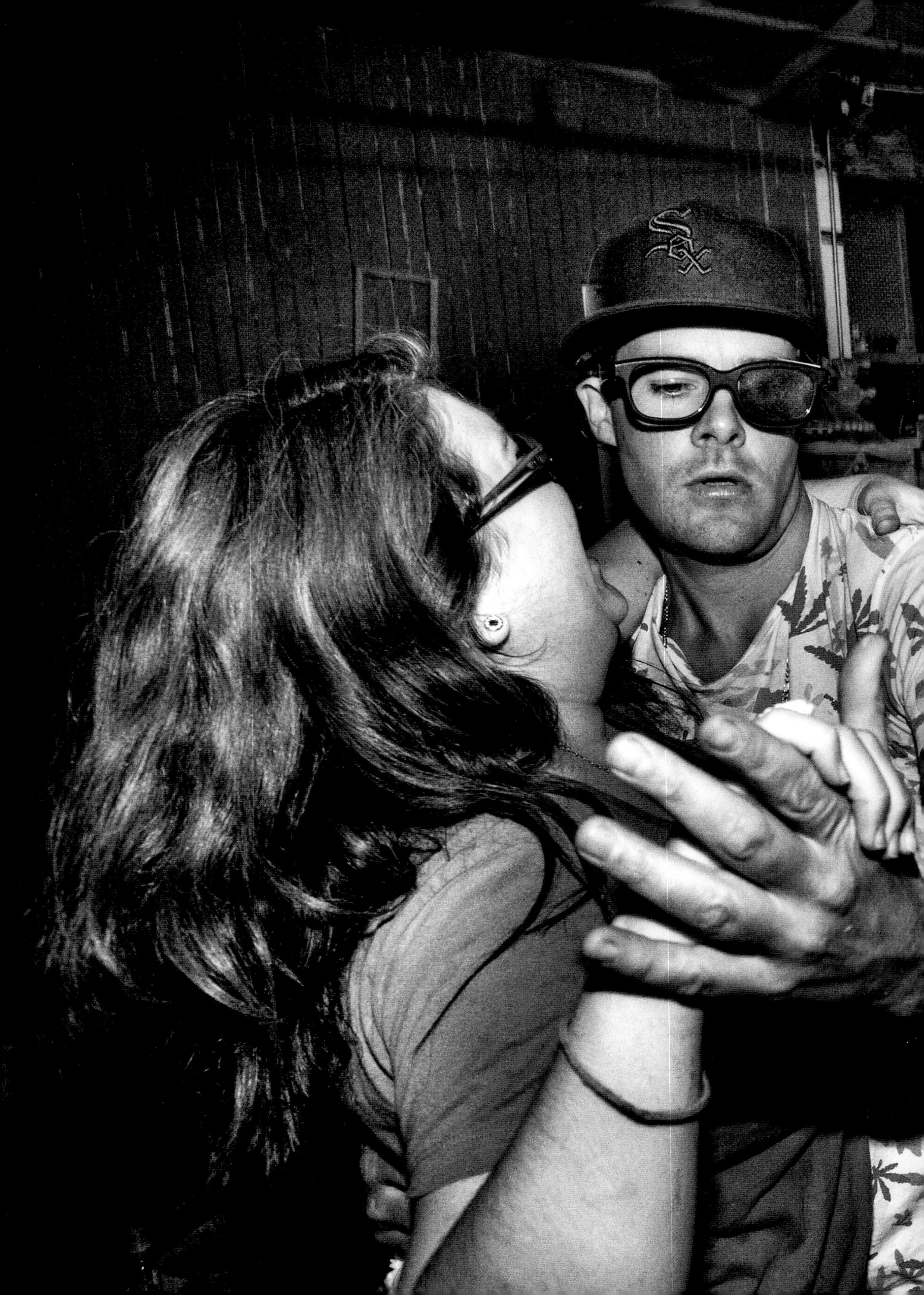
SOX

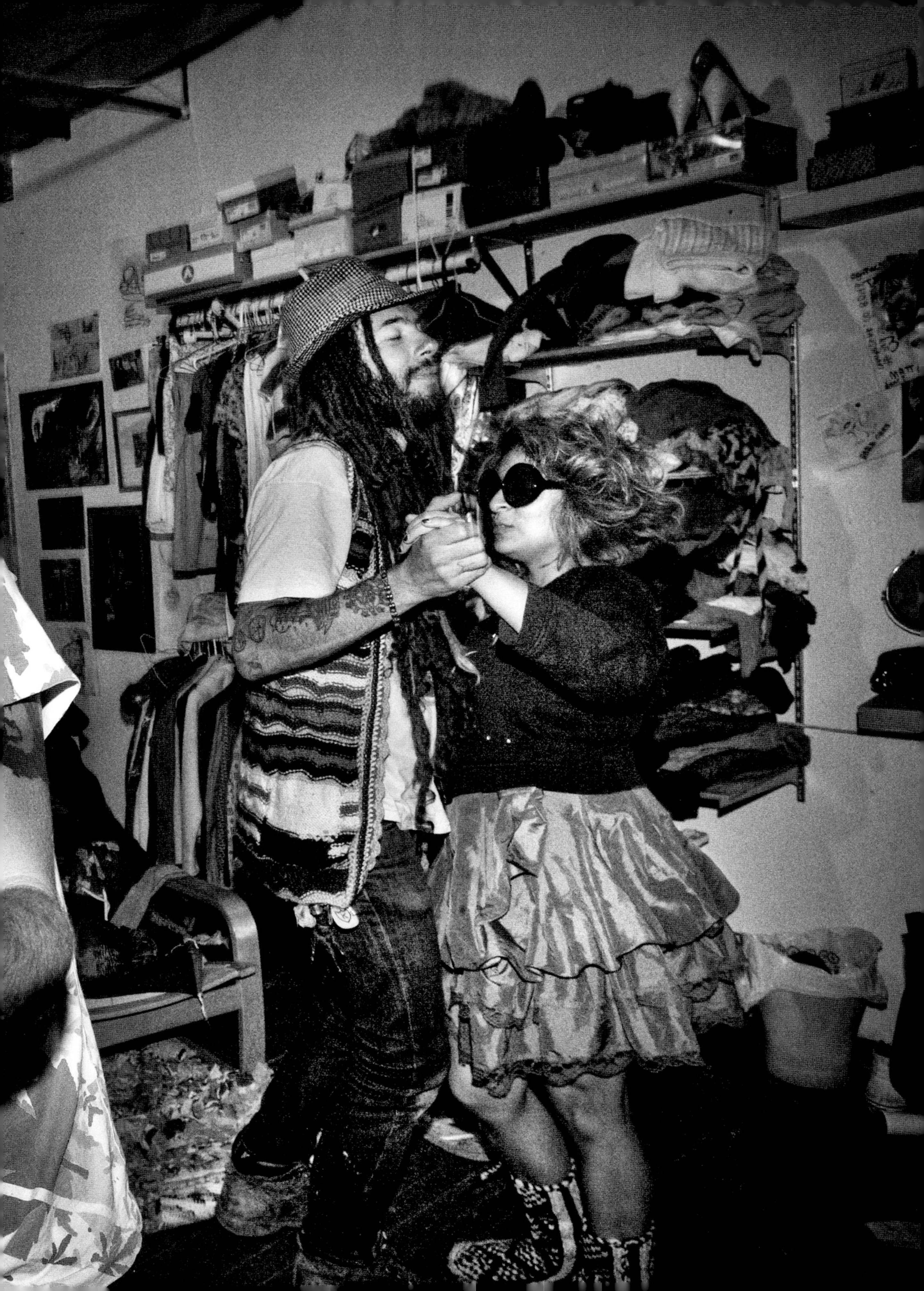

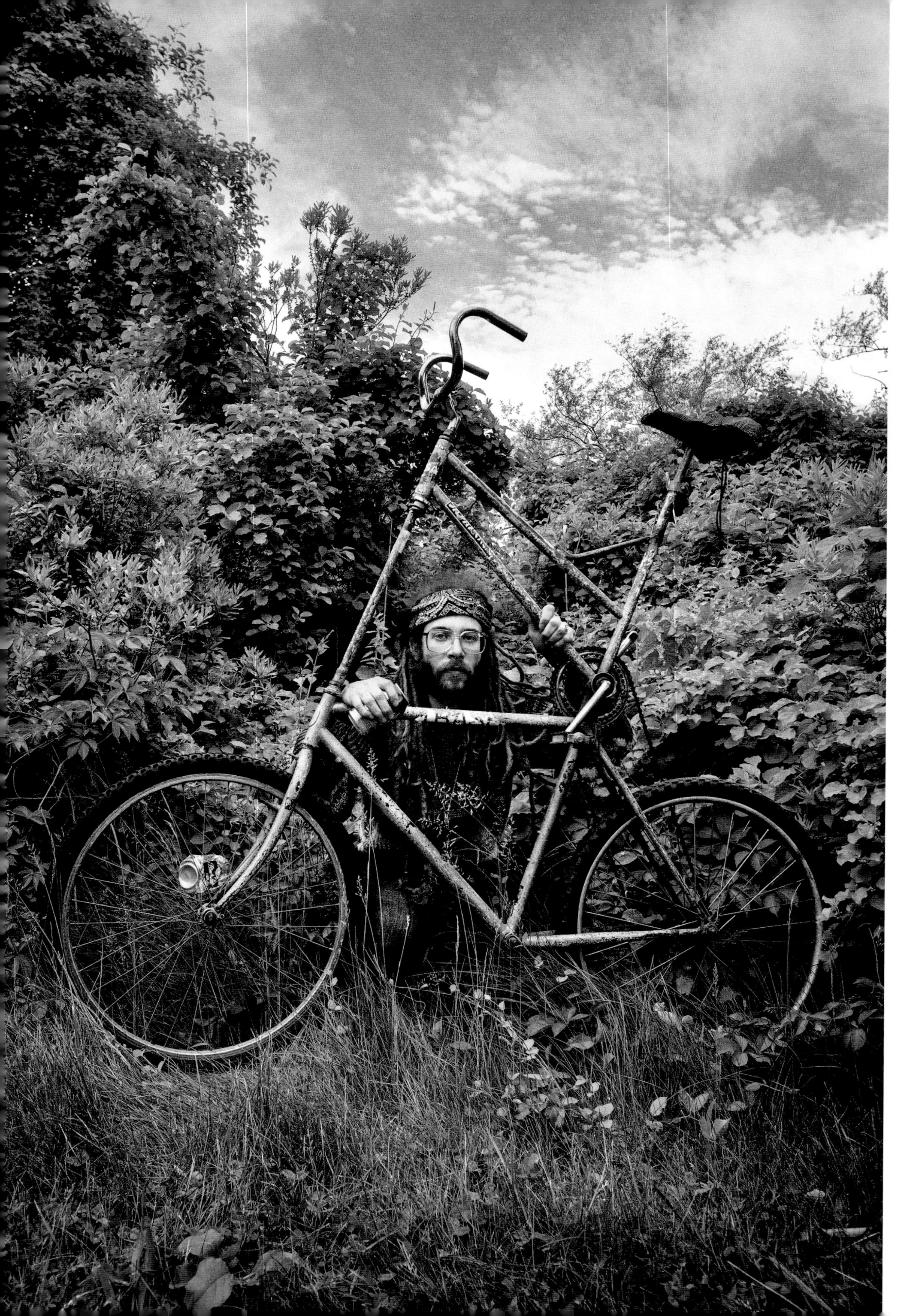

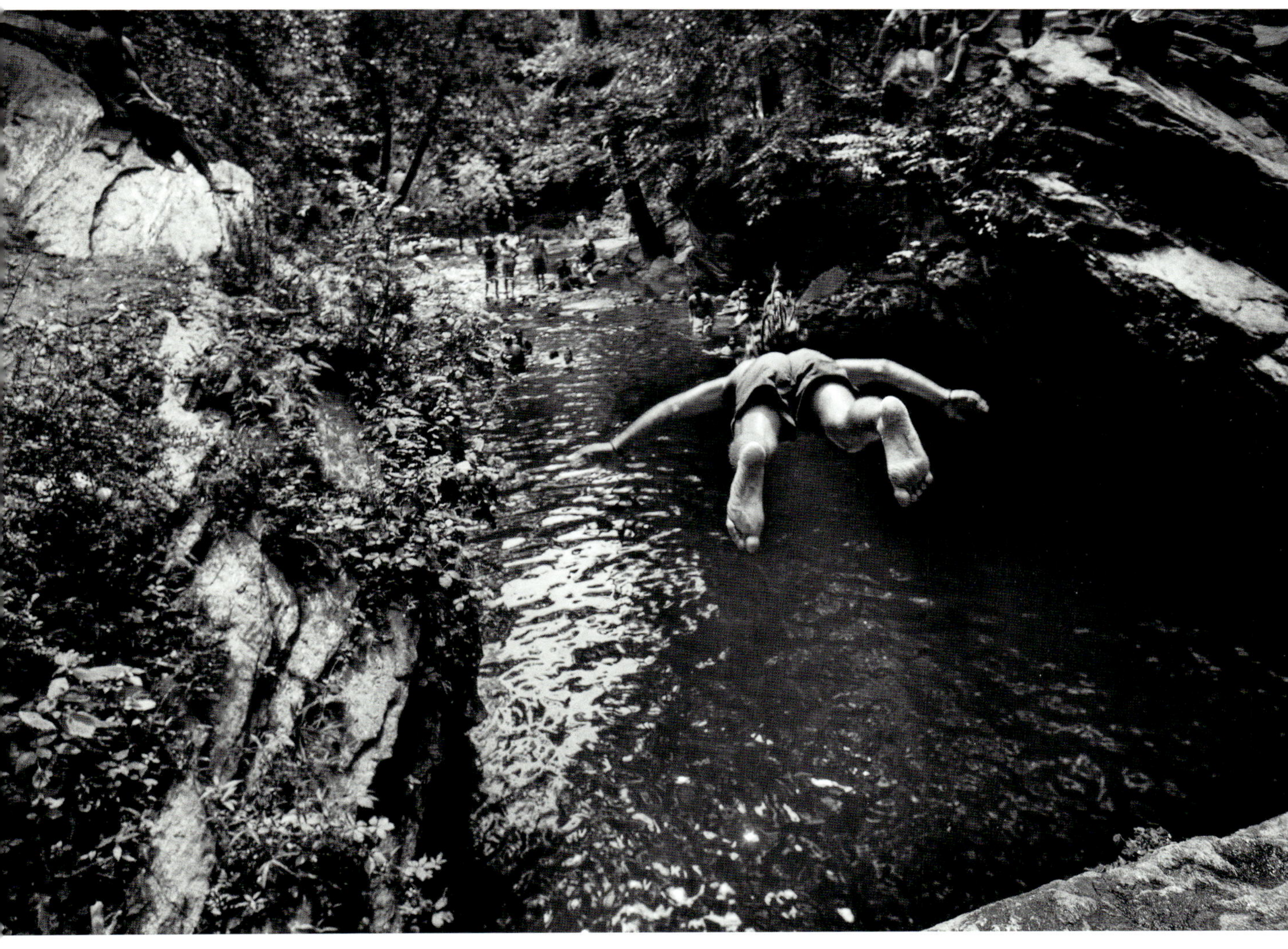

"Their community is mainly based on the bike culture, art, and on the real value of relationships. These simple values that seem to have disappeared."

Julie Glassberg

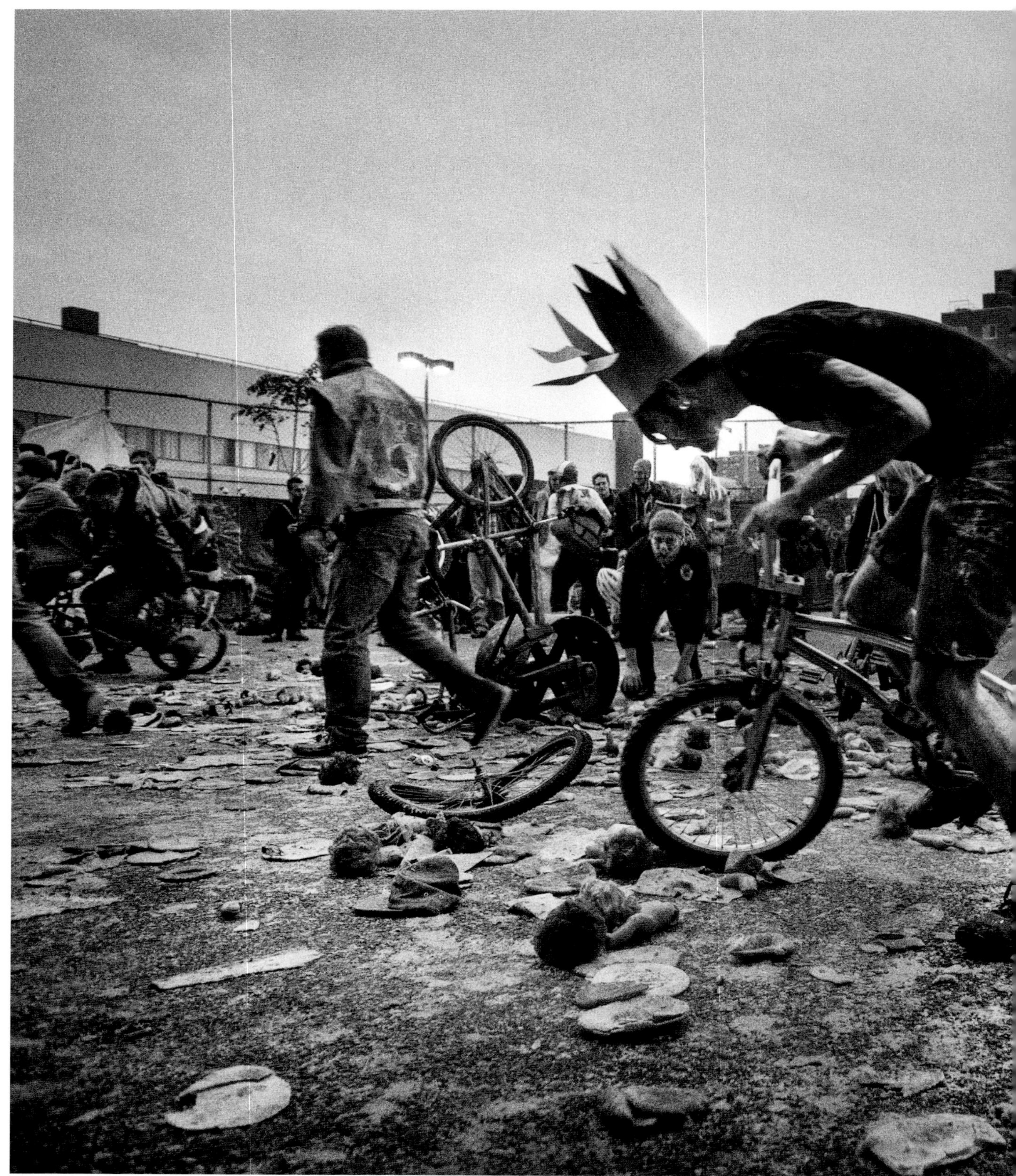

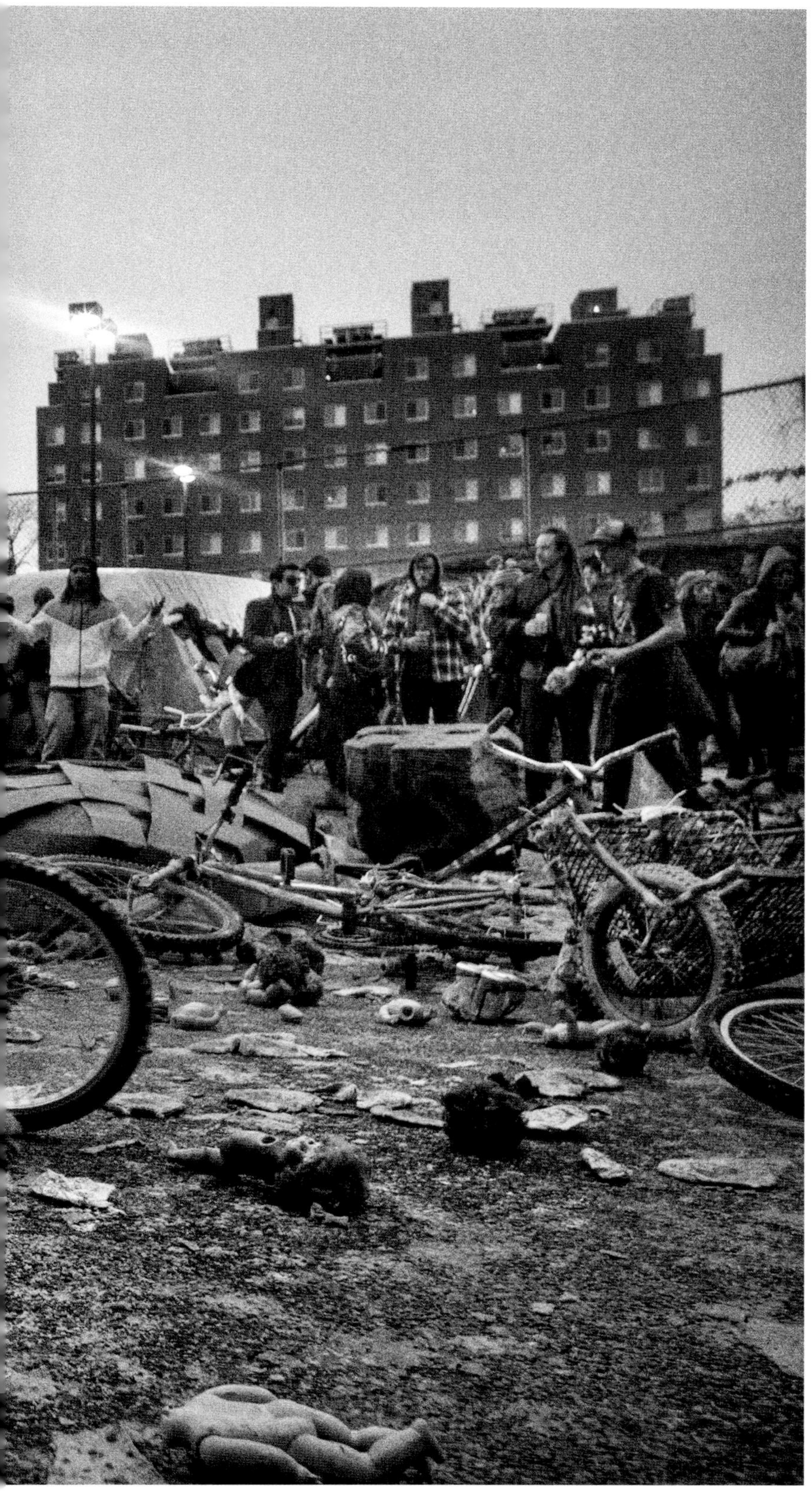

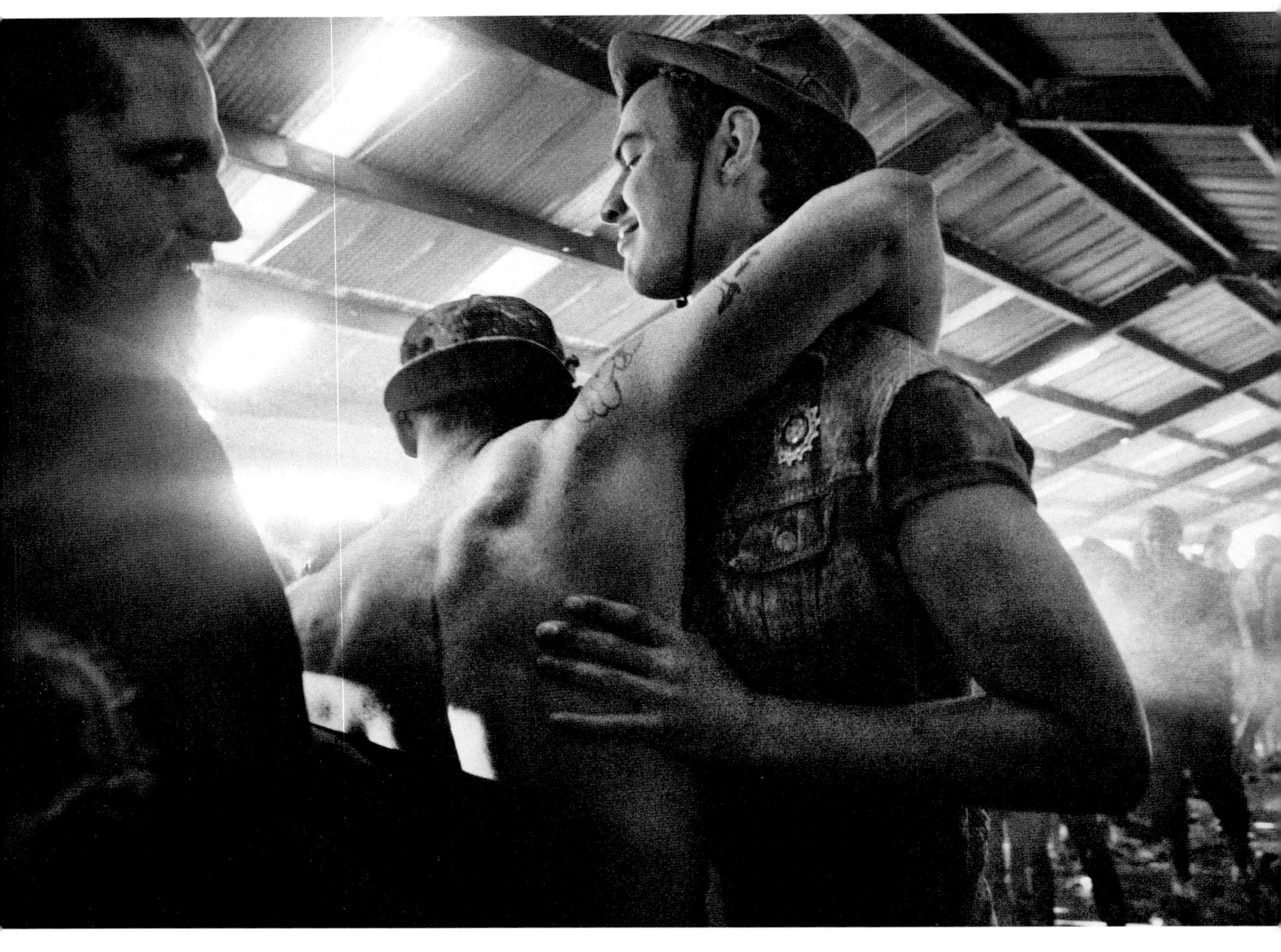

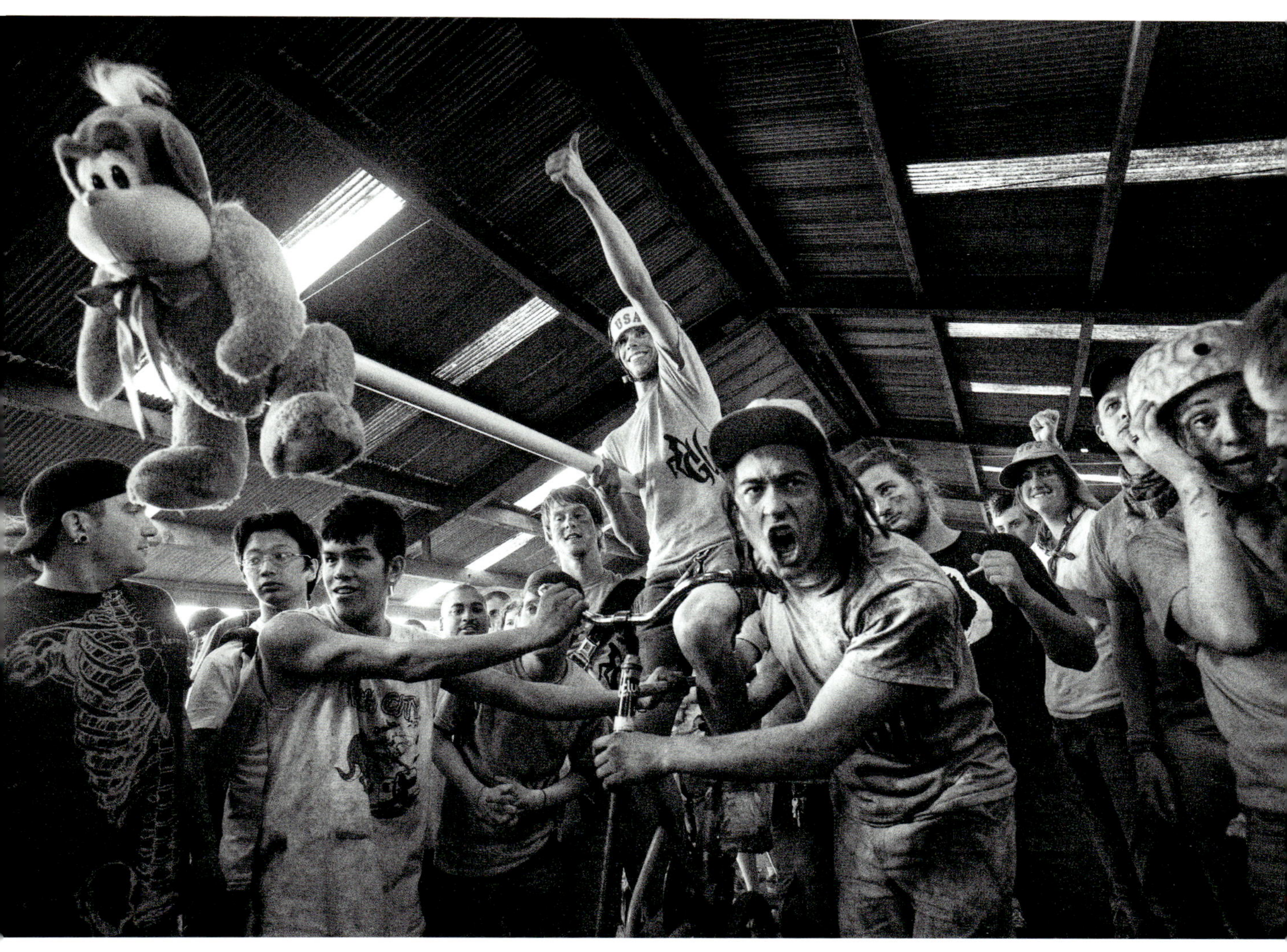

"It is interesting to see this destructive, rebel culture, revolving around such a non-threatening object: the bicycle."

Julie Glassberg

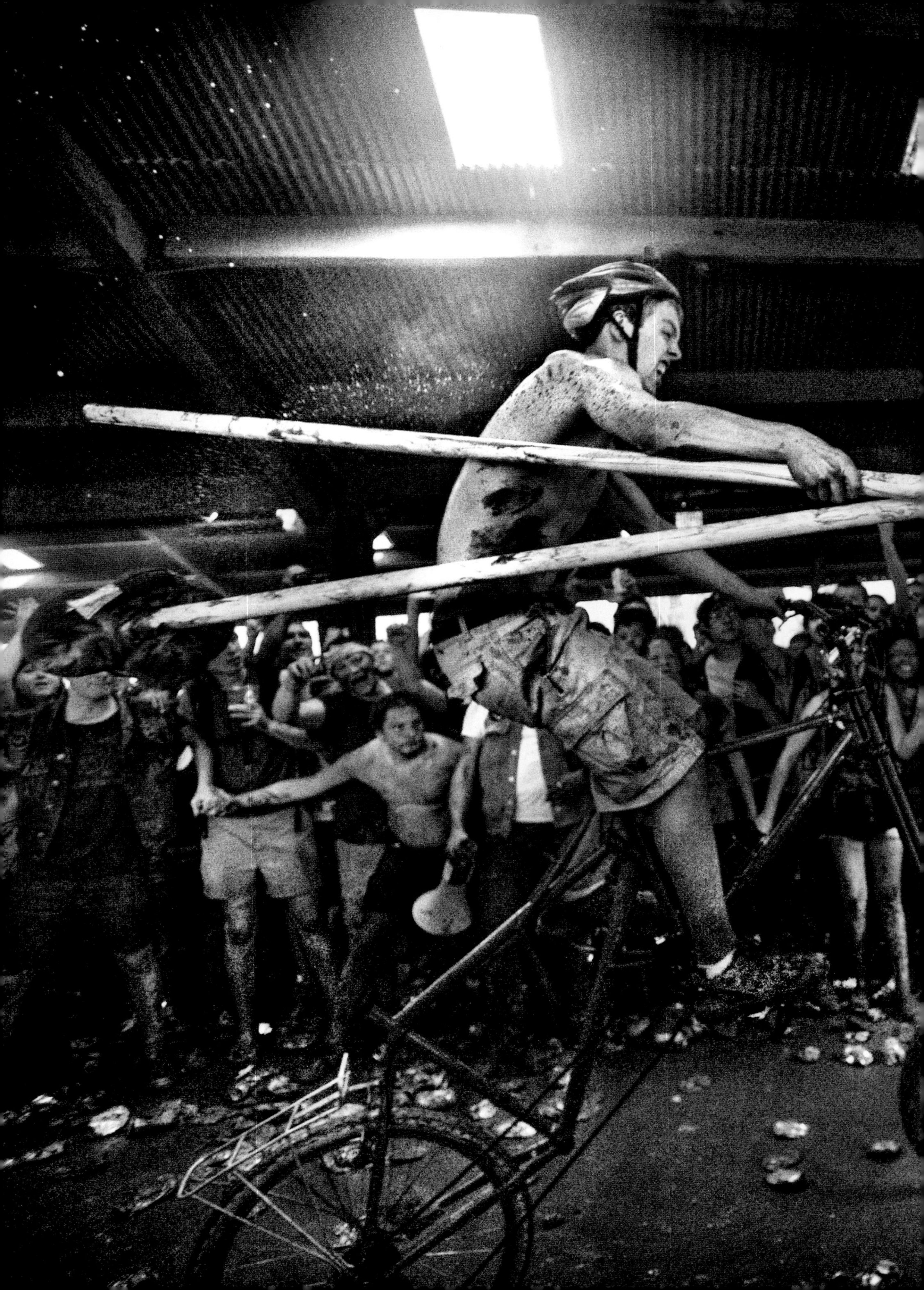

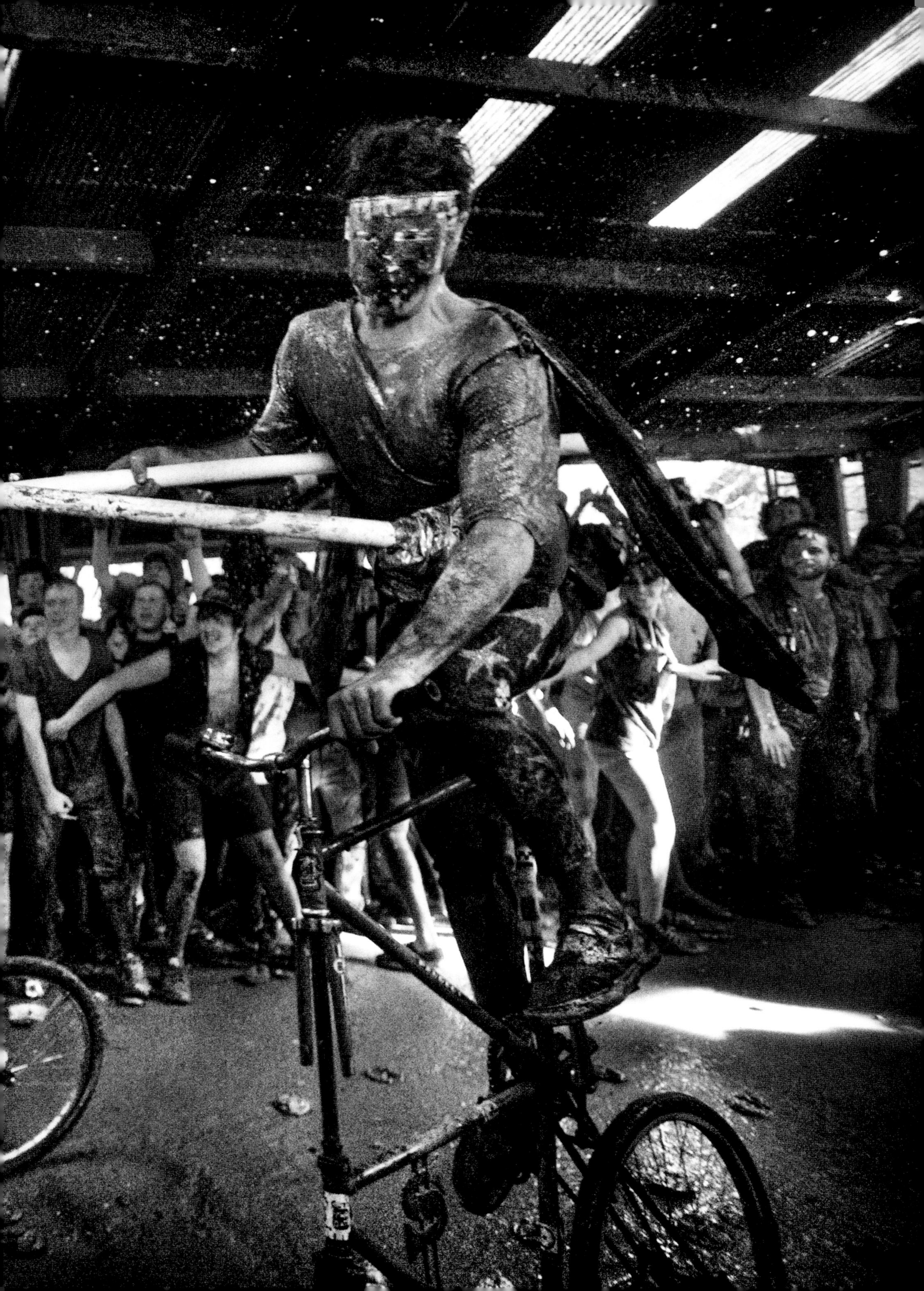

Sculptures on Wheels

New York—An epic yearly festival of mutant bikes

Photos
Tod Seelie

The competitors look like apocalyptic knights. With long lances padded at their ends, they ride toward one another, seeking to knock their opponent off their bike. Those who fall either land on the ground or are caught by the roaring crowd. Those who remain upright are meanwhile celebrated as champions. This sunset tournament is the crowning event of Bike Kill in New York, a yearly festival for "mutant bikes" hosted by the Black Label Bicycle Club. Each year, a new and suitable location must be found. Therefore, the outcome of each Bike Kill can depend upon how much the New York Police Department decides to hassle the bike freaks. Some Bike Kill attendees have come every year for nearly two decades; for many people, it rivals Christmas in anticipation, and old friends gather from far and wide to come together for it.

Aside from the tall bikes and mini-bikes, many other unique creations are present. Every bike is a testament to the ingenuity of its creator. Each one is a sculpture on wheels. The riders are subjected to objects being thrown at them, being shoved by spectators, and having oil drums rolled into their way. And while the event can be rough-and-tumble—falls and collisions are common—the overall feeling of the day is one of joy, of community, and introducing newcomers to the pleasures of trying to ride these strange bikes with friends.

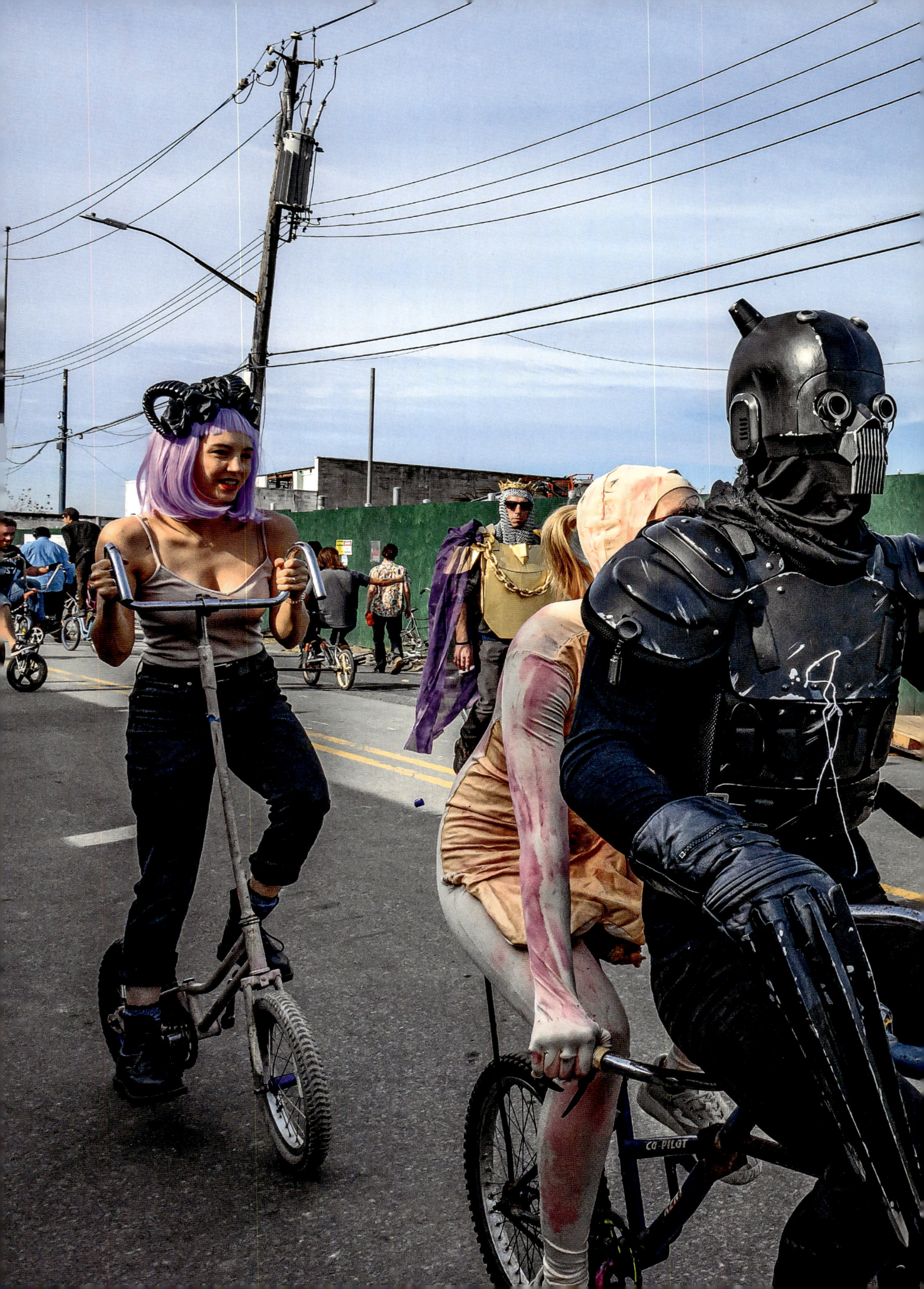
CO-PILOT

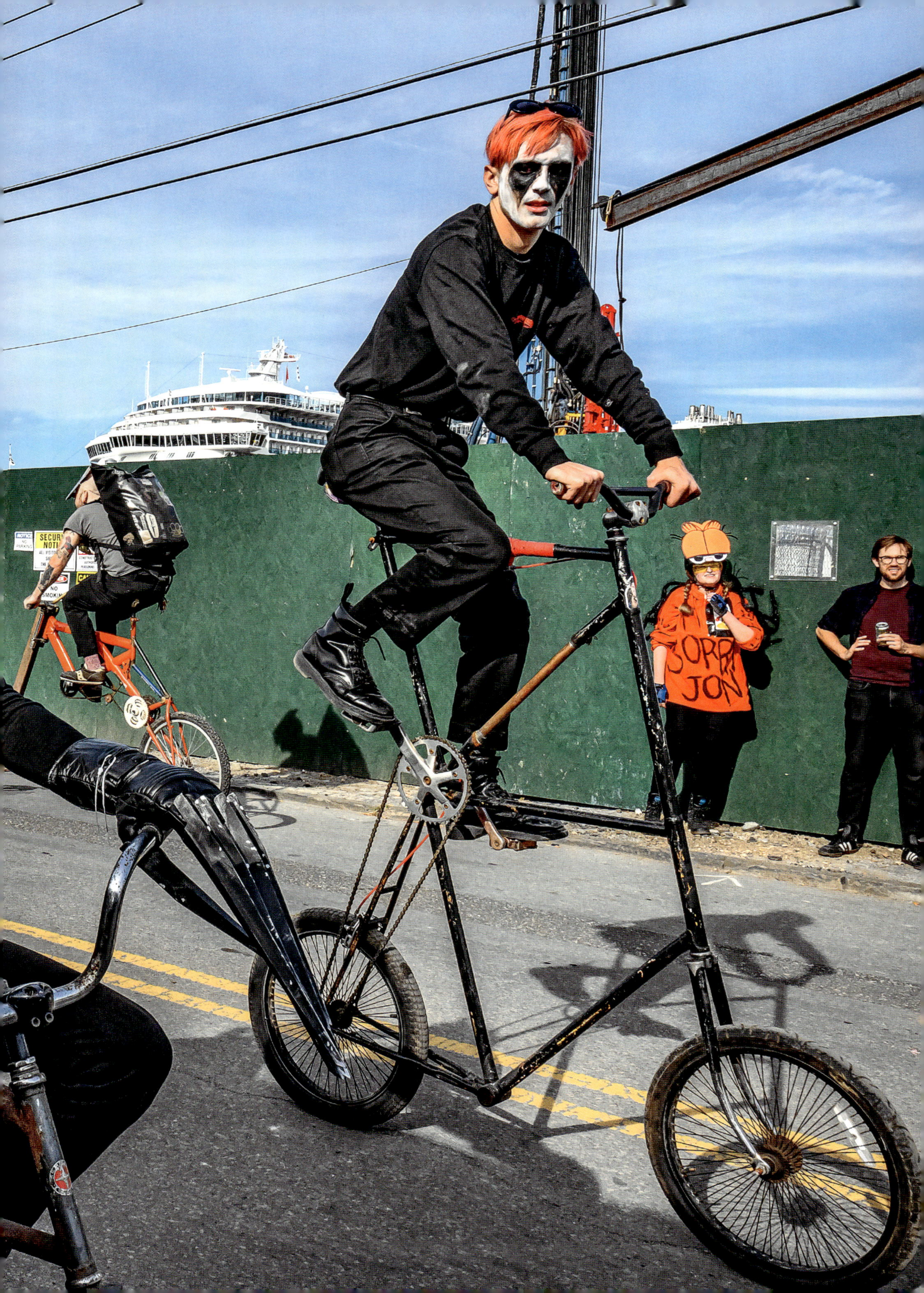
JON

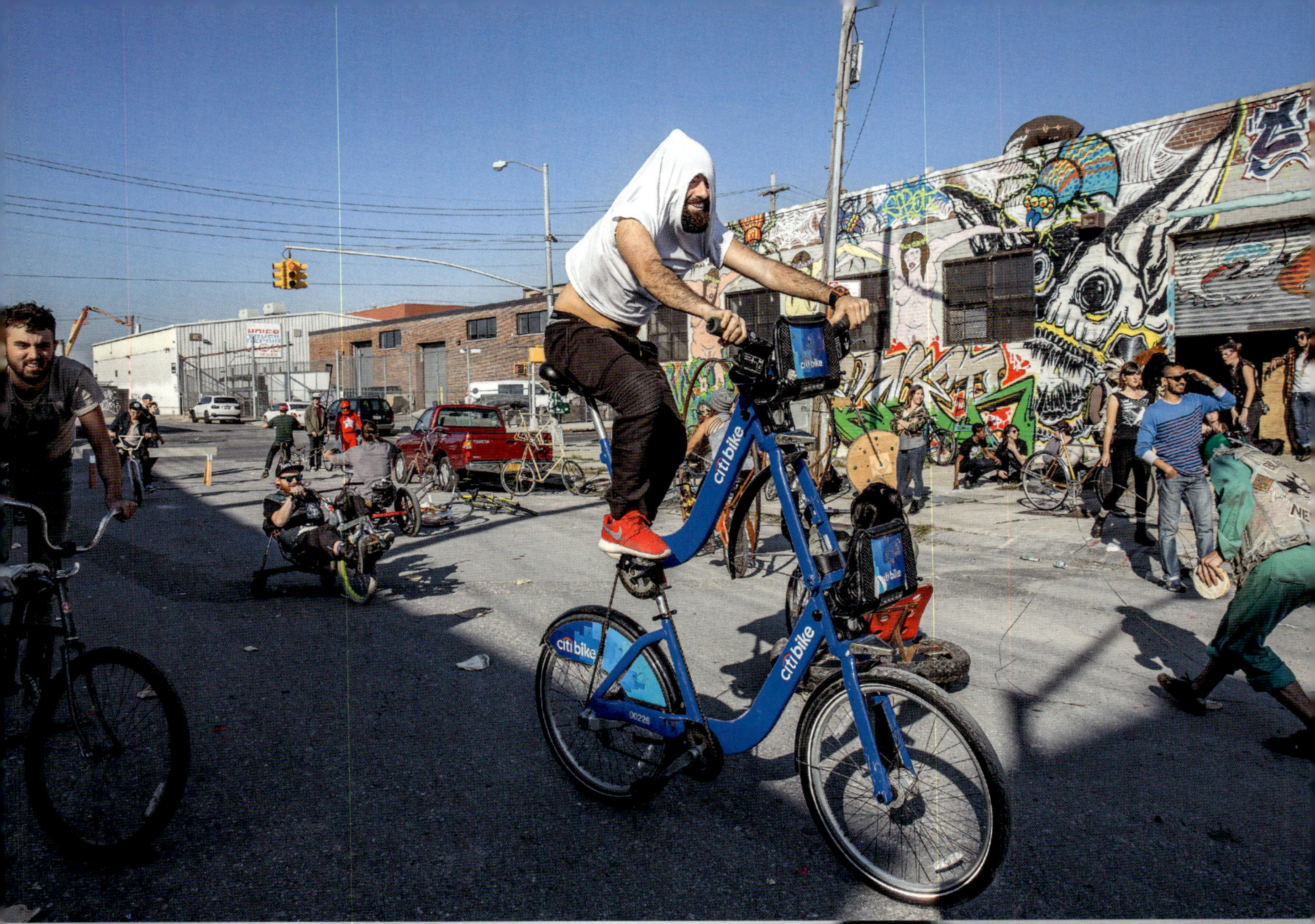

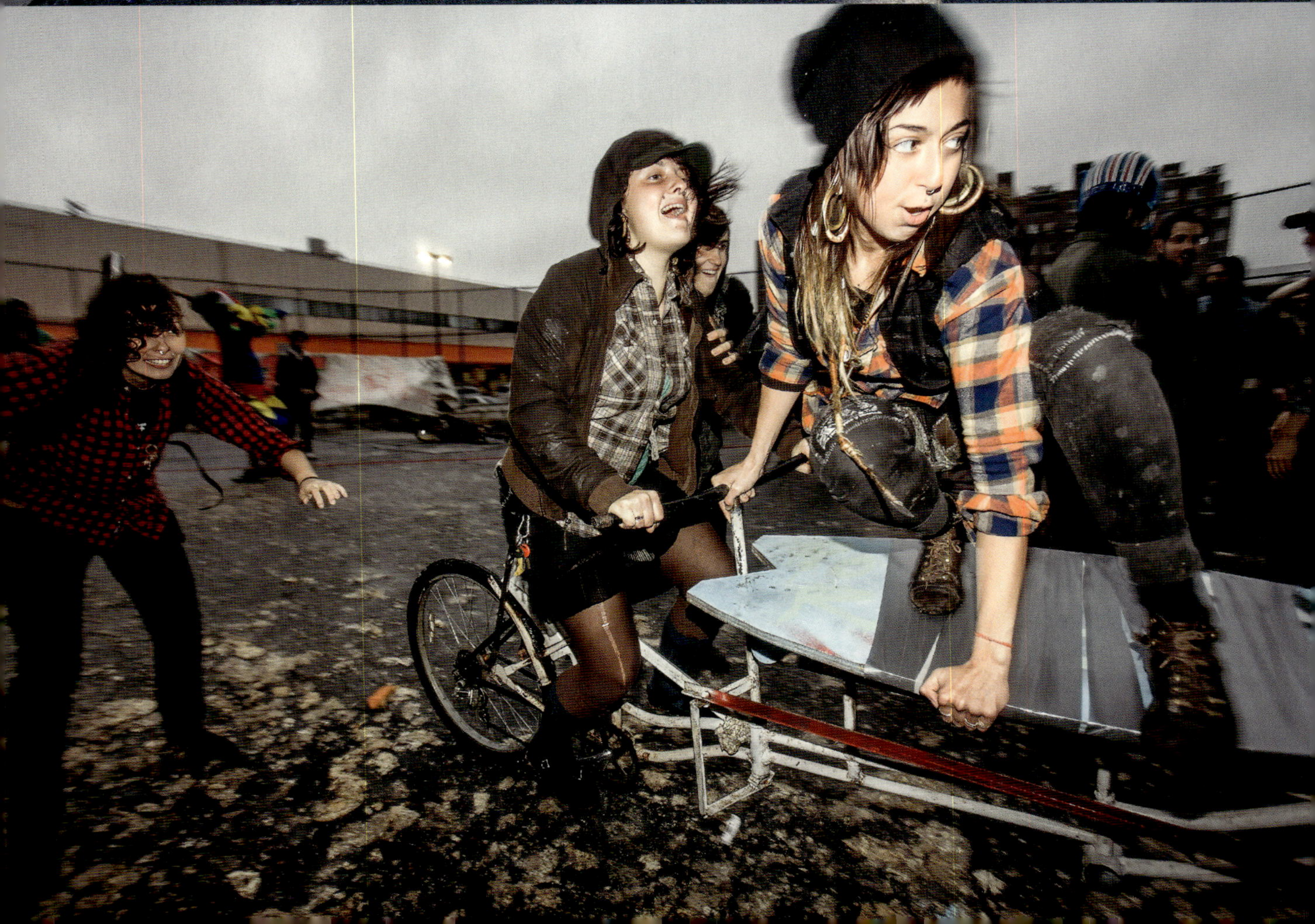

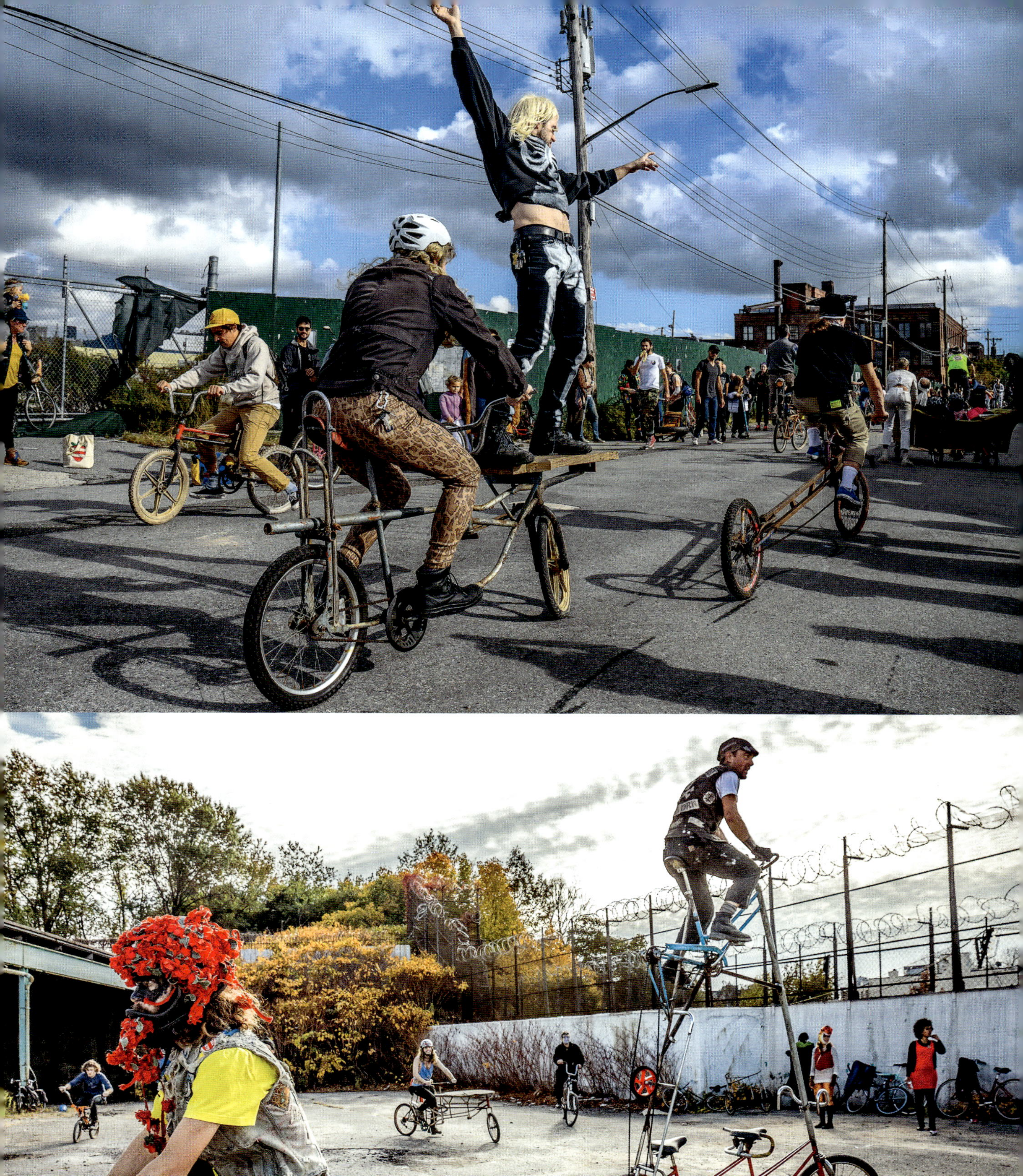

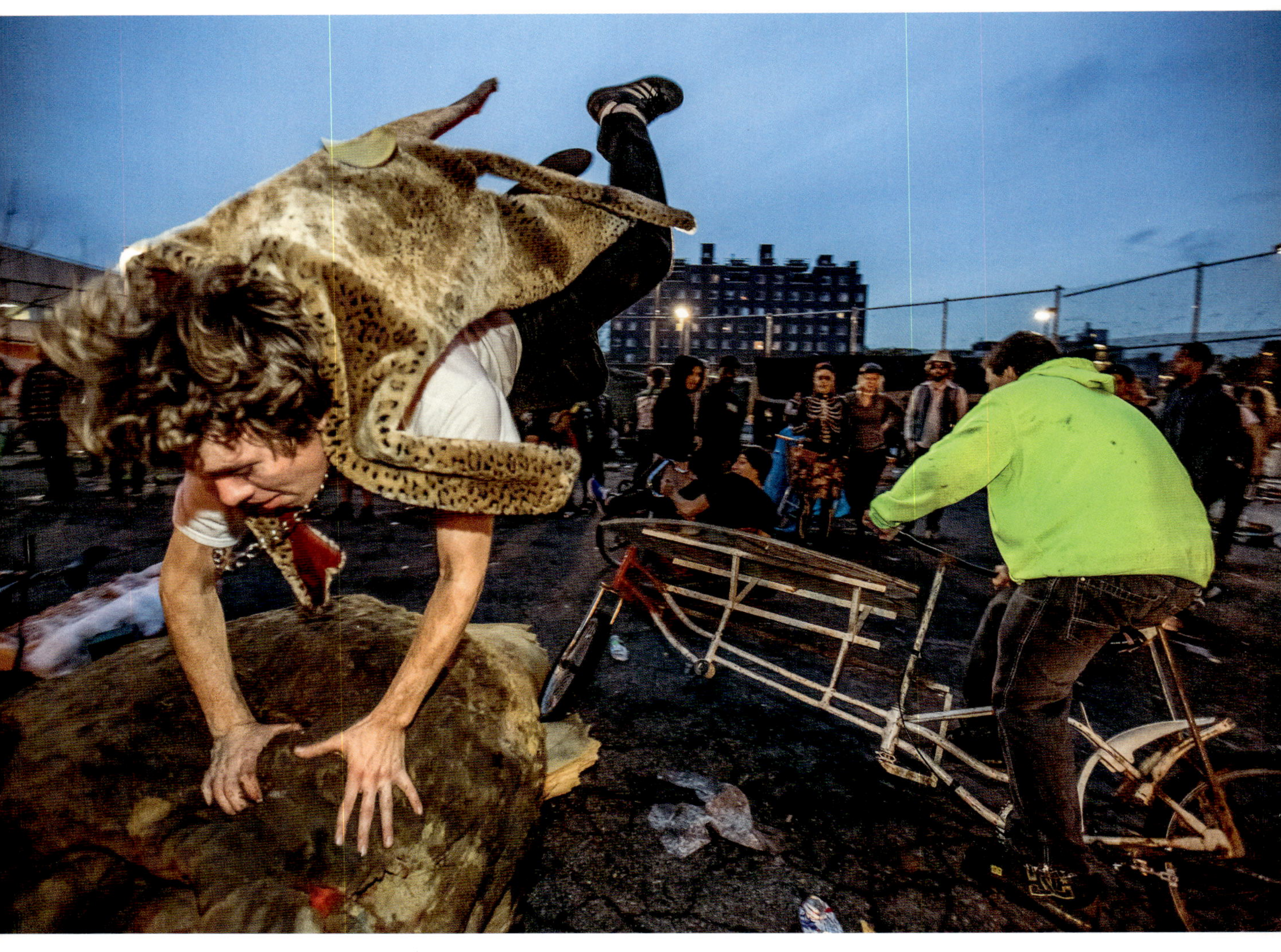

"Sometimes it feels like the apocalypse, and you're about to watch someone die, and other times it's like 'people should bring their kids to this.'"

Caledonia Curry a.k.a. Swoon

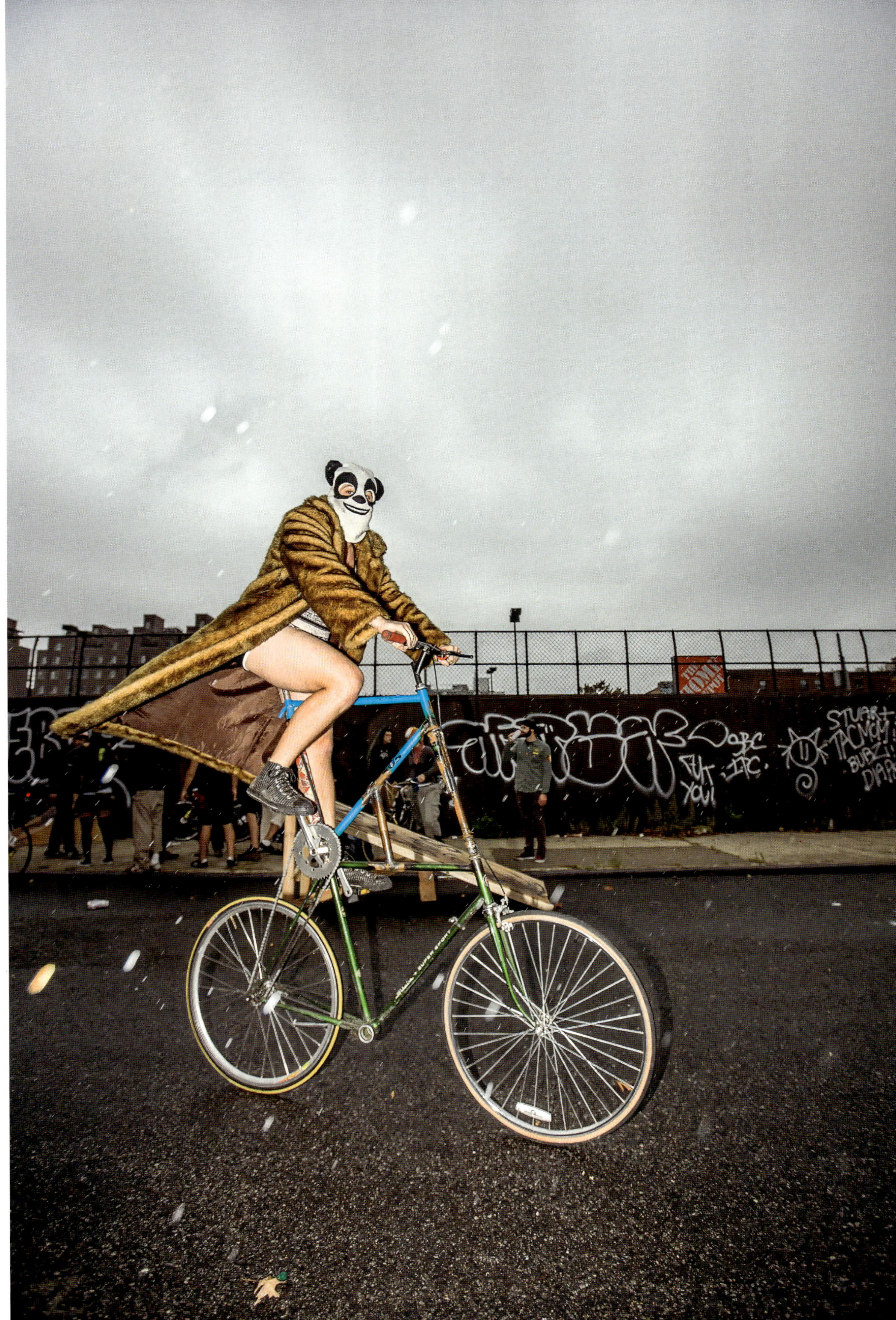

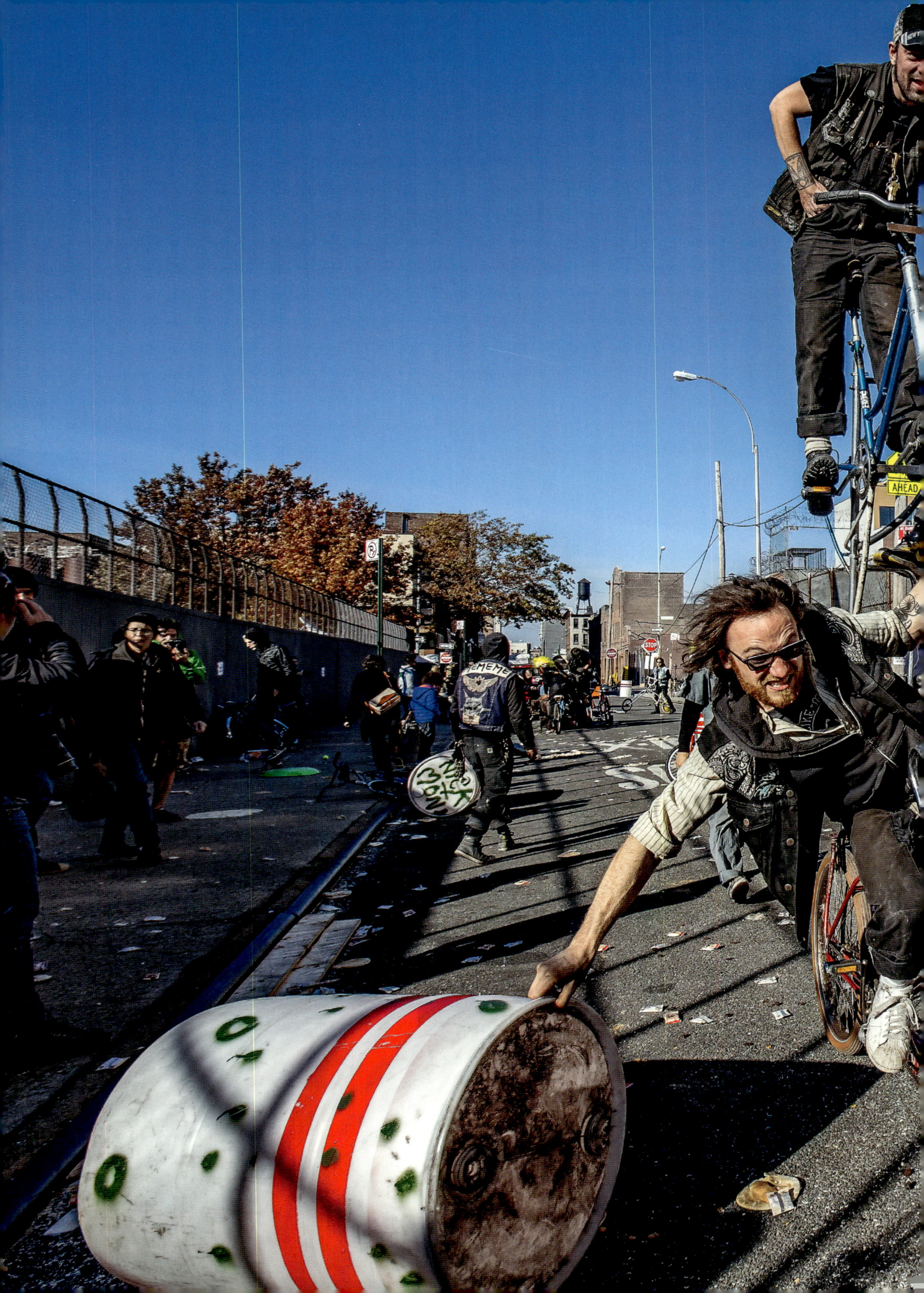
AHEAD
STOP

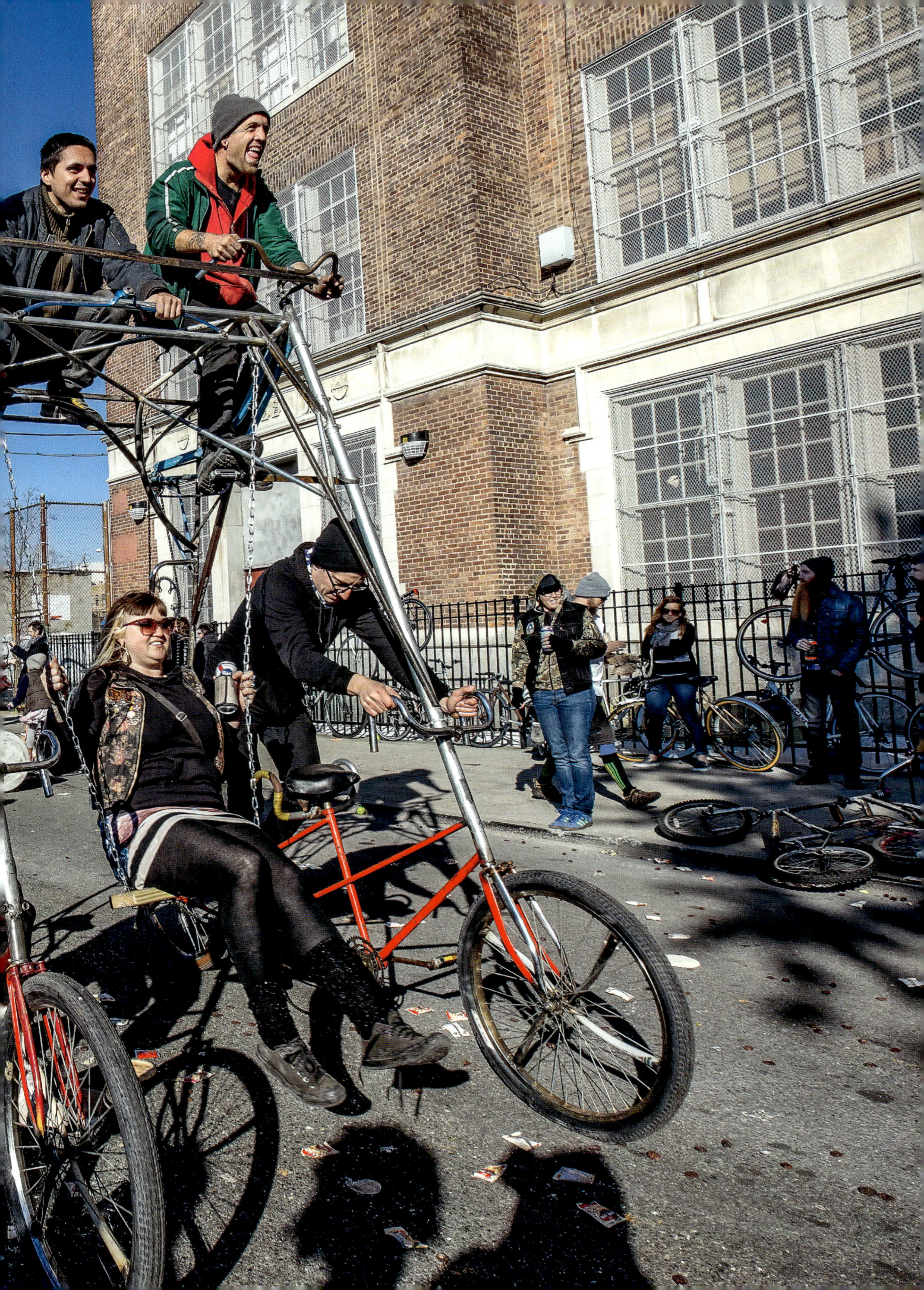

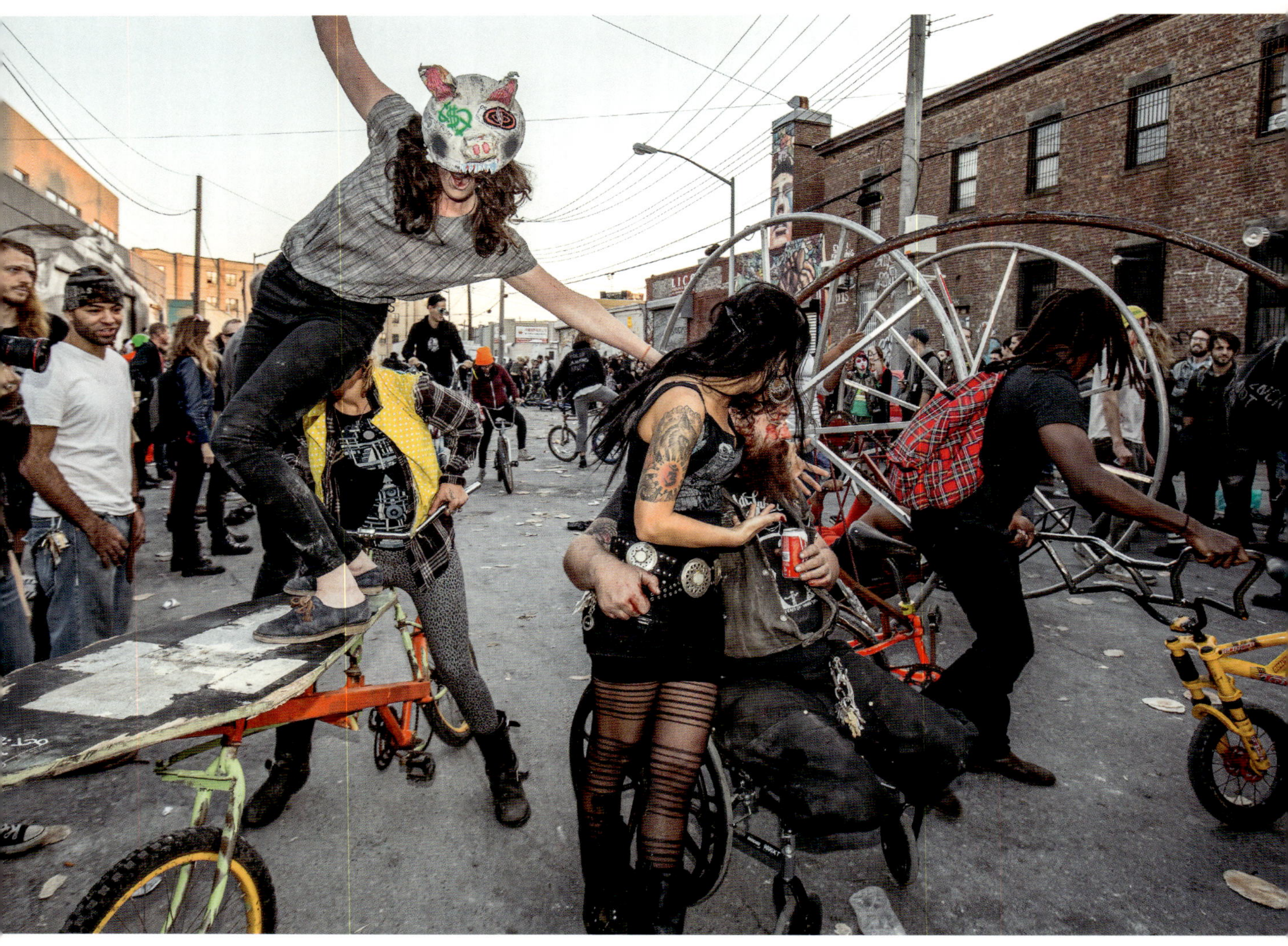

"It's about creativity and it's not about money.
It's all about being as anti-consumerist and
anti-materialist as we can be."

Collin

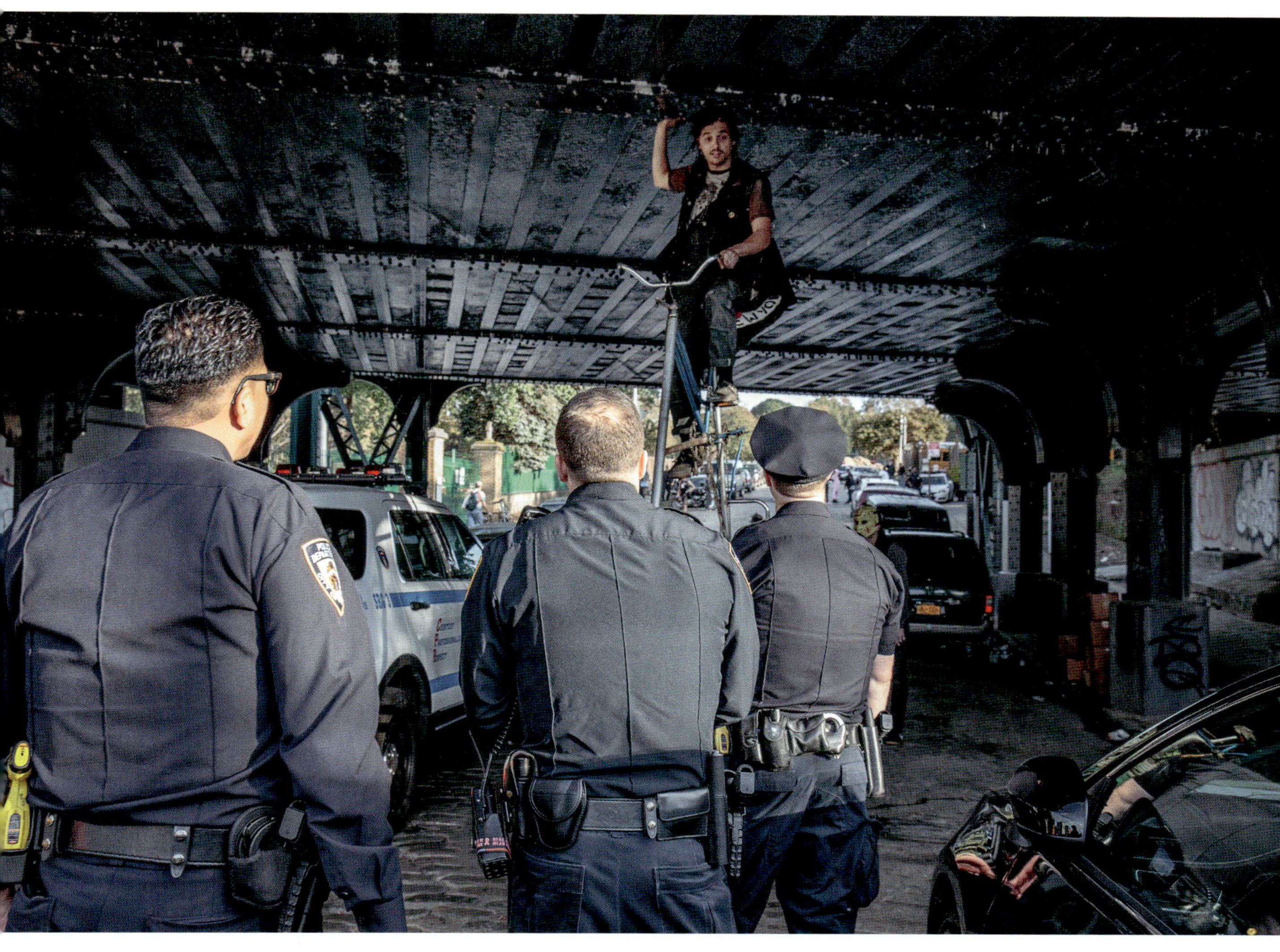

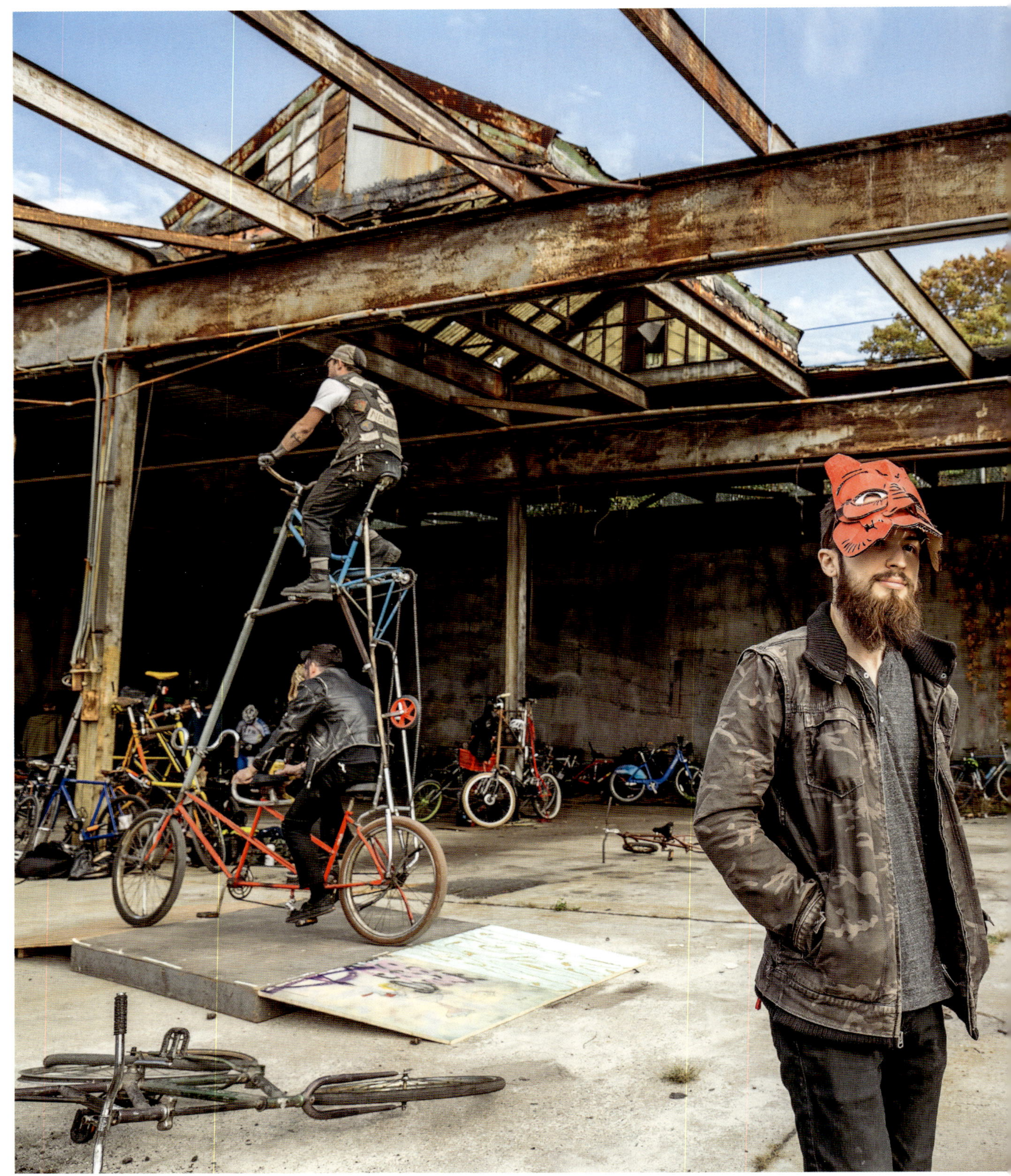

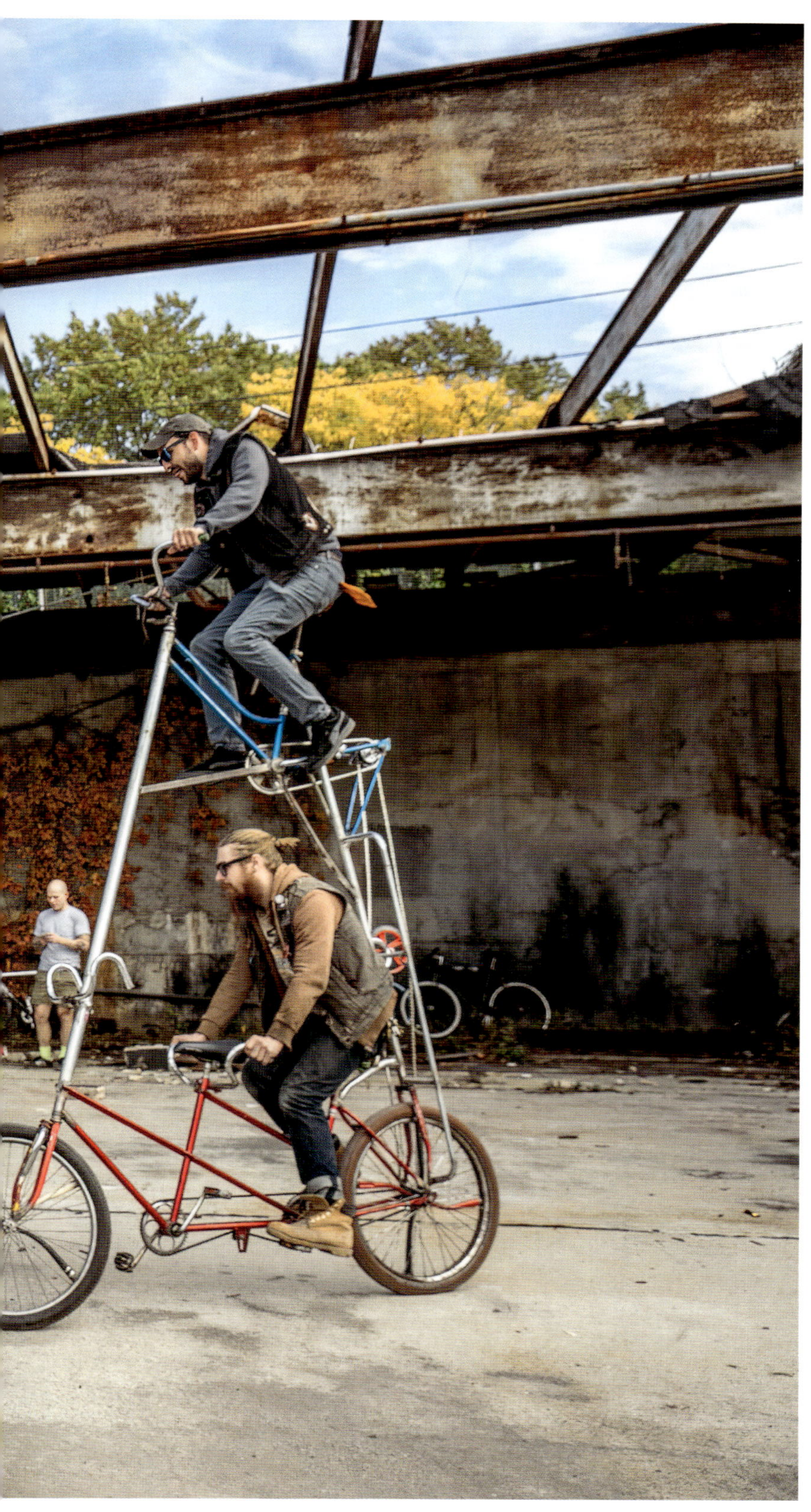

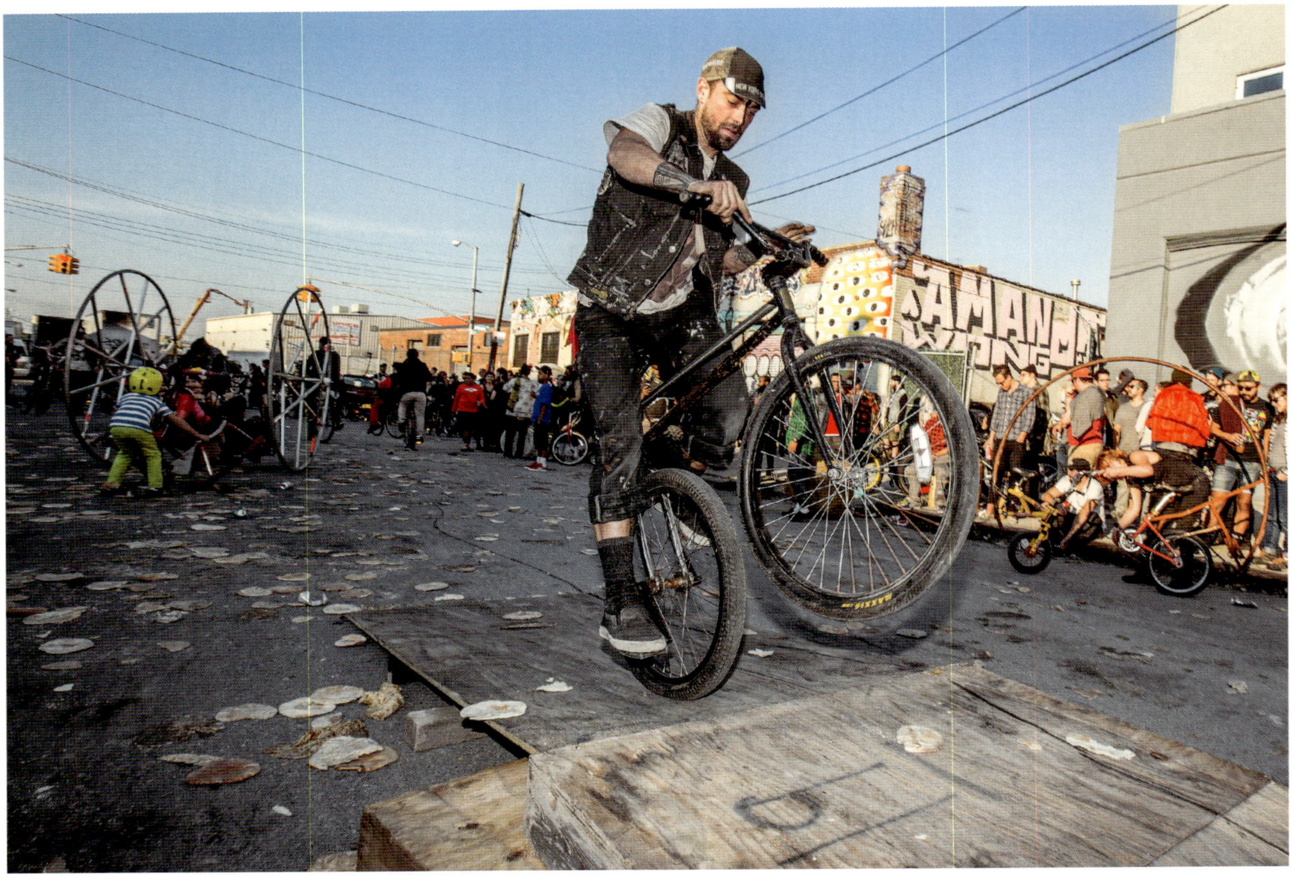

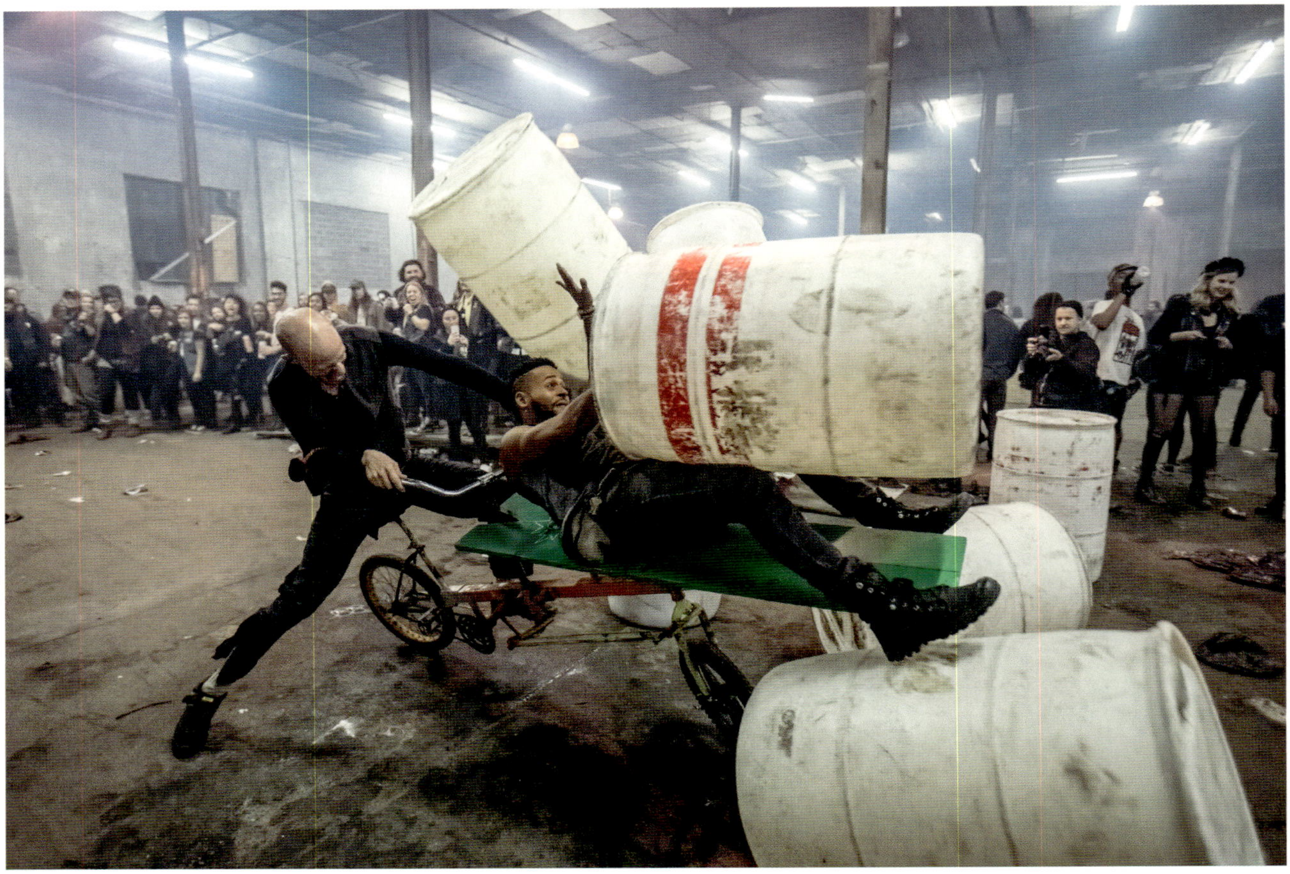

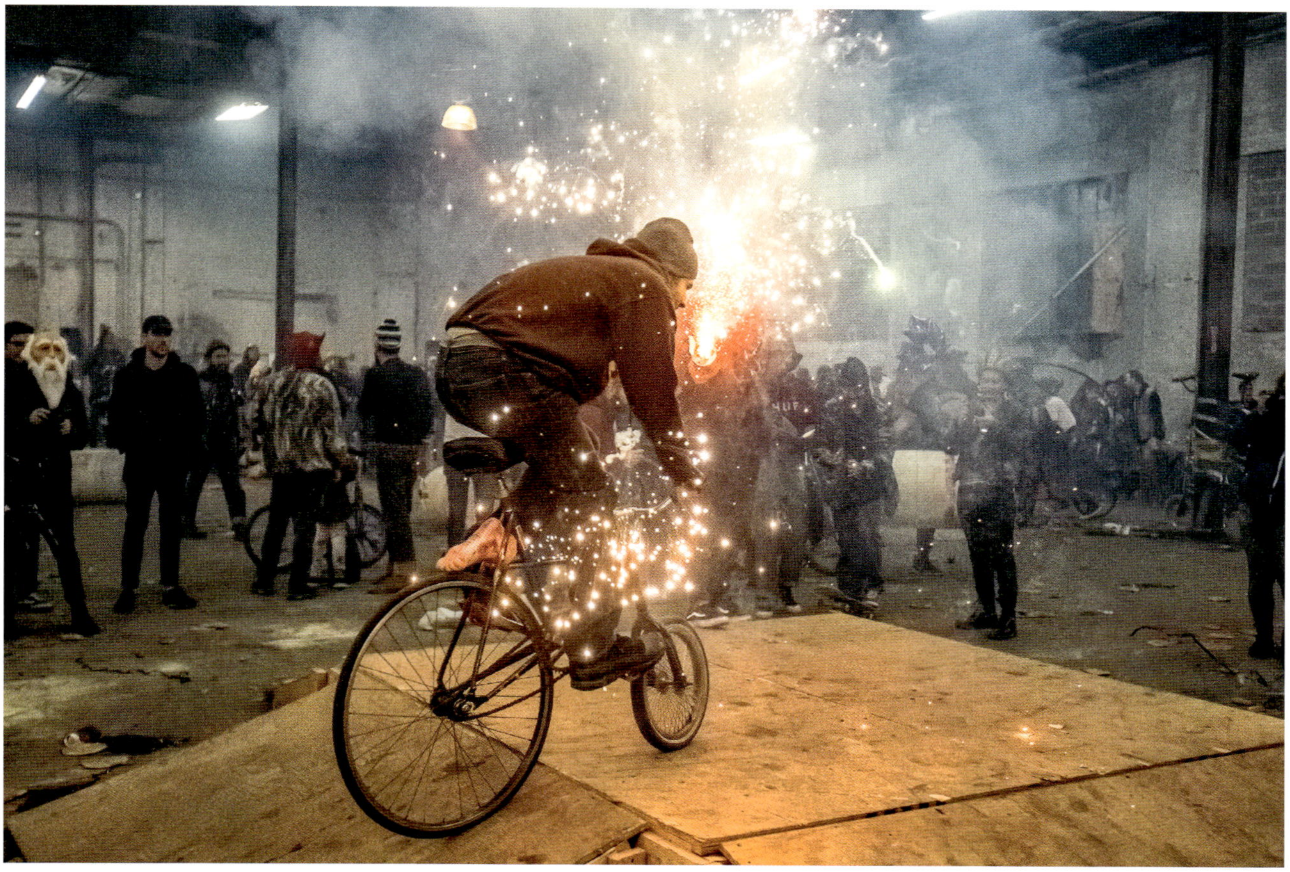

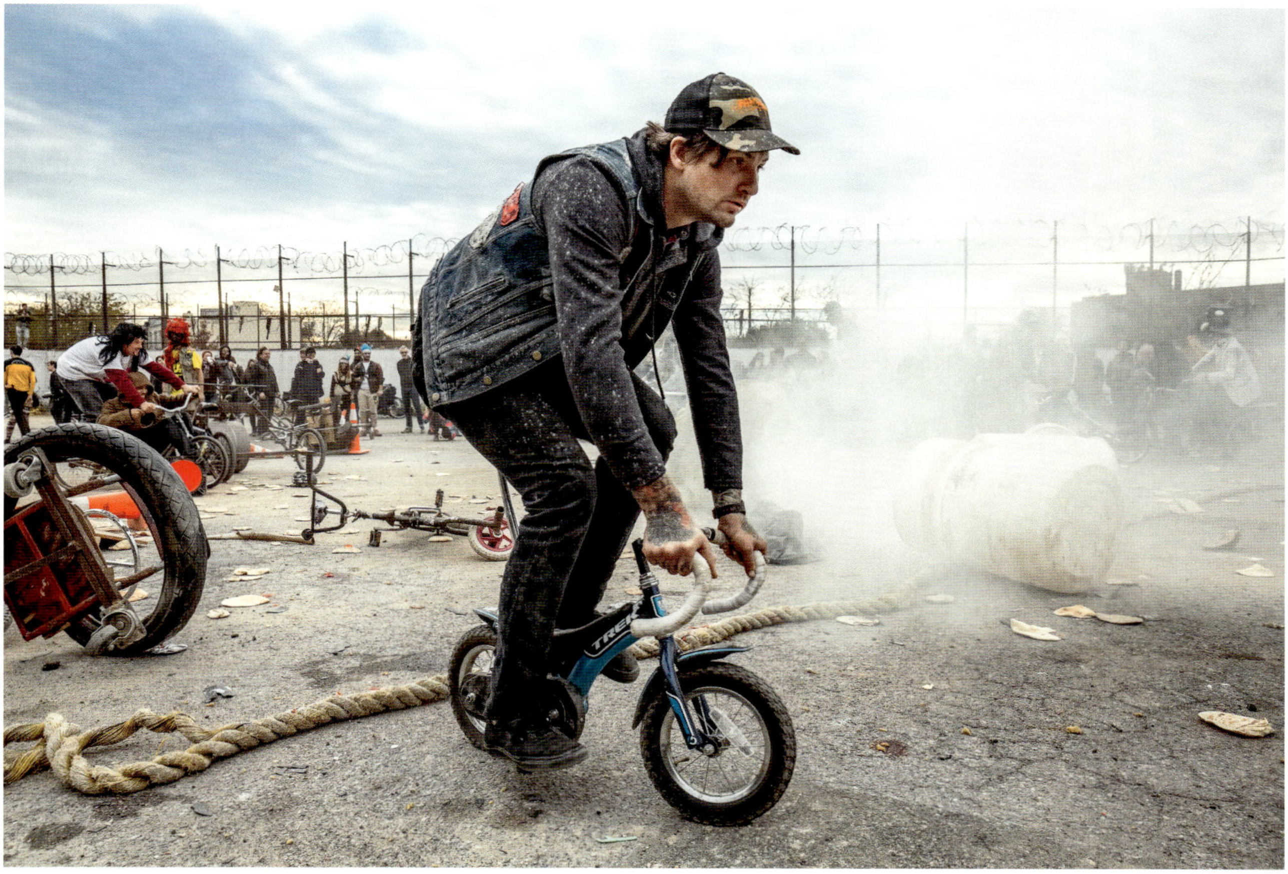

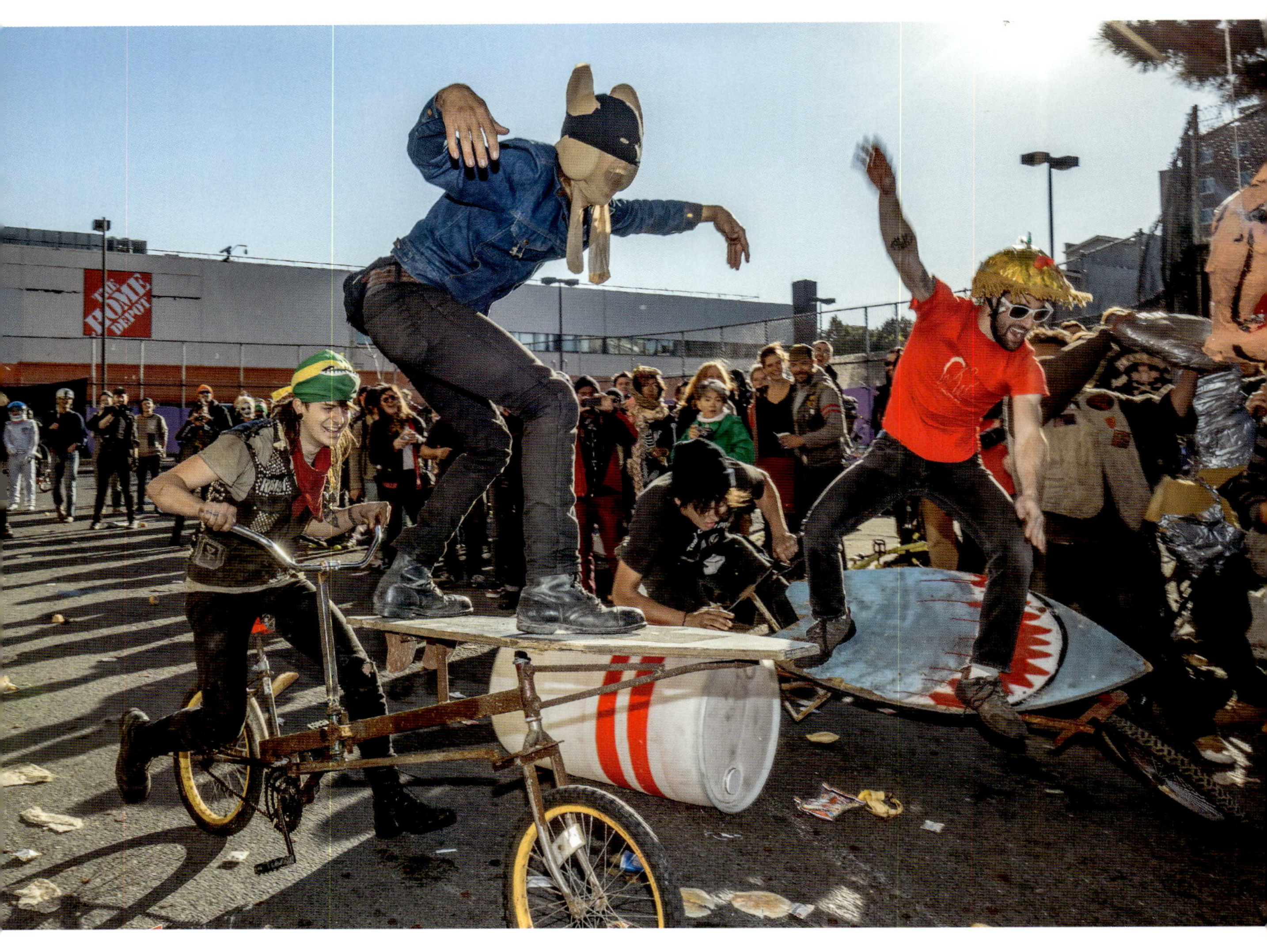
THE HOME DEPOT

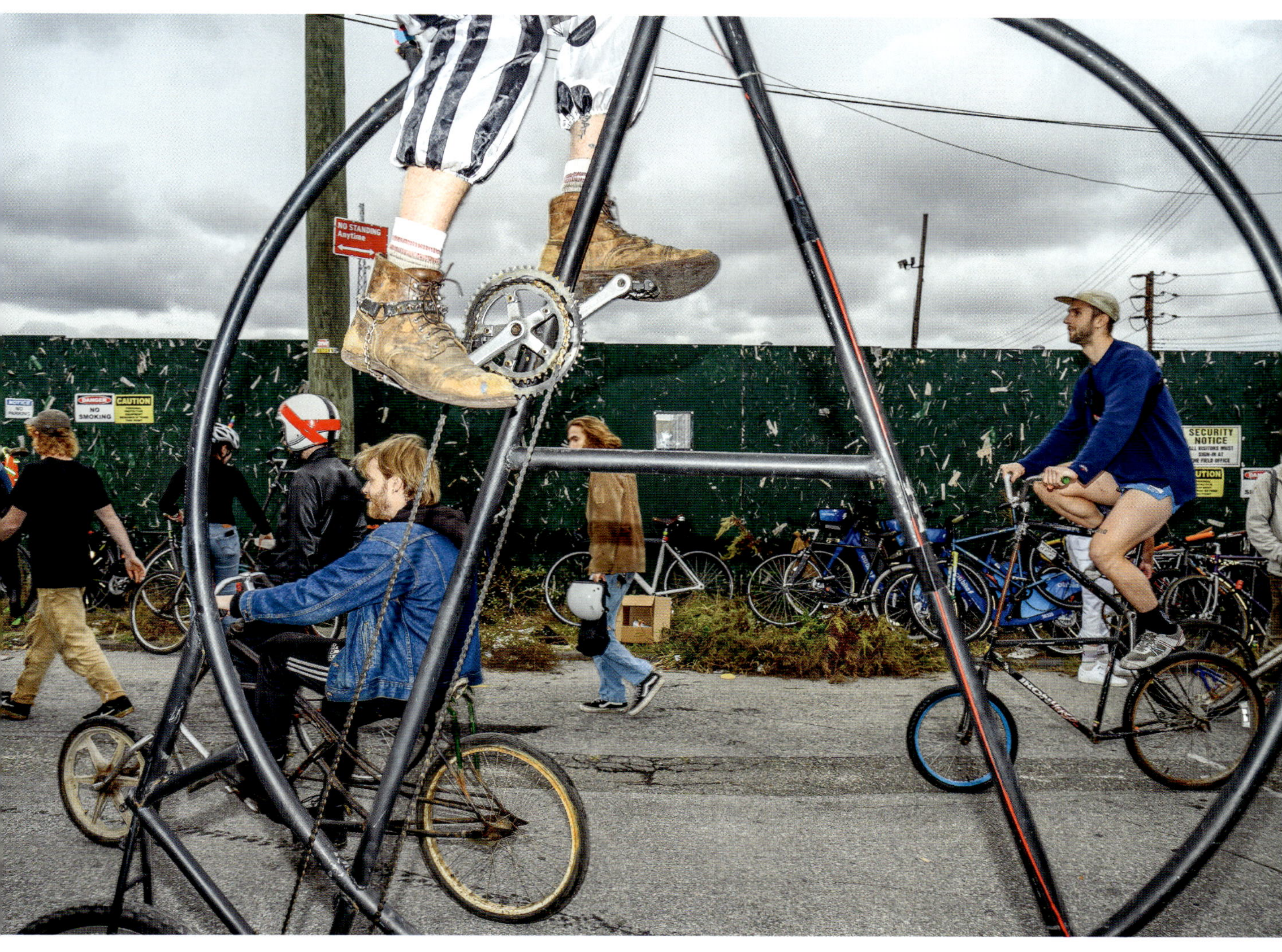

"Bike Kill is a chaotic and creative energy that inspires us to work on our own cool shit. They've taught us how to get away with something like this, how not to step on toes, and to make art. Who wouldn't want to be a part of something like this?"

Matt Porr

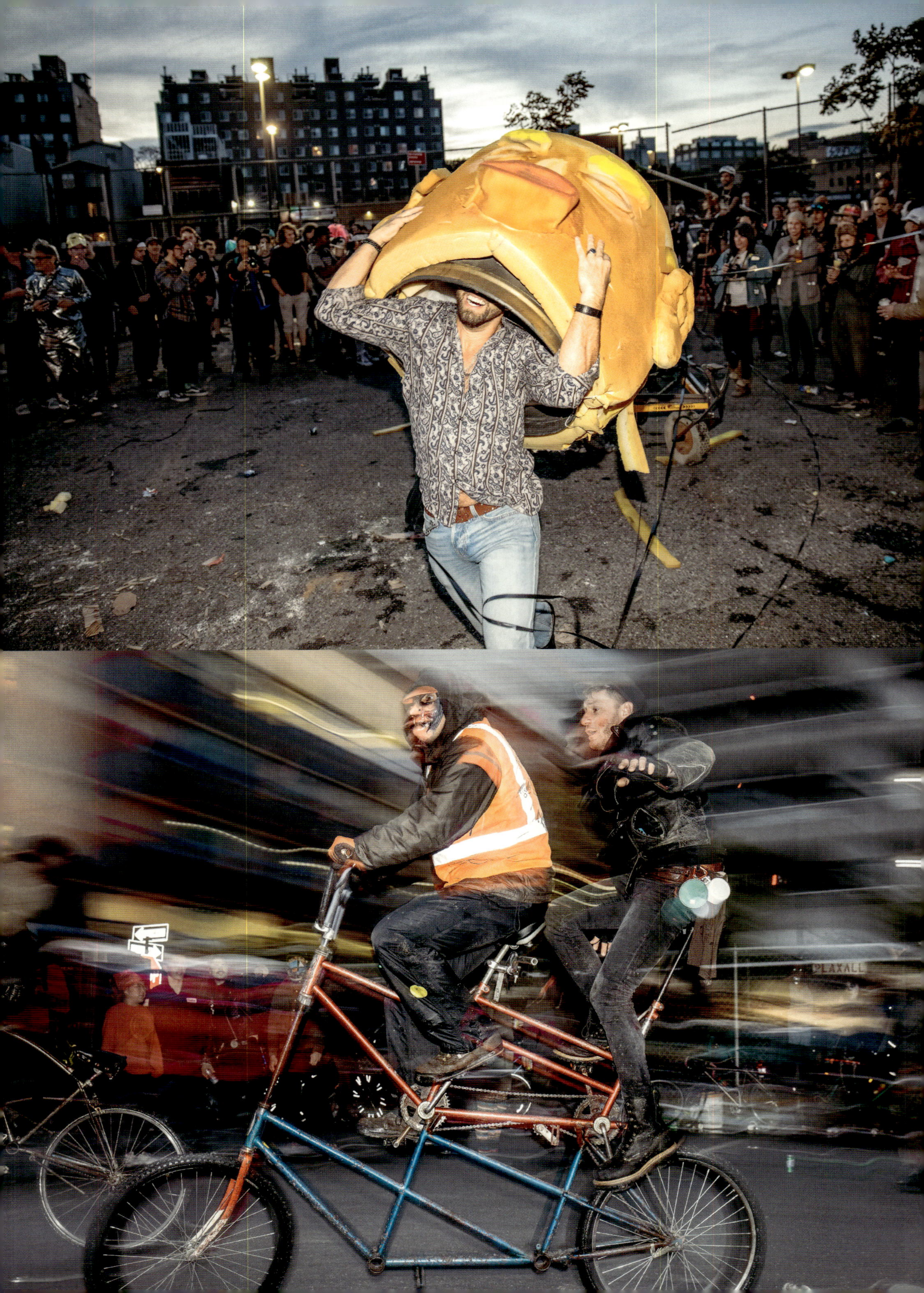
PLAXALL

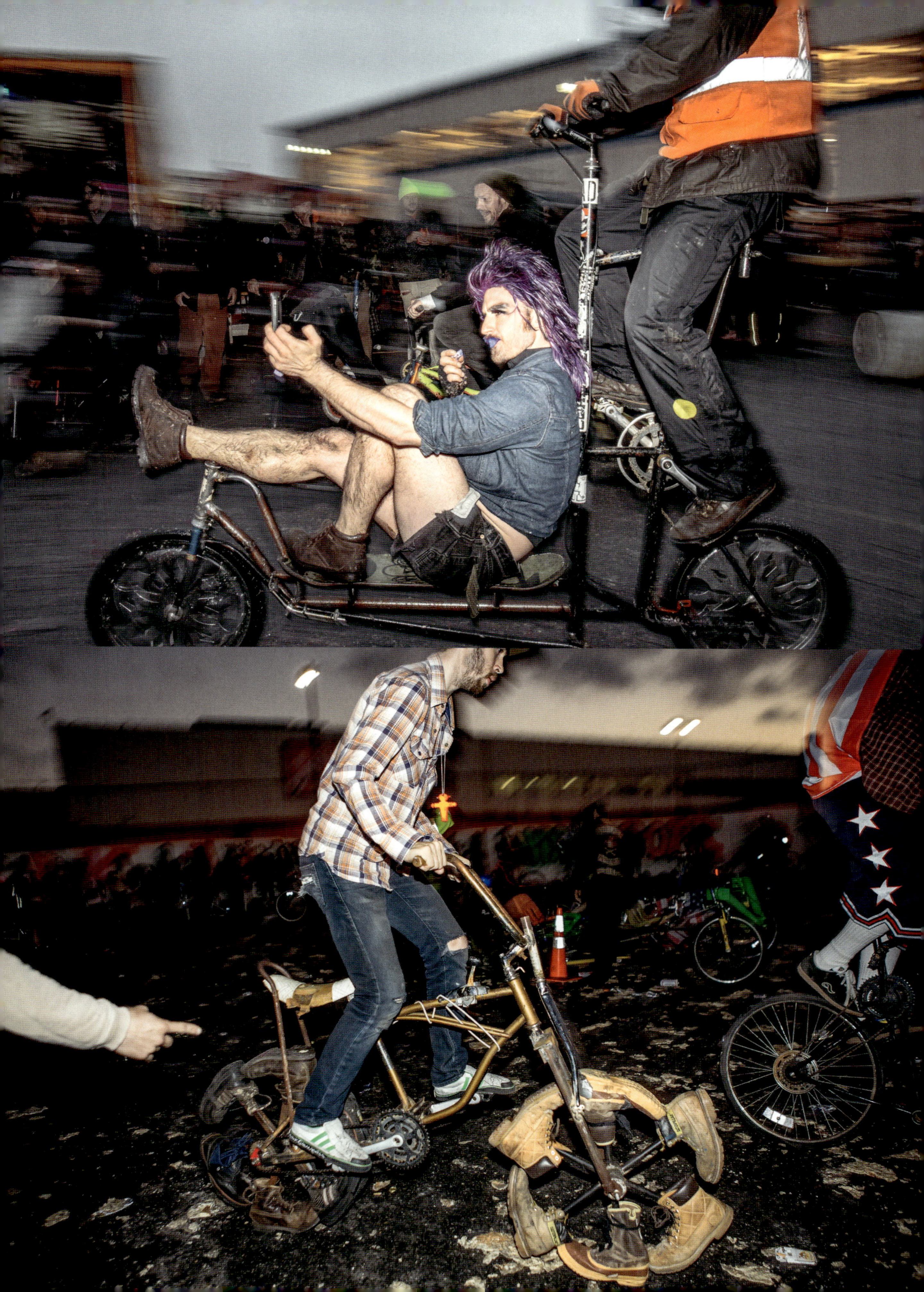

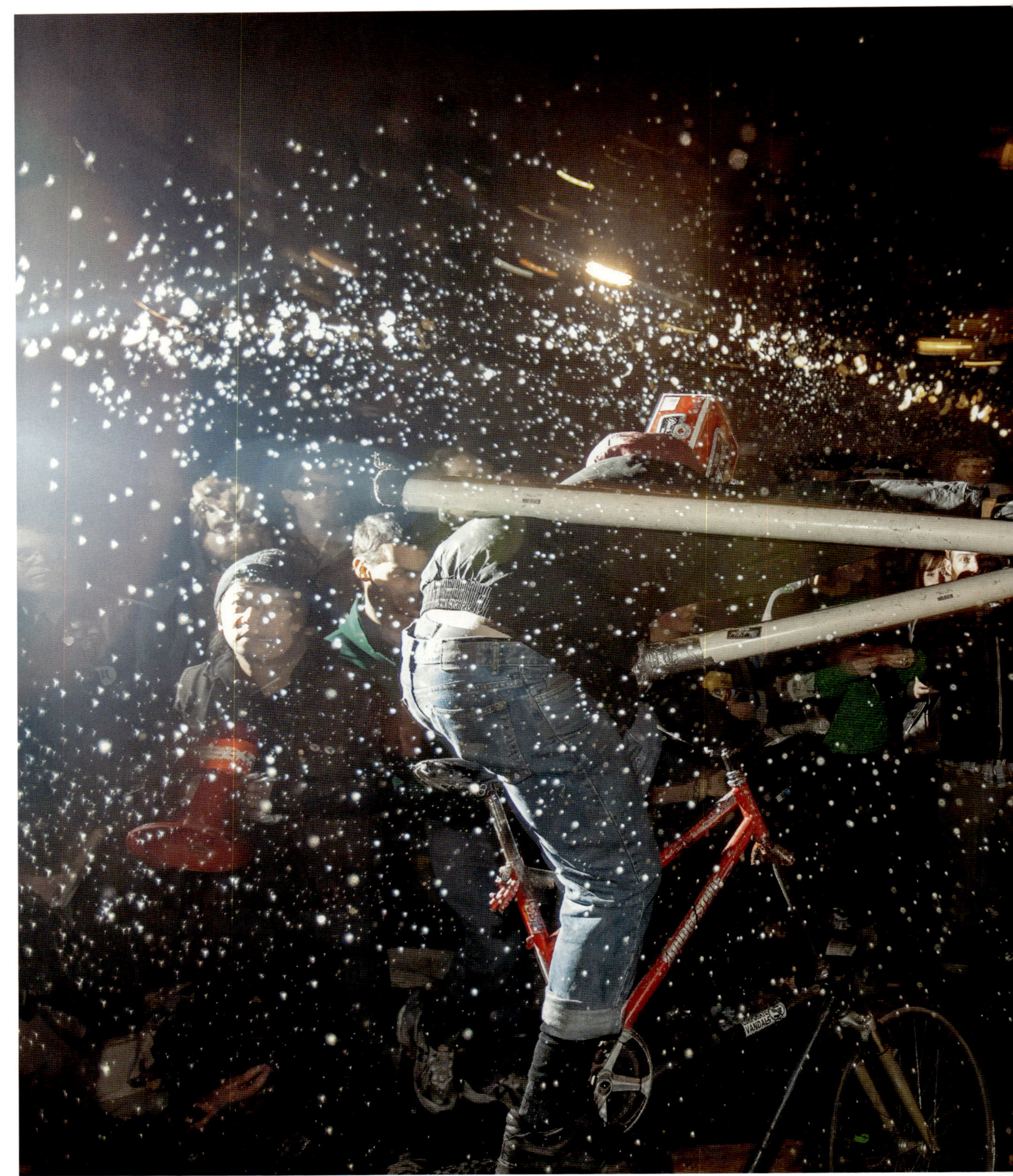

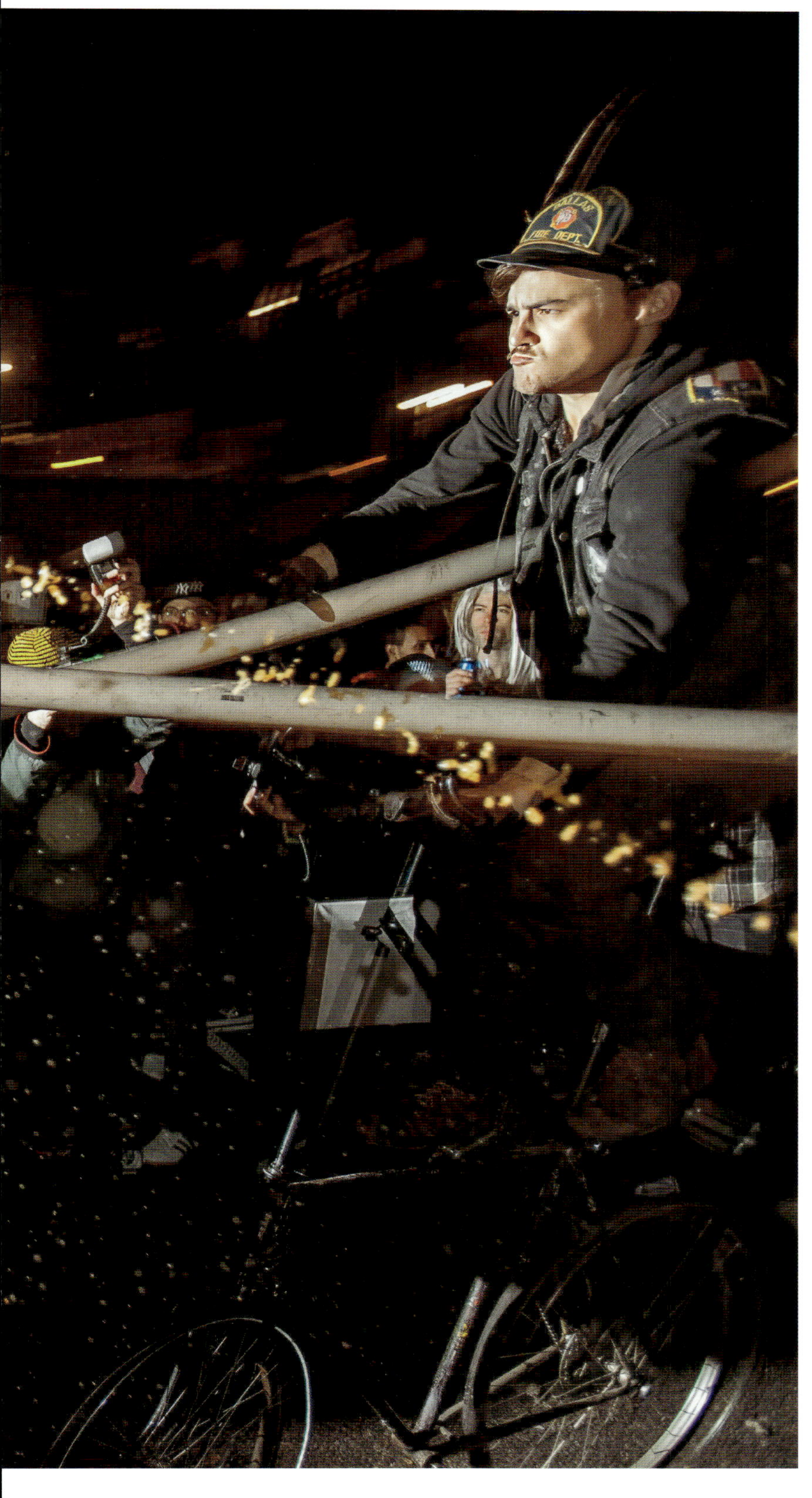

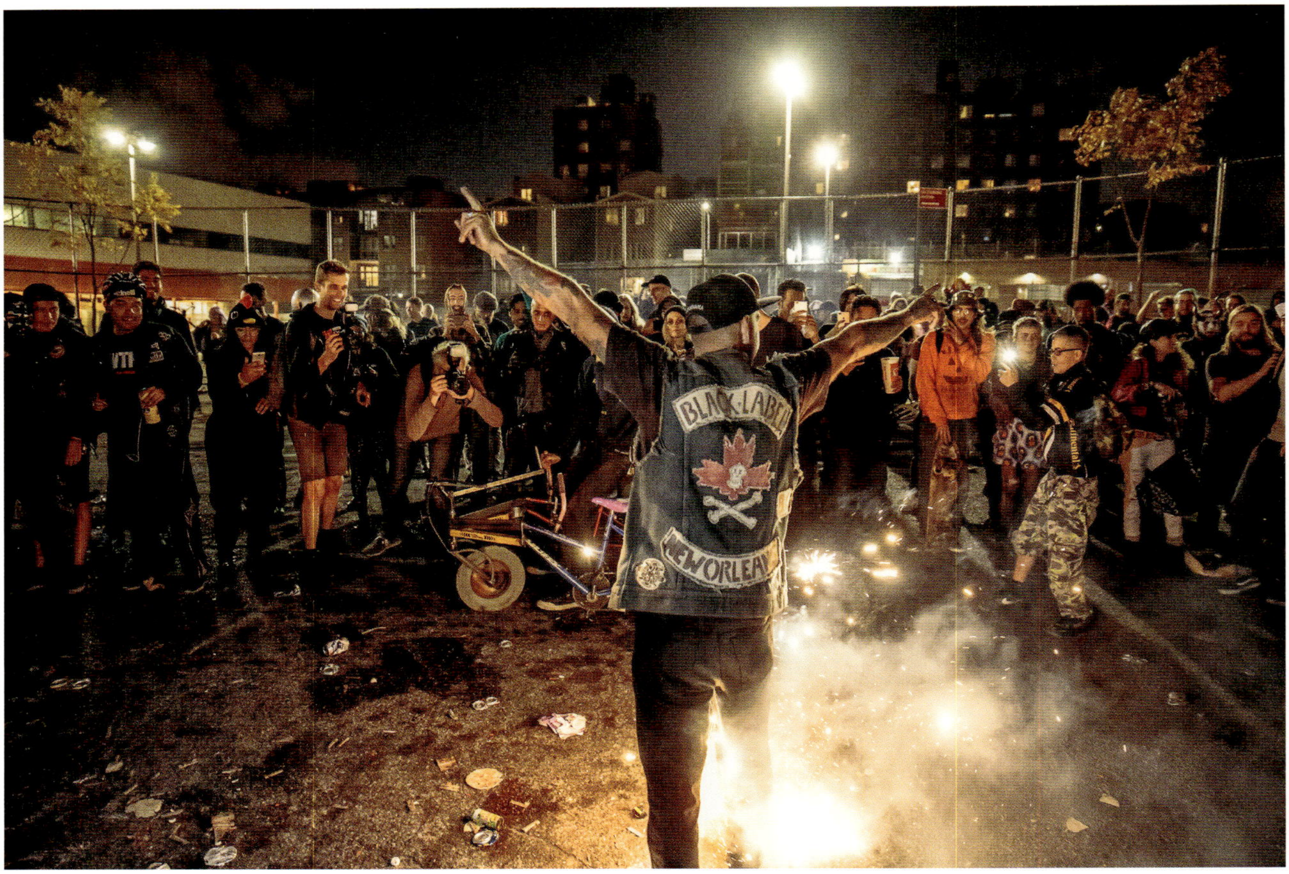
BLACK LABEL
NEW ORLEANS

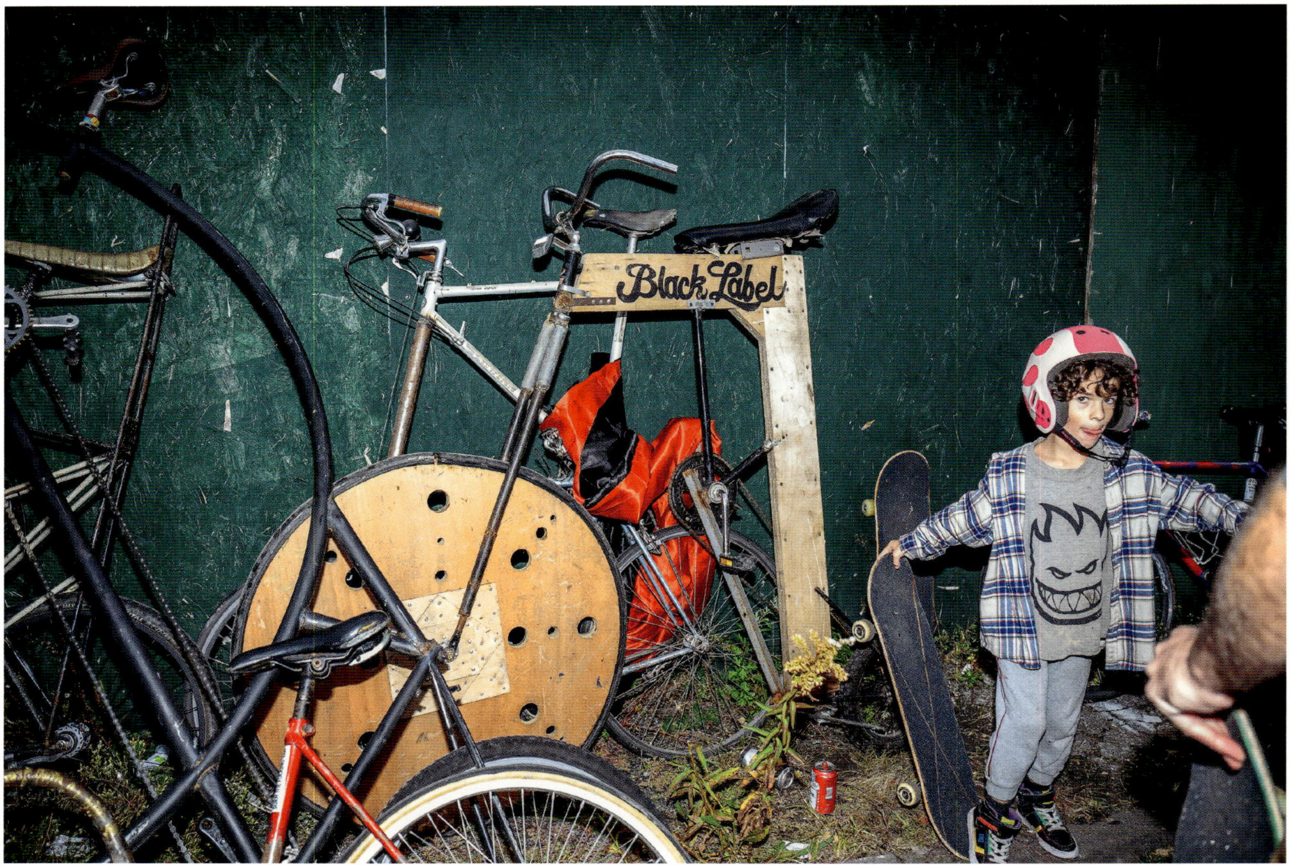
Black Label

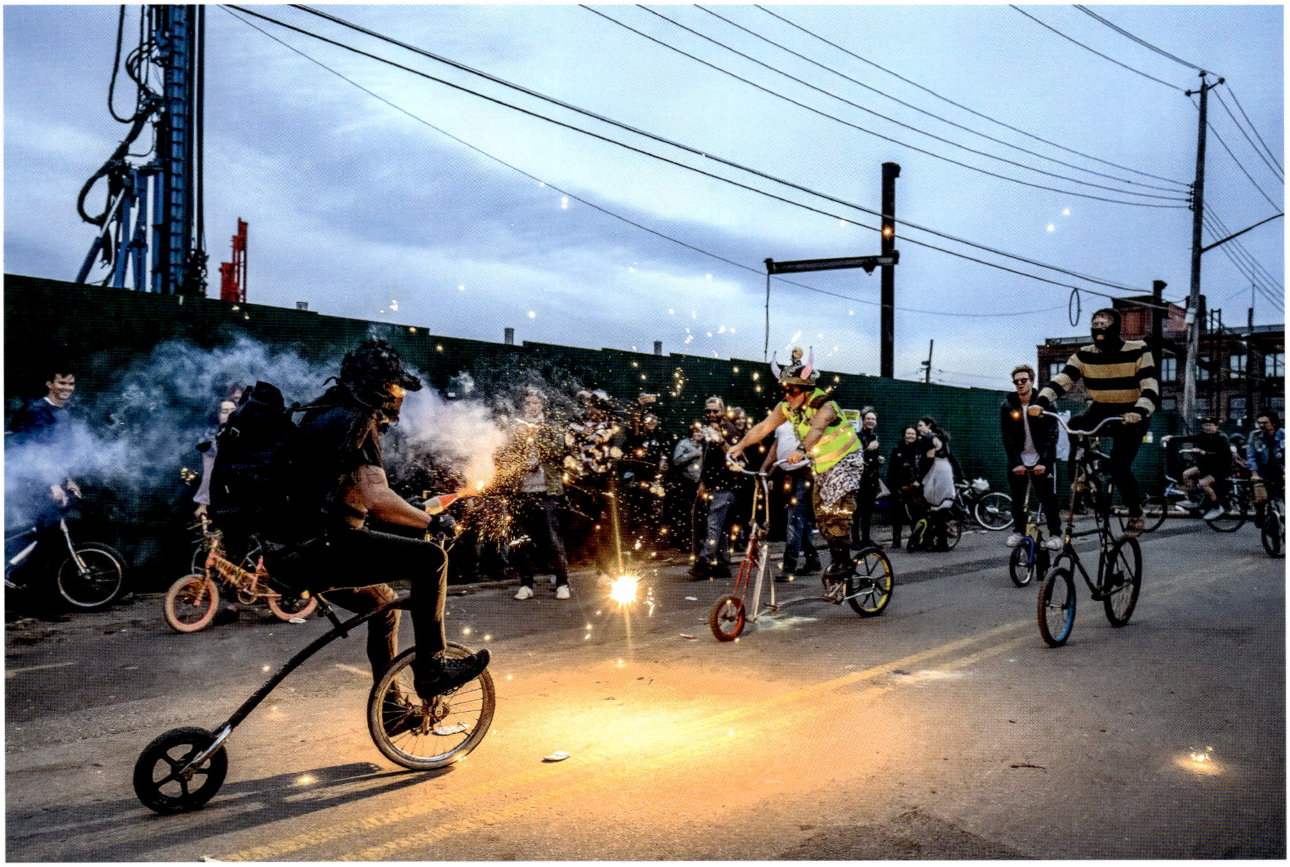

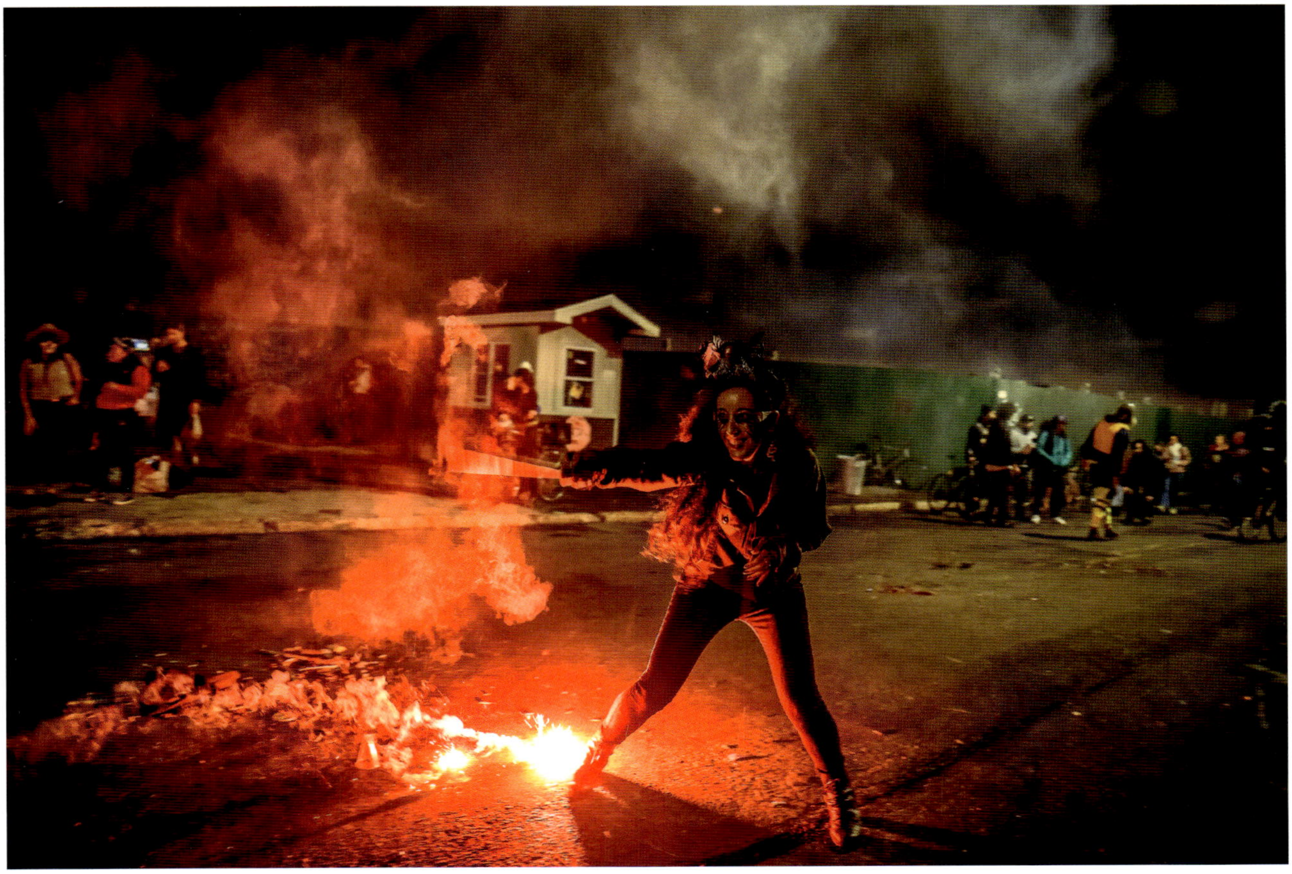

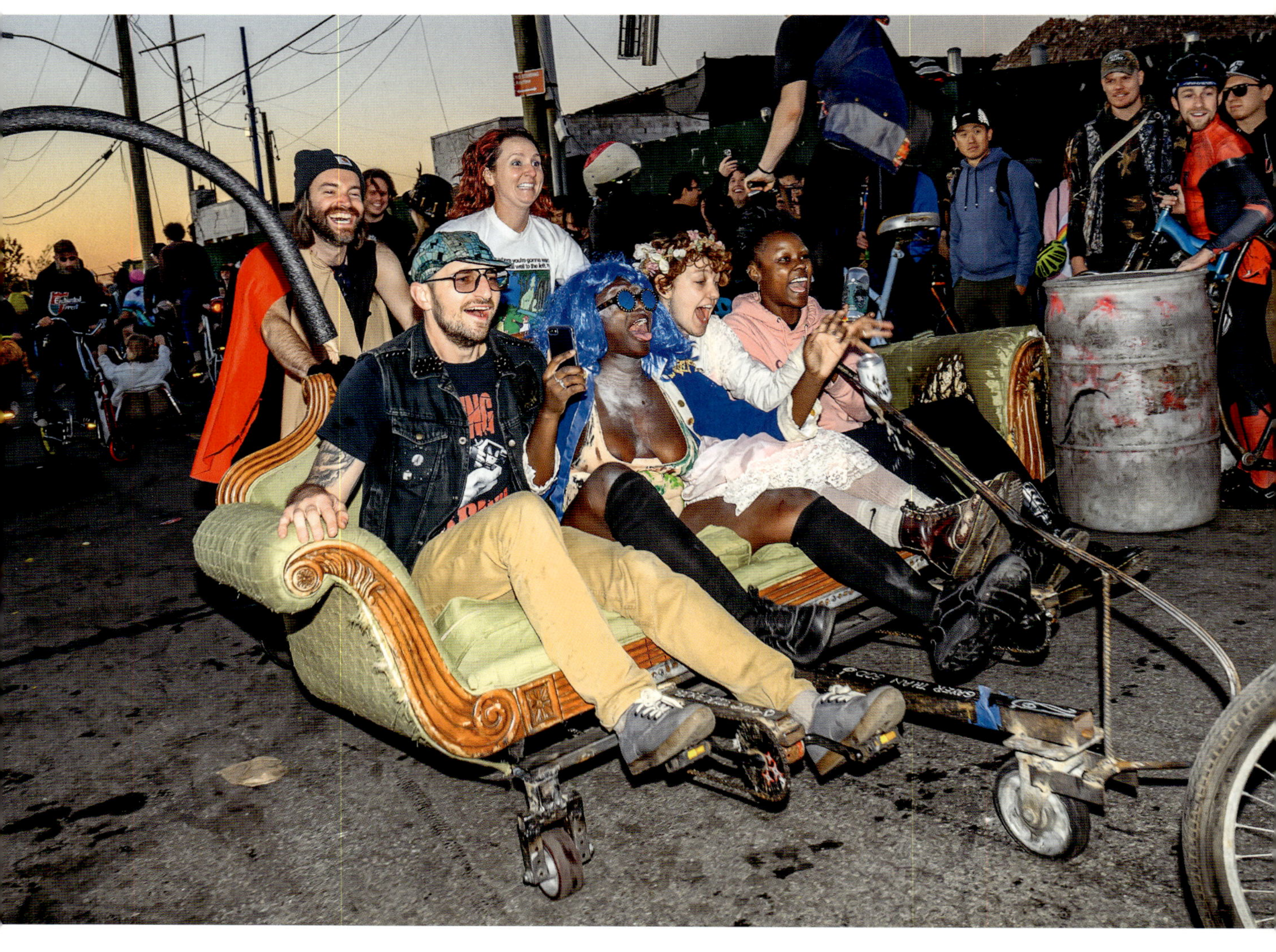

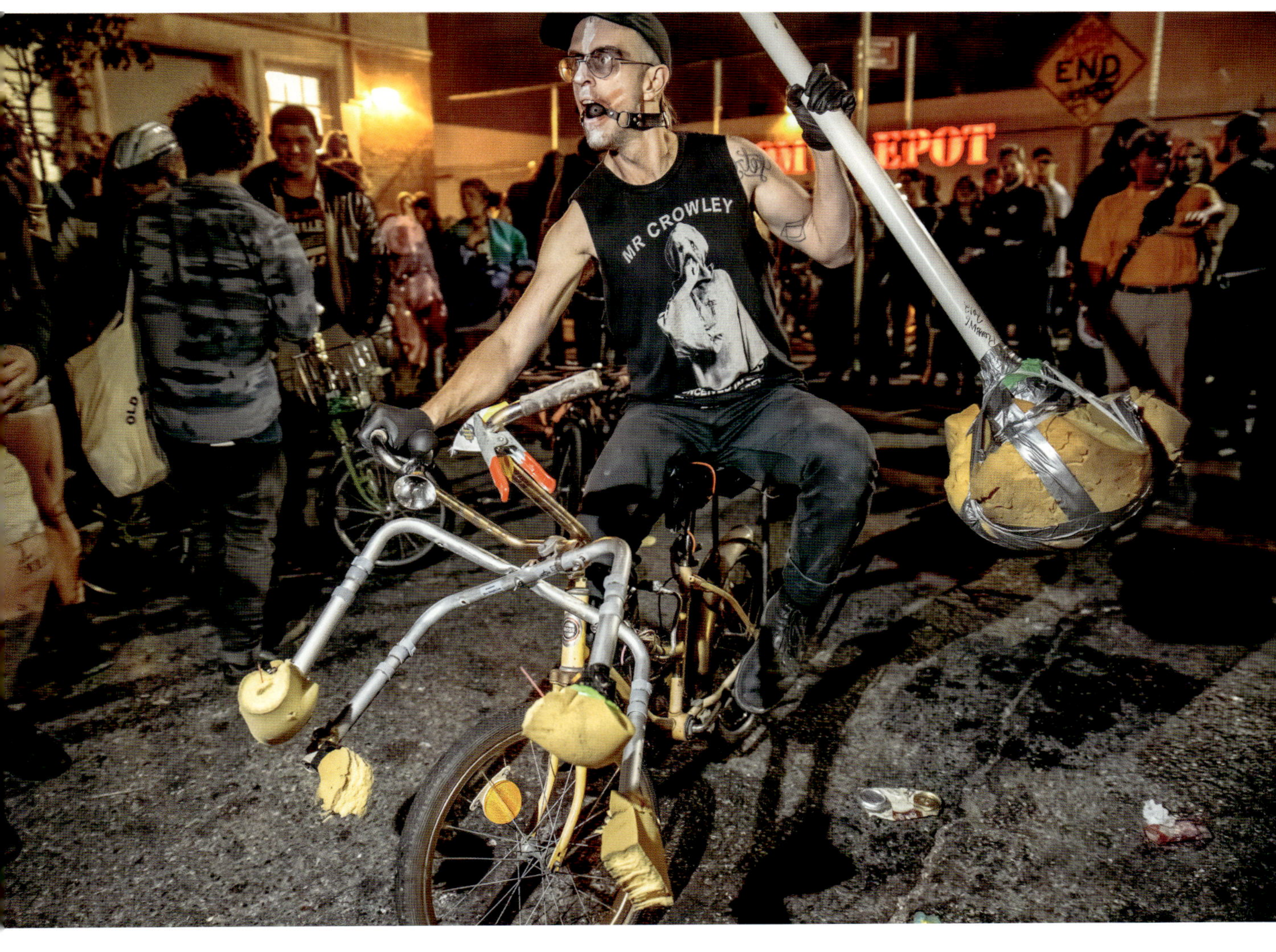
END
EPOT
MR CROWLEY
OLD

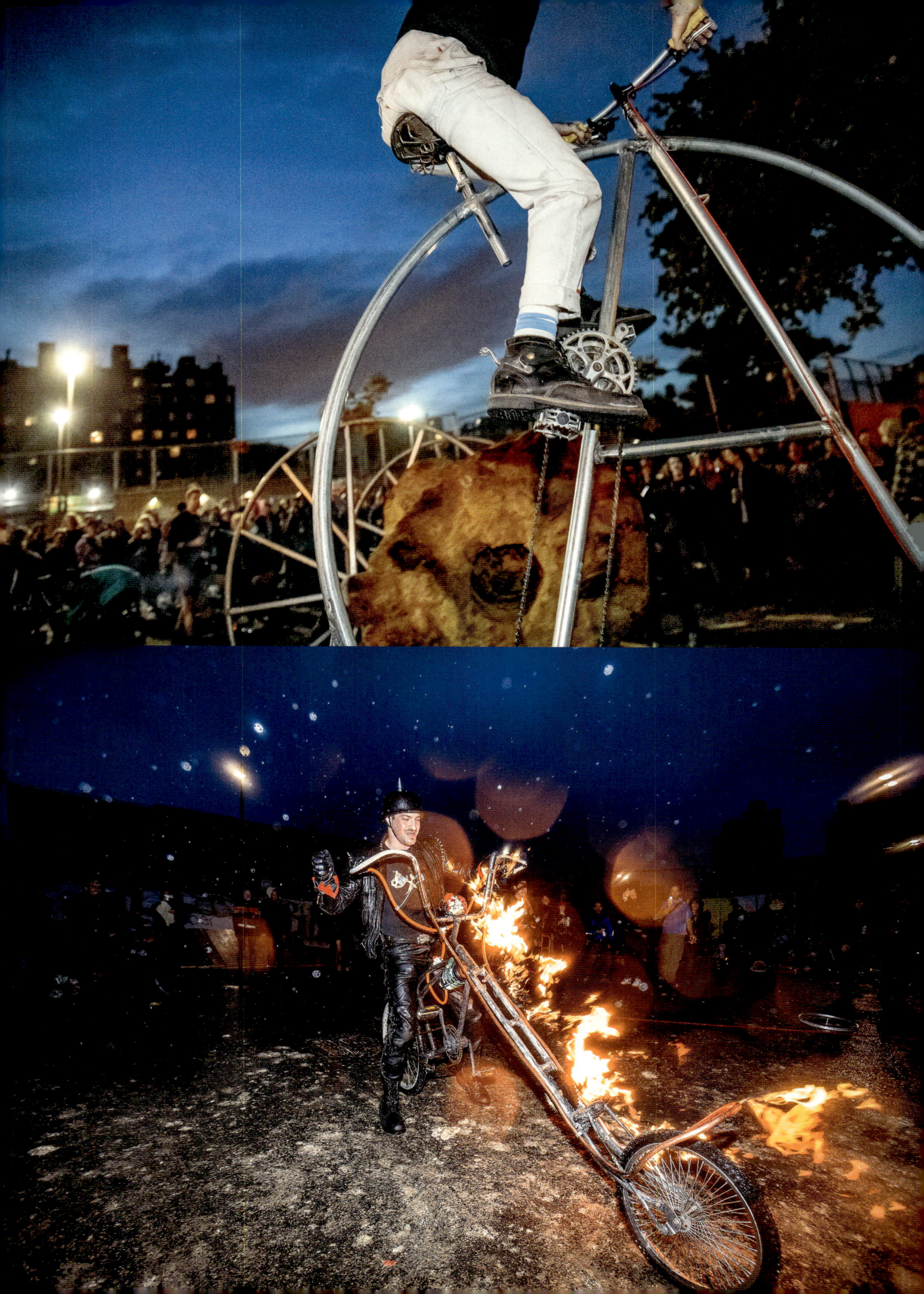

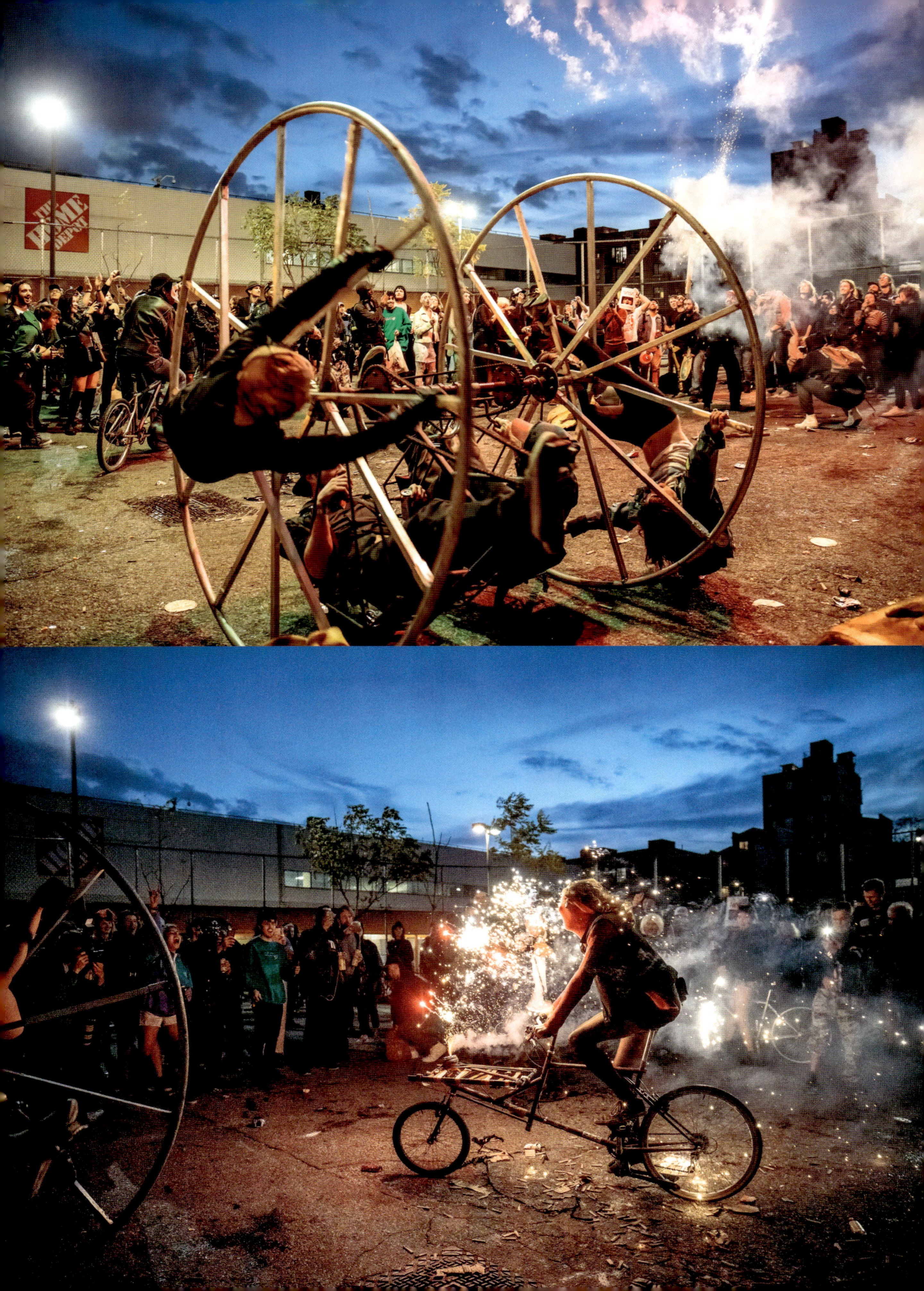
THE HOME DEPOT

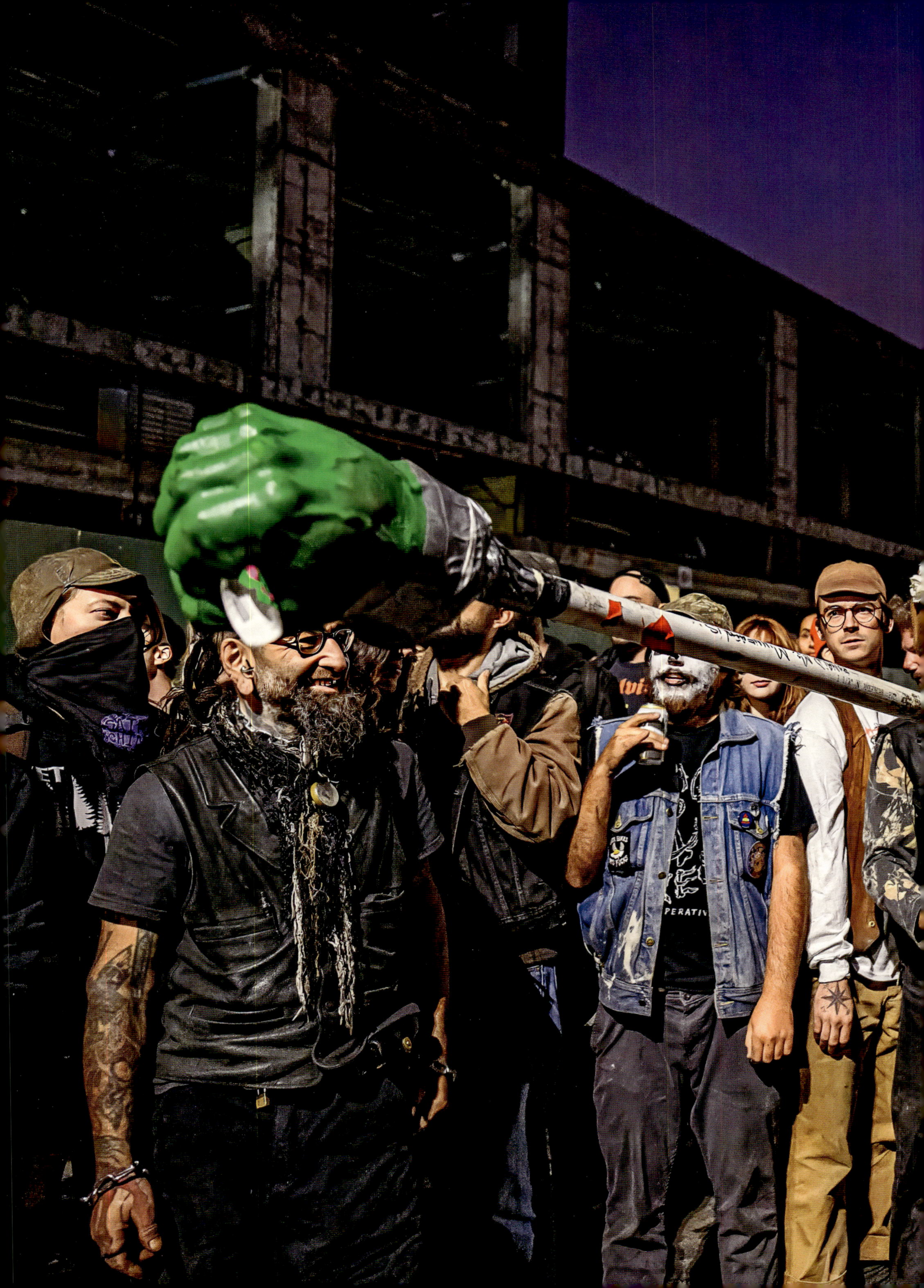

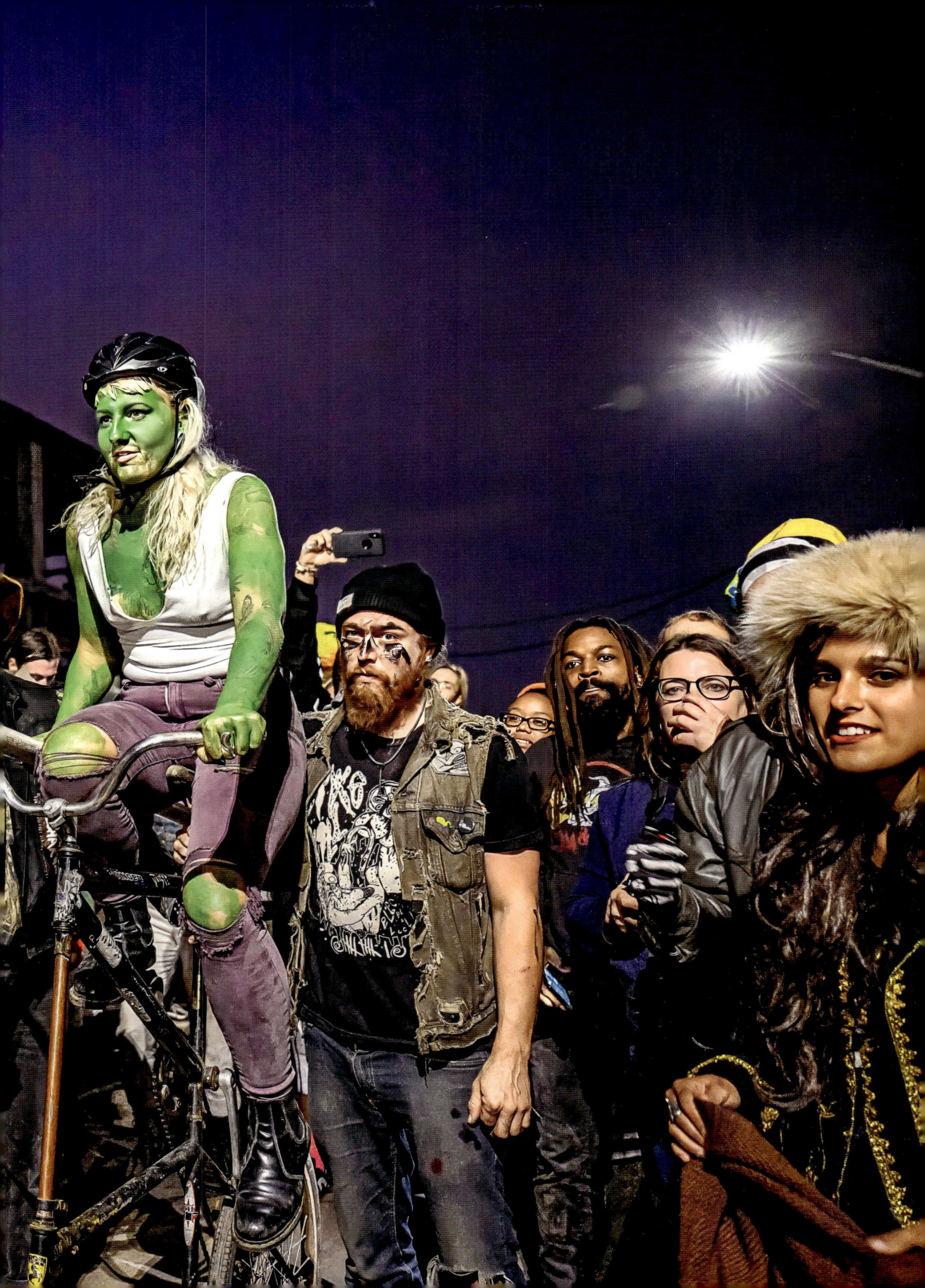

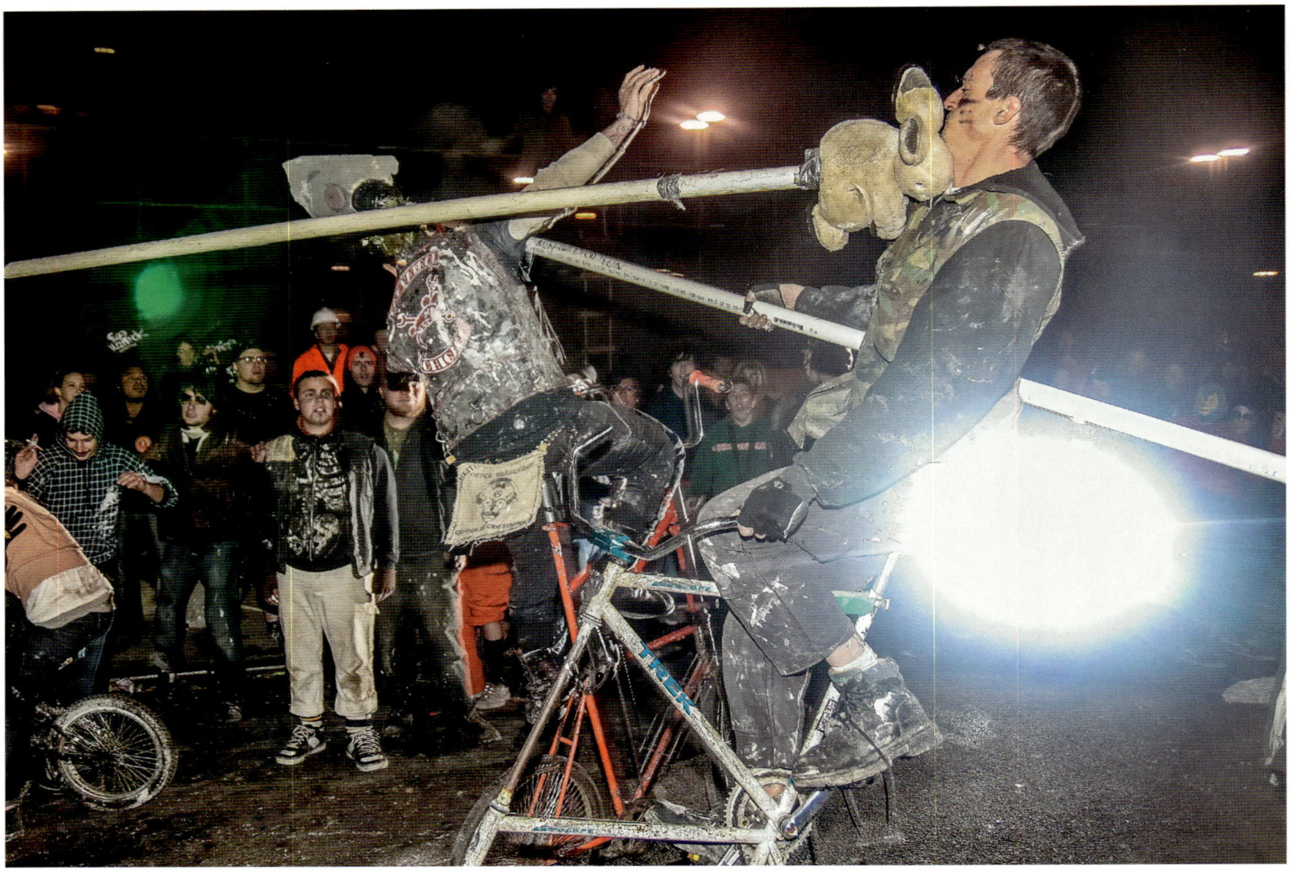

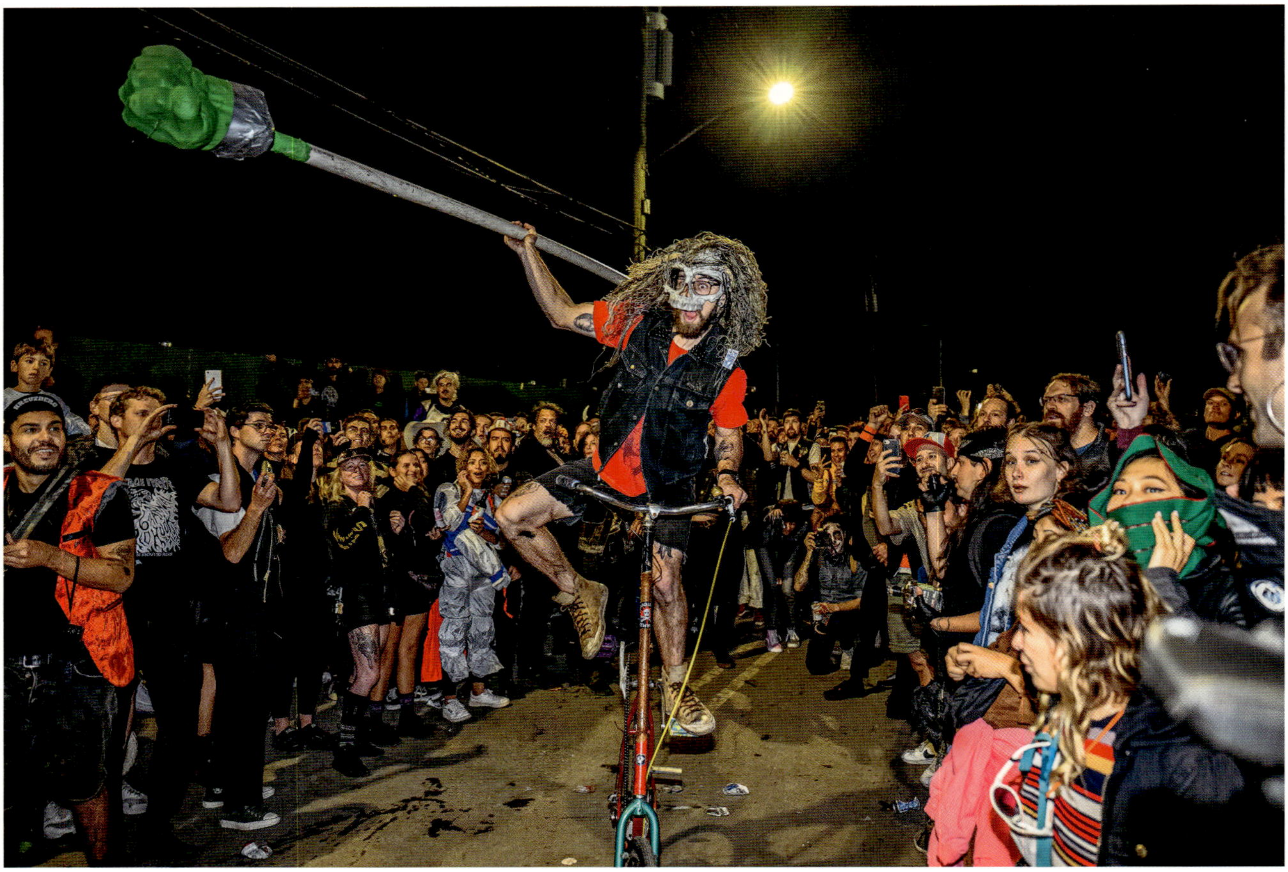

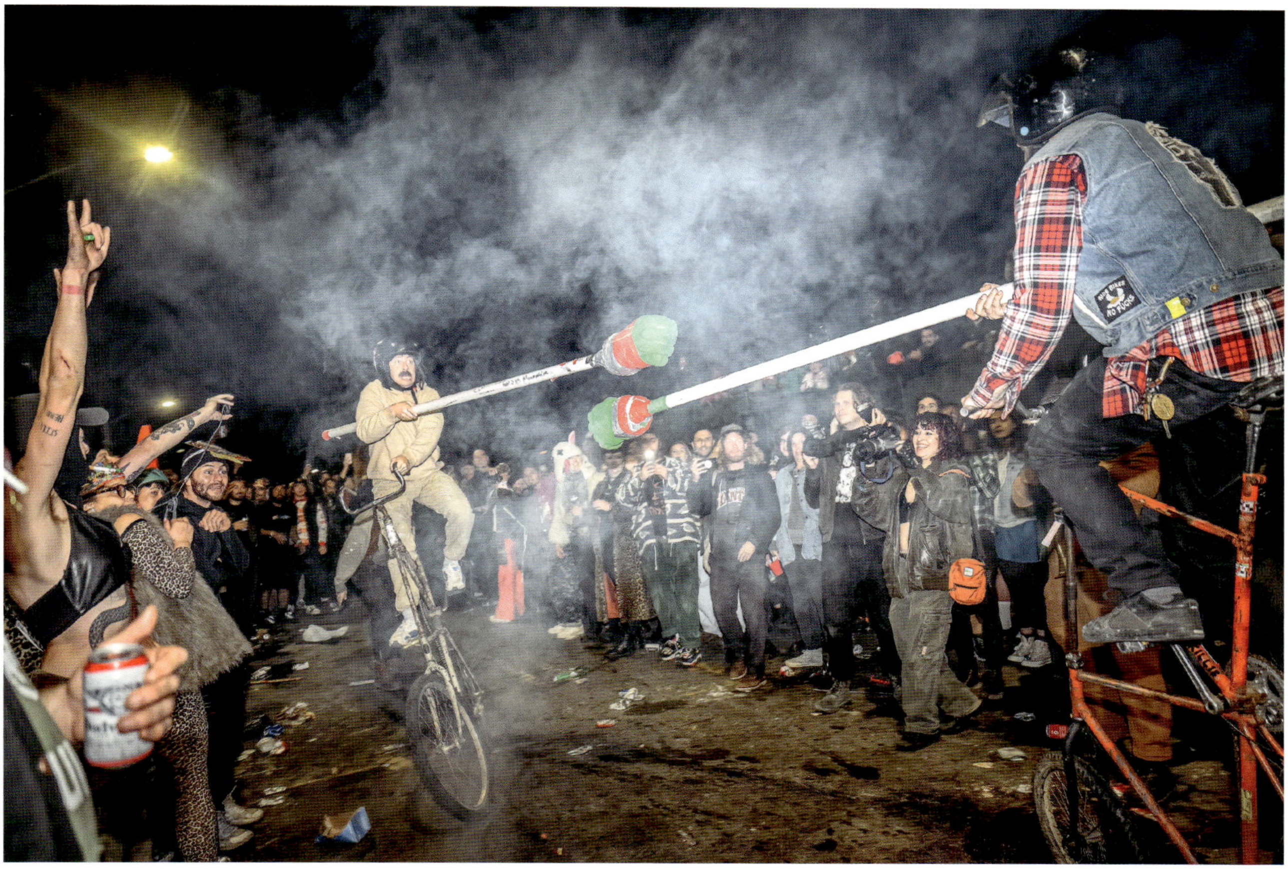

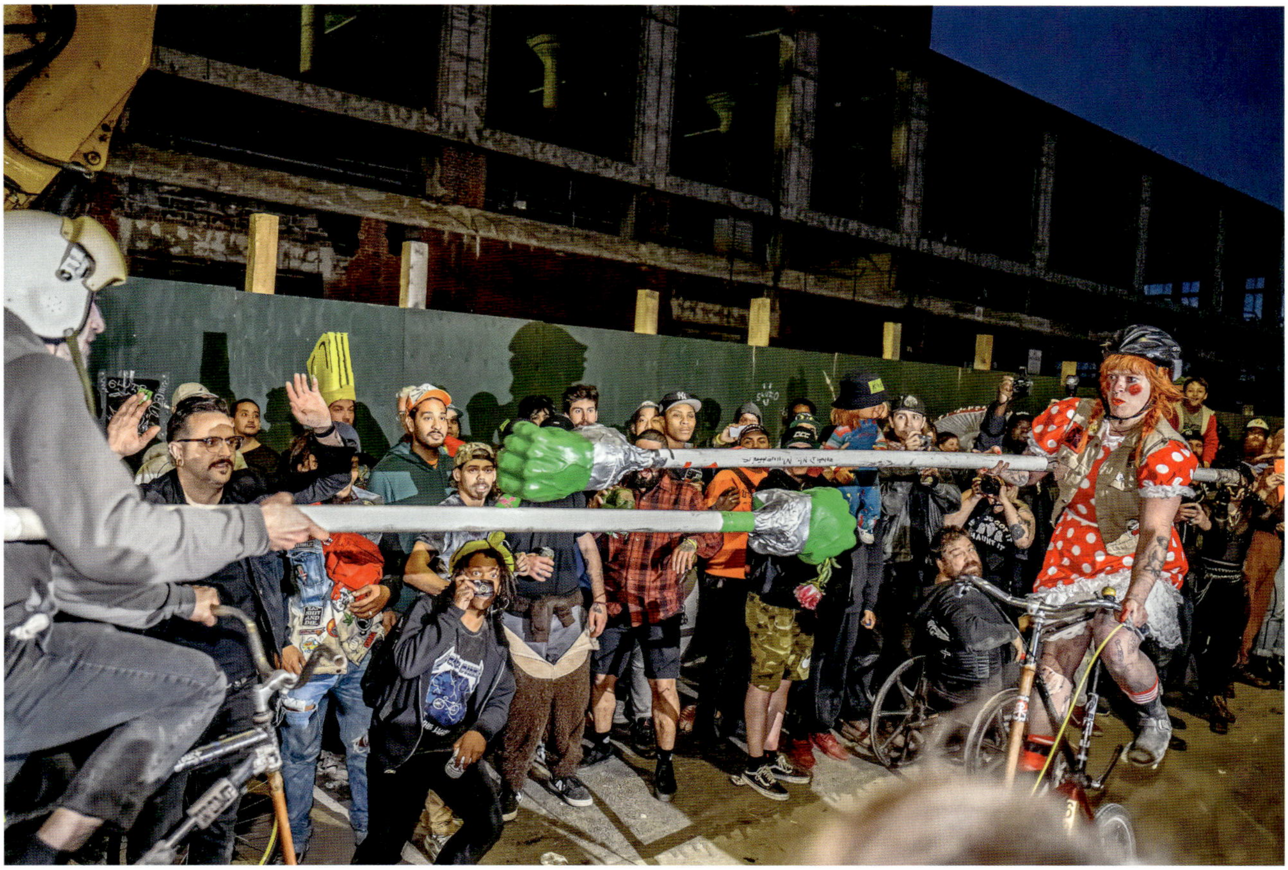

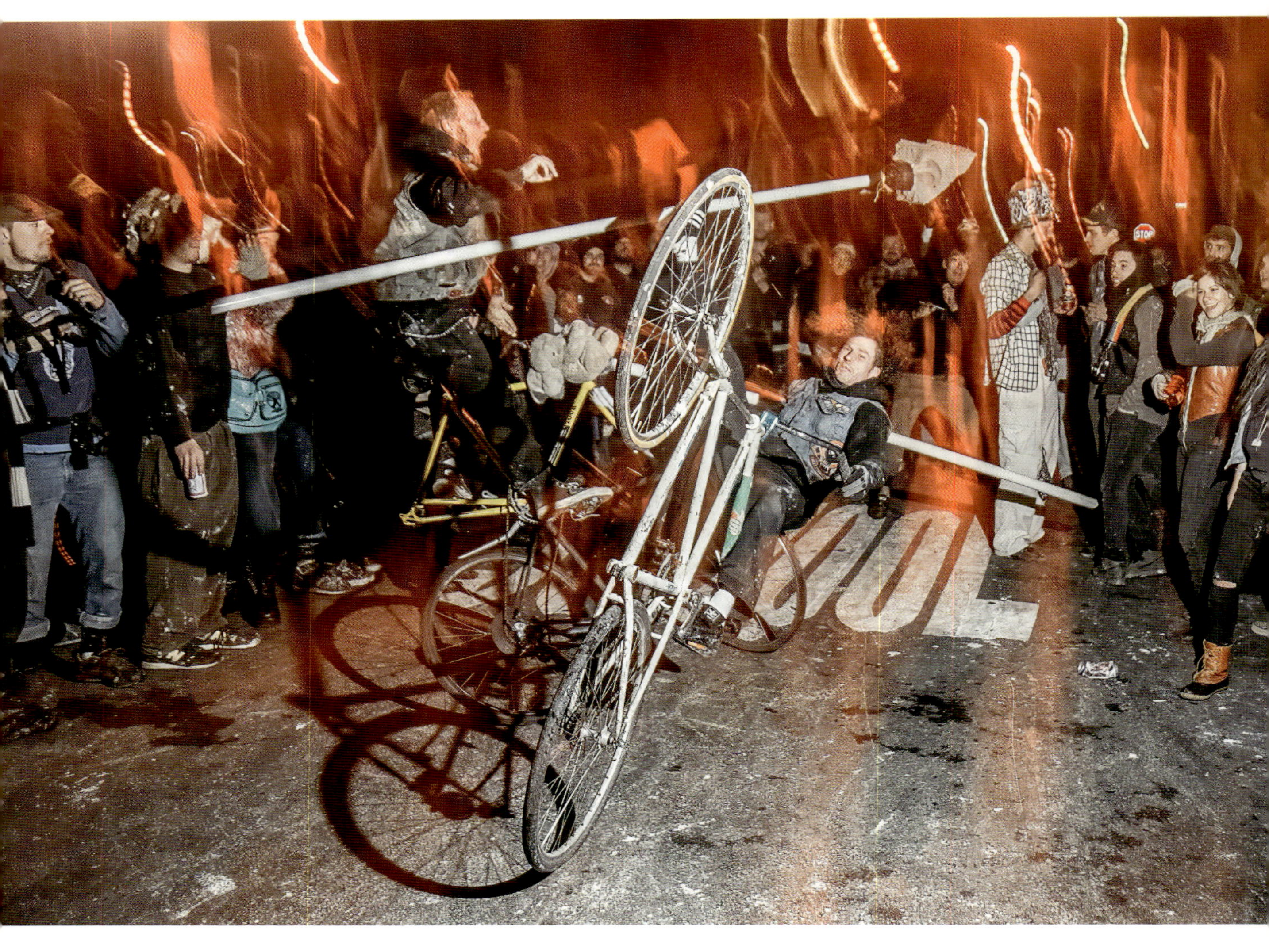

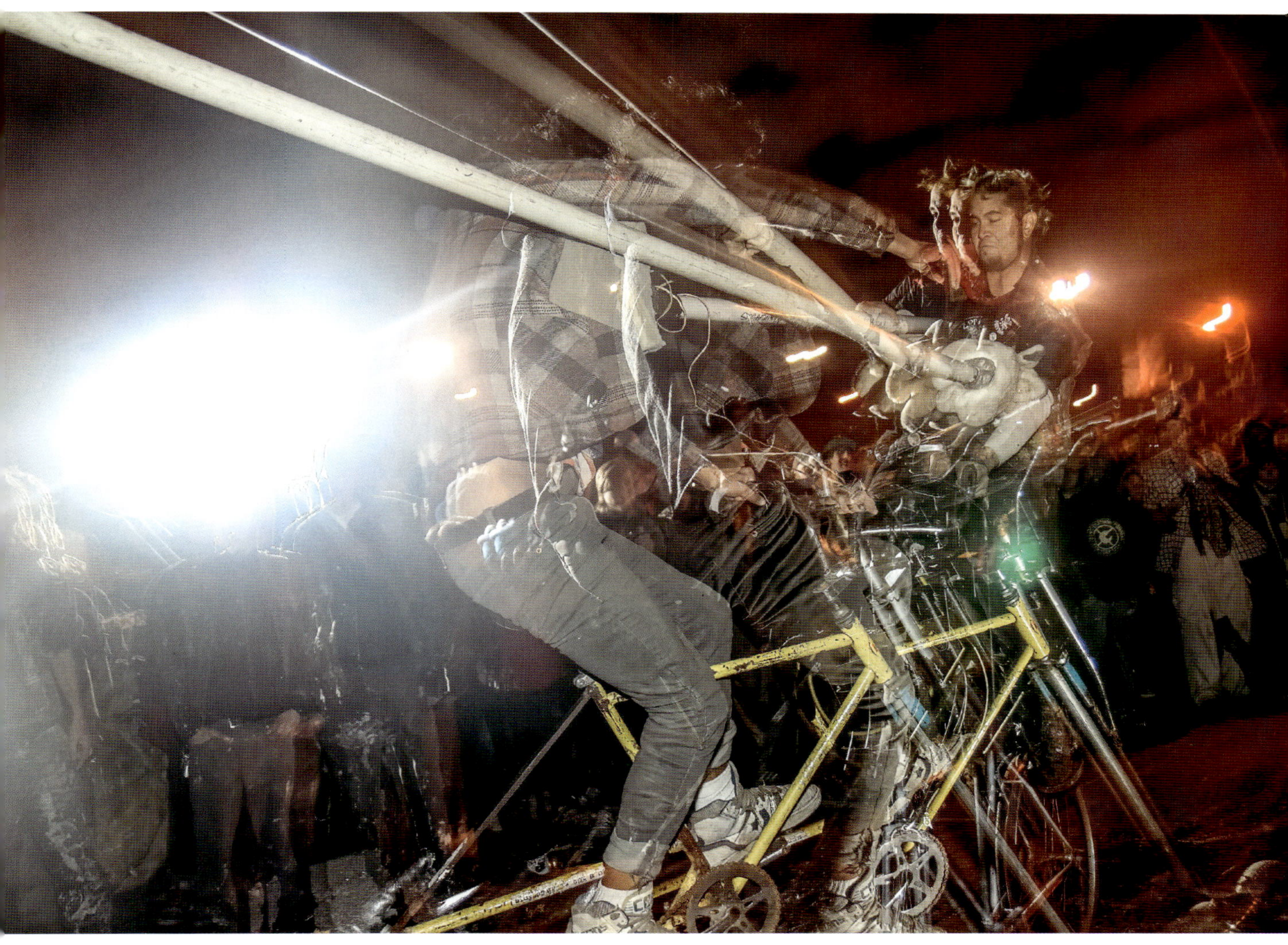

"The energy during the jousting is a bit of benevolent bloodlust. Everyone is excited, cheering, and crowding forward to see the hit, but no one wants anyone to get seriously hurt."

Tod Seelie

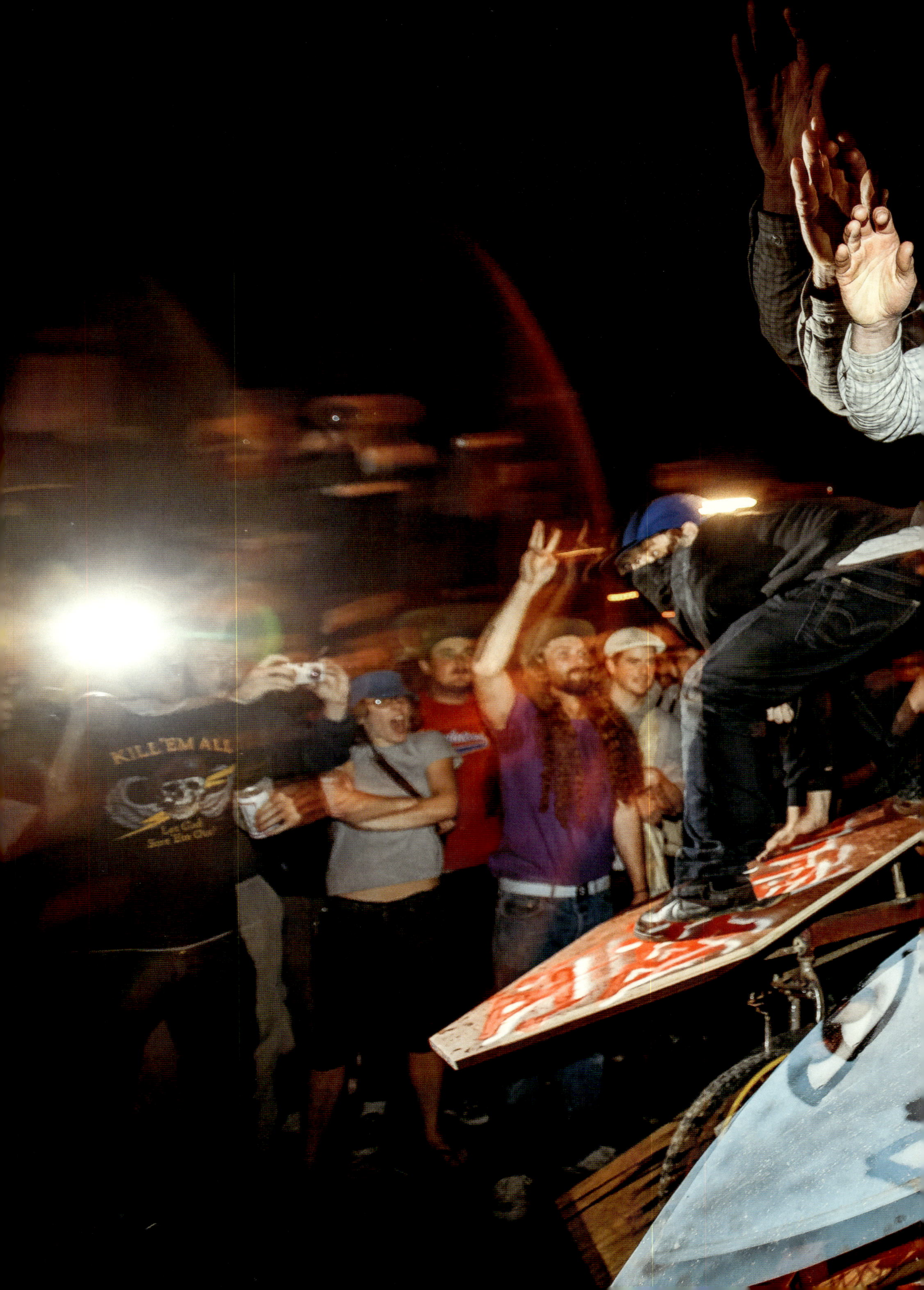
KILL 'EM ALL

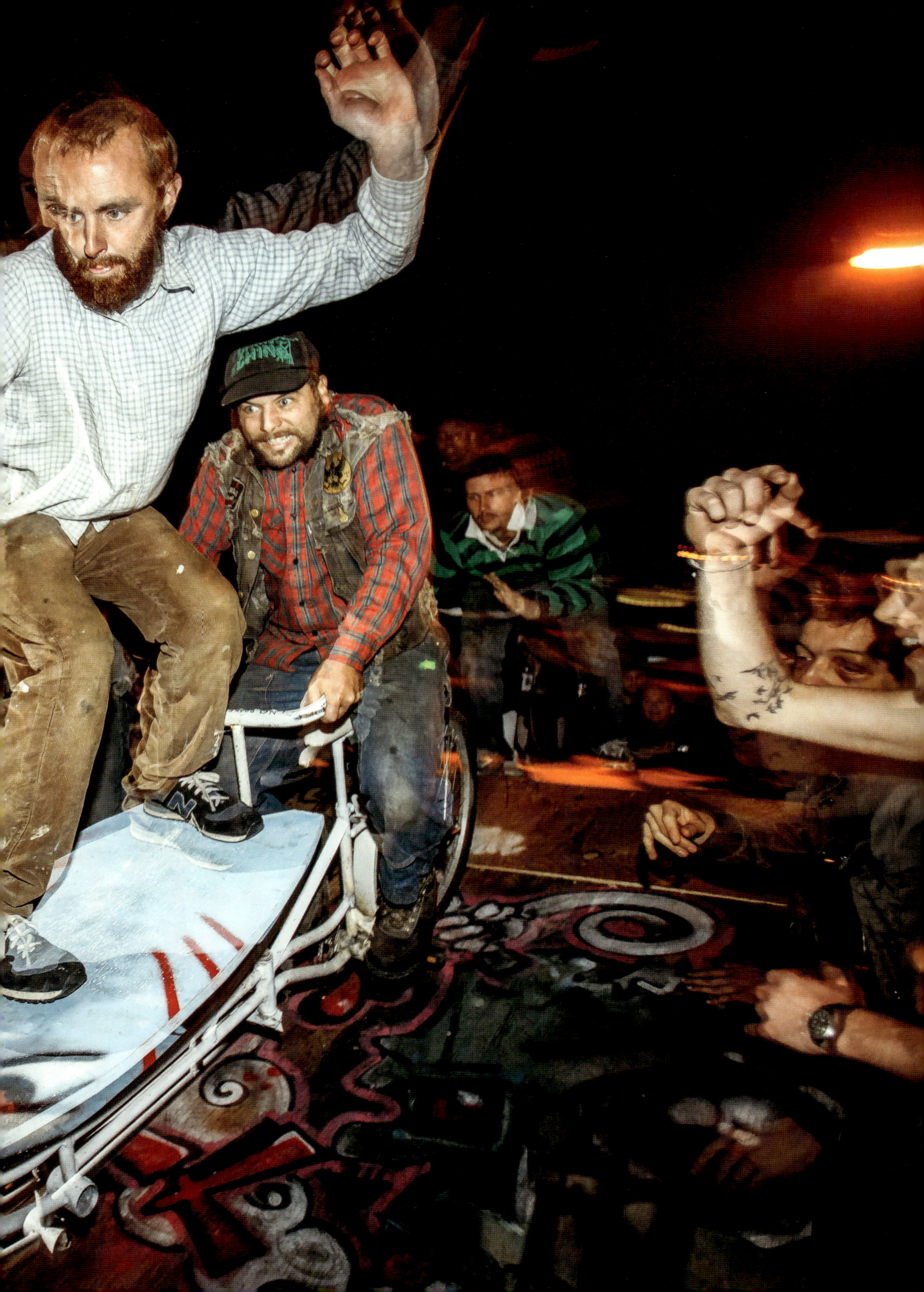

Bikes Bring Bonds

Berlin—Punks, bikes, and a different kind of street fight

Photos
Christophe Gateau

From a distance some bikes appear like ordinary road bikes—stripped down to the bare minimum. Others have oversized tires, spikes on the front, or reinforced spokes. When the gladiators gather for the "battle on two wheels," the objective is to destroy the tires of all other opponents. The gladiator's own bike must remain rideable. The last person remaining wins. This competition is one of three at the Bike Wars tournament in Berlin. The "battle of the big machines" follows the same principle. However, these vehicles are allowed to have three or more wheels. Lastly, the "tournament of the tall bikes" is a jousting tournament where the riders seek to dismount their opponents with a lance.

The aggressiveness of the competitors and their body-checking is infectious upon the crowd. Soon water-balloons are thrown into the fray. Ultimately, it is all about the experience. Painful crashes are met with boisterous oohs and ahhs from the crowd.

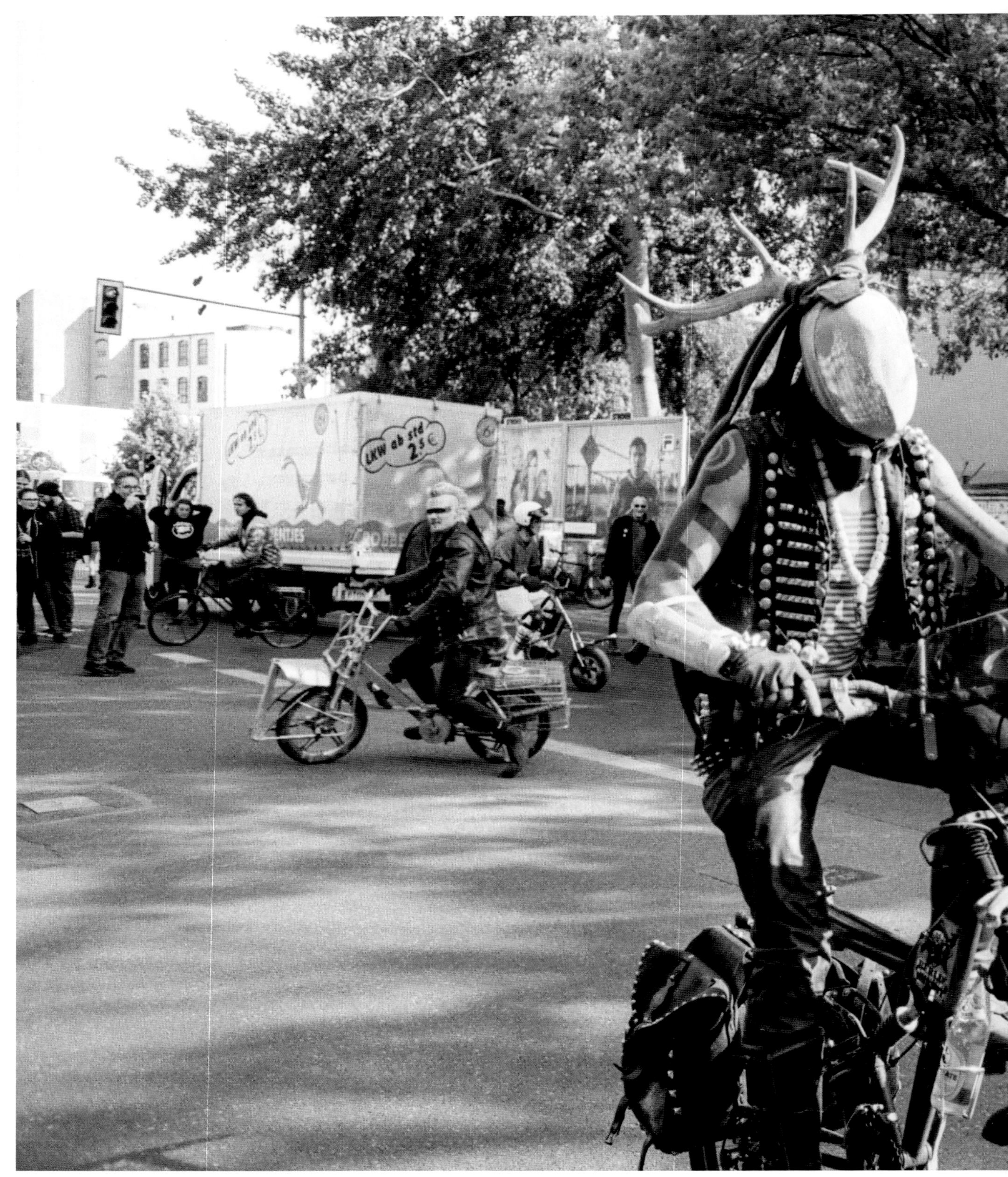
LKW ab std 2,5 €

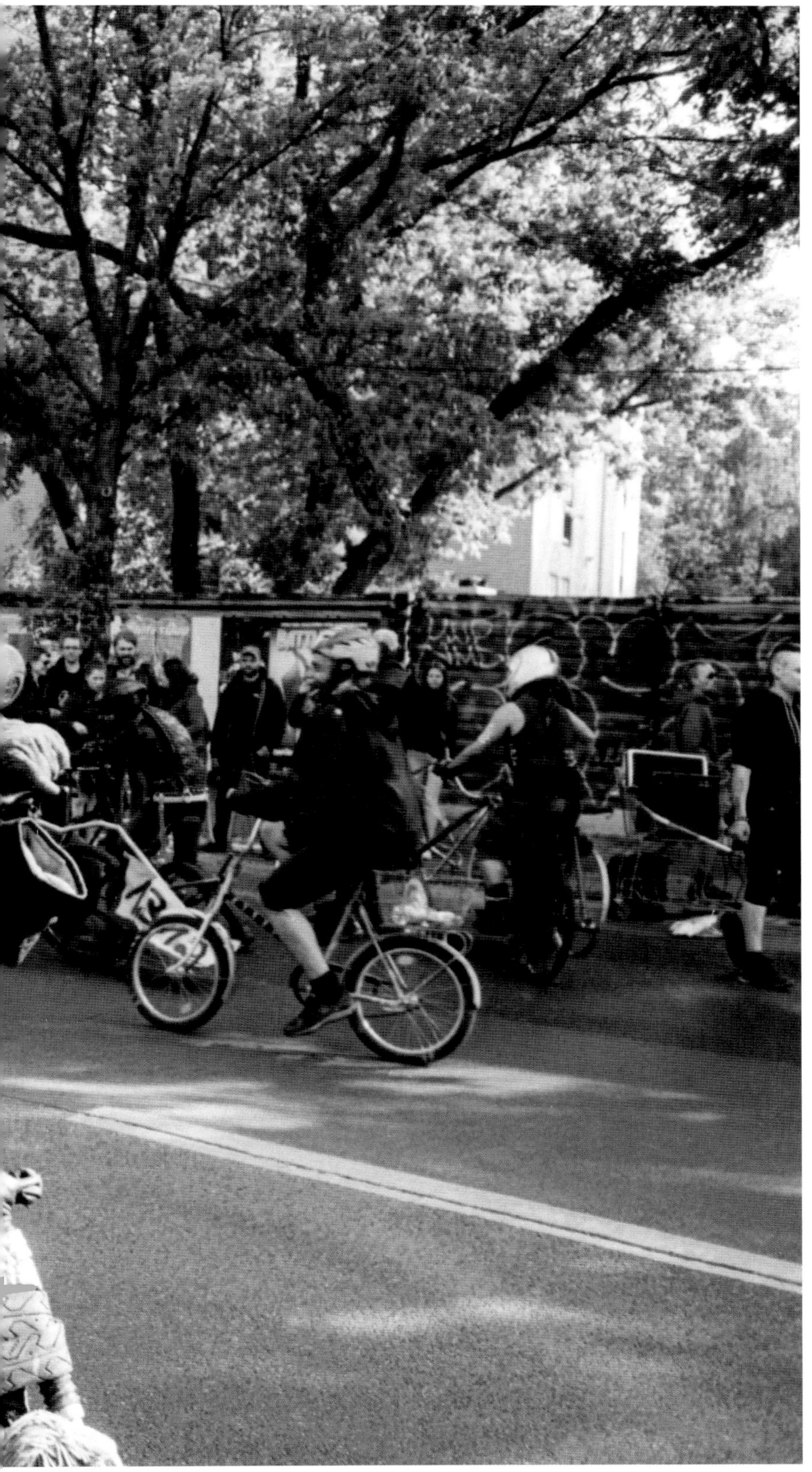

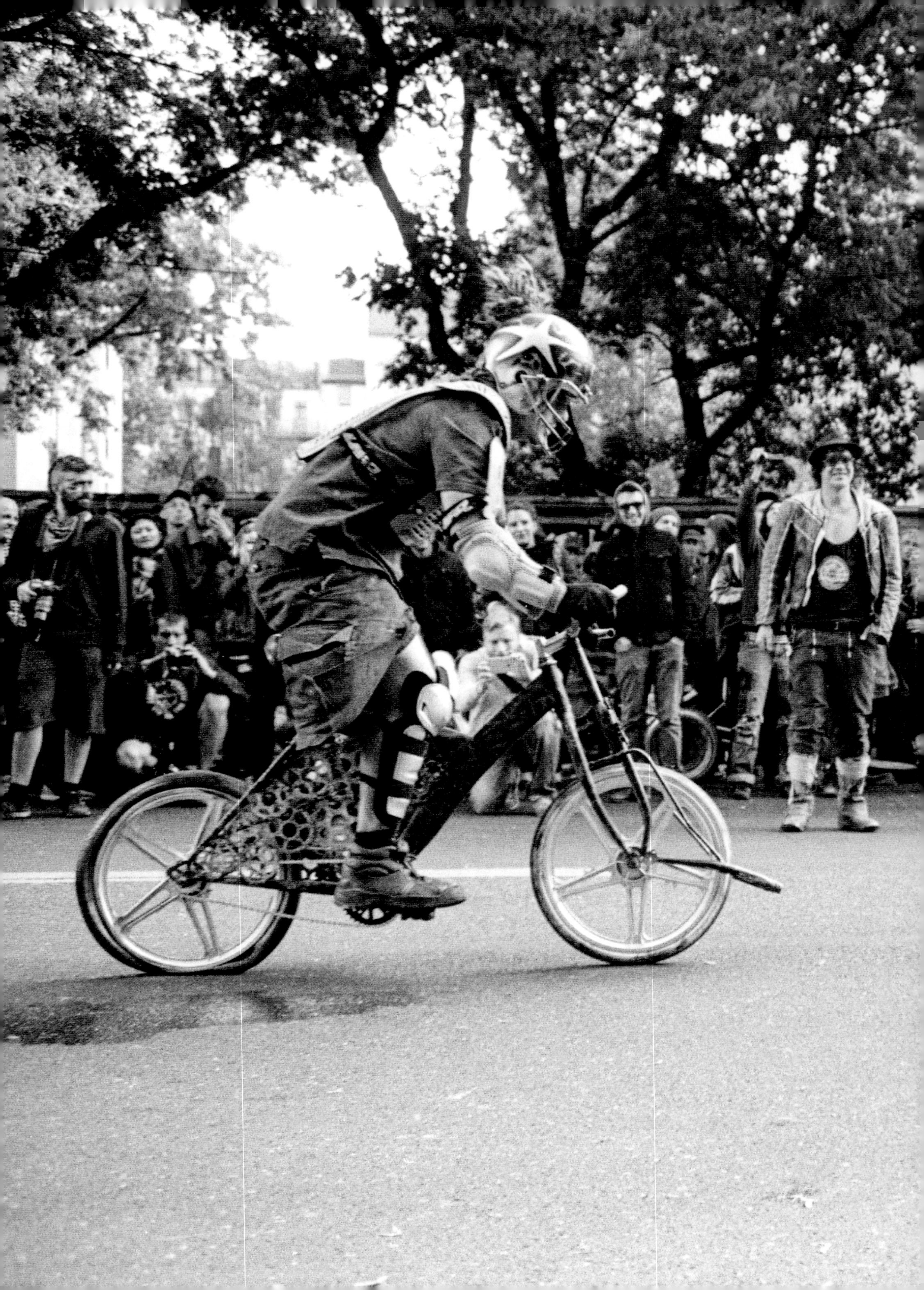

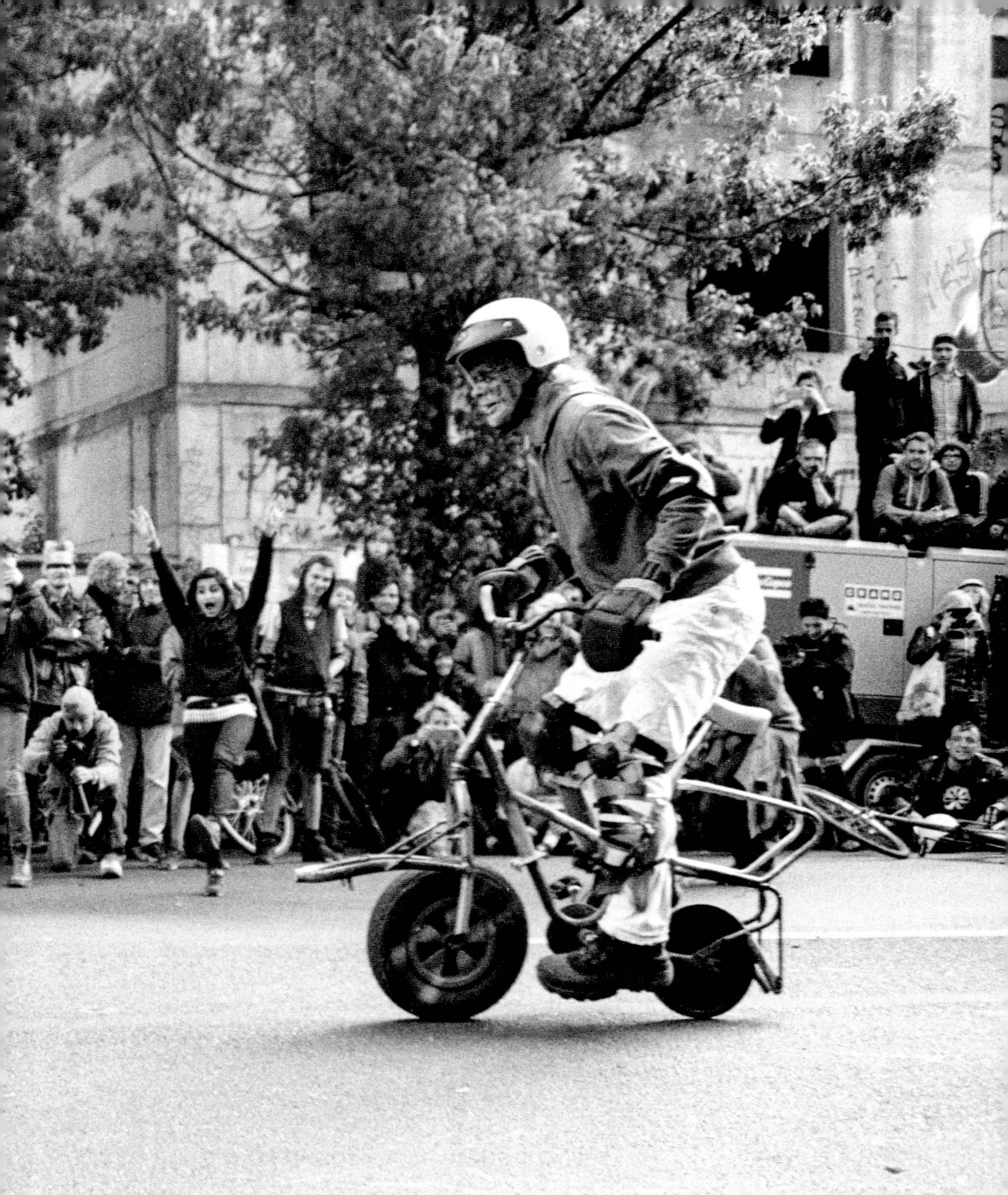

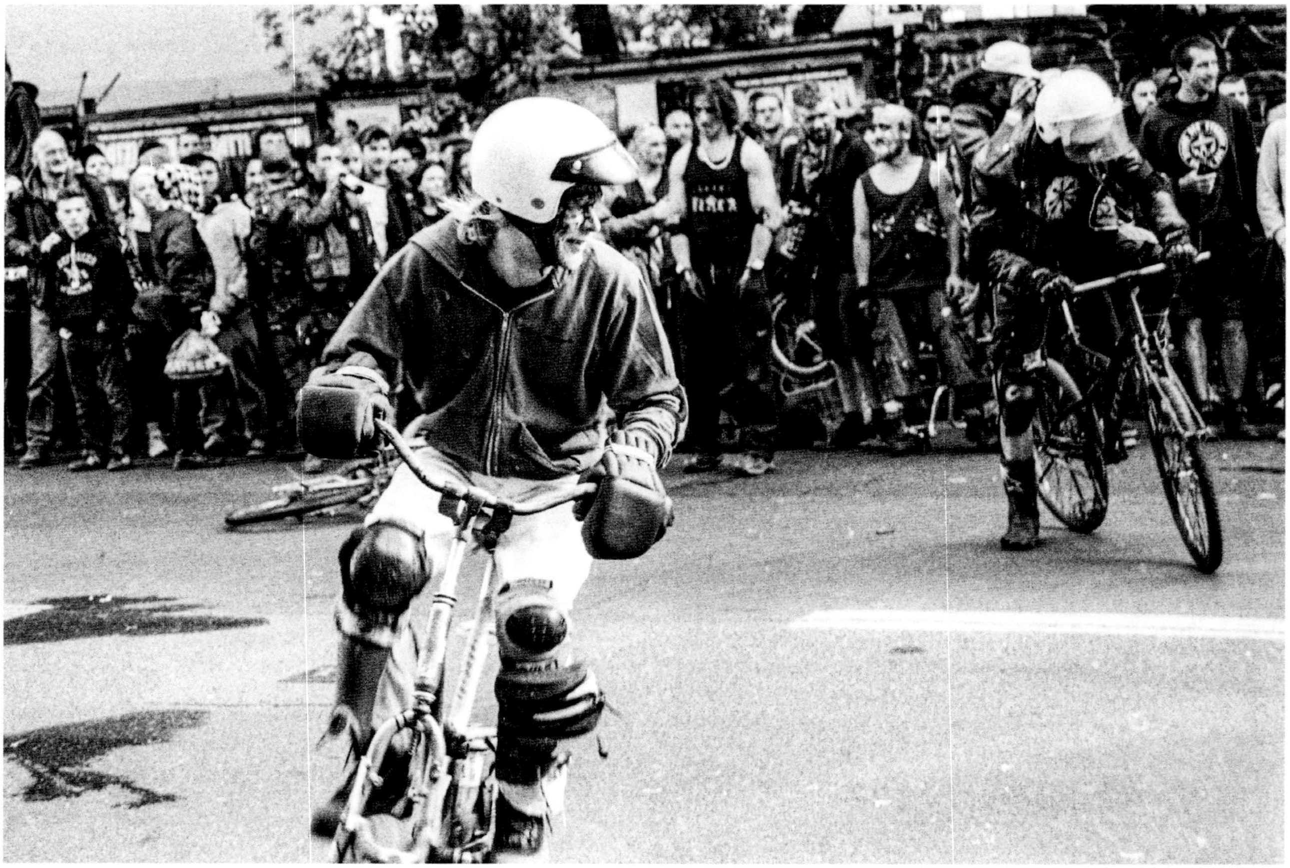

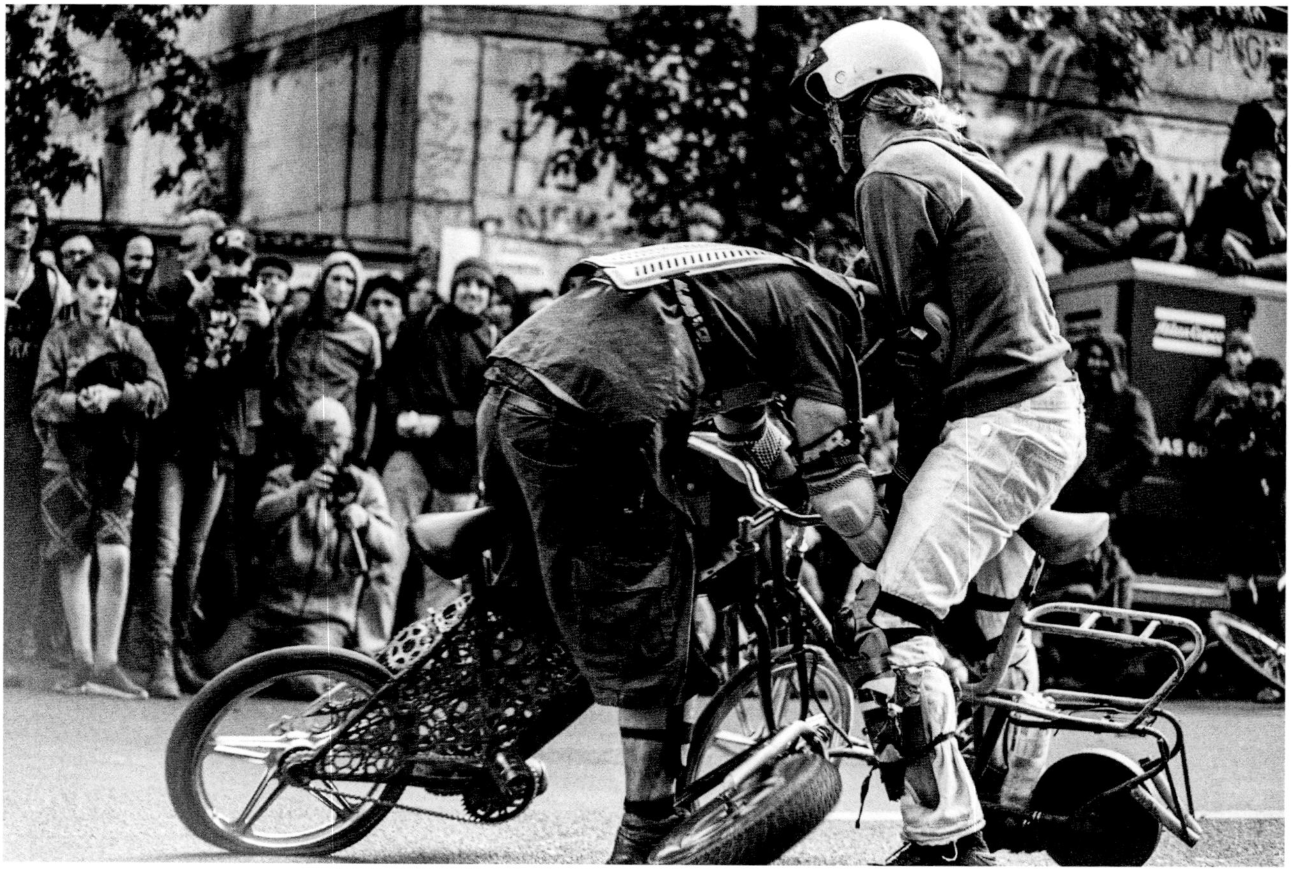

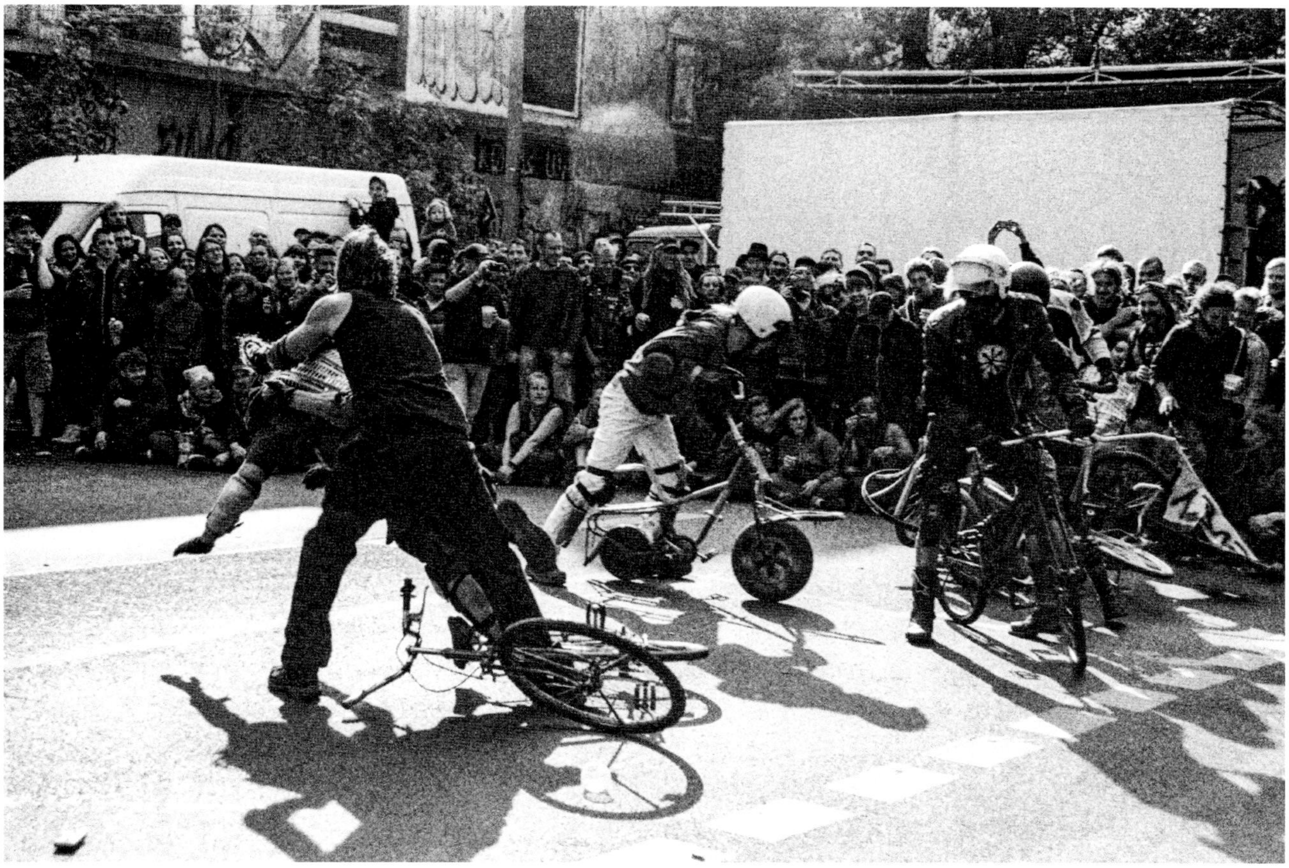

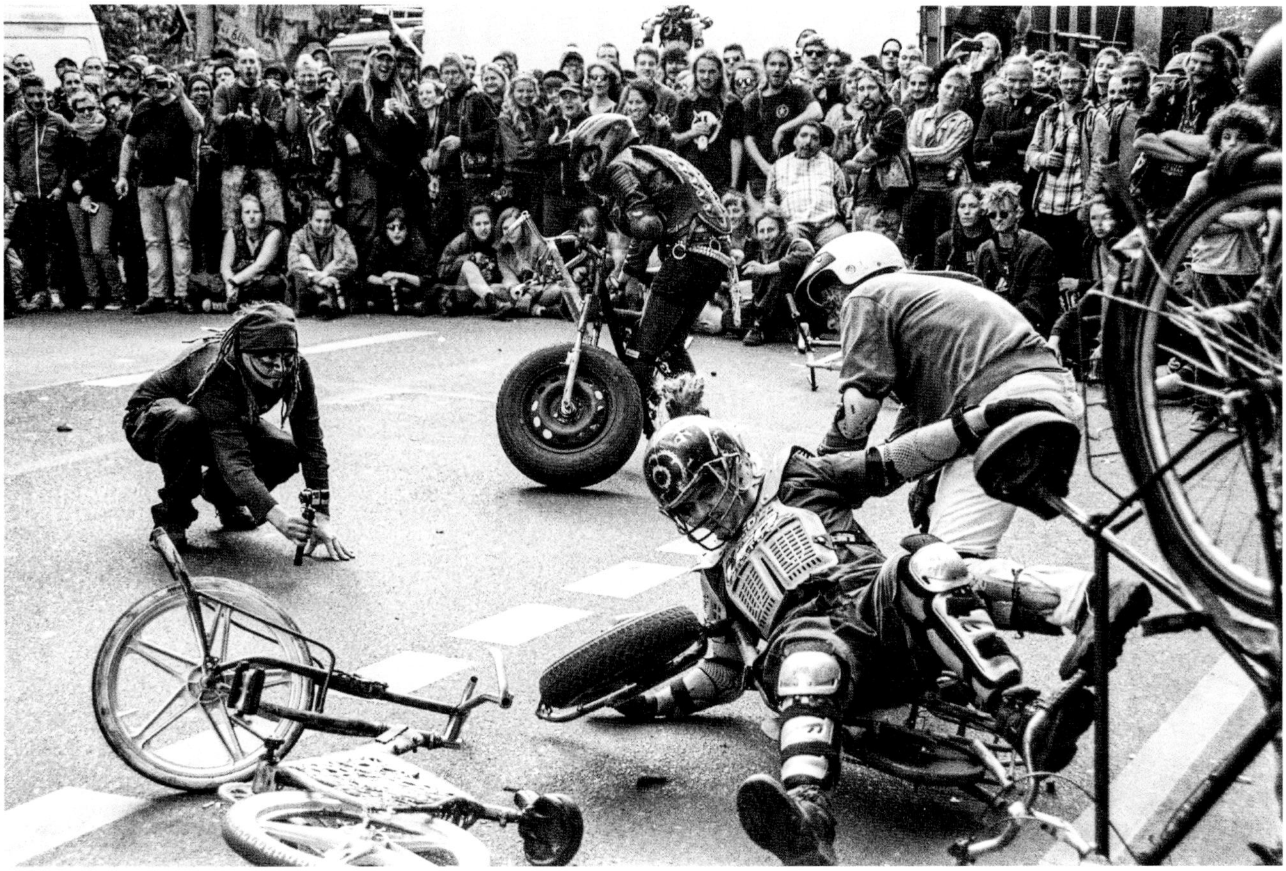

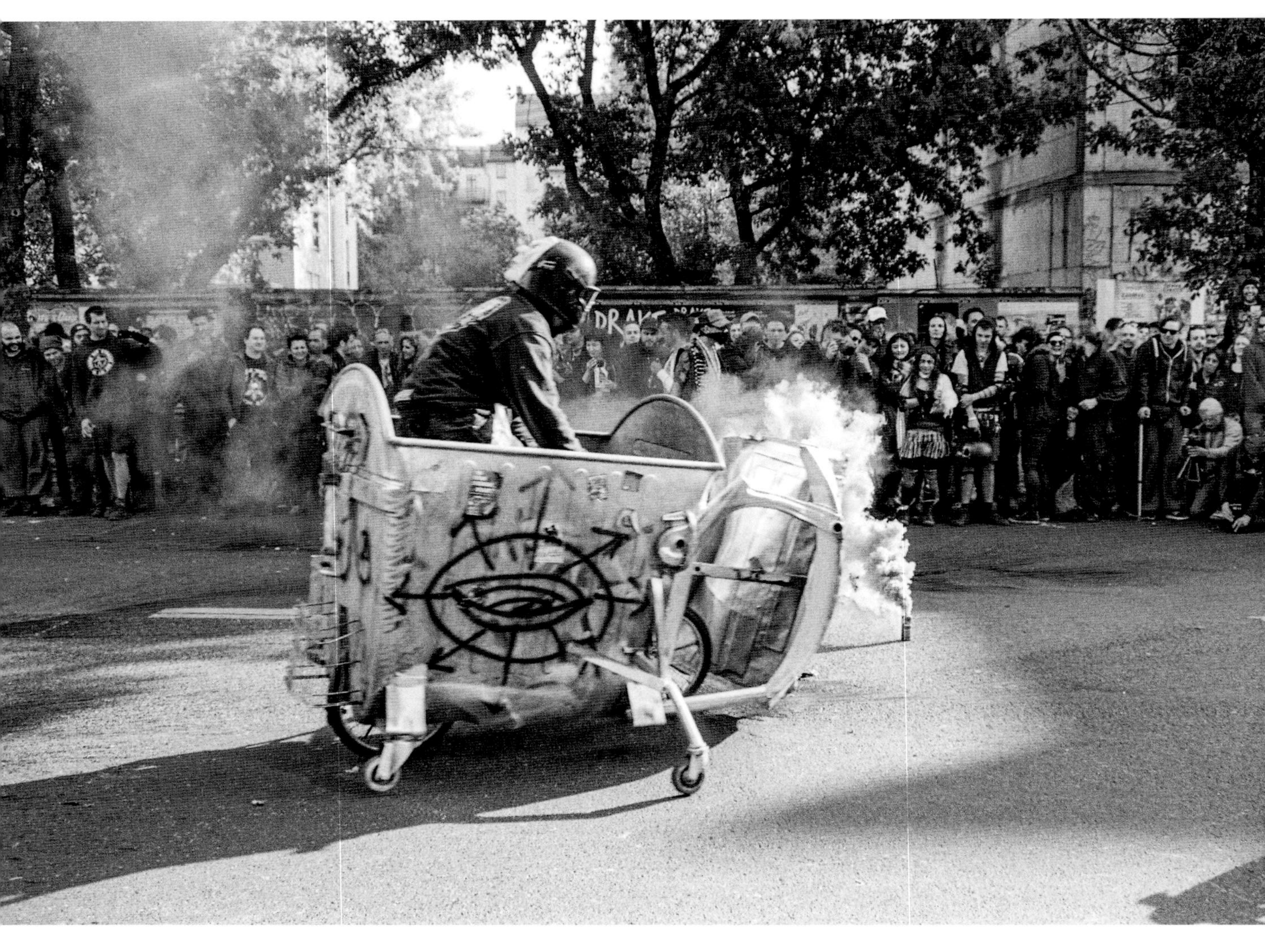

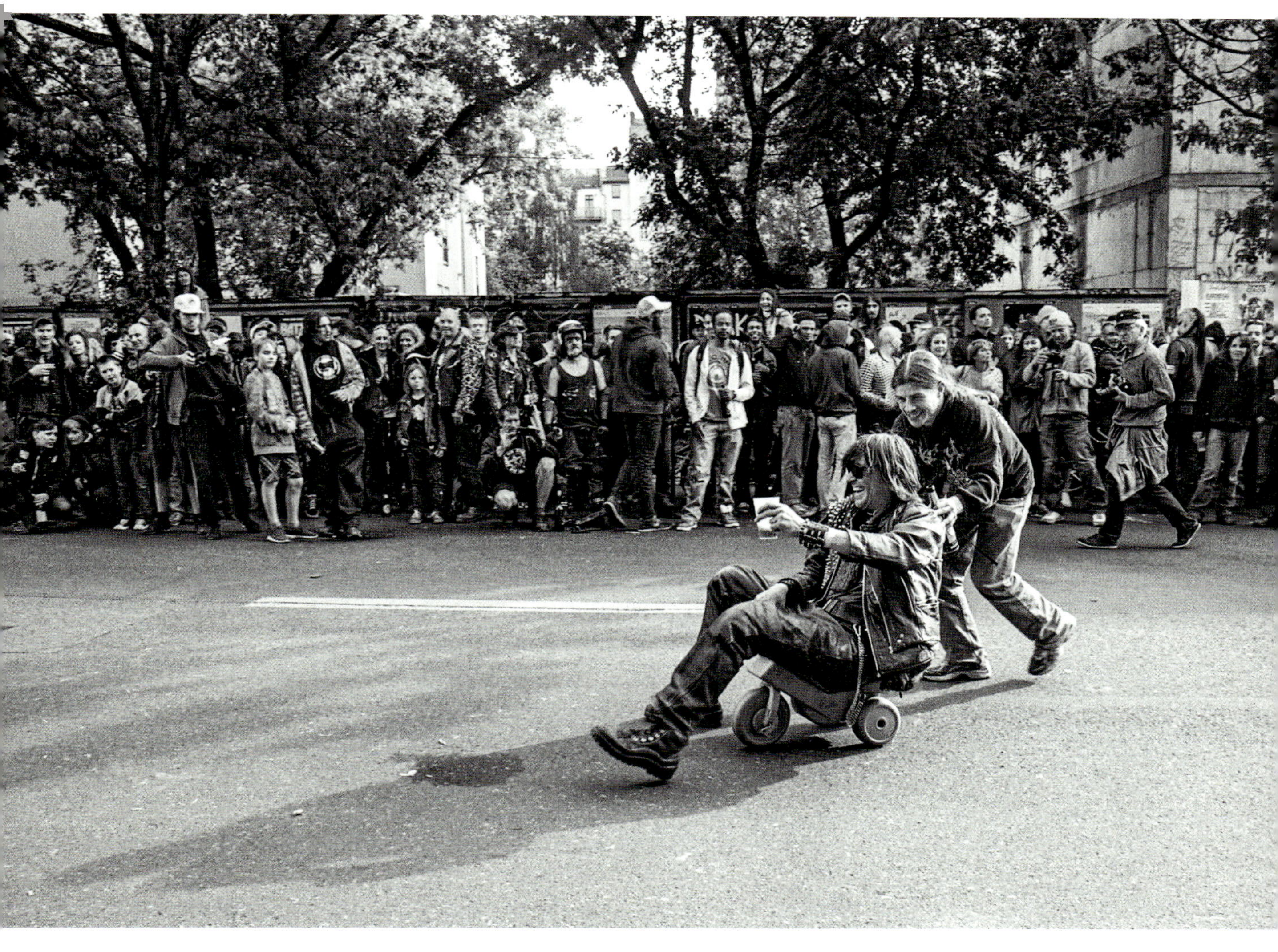

"Come—build—destroy. The idea is that you build something really beautiful with a lot of love and effort, but then you're not afraid to lose it. It's kind of a Buddhist attitude. Apart from that, of course, it should look spectacular!"

Sev

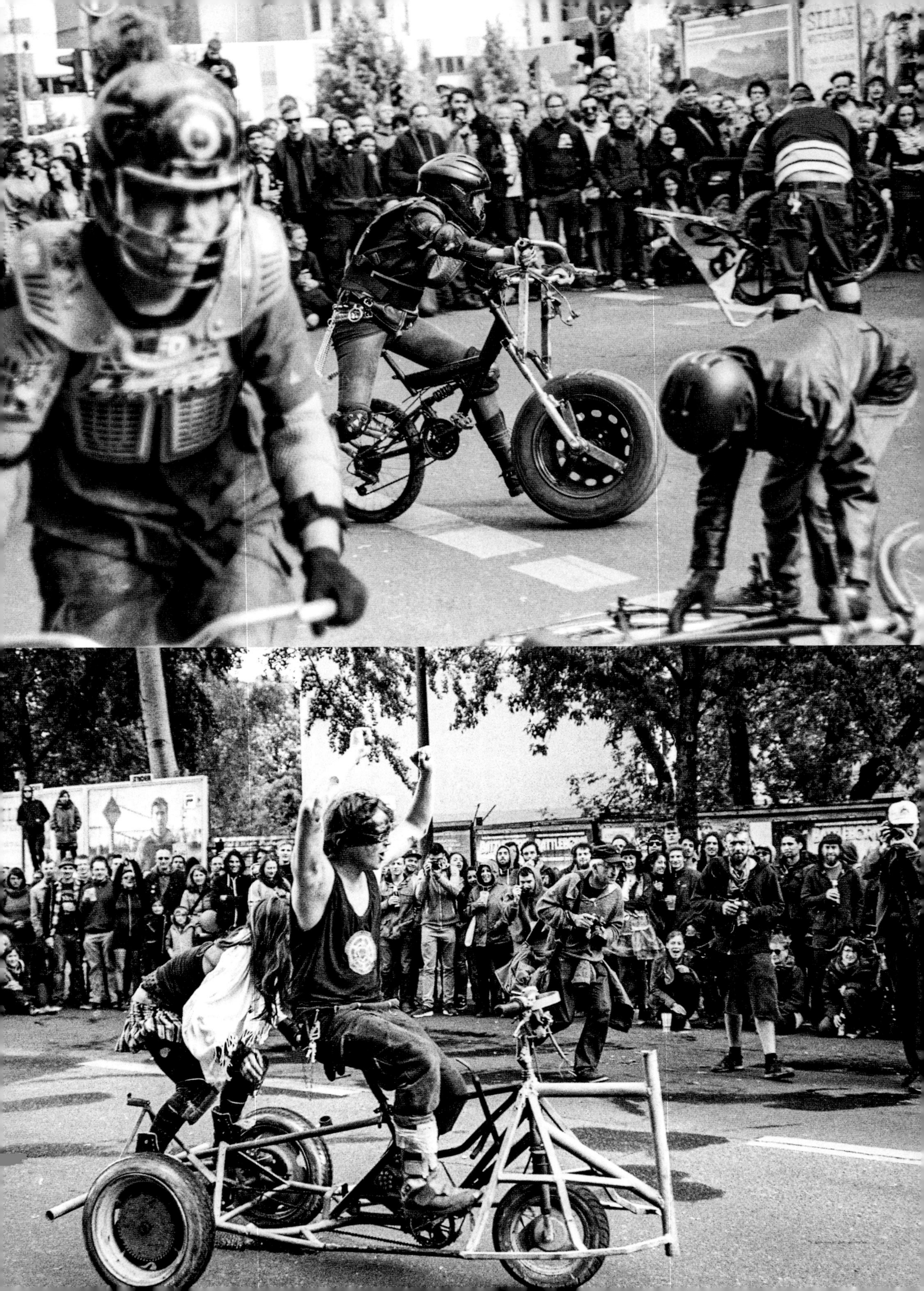

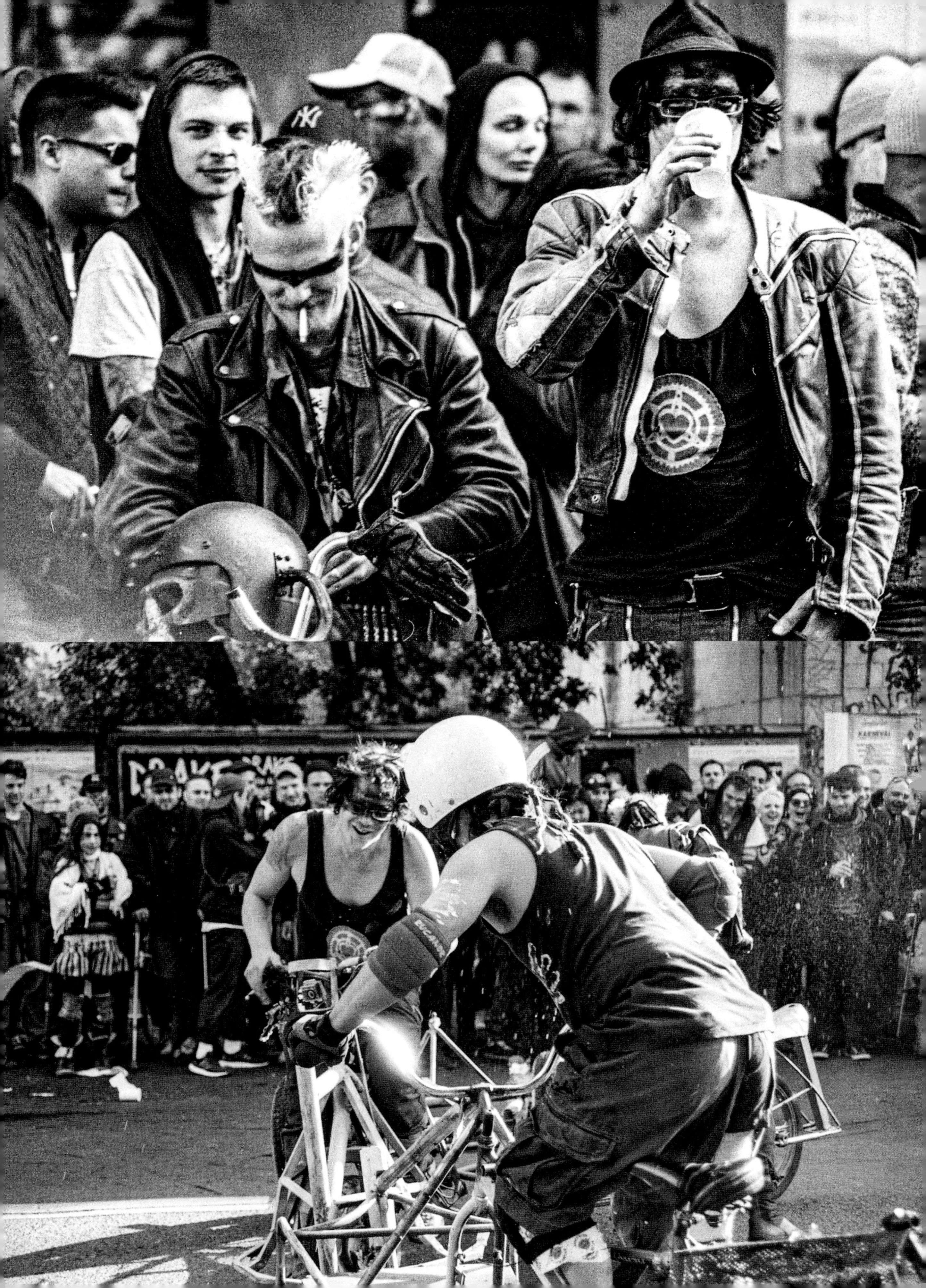

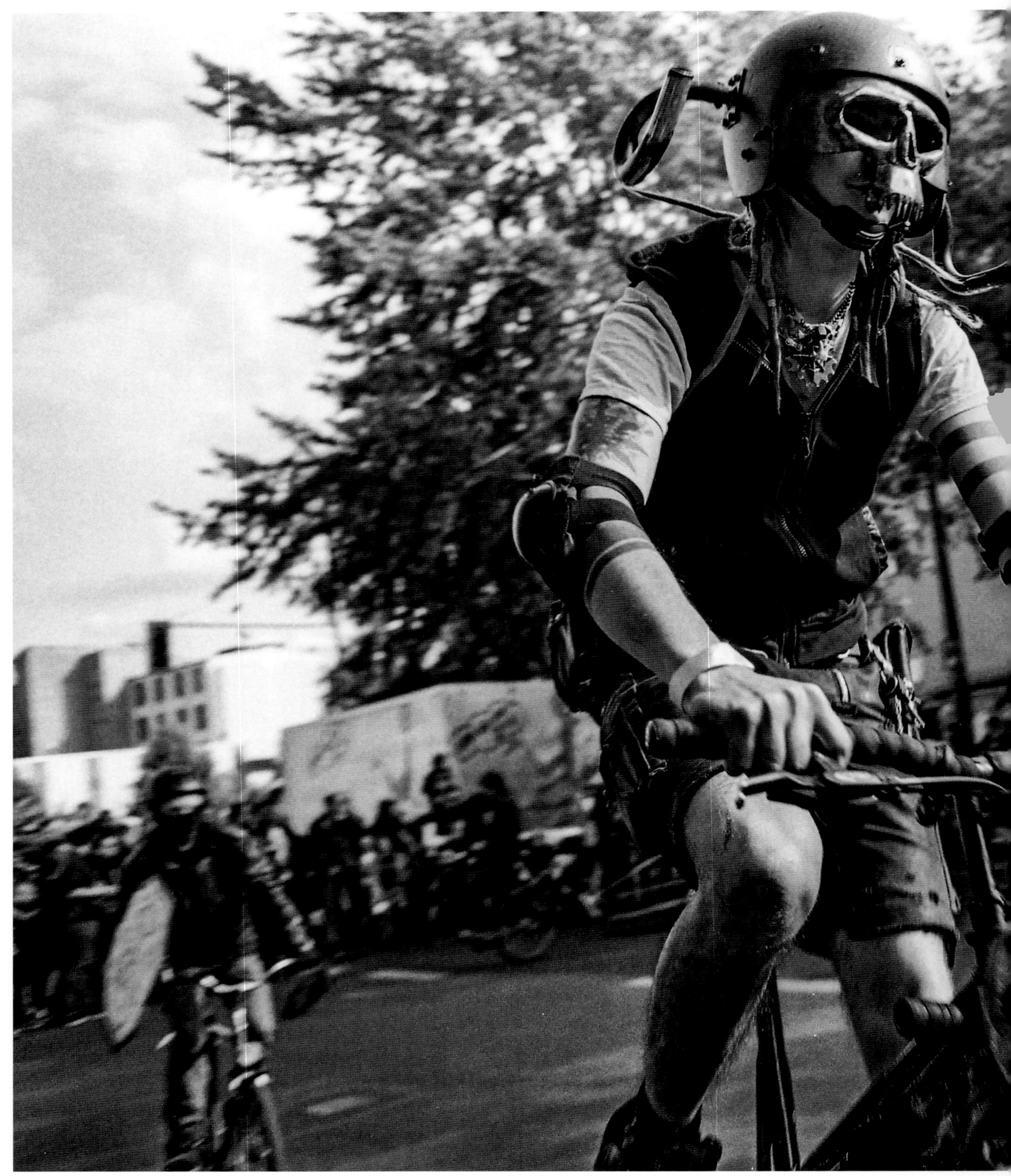

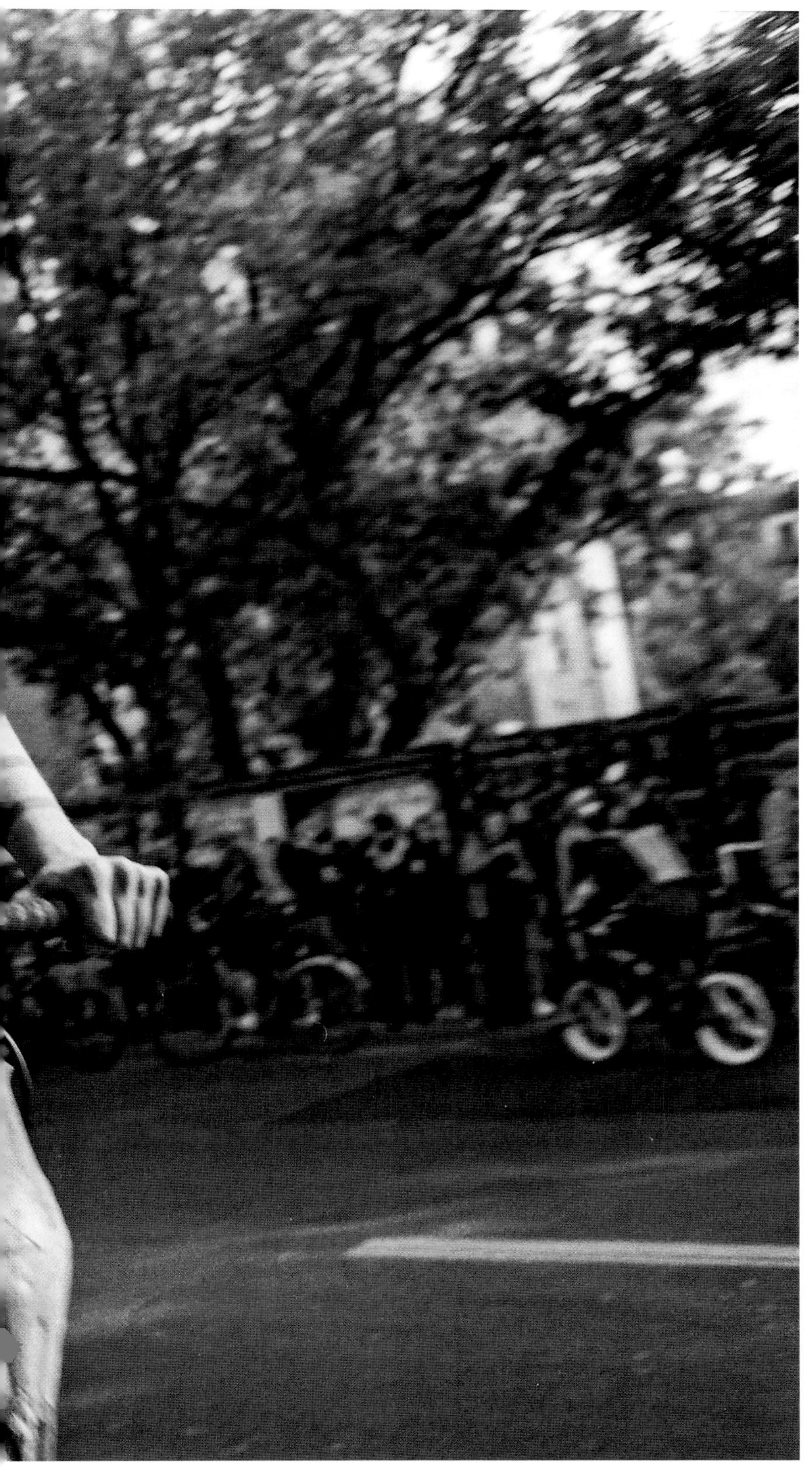

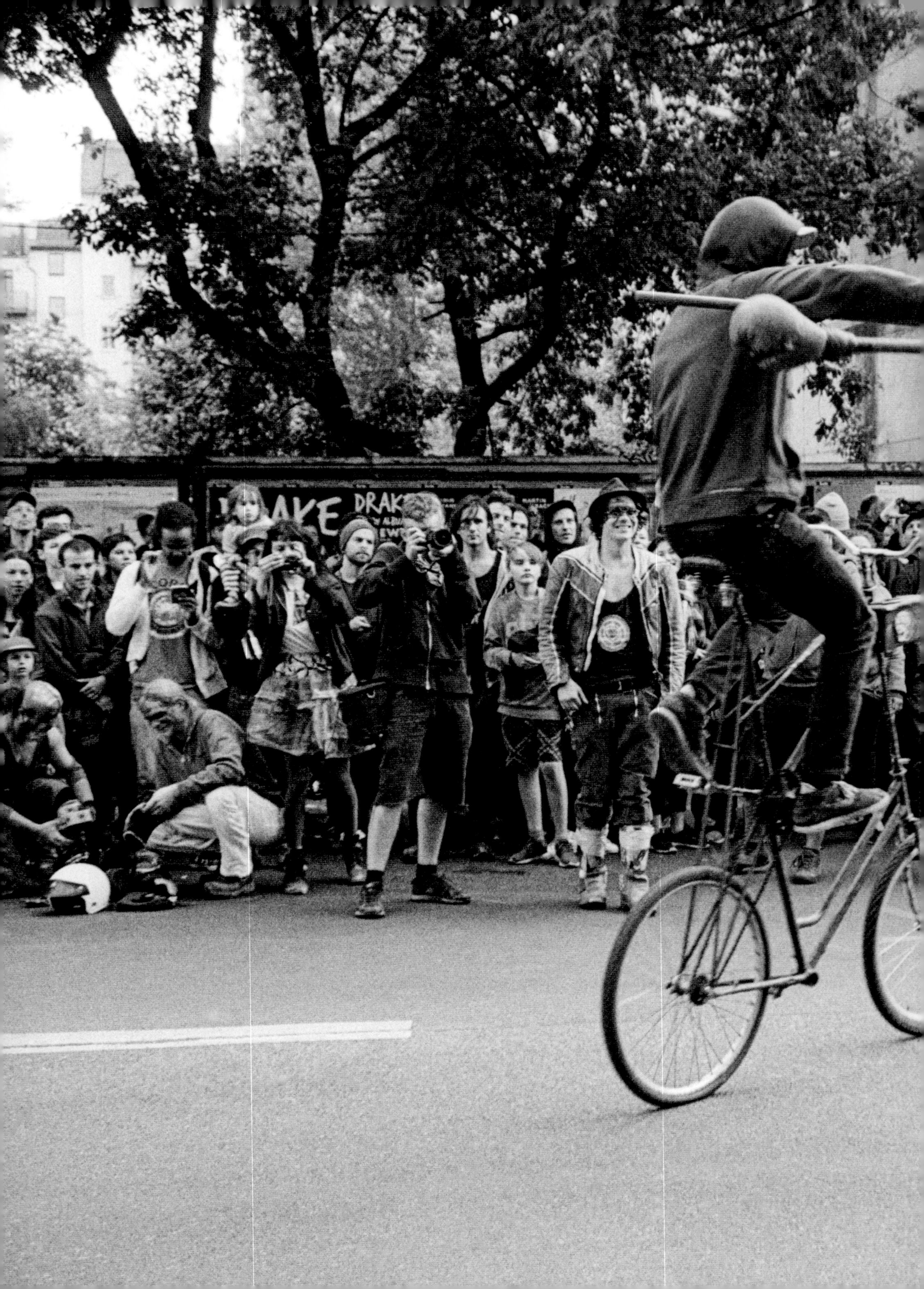

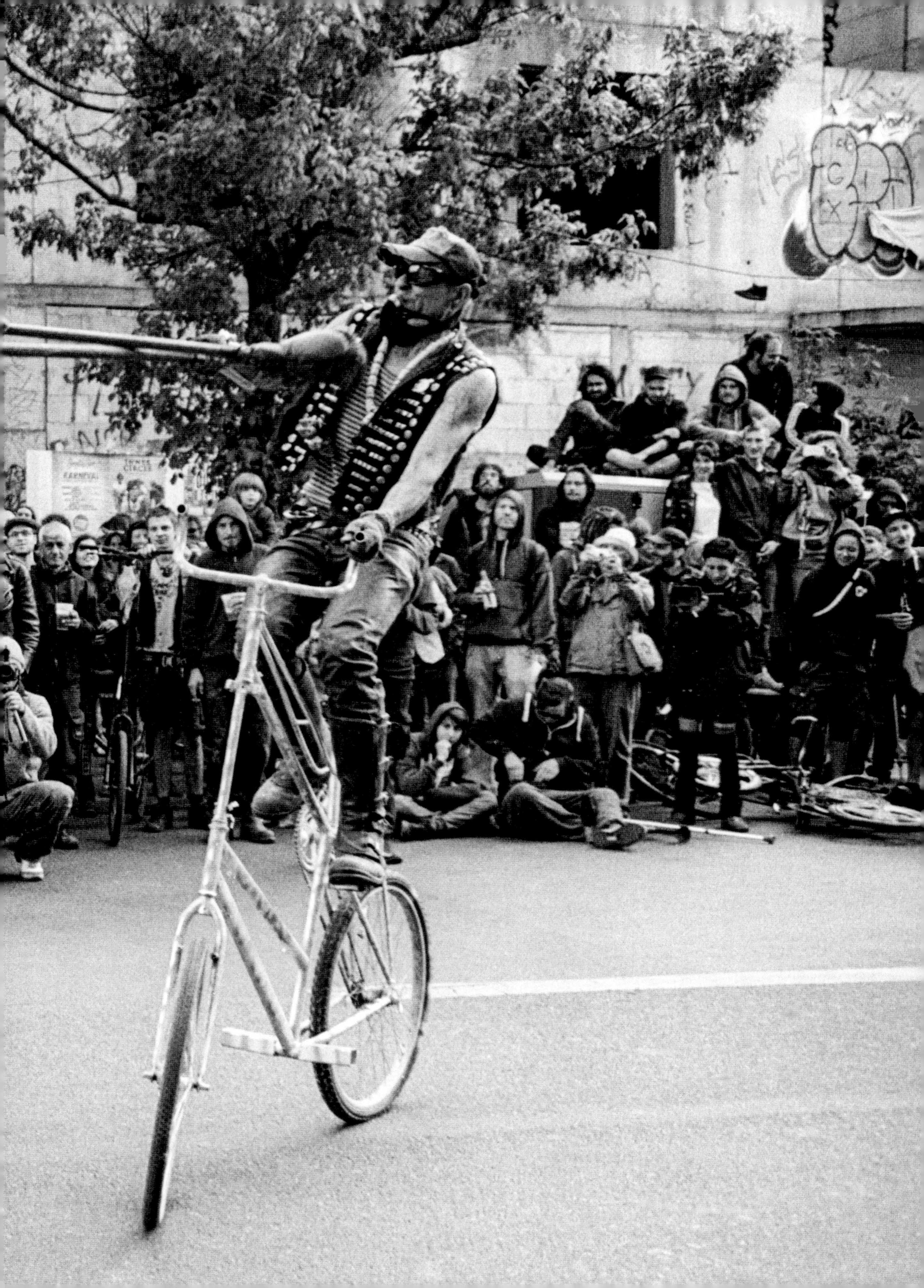
KARNEVAL

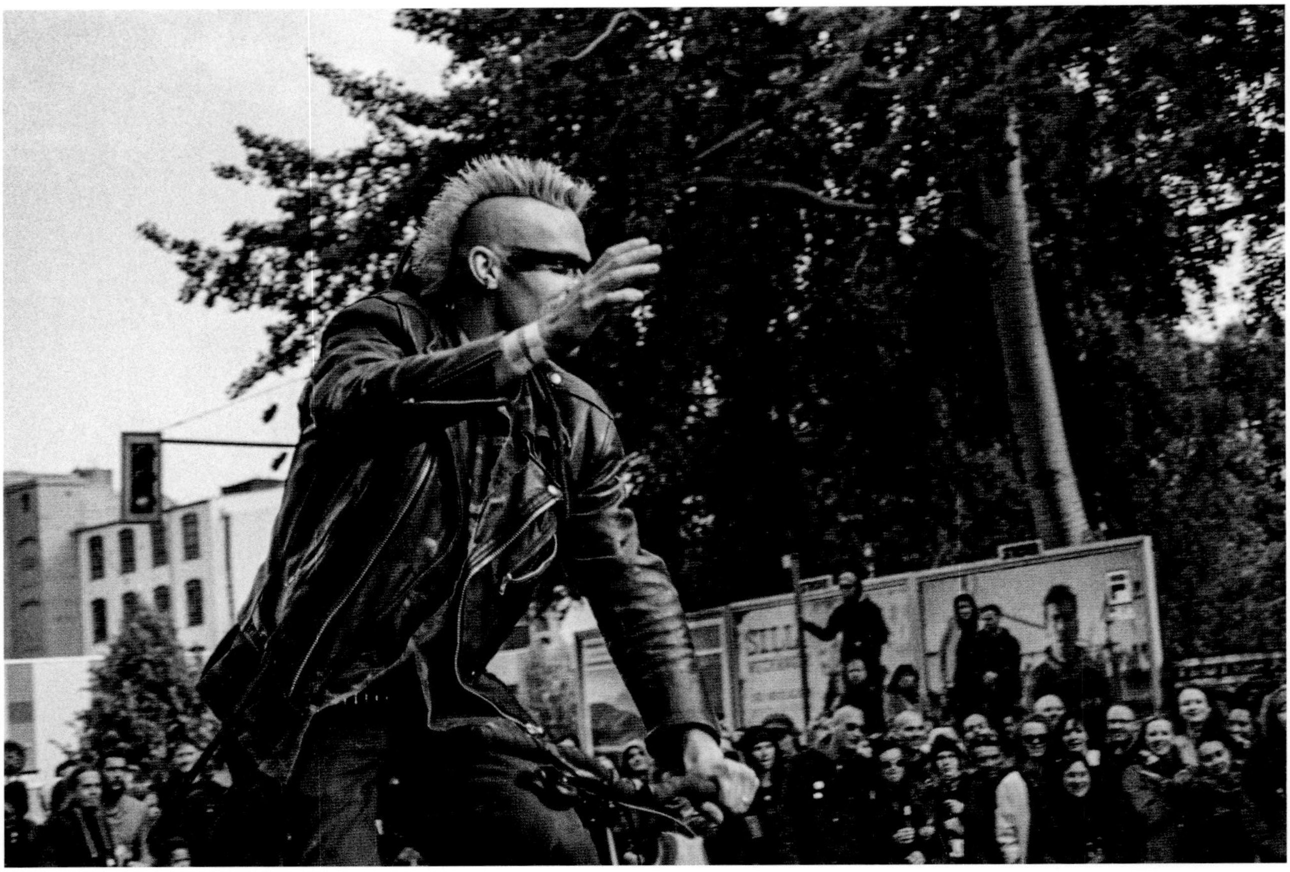

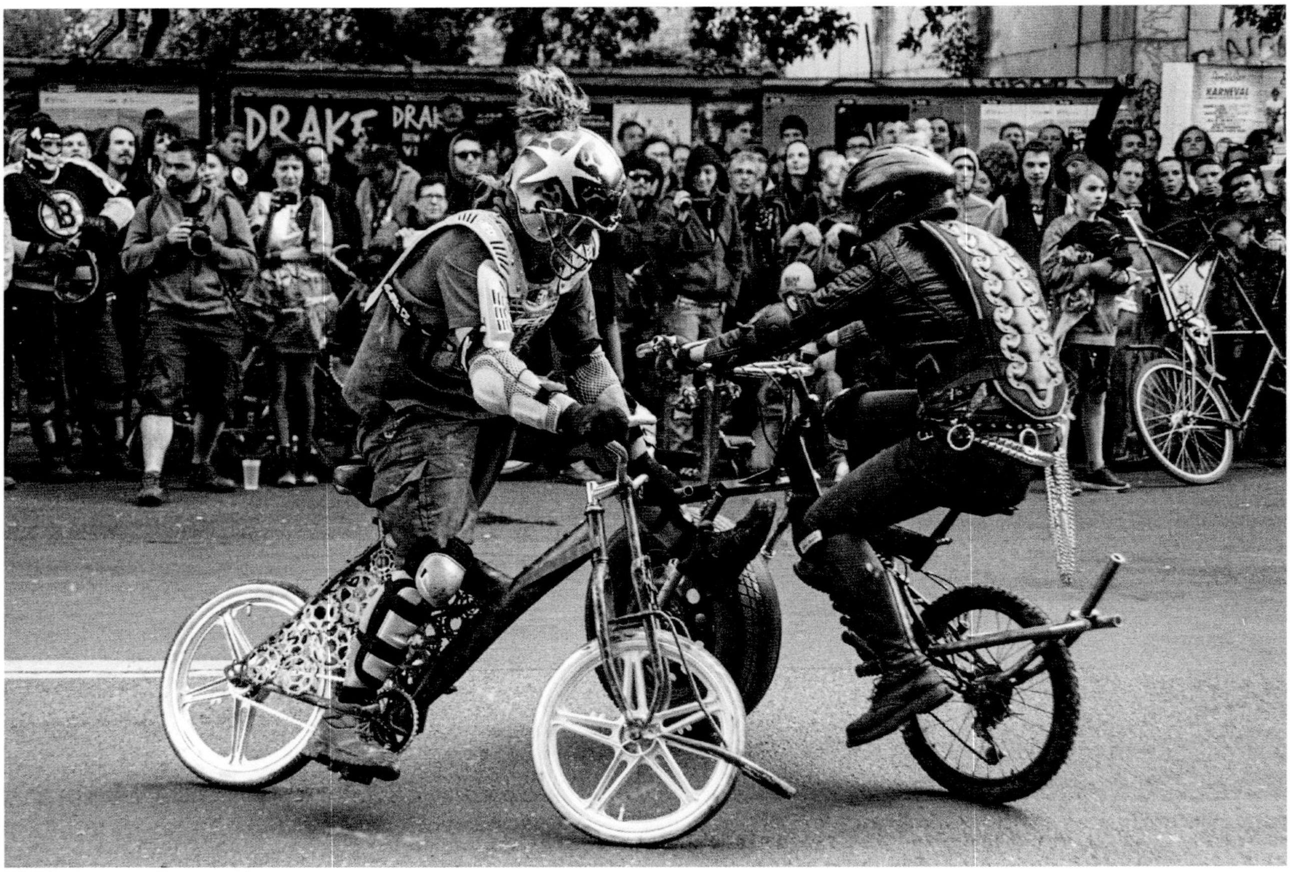

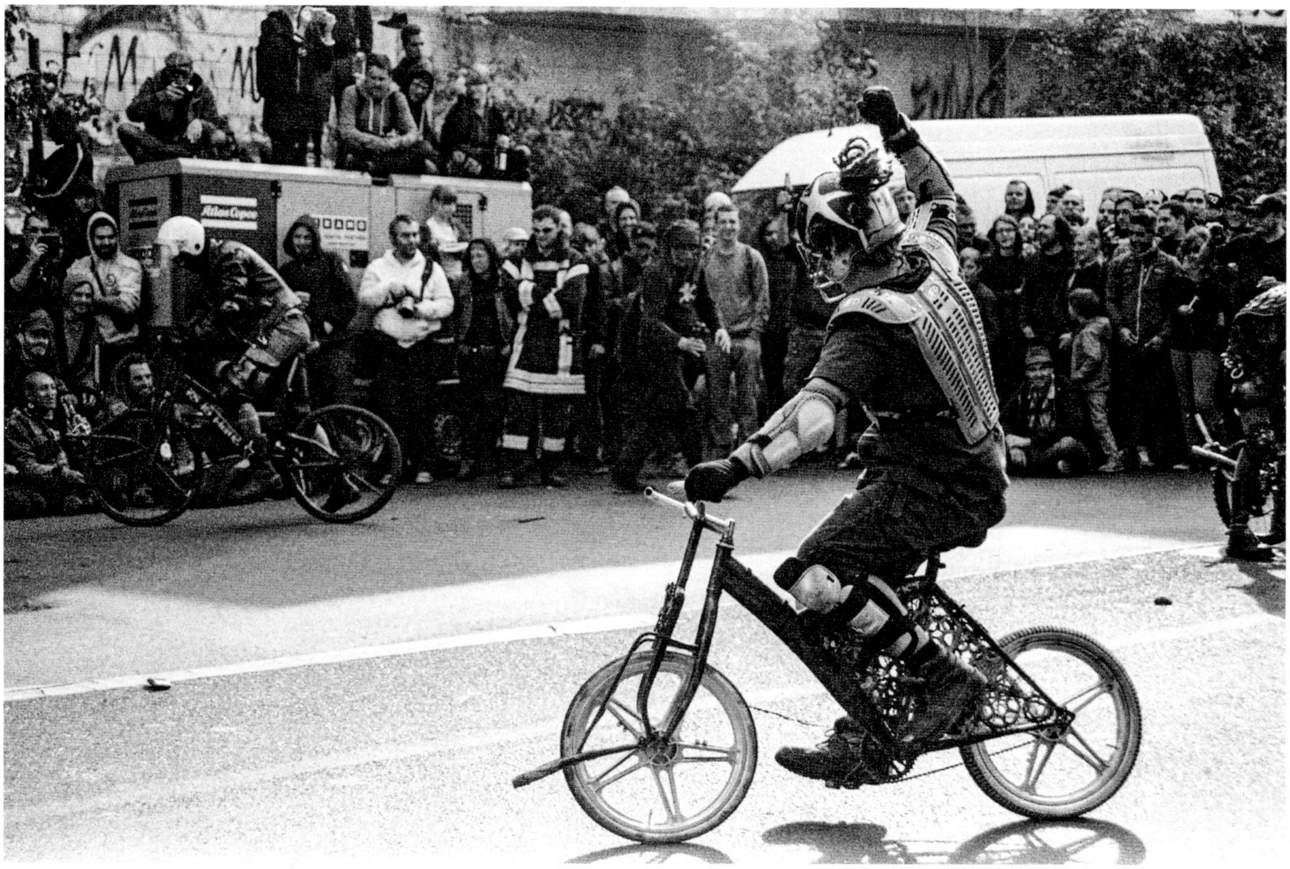

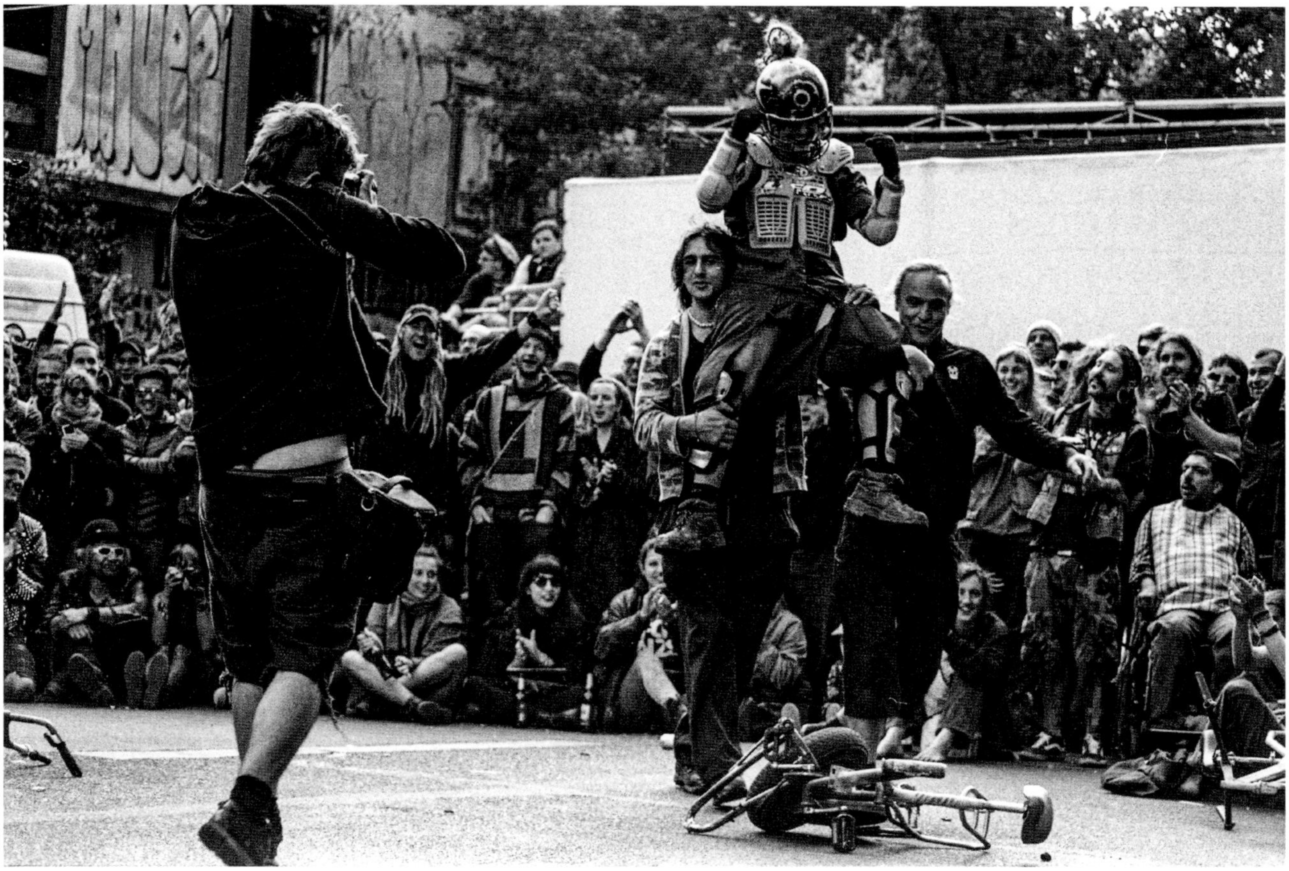

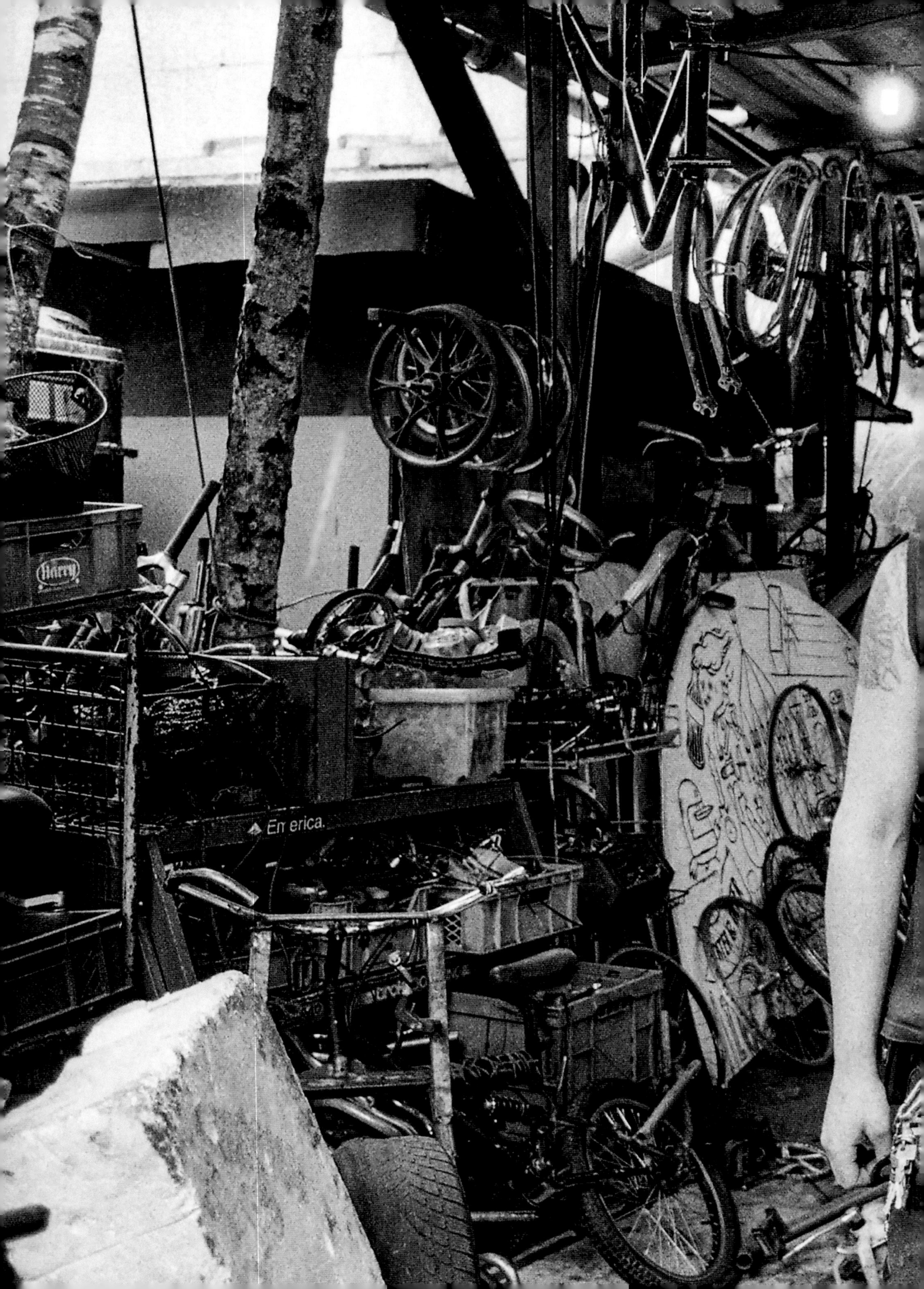
Harry
Em erica.

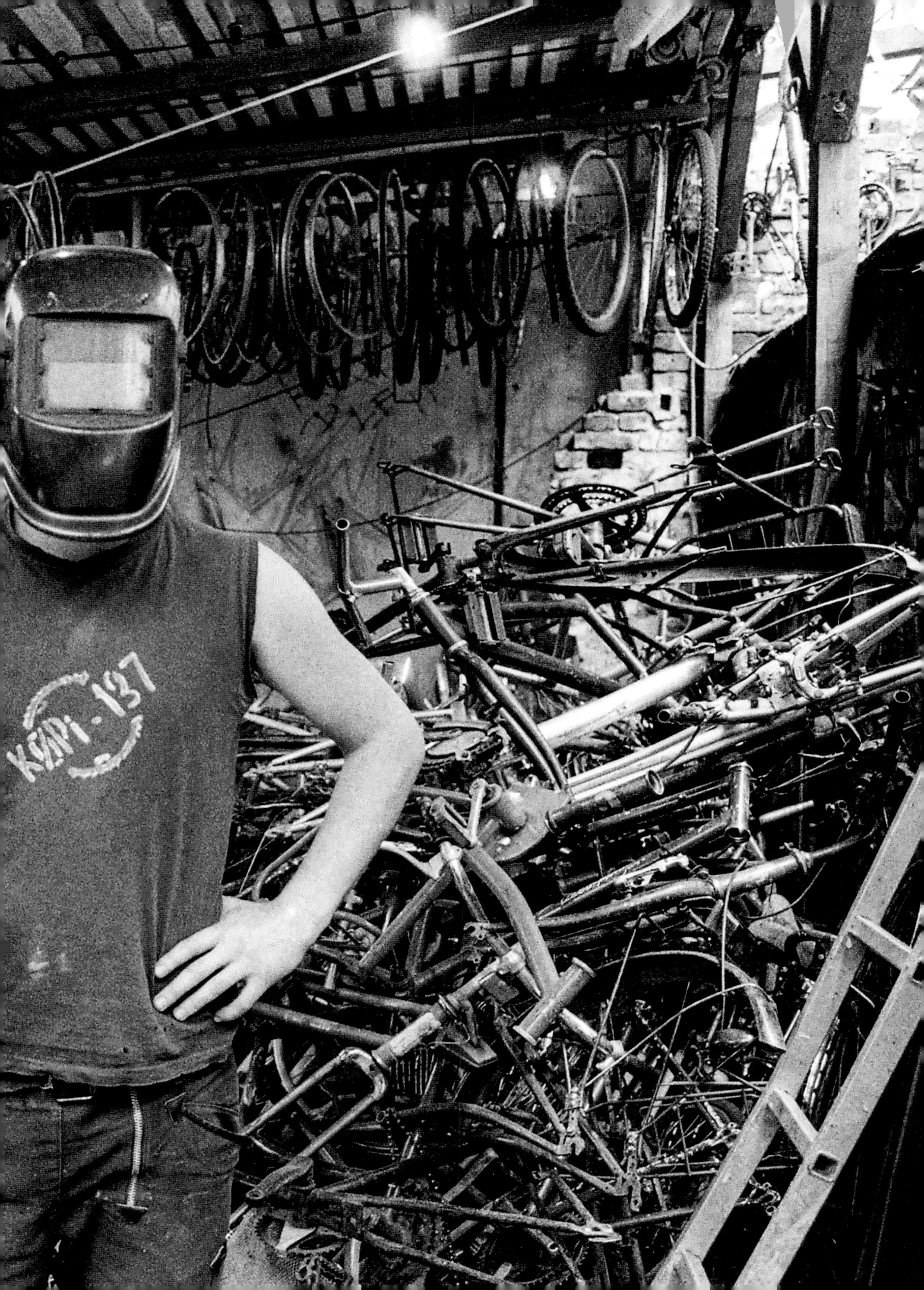
KöPi - 137

Easy Rider Road Show

The mobile exhibition

Photos
Philipp von Recklinghausen
Tod Seelie

The Easy Rider Road Show is an exhibition about bicycles on bicycles. It consists of five converted cargo bicycles displaying the photographic narratives which are presented in this book. As the Easy Rider Road Show moves through the city in a convoy, large-format photos can be seen on both sides of each bike. As soon as the Road Show has reached its location and the cargo bikes have formed a wagon, a castle, or spread out on the grounds, another four photos become visible on each cargo bike.

Unfolded like the solar sails of a spaceship, they project out into a photo exhibition in the middle of the urban space. All of the photographic projects shown have in common the intention of depicting communities in whose lifeworld the bicycle is essential. The architecture of the exhibition itself is mounted upon the bicycle, clearly illustrating that the bicycle is more than just an ideal means of urban transportation. This mobile exhibition demonstrates that the bicycle is a promise of freedom, a bringer of happiness, and a utopia unto itself.

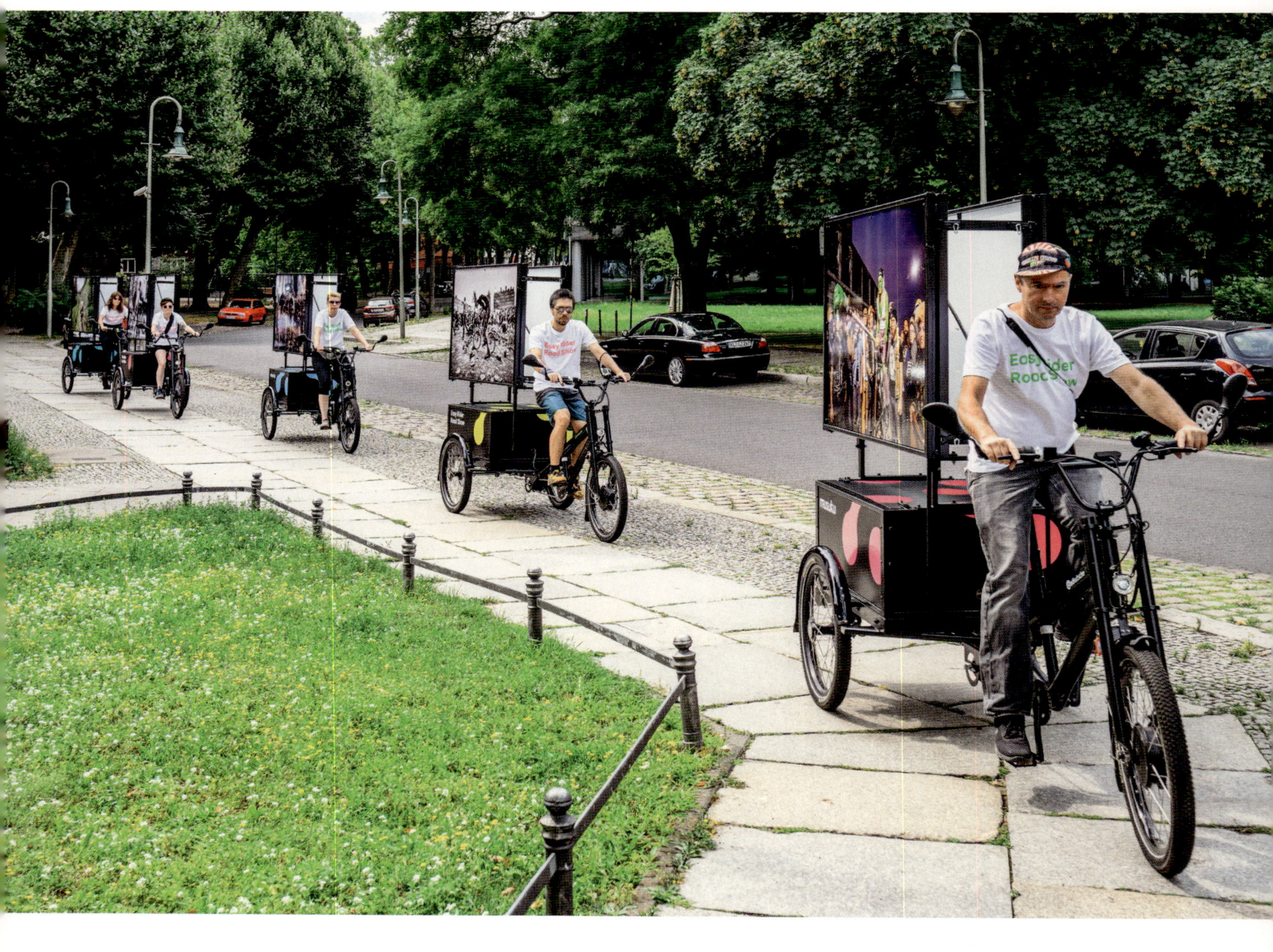

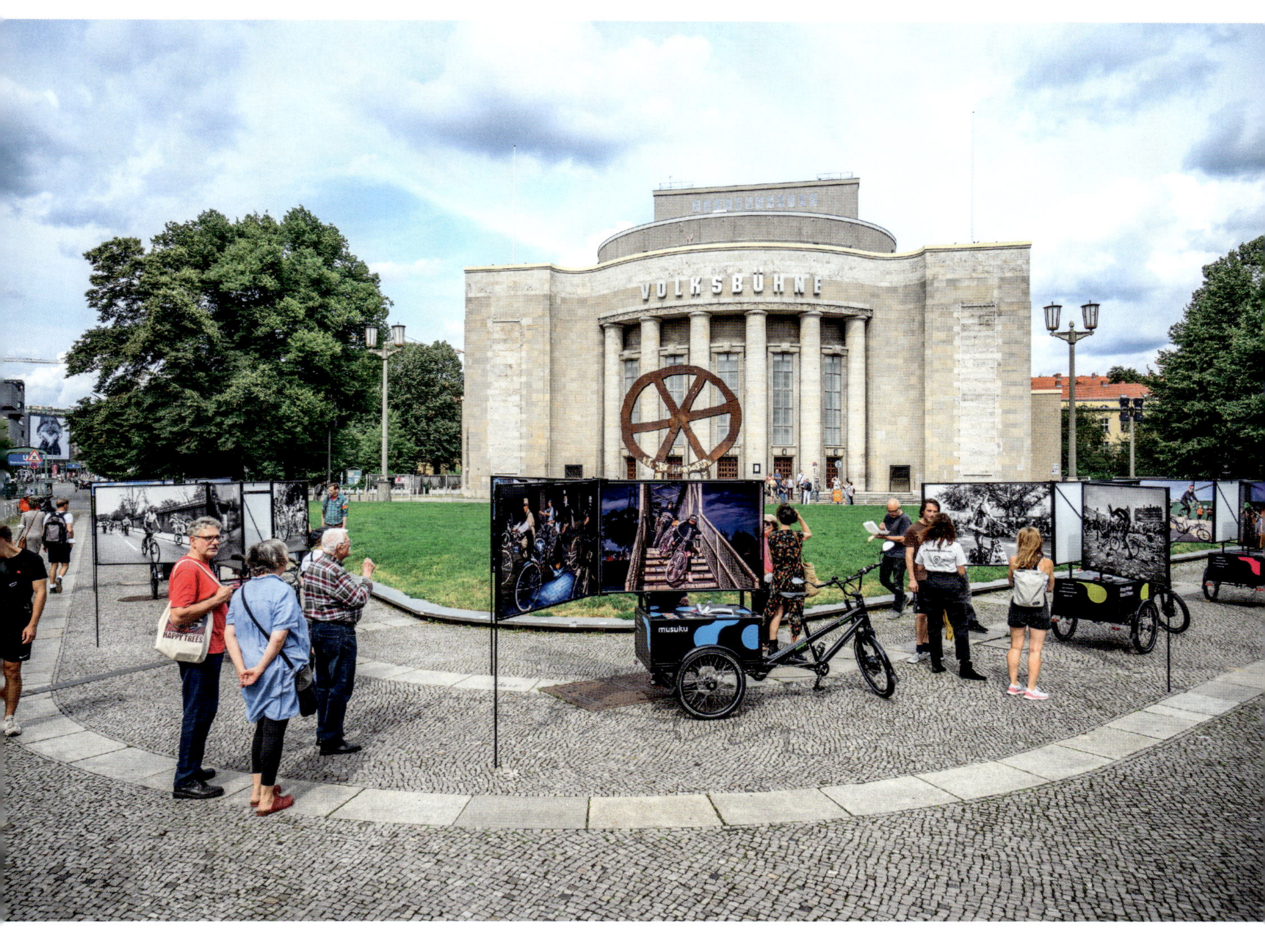
VOLKSBÜHNE
musuku
HAPPY TREES

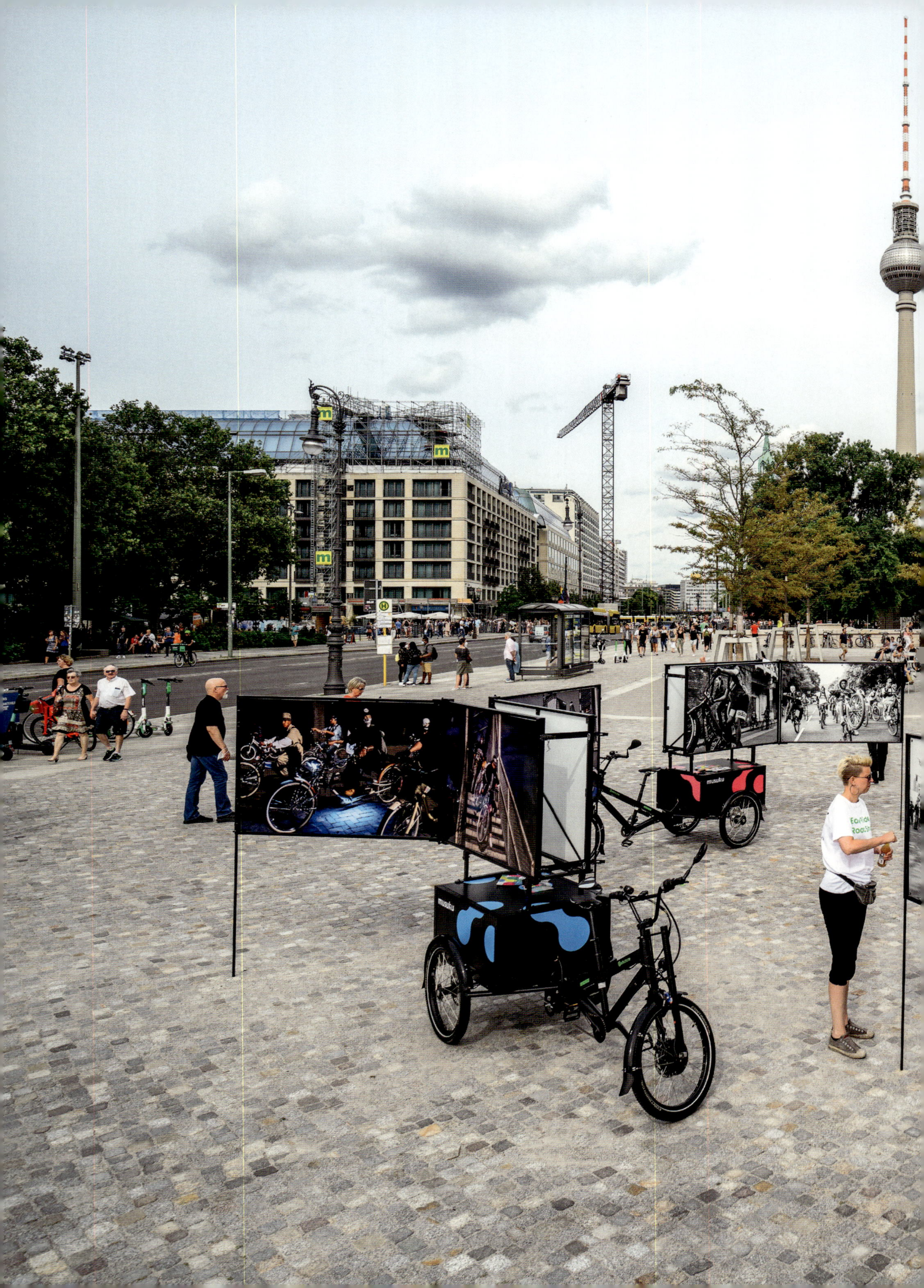

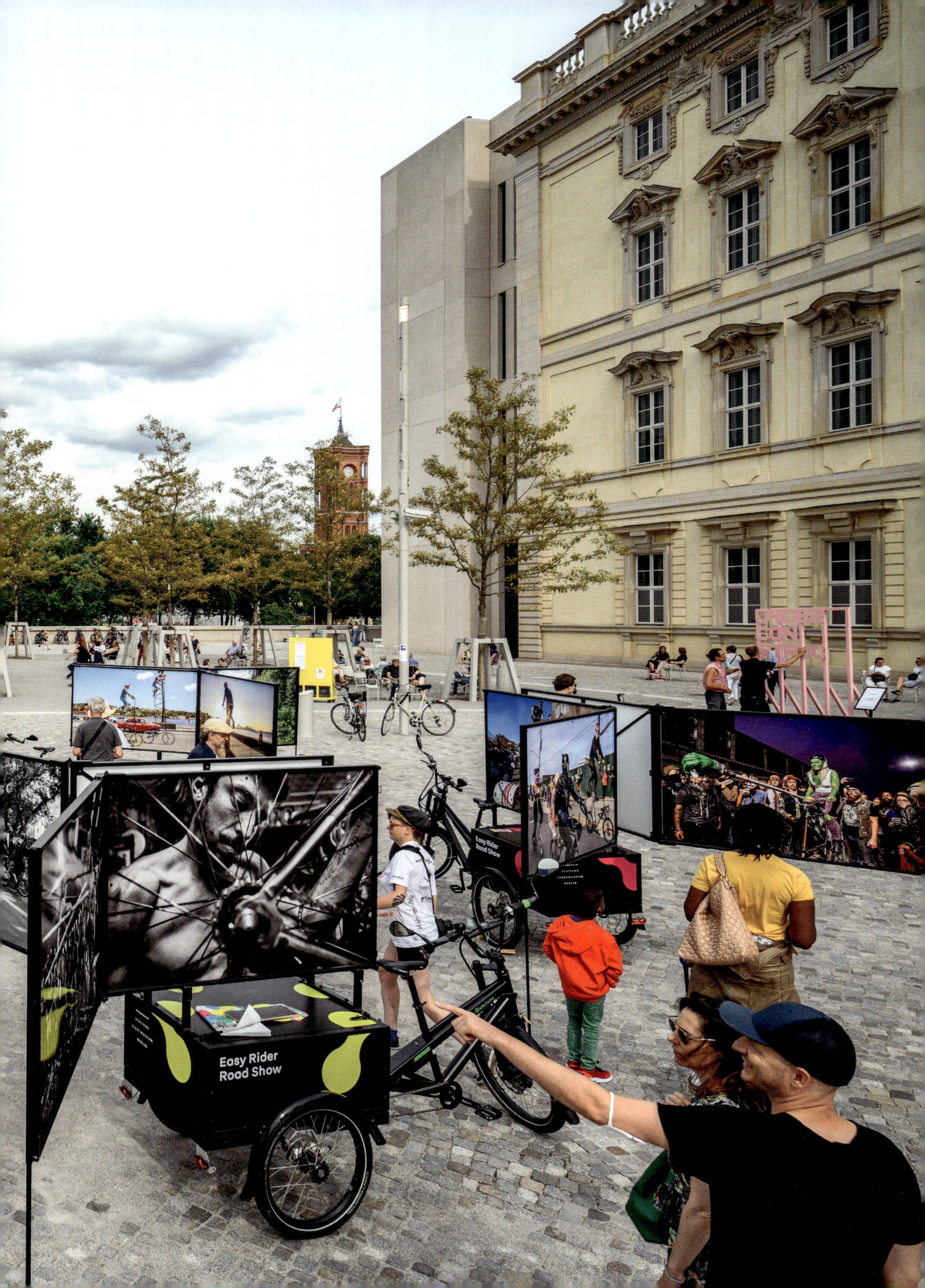
Easy Rider
Road Show

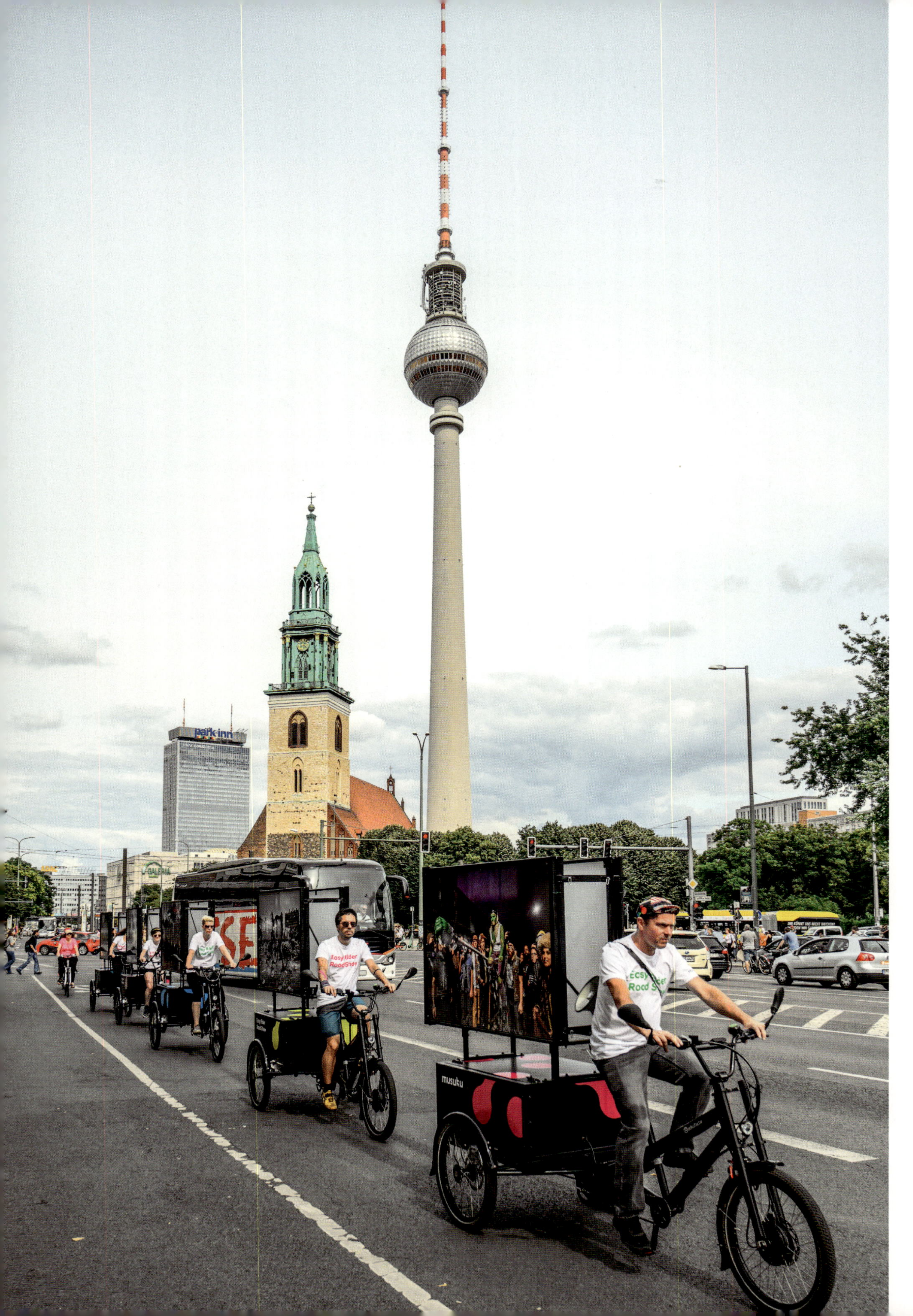
park inn
musuku

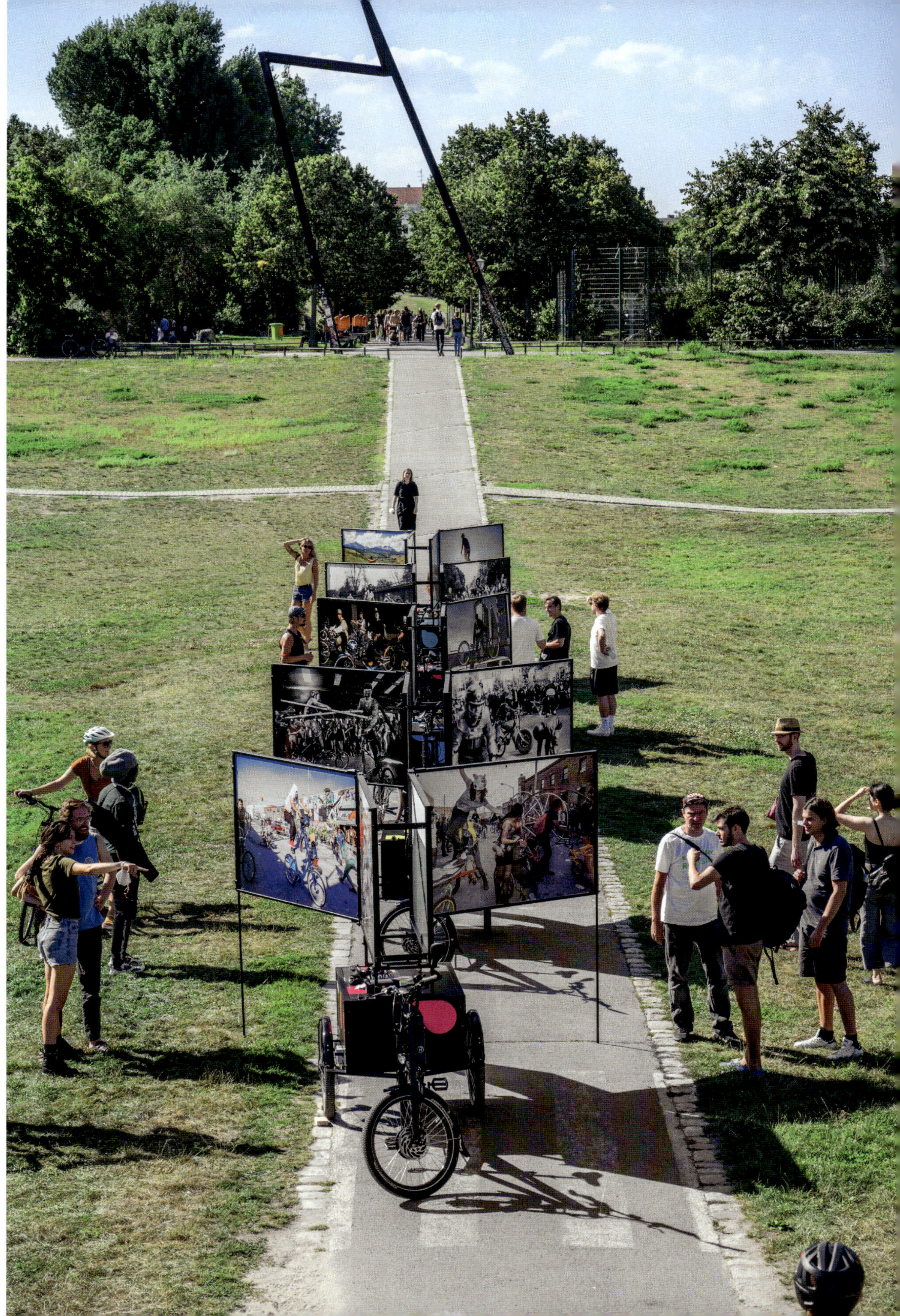

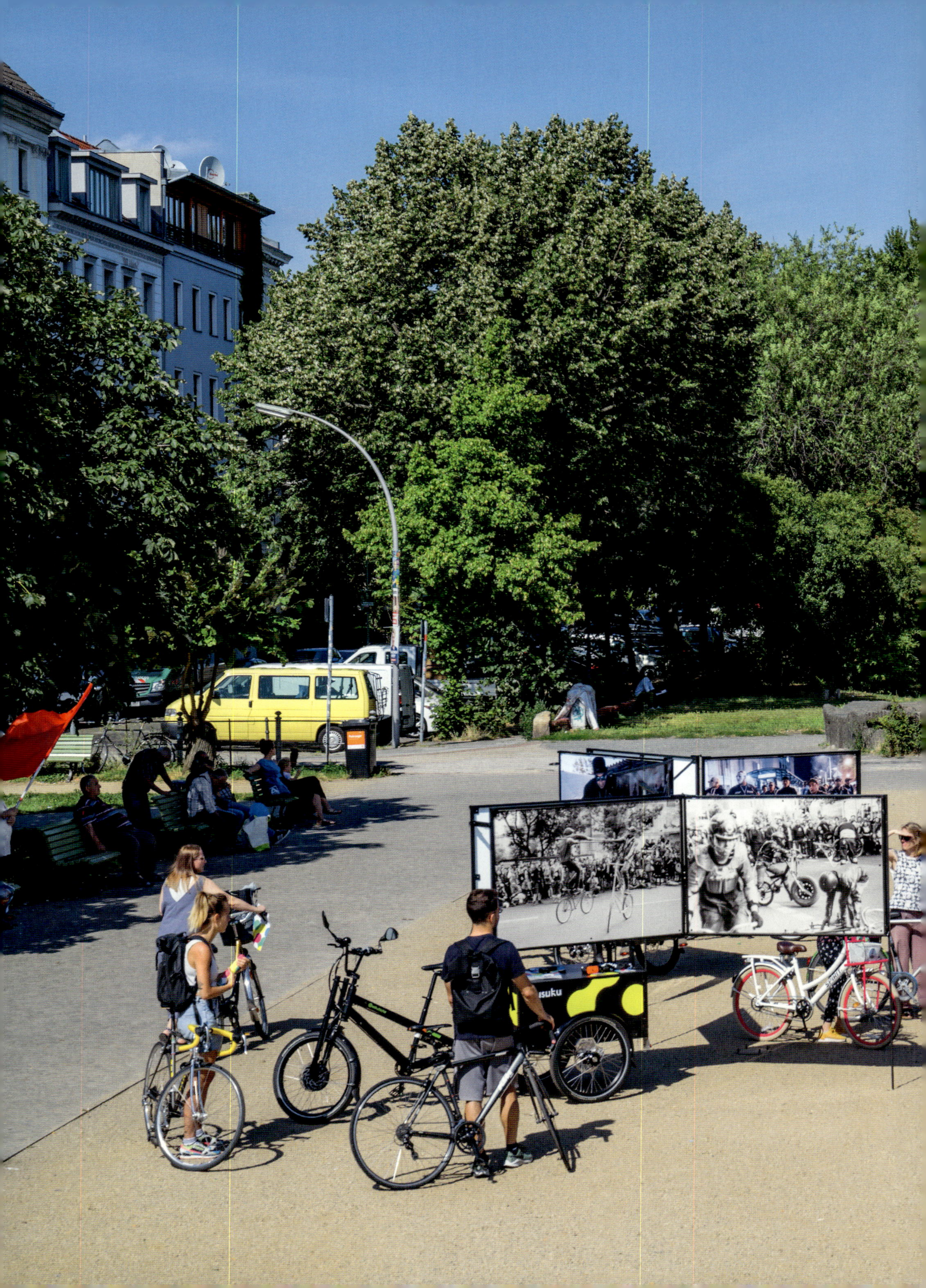

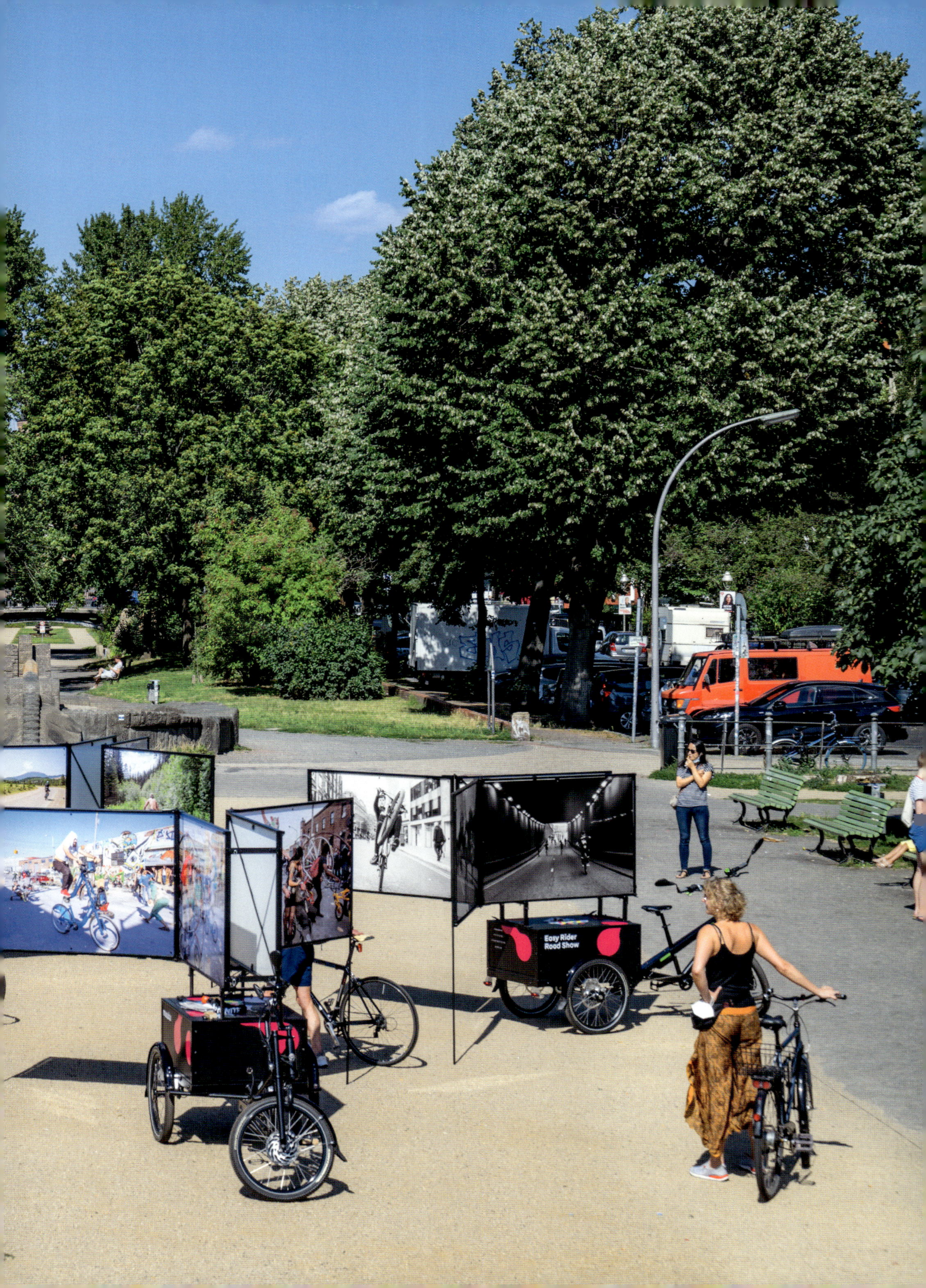
Easy Rider
Road Show

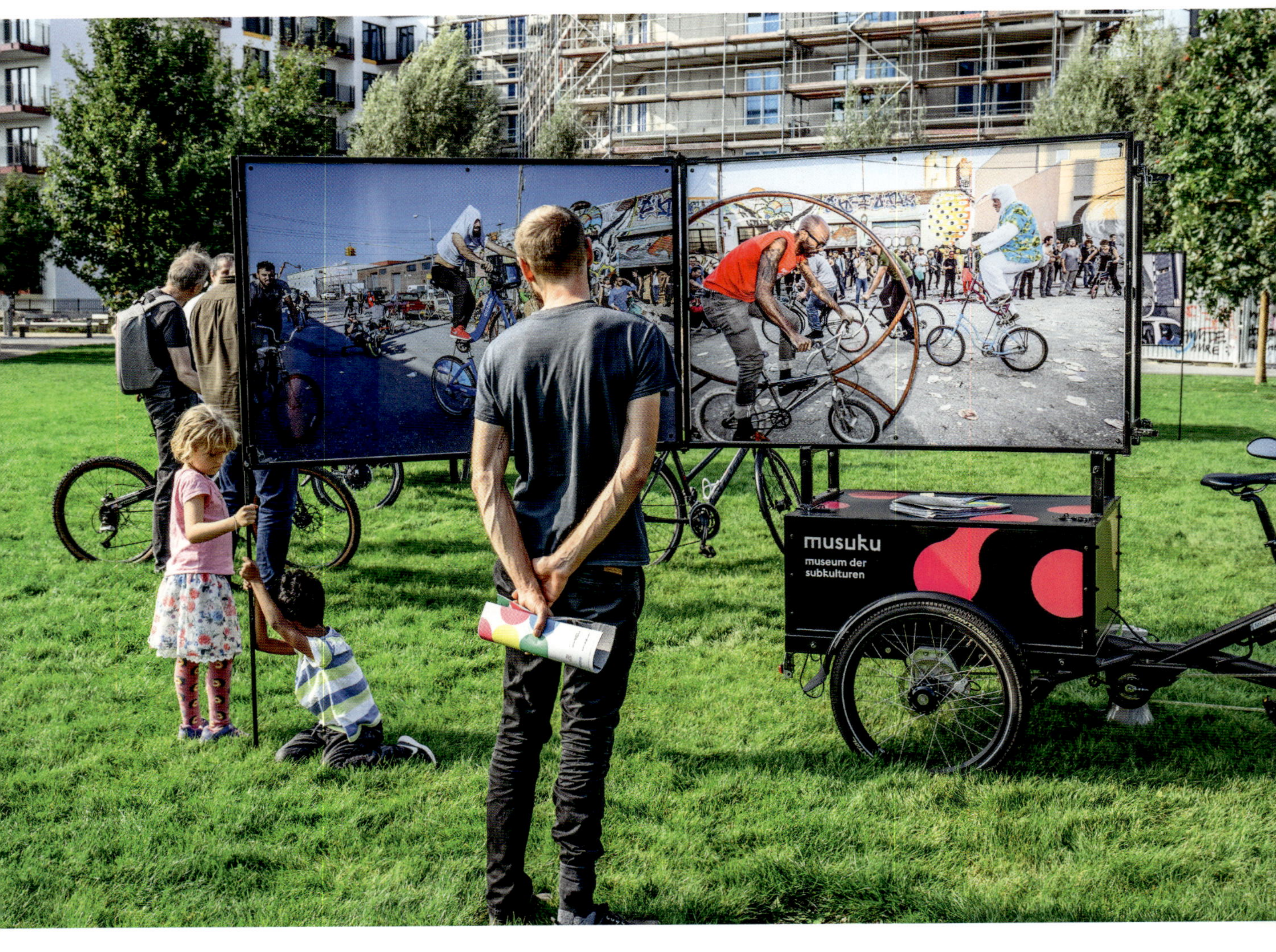
musuku
museum der
subkulturen

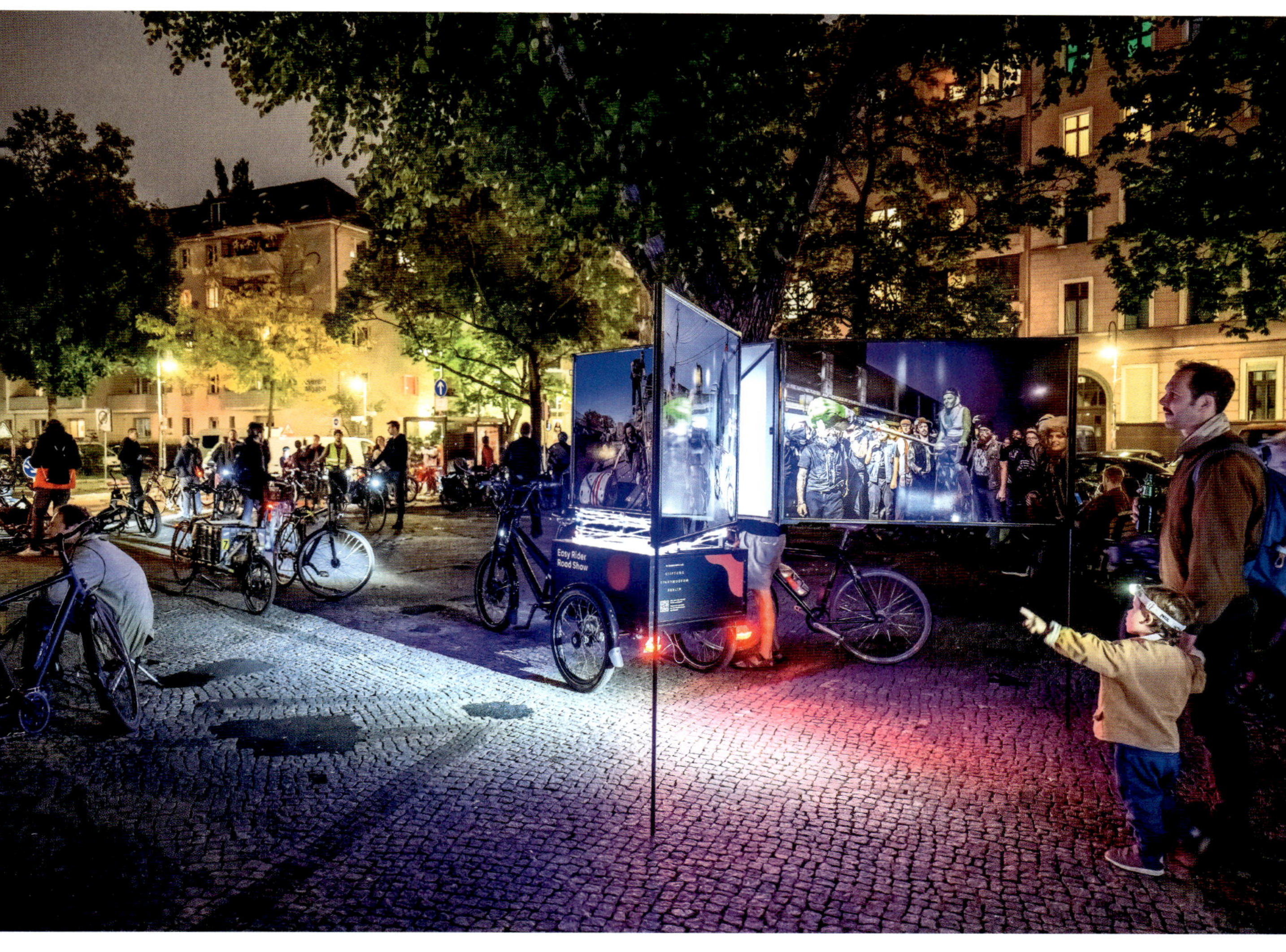

"Too little consideration is given the idea that cycling is a lifestyle, being cultivated in Berlin and around the world right now, with a lot of utopian potential."

Susanne Messmer

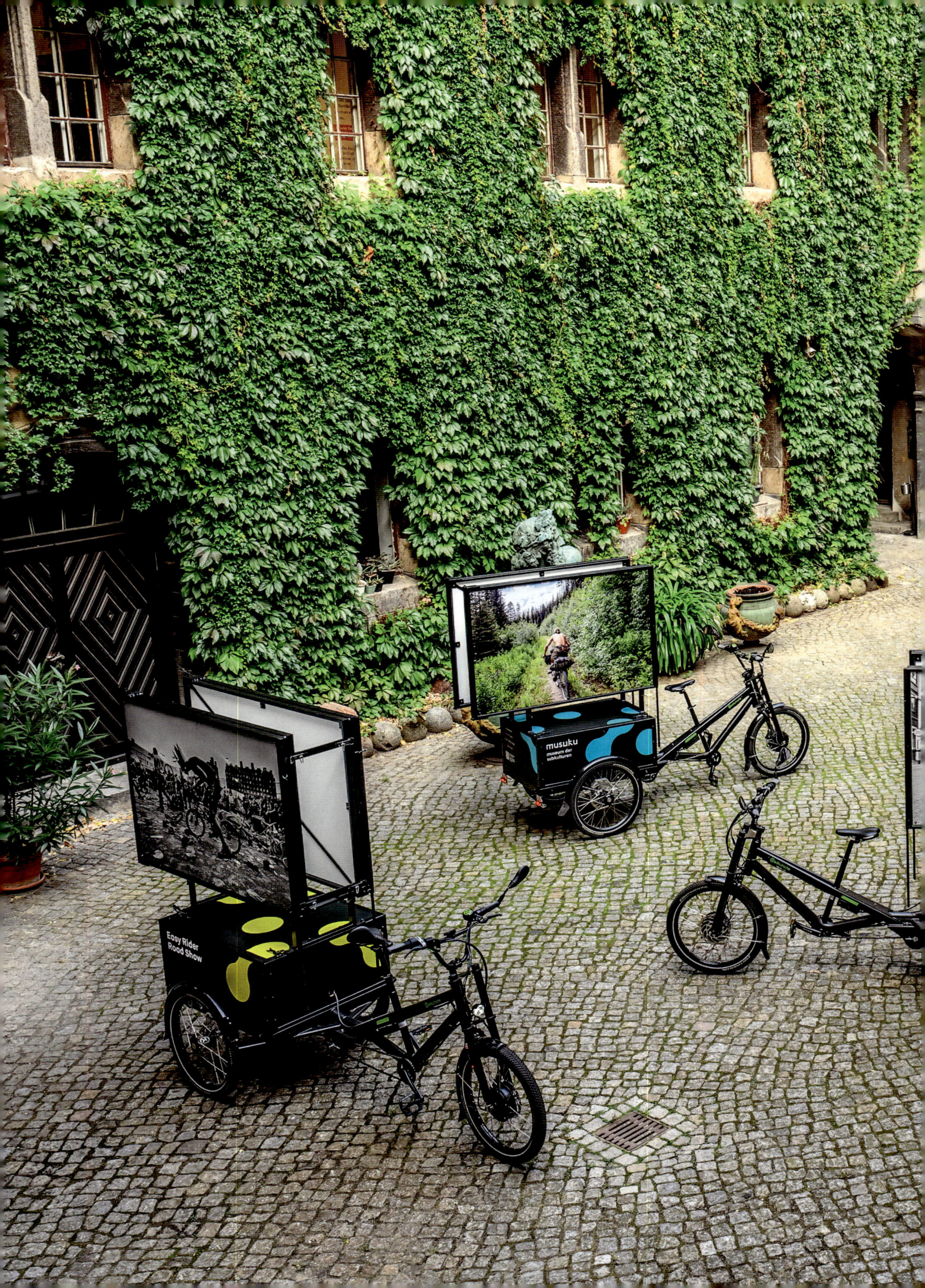
musuku
museum der
subkulturen
Easy Rider
Road Show

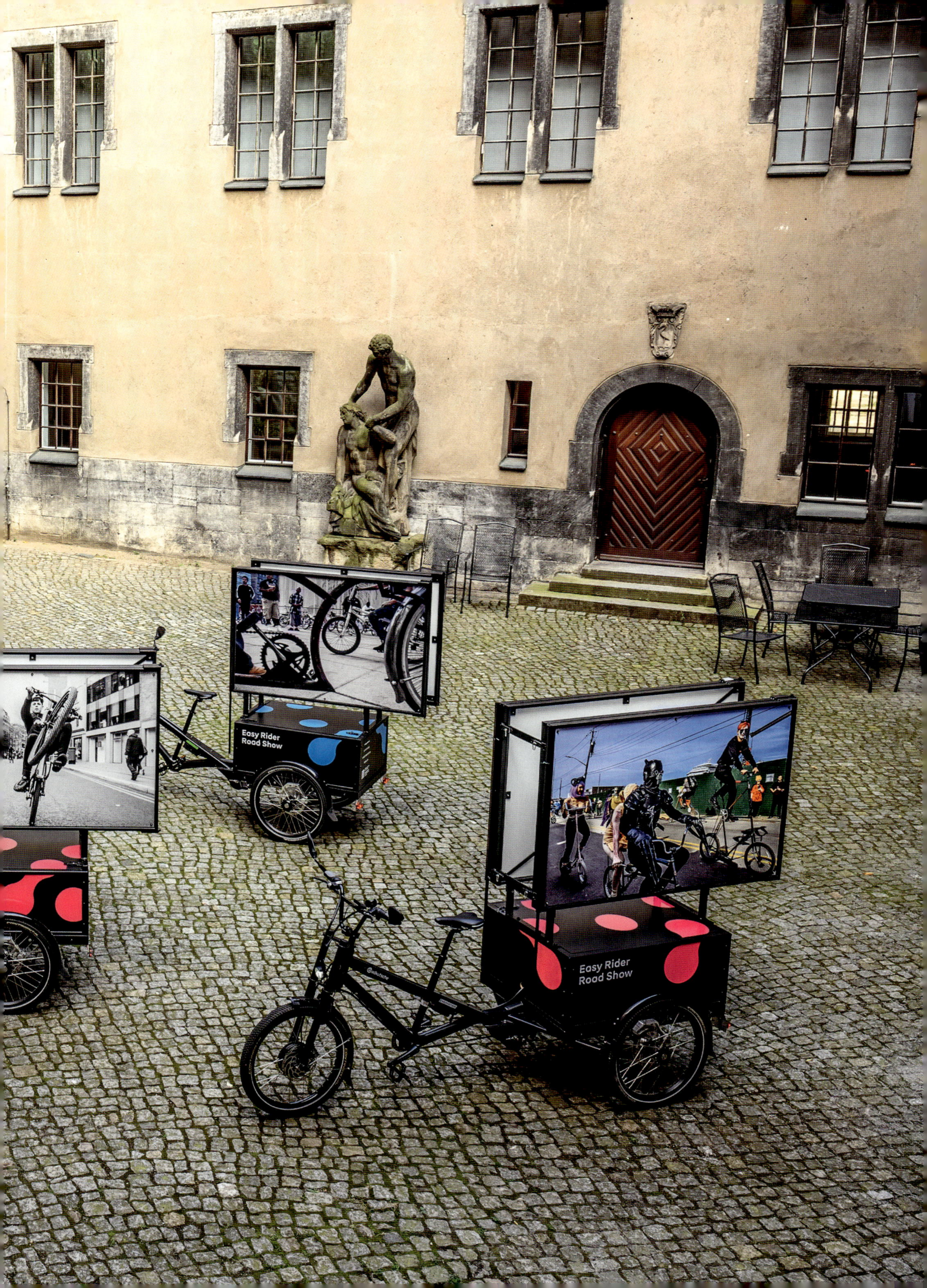
Easy Rider
Road Show
Easy Rider
Road Show

Appendix

Photographers

Adam Corbett

is a photographer and filmmaker based in London. Driven by his desire to capture the defining moment, his work is centered around movement, culture and identity. Documenting projects such as BikeStormz, Adam uses his photography to champion and support young people and the communities who use sport and movement as a way to engage and create change. Inspired by the relationships he explores through his camera, Adam has worked on philanthropic projects with charities and organisations in the UK, India, Ethiopia, Brazil, and the US.

Christophe Gateau

is a Berlin-based photo and video journalist. Before he began his training as a photographer at the Lette Verein Berlin, his interest in storytelling took him to Albania and Kosovo for a year in order to document the culture, people, and stories from the region. In 2017, he started a two-year internship as a photojournalist at the German Press Agency (dpa).

Julie Glassberg

was born in Paris, France. After studying graphic design, she decided to turn her passion for photography into a career and moved to New York. She is particularly interested in the diversity of world cultures, subcultures, underground scenes and social misfits and outsiders. Her first small edition book on this project was shortlisted by Paris Photo in 2018, followed by another edition of the book *B.L.B.C.N.Y* in 2023 with the independent French publisher Serious Publishing.

Jeoffrey Guillemard

was born in 1986 in Nancy, France. He has been living in Mexico since 2006. He beganas a self-taught photographer and then, in 2014, followed the EMI-CFD photojournalism training in Paris. Focusing on contemporary social issues, his documentary work explores topics such as migration, sexuality, religious practices, and social movements.

Tod Seelie

is an American photographer who has photographed across the United States and in twenty-five other countries across the five continents. His work reflects on his own life, which often intersects with what are often called "subcultures." He has exhibited internationally and published a monograph, *BRIGHT NIGHTS*, with Prestel Publishing in 2013.

Crew

The Art of Being a Part

The musuku—Museum der Subkulturen (Museum of Subcultures) is an initiative of artists and cultural workers from Berlin. It is a nomadic exhibition and storytelling space and shows its projects at changing locations and in cooperation with various partners, artists, and institutions as well as in public space. The musuku exhibitions are collaborative and multi-voiced. They provide a counter-narrative to the narrative of the divided society and the individual isolated within it, and explore the opportunities and possibilities that arise when we engage in a different way of looking at things: The Art of Being a Part.

The *Easy Rider Road Book* is the third publication by Anke Fesel and Chris Keller after *Berlin Wonderland,* 2014 (bobsairport) and *Berlin Heartbeats,* 2017 (Suhrkamp).

The *Easy Rider Road Show* in Berlin 2021/2022 was a cooperation with the Stiftung Stadtmuseum Berlin.

We thank

Bettina Hertrampf, who together with us brought the Easy Rider Road Show on the road. Paul Spies and the team at the Stiftung Stadtmuseum, especially Bianca Schrauwen and Ines Wenzel. Mario Kohler, Termindruck & Berlin Feinartprinters, Hahnemühle, Filmolux, Radkutsche, Daniel Weissroth Metallwerkstatt, Marina Nowitzki, Lukas Hartwig / Tischlerei Holzmanufaktur in Berlin, Denise "Nietze" Schmidt, Frank Blum, Tod Seelie and Anna Merlan, Jesse E. Lillefjeld, Ulrich Gutmair, Philipp von Recklinghausen, Henner Merle, Ludwig Lohmann, Aino Stratemann, Ralf Metzler, Christoph Dettmeier, Køpi Bicycle Workshop, Rob Cairns, and @deythos aka Matthias Reisch/ FxD.BLN, Rainer Balke, Rückenwind e.V., Dustin Nordhus/cicli berlinetta, Mr. Stock, Peter Langbauer, Sarah Glöckner, Guilherme Cadeco da Silva, Britta von Willert, Isabell Eberlein and Kim van Dijk / Velokonzept, Anne Hübschmann and Josef Maaß / Dunkelstrom Lichtkollektiv, Stefan Hirtz / Artefakt Kulturkonzepte, Kathrin Cluss, Stefanie Werk, Leo Solter, Nils Clausen / Containermanufaktur, Torsten Lund, Stephan Meinke, Hazim Zuber.

Credits & Imprint

Photos

Adam Corbett

Cover, 12/13, 14, 15, 16, 17, 18/19, 20, 21, 22, 23, 24/25, 26, 27, 28, 29, 30/31

Christophe Gateau

152/153, 154/155, 156, 157, 158, 159, 160, 161, 162/163, 164/165, 166, 167, 168/169

Julie Glassberg

96/97, 98, 99, 100, 101, 102, 103, 104/105, 106, 107, 108/109, 110, 111, 112/113

Jeoffrey Guillemard

52/53, 54, 55, 56, 57, 58/59, 60, 61, 62/63, 64, 65, 66, 67, 68, 69, 70, 71

Philipp von Recklinghausen

172, 173, 174/175, 176, 177, 178/179

Tod Seelie

34/35, 36, 37, 38, 39, 40/41, 42, 43, 44/45, 46, 47, 48/49, 74/75, 76, 77, 78, 79, 80, 81, 82, 83, 84, 85, 86/87, 88, 89, 90, 91, 92/93, 116/117, 118, 119, 120, 121, 122/123, 124, 125, 126/127, 128, 129, 130, 131, 132, 133, 134/135, 136, 137, 138, 139, 140, 141, 142/143, 144, 145, 146, 147, 148/149, 180, 181, 182/183

Text credits

Page 15, 21, 23, 28
Huck Magazine
Inside the fearless bike movement tearing up London
Text by Alex King
Published August 02, 2017
www.huckmag.com/article/bikestormz-movement-cycling-bikelife-survival-london

Page 39, 47
BBC Travel
The Cuban building the world's tallest bike
Text by Anna Merlan
Published April 12, 2017
www.bbc.com/travel/article/20170406-the-cuban-building-the-worlds-tallest-bike

Page 55, 67, 70
Hiya!
Chilango Lowbike Club Interview par Veneno
Text by Veneno
Published June 18, 2021
www.hiya.fr/2021/06/18/chilangos-lowbike-club-interview-par-veneno

Page 77, 79, 83, 89
The Radavist
DFL the Divide: A Friend Tour with Bikes
Text by Hannah Kirby, Adam and Serena Rio
Published August 20, 2018
www.theradavist.com/dfl-the-divide-a-friend-tour-with-bikes

Page 103, 107, 111
First Edition Photobook
Text by Julie Glassberg
Published 2018
www.julieglassberg.com/bike-kill/00

Page 120, 131
Gothamist
Photos: Bike Kill's Gathering Of 'Mutant Bikes' Takes Over Lot In Red Hook
Text by Max Rivlin-Nadler
Published Nov 1, 2021
www.gothamist.com/arts-entertainment/photos-video-bike-kill-brooklyn-2021

Page 124
Movie *Bike Club*
Directed by: Jacob Septimus & Anthony Howard
Produced by: Fredric King & Jacob Septimus
2006
bikeclubfilms.com

Page 147
Digital Photography Review
Behind the Photo: Tod Seelie on capturing tall bike jousting
Text by Jeanette D Moses
Published Dec 13, 2022
www.dpreview.com/articles/0525978272/behind-the-photo-tod-seelie-on-capturing-tall-bike-jousting

Page 159
Vice
Wenn Punks sich auf Fahrrädern prügeln – Willkommen auf den Berliner »Bike Wars«
Text by Christophe Gateau
Published June 13, 2016
www.vice.com/de/article/jm4mbk/wenn-punks-sich-mit-fahrrdern-pruegeln-willkommen-auf-den-berliner-bike-wars

Page 181
taz
Gewohntes mit anderen Augen sehen
Text by Susanne Messmer
Published Nov 8, 2021
www. taz.de/Die-Wochenvorschau-fuer-Berlin/!5810473

Imprint

Editors
Anke Fesel and Chris Keller
www.musuku.de

Project management
Anna Warnow

Copyediting
George MacBeth

Translations
Jesse Lillefjeld

Graphic design
Anke Fesel

Typeface
Round, Bureau Brut

Production
Alise Ausmane

Reproductions
DruckConcept, Berlin

Printing and binding
Graspo CZ, a.s.

Paper
GardaPat 11, 150 g/m²

Cover illustration
Adam Corbett

Published by

Hatje Cantz Verlag GmbH
Mommsenstraße 27
10629 Berlin
www.hatjecantz.com

A Ganske Publishing Group
Company

ISBN 978-3-7757-5570-2

Printed in the Czech Republic